MW00911464

Roland Hammond

A History and Genealogy of the Descendants

of William Hammond of London, England, and His Wife Elizabeth Penn

Roland Hammond

A History and Genealogy of the Descendants
of William Hammond of London, England, and His Wife Elizabeth Penn

ISBN/EAN: 9783744755757

Printed in Europe, USA, Canada, Australia, Japan

Cover: Foto ©ninafisch / pixelio.de

More available books at **www.hansebooks.com**

ROLAND HAMMOND, M.D.

A

HISTORY AND GENEALOGY

OF THE

DESCENDANTS

OF

WILLIAM HAMMOND

OF LONDON, ENGLAND,

AND

HIS WIFE ELIZABETH PENN;

THROUGH THEIR SON

Benjamin of Sandwich and Rochester, Mass.

1600—1894.

BY

ROLAND HAMMOND, A.M., M.D.

FELLOW OF THE MASS. MEDICAL SOCIETY, ETC.

BOSTON:

DAVID CLAPP & SON, PRINTERS.

1894.

TO

THE MANY MEMBERS OF THE HAMMOND FAMILY

WHO HAVE SO KINDLY AND PATIENTLY ASSISTED IN

FURNISHING THE MATERIALS FOR THIS WORK,

THIS BOOK IS GRATEFULLY DEDICATED,

WITH THE KIND REGARDS OF THEIR FRIEND,

THE AUTHOR.

" Here lies the volume thou boldly hast sought."—*Sir W. Scott.*

" A chiel's amang ye taking notes, and faith he'll prent it."—*Anon.*

" Your pardon, good sirs, the table is spread."—*Old Play.*

" Go, little booke, God send thee good passage,
And specially let this be thy prayere,
Unto them all that will thee read or hear,
Where thou art wrong, after their help to call,
Thee to correct, in any part or all."—*Chaucer.*

" We live in deeds, not years; in thoughts, not breaths;
In feelings, not in figures on a dial.
We should count time by heart-throbs. He most lives
Who thinks most, feels the noblest, acts the best.
And he whose heart beats the quickest, lives the longest;
Lives in one hour more than in years do some
Whose fat blood sleeps as it slips through their veins."—*P. J. Bailey.*

PREFACE.

The present work, commenced eight years ago amid the exacting cares and duties of a large professional practice, was completed during a long and tedious convalescence. And although many times it was extremely trying and disheartening, yet on the whole it has been a fascinating and, at times, a pleasant pastime.

When the writer first commenced collecting statistics it was with no idea of publication. But the work grew to such dimensions that it seemed best to carry it to completion for the benefit of the name of which it treats.

A few words are desirable as to the scope of the work, its plan, and the sources from which the materials have been obtained.

As to its *scope*, the idea has been to give as complete a history and genealogy as possible of all the descendants of William Hammond, who died in London, Eng., previous to 1634, and of his son Benjamin, who, born at London in 1621, came to Boston in 1634 with his mother, Elizabeth [Penn] Hammond, and three sisters, and died at Rochester, Mass., in 1703, leaving four sons, Samuel, John, Nathan and Benjamin, all of whom married and left children. As far as has been within range of possibilities, the history and genealogy of these four sons and their descendants have been carefully and conscientiously traced down to the present time.

No one, however, can be more painfully aware than the writer that many branches have disappeared, probably beyond all possibility of recovery or discovery. Possibly the publication of this Genealogy may be the means of bringing some of the lost tribes to light. And the author would esteem it a favor if any parties, knowing themselves to be related to the Hammonds described in this book, will communicate with him personally, giving all the information possible of their branches of the name.

On the other hand, great care has been taken to include none in this work unless the writer has felt morally certain that they actually belonged to this line of Hammonds.

The *plan* of the work has been to give first a person's place of residence, his business or occupation, and such other facts of his life as it seemed desirable to place on record. Then follow the facts of his marriage, viz: wife's maiden name, date of marriage, and the names and dates of birth of his children. Then the children who died young, all who did not marry, and the daughters who married, and also the sons who married but left no issue, are first disposed of. Finally, the sons who married, and left issue that carried on the family or line, are taken up, each in turn, and his record brought down to the present time, or until the branch runs out or could be traced no further. Then the next son is taken up, and his record traced out in like manner.

Thus it will be seen that no attempt has been made to arrange the work by generations. The writer first tried this plan, but afterwards abandoned it for the one here adopted. The latter plan being more desirable from the fact that it enables anyone to get a clearer idea of the different branches and families, because they are kept together better.

To enable a stranger to follow out the record more readily, each branch, and the different sub-branches or families, have been designated by a series of numbers. The head of the family being designated by the †, and the sons who carry on the line, each by the number of his birth in the family, and the later sons in a similar manner, etc. For example, †–5–8. Thomas, means that Thomas was the eighth child of 5, and that 5 was the fifth child of †, or the head of the family or branch.

The record of daughters,—unless there were some good reason to the contrary,—has usually been dropped after giving their places of residence and the facts relating to their husbands and children. Where good reasons seem to exist, the record has been carried further,—even down to the present time.

Every available *source* known to the writer has been drawn upon to obtain materials for this Genealogy,—town records, church records, probate records, private records, head stones in cemeteries, etc. But, after all, a great part of the facts and statistics have been obtained from a very extensive correspondence with parties living in nearly all the northern and middle, and in many of the western and southern states. The writer has received more than one thousand letters and postal cards, and has written many more than that number.

The writer is not so sanguine as to suppose that a work like the present, containing so many facts gathered from so many sources, is entirely free from errors. But every effort has been made to have the facts *as correct as possible.*

A "Coat of Arms" is figured and described as a relic of our English Ancestry, though an interesting one even to Americans.

The "half-tones" are the best it has been possible to obtain under the circumstances. Some of the photographs and steel prints, from which they have been made, being very old and much faded, rendered it impossible to obtain fine work in such cases. Where a fresh photograph could be obtained the quality of the work is all that could be desired.

With these explanatory remarks the author sends the Genealogy forth, hoping it may afford in its perusal as much pleasure to its readers as it has to the writer in its preparation.

                                        ROLAND HAMMOND.

CAMPELLO, MASS., JANUARY 5, 1894.

CONTENTS.

INTRODUCTION.

It is said that the first mention of the name of "Hamon" or "Hamond" is in connection with the conquest of England by William the Conqueror in 1066. He caused an Abby to be erected on the battlefield at Hastings in honor of his victory over Harold, the last of the Saxon kings. In this, which is called "Battle Abby," there were deposited the names of all the nobles or barons, as they were called, who came with William from Normandy. Among these names is that of Hamound, afterwards written Hammond.

The name of Hammond may arise from one of three sources, viz.: 1. Hammonet, a town or house, or an elevation; 2. Hamon, faithful; 3. St. Amand, in regard to which Burke's Landed Gentry, Vol. I., says, "The family of Hammond is of considerable antiquity in England, and it is probable may have derived its origin from a branch of the Norman House of St. Amand."

At any rate the Hammonds have been in England for many centuries, and there were and are in that country many eminent families bearing the name.

A family of special interest to us is that of William Hammond of London, Co. Kent, whose descendants form the subject of this Genealogy. He married Elizabeth Penn, sister of Admiral Sir William Penn, and aunt to William Penn the Quaker, and had a son Benjamin and three daughters who with their mother afterwards came to Boston. This family is known among genealogists as that of "William of London."

Another family whose descendants have played an important part in the affairs of this country, is that of Thomas Hammond of Lavenham, Co. Suffolk, England. He married Rose Trippe, and had, besides several daughters, two sons, William and Thomas, who after marrying and having children, came to Boston, and were known respectively as "William of Watertown," and "Thomas of Newton."

2

A celebrated family in England is that of St. Albans Court in Nonington, Co. Kent. John Hamon, the first known in this line, was a tenant under the Culpeppers of St. Albans, and began the purchase of the "manor" as it was called. His son, Thomas Hamond, completed the purchase of the manor in 1551. To him was granted a coat-of-arms in 1548, in the second year of Edward VI., by Barker, Garter King-at-Arms. This coat-of-arms, perhaps the oldest granted to any Hammond, has been selected after much consideration as the best to represent the name of Hammond in this Genealogy.*

Sir William, b. 1579, d. 1650, grandson of this Thomas Hammond, was knighted by James I., in 1607–8, and had a brother Thomas. To this Thomas the descendants of "William of Watertown" and "Thomas of Newton" have endeavored to trace their line of descent without avail. The present representative of the St. Albans family is William Oxenden Hammond, Nonington, Co. Kent, England.

There is quite a general impression and a strong probability that William of London is descended from one of the younger sons of the family of St. Albans Court, possibly from one of the brothers of Sir William, of whom there were several,† though the connection has not been traced out, as the English genealogies preserve full records of the first sons only, later sons and daughters being usually merely alluded to. There are also reasons for believing that William of London and Thomas of Lavenham may have been more or less distantly related, but certainly not nearer than cousins if the relationship was as near as this.

There are many other noted families bearing the name in England, one of the later being that of Baron Edmund Hammond who was raised to the Peerage in 1874, and recently deceased. The Chaplain, and the Keeper, at the Isle of Wight, and one of the Judges of Charles I, were Hammonds.

There are several distinct branches or lines of Hammonds in this country.

First is that of which William A. Hammond, M. D., of Washington, D. C., late Surgeon-General of the U. S. Army, is a member. His great grandfather, Philip Hammond, the first ancestor of this line in this country, is said to have come

---

* The design with description is given on page 6.
† Sir William's brothers were:—John, Edward, Thomas, Col. Francis and Col. Robert.

from Co. Kent, and landed in Ann Arundell Co., Maryland, in 1607. Philip's brothers, Thomas and Rezin, came over soon afterwards and settled at Jamestown, Va., in 1608, and were called "Cavaliers" because they favored Charles I. The Puritans were called "Round Heads" because they favored Cromwell.

There is another line whose ancestor is said to have settled in Kittery, Me., and the family is known as that of "William of Kittery," Maine. When the family came to this country is not known by the writer.

In 1632 William Hammond, son of Thomas of Lavenham, Eng., before referred to as William of Watertown, came to Boston, and some years afterwards settled in Watertown, Mass. Two years later his family, consisting of his wife Elizabeth Payne Hammond, two sons, Thomas and John, and three daughters, Anne, Elizabeth, and Sarah, rejoined him, arriving at Boston in the ship Francis in April, 1634.* William Hammond lived and died at Watertown, the family being transmitted by his sons Thomas and John. Let it be especially noted that he did not have a son Benjamin as claimed by Savage, this Benjamin being the son of William of London.

In the same year, 1634, Mrs. Elizabeth Penn Hammond, widow of William of London, with her son Benjamin and three daughters, Elizabeth, Martha and Rachel, came in the ship Griffin, landing at Boston Sept. 18, 1634. From the son Benjamin, who settled in Sandwich, Mass., and married Mary Vincent, all this family has descended.

In 1636, Thomas, son of Thomas of Lavenham, with his wife Elizabeth [Cason] and children Elizabeth and Thomas, came to Boston, and settled at Hingham, Mass. In 1640 he removed to Newton, where he afterwards lived and died, and is known as "Thomas of Newton." At Newton, Sarah and Nathaniel were born to him. The two sons Thomas and Nathaniel transmitted the family.

Owing to the similarity of the names of the two William Hammonds, only one of whom came to this country; and of those of their wives, Elizabeth Penn and Elizabeth Payne, both also having brothers named William; and to the further fact that Elizabeth Penn's brother the admiral, and nephew the Quaker, were both named William; and especially to the singular coinci-

* Elizabeth Payne, wife of William Hammond, was a sister of William Payne, an extensive property holder in New England.

4   HAMMOND GENEALOGY.

dence that both Elizabeth Hammonds with their children came to
Boston in the same year, 1634, Savage, and after him Farmer
and other early genealogists, got badly confused in regard to
the two families of William of London and William of Watertown, thought there was only one William Hammond, that he
married Elizabeth Payne, and denied that Elizabeth Penn was
the ancestress of any Hammonds in this country.

The facts contained in the memorandum book* of Captain
Elnathan Hammond of Newport, R. I., and the admirable arti-
cle, based on these facts, in regard to the descendants of Benjamin Hammond, son of William of London, published in the
Historical and Genealogical Register for January, 1876, by
Philip Battel of Middlebury, Vt., have effectually dispelled all
doubts as to the above points, and have firmly established
Elizabeth Penn as the wife of William Hammond of London,
and these two as the parents of Benjamin of Sandwich, Mass.,
whose sons Samuel, John, Nathan, and Benjamin settled in
Rochester, Mass., about 1680–84, and whose genealogy is
traced as certainly and as surely as that of any name in this
country. The writer of this Genealogy can personally point to
the exact spots where these four sons lived, reared their families,
and died.

Previous to the year 1787 there were on the shores of Buzzard's Bay, Mass., the two great towns of Dartmouth and
Rochester, Dartmouth lying to the west of Rochester. In 1787
the towns of Westport and New Bedford were set off from Dartmouth. In 1812 the town of Fairhaven was set off from New
Bedford; and in 1860 the town of Acushnet from Fairhaven.
Hence the old town of Dartmouth constituted the present towns
of Dartmouth, Westport, New Bedford, Fairhaven and Acushnet.

The principal localities of the old town of Rochester were
North Rochester, lying in the northwest part of the town;
Rochester Centre, in the central part; Sippican Village, lying
in the southeast; Mattapoisett Village in the south, on Mattapoisett Harbor, a branch of Buzzard's Bay; Hammondtown in
the southwesterly part; and Mattapoisett Neck in the extreme
southwest, the latter being a point of land extending some two
miles south into Buzzard's Bay.

The town of Rochester was incorporated in the year 1686.

* For further account of the memorandum book see record of Capt. Elnathan Hammond.

As early as 1638, it appears that the colony court of Plymouth granted lands at Sippican to a committee of the Church of Scituate, for the seating of a township and a congregation. The territory, however, remained unoccupied till 1651, when it was granted for the benefit of the town of Plymouth. It was probably purchased of the natives the same year. The town is said to have taken its name from the ancient city of Rochester, in Kent, England, a shire from whence many of the first planters of Scituate, and of course Rochester, emigrated. The first settlers appear to have come into the place from Sandwich, Marshfield and Scituate about the year 1680. Among them were the following: Rev. Samuel Arnold, Moses Barlow, Aaron Barlow, Jacob Bumpus, Joseph Burgess, Joseph Dotey, Samuel Hammond, John Hammond, John Haskell, Abraham Holmes, ——— Sprague, Samuel White, and Job Winslow.

In 1854, the southeasterly part of the town of Rochester, containing Sippican Village and adjacent territory, was set off as the present town of Marion. In 1857 all the southerly part of Rochester, including Mattapoisett Village, Hammond-town and Mattapoisett Neck, was set off as the present town of Mattapoisett, leaving in the present Rochester, Rochester Centre and North Rochester. It is probable that but few, if any, Hammonds lived within the limits of the present town of Rochester.

Mattapoisett Village is about six miles east of New Bedford, five miles west of Sippican Village, and five miles south of Rochester Centre. The most of the early Hammonds of Rochester lived within the limits of the present towns of Marion and Mattapoisett.

The Indian word Mattapoisett is said to signify "The place of Rest." The Indians living five or six miles north of the Village used frequently to come down to the shore for the purpose of obtaining clams and fish; one or two miles north of the Village, they used to stop at a spring and rest. From this circumstance, it is said, the river and place derived their names.

The first meeting-house was built in the vicinity of Sippican Harbor, and at this place, it is probable, the first settlers located themselves. The Rev. Samuel Arnold was the first minister. Mr. Arnold was succeeded by Rev. Timothy Ruggles, who was settled here in 1710. While he was minister, the inhabitants of the southwestern part of the town, now Hammondtown, Mattapoisett Neck and the Village, living remote from the place of worship, proposed to be set off into a distinct parish. This

was done about the year 1733, and Rev. Ivory Hovey was
ordained their minister. This parish comprised that part of the
town which still retains the Indian name Mattapoisett. The
church was located in Hammondtown. Mr. Hovey was succeeded in 1772, by Rev. Lemuel LeBaron. The LeBarons of
Plymouth County are descendants of Dr. Francis LeBaron, the
celebrated surgeon who was wrecked from a French privateer
in 1696 in Buzzard's Bay, and afterwards settled in Plymouth,
Mass. Rev. Thomas Robbins, D. D., the successor of Mr.
LeBaron, possessed for those times one of the most valuable
private libraries in the State, consisting of about 3000 volumes
and 4000 pamphlets, some of which were very rare.

A third Congregational society was formed from several bor-
der towns, about 1748, of which Rev. Thomas West was for
many years pastor. This church was located in North Rochester.

Much of the land in Mattapoisett was purchased of King
Philip, the great Indian Chief. Many of the original settlers
of Scituate, Mattapoisett and adjoining towns, came from Co.
Kent, England, and there is a street at Scituate Harbor named
by them, and still known as Kent Street. In addition to the
original settlers of Rochester already given, may be mentioned
the names of Annable, Turner, Lombard, Lothrop, Parker,
and Stedman, some of whom afterwards intermarried with the
Hammonds.

It is said that the "First purchase of the town of Rochester
was by Joseph Lothrop, Barnabas Lothrop, Knellan Winslow,
and William Clark, of Joseph Winslow, Governor of Plymouth,
for the sum of £200 current money, Jul. 2, 1679." That
"The town of Rochester was divided into 33 shares, every
33rd being reserved for the support of the Ministry." That
"Benjamin Hammond the son of William of London, the first
in our line from England, moved from Sandwich to Rochester
in the year 1684, and purchased half a share, or grant, of the
town of Rochester. The deed certifies that he payed 20 and 6
pounds."

DESCRIPTION OF THE COAT OF ARMS.

This Coat-of-Arms was granted by Barker, Garter King at
Arms, to Thomas Hammond of St. Alban's Court, in 1548,
second year of Edward VI.

Arms.—Argent, on a chevron sable, between three pellets each charged with a martlet of the field, as many escallops or, a bordure engrailed vert.

Crest.—A hawk's head collared gules, rays issuing or.

Motto.—Pro Rege et Patria. [For king and country.]

Seat.—St. Alban's Court, Nonington, Co. Kent, England.

There is another armorial ensign or bearing, a copy of which is in the possession of the author, which is said to have been granted to the Sirname of Hammond. The shield is Norman, or heart-shaped, and the grant, if genuine, is undoubtedly very ancient and of Norman origin. The only reason this beautiful coat-of-arms is not given the preference in this work is because its genuineness is not so well attested as that of the one given above. The description is as follows : —

Arms.—Field, argent, a cheveron sable charged with three escollops argent. Between three pellets sable each charged with a martlet argent, within a bordure engrailed gules.

Crest.—On a helmet and wreath of three colours, a lion's head erased gules.

Motto.—Tentanda Via Est. [A way must be tried.]

Extract from the records in [the office of] the King-at-Arms in London.

A coat-of-arms, in olden times, was a short coat with short sleeves, worn over his armor by a knight, and on which his armorial bearings were worked in bright colors. Hence the origin of the term, coat-of-arms.

Below is an explanation of some of the terms used in heraldry :—

Cheveron, an honorable ordinary, representing two rafters of a house meeting at the top.

Martlets, birds of the swallow kind without feet, denoting a younger son having no landed inheritance.

Escollops denotes that the bearer or his ancestors had made long voyages or pilgrimages, or had been engaged in the Crusades.

Bordure, an additional honor or mark of cadency distinguishing one branch from another.

Engrailed, endented or wavy edges, denoting that the honor was obtained with difficulty.

Erased, when the head is torn from the body and presenting

at the neck a rough or ragged appearance instead of straight, showing strength as against skill with the sword.

Argent, silver, or white, referring to the shield, purity. Gules, red, referring to the crest, courage. Or, gold, goodness. Azure, light blue, truth and purity. Sable, black, denoting antiquity of lineage. Vert, green, denoting life and vigor.

PART I.

WILLIAM HAMMOND OF LONDON, ENGLAND.

---

†. **William Hammond**[1] was born in London, County Kent, Eng., and there married **Elizabeth Penn**, sister of the Admiral, Sir William Penn, and aunt to William Penn, the Quaker. William Hammond died and was buried in London, and was probably descended from the Hammonds of St. Albans Court, County Kent, Eng. His children were:

1. Benjamin.	b. in 1621.	d in 1703.
2. Elizabeth,	b.	d.
3. Martha,	b.	d.
4. Rachel,	b.	d.

These children were all born in London, County Kent, Eng. Elizabeth Hammond, widow of William, with her son Benjamin and three daus., all young, left a good estate in London, and came over to New England in the troublesome times of 1634, from a desire to have the liberty to serve God according to the dictates of their consciences. They arrived in Boston, Sep. 18, 1634, in the ship Griffin, and had with them the Rev. John Lothrop,* their minister. Mrs. Hammond lived in Boston and in Watertown, Mass., until the year 1638, when she joined Rev. John Lothrop's church in Scituate, Apr. 16, 1638, being the 33d member of said church.

Mrs. Elizabeth [Penn] Hammond probably returned to Boston near the close of the year 1639, as she died and was buried there A.D. 1640.

* Rev. John Lothrop established a church at Scituate Harbor, Mass., and afterwards one at Barnstable, Mass. He is said to have married for his second wife, Anna, widow, daughter of William Hammond of Watertown, Mass., and had Barnabas, Abigail, Bathsheua and John. But the evidence that the widow Anna was the daughter of William Hammond is far from convincing. Rev. John Lothrop received the degree of A.B. from Queen's College, Cambridge, Eng., in 1605, was admitted to the living in Egerton in 1611, renounced his Orders in 1623, and became an independent preacher, before coming to Boston.

Of the three daughters of William Hammond and Elizabeth Penn,—Elizabeth, Martha and Rachel,—nothing further can be learned.

1.—BENJAMIN HAMMOND OF SANDWICH AND ROCHESTER, MASS.

†-1. **Benjamin² Hammond,** son of William and Elizabeth, went to Sandwich, and there in 1650 married Mary Vincent, dau. of John Vincent, who was born in England in 1633. Nothing is known as to his whereabouts from his arrival in Boston, in 1634, to his marriage to Mary Vincent in 1650, except that he was at Yarmouth in 1643. Benjamin Hammond and Mary Vincent had issue, as follows:

1. Samuel,	b. in	1655.	d.
2. John,	b. Nov. 30, 1663.		d. Apr. 19, 1749, O S.
3. Nathan,	b. in	1670.	d.
4. Benjamin, 2d,	b. Nov.	1673.	d. March 29. 1747.
5. Rose,	b.		d. Nov. 20, 1676.
6. Mary,	b.		d. young.

Samuel Hammond and his brother John probably came from Sandwich to Rochester, Mass., about 1680. Benjamin Hammond with his wife and two sons, Nathan and Benjamin 2d, probably came to Rochester about 1684. Benjamin died there in 1703, æ. 82; and Mary, his widow, in 1705, æ. 72.

PART II.

SAMUEL HAMMOND, OLDEST SON OF BENJAMIN.

---

†. **Samuel[3] Hammond** [oldest son of Benj.,[2] William[1]] was born at Sandwich, Mass., in 1655, came with his brother John to Rochester, Mass., about 1680, and settled in the extreme southwesterly part of the town, known as the "West Neck," where he died at a ripe age much respected. He was one of the founders and a prominent member of the first Congregational Church in Rochester, located in the present town of Marion. He was an extensive land-holder, and settled four of his sons around him, viz: Seth, Josiah, Barnabas and Jedediah, the latter of whom afterwards moved to Scituate. He bought his land of Hugh Cole of Swansey, and he of King Philip, Sachem of Pokanoket, in 1671.* A house built by his son Barnabas in 1767 is still standing. Samuel Hammond m. about 1680 Mary Hathaway, and had issue :

1.	Benjamin,	b.	Dec. 18, 1681.	d.	
2.	Seth,	b.	Feb. 13, 1683.	d.	in 1736-7.
3.	Rosamond,	b	May 8, 1684.	d.	
4.	Samuel, 2d,	b.	Mch. 8, 1685.	d.	
5.	Thomas,	b.	Sep. 16, 1687.	d.	
6.	Jedediah,	b.	Sep. 19, 1690.	d.	
7.	Josiah,	b.	Sep. 15, 1692.	d.	
8.	Barnabas,	b.	Jan 20, 1694.	d.	
9.	Maria,	b.	Jan. 27, 1697.	d.	
10.	John,	b.	Oct. 4, 1701.	d.	
11.	Jedidah,	b.	Sep. 30, 1703.	d.	

Of these children, **Rosamond[4]** m. Jun. 20, 1705, John Spooner of Rochester, and had issue : Peter, Elizabeth, Rose, Jeduthan, Benjamin, John, Thomas, Hobbs and Mary.

* A copy of King Philip's Deed will be found near the end of Part II.

9. **Maria⁴** m. July 15, 1717, David Clark of Rochester, and lived near the Butts place, West Neck. Issue: Mary, who m. her cousin Barnabas, son of Samuel 2d; and probably others.

11. **Jedidah⁴** m. Dec. 17, 1719, Joseph Turner of Rochester. Of **Benjamin** nothing further is known, but he probably died young.

I.—SETH HAMMOND OF ROCHESTER, MASS.

†. **Seth⁴ Hammond,** second son of Samuel³ [Benj..² William¹], who was a farmer living near his father, m. Mch. 4, 1706, Mary Randall, and had issue:

1. Jerusha,	b. May 2, 1708.	d.
2. Archelus,	b. Sep. 15, 1709.	d.
3. Jedediah,	b. Sep. 16, 1711.	d.
4. Seth,	b.	d.
5. Jonathan,	b.	d.
6. Sylvanus,	b.	d.

Seth may have m. 2d, in 1714, Elizabeth Stewart of Chatham, and, if so, the last three children were born by the 2d marriage. But the Will, proved Feb. 28, 1837, names the widow Mary.

Of Seth's children, 1. **Jerusha⁵** m. Nov. 25, 1733, Barzillai Randall of Rochester.

†-2. **Archelus⁵** m. Dec. 10, 1729, Elizabeth Weeks, and lived near the Noble Gelett Place in Fairhaven, just over the Rochester line. Issue: 1. Amaziah, 2. Charles, and 3. Judah.

Of these children, 2. **Charles⁶** probably m. Oct. 4, 1764, his cousin Eliphel, dau. of Jedediah Hammond.

†-2-1. **Amaziah⁶** m. about 1756, Lydia Gardner of Nantucket, and had issue:

1. Gardner,	b. in 1757.	d.
2. Archelus,	b. in 1759.	d. in 1830.
3. Ruth,	b. in 1764.	d.

Of these children Archelus was a sailor, and was noted as a great whaleman.

†-5. **Jonathan,⁵** probably fourth son of Seth, m. Mch. 3, 1743, Sarah Jones of Plymouth, and had issue:

Barnabas Hammond House.

1. David,   b. Jun. 20, 1745.   d.
2. Jonathan,   b. Feb. 3, 1747.   d.

Of these children David probably m. Nov. 14, 1766, Abigail Taber at Dartmouth.

†–6. **Sylvanus,**[5] fifth son of Seth, m. Feb. 7, 1749, Harriet Randall, and had issue :

1. Ebenezer, }   d. young.
2. Sylvanus, Jr., } b. Mch. 19, 1756. d.
3. Ebenezer,   b. Mch. 15, 1762. d. Jun. 19, 1841.

†–6–2. **Sylvanus, Jr.,**[6] married Charity ———, and lived at Rochester. Issue :

1. Sylvanus,   b. Jan. 10, 1786.   d.
2. Ebenezer,   b. Apr. 5, 1788.   d.
3. Charity,   b. Aug. 8, 1790.   d.
4. Elisha,   b. Nov. 26, 1792. d. Jan. 7, 1793.
5. Seth,   b. Dec. 25, 1793. d.

†–6–3. **Ebenezer,**[6] who probably lived in New Bedford, m. Jan. 4, 1790, Prudence Sherman, who was b. May 10, 1769, and d. Jan. 27, 1848. Issue :

1. Polly,   b. Sep. 8, 1790.   d. Apr. 6, 1796.
2. Charles,   b. Jan. 20, 1792.   d.
3. Mercy,   b. Oct. 1, 1794.   d. Apr. 6, 1796.
4. David,   }
5. Jonathan, } b. Mch. 26, 1797. d. May 6, 1798.
6. Betsey,   b. in   1800.   d. Nov. 27, 1868.

†–6–3–2. **Charles**[7] m. Jun. 20, 1819, Lucinda Parlow, and lived at Rochester. Issue :

1. Caleb,   b. Mch. 6, 1820.   d.
2. Mary Ann,   b. Mch. 3, 1822.   d.
3. Caroline M., b. May 2, 1824.   d.

3.—JEDEDIAH HAMMOND OF DARTMOUTH AND ROCHESTER, MASS.

†–3. **Jedediah**[5] **Hammond,** second son of Seth[4] [Samuel,[3] Benj.,[2] William[1]], lived in the town of Dartmouth until after the birth of his eighth child, Phineas, when he removed to the town of Rochester, where the remainder of his children were born. He m. 1st, Mch. 29, 1737, Elizabeth Jenney, who died Dec. 14, 1747. Issue :

1. Zilpha,   b. Jul. 5, 1738.   d.
2. Jeduthan, b. Apr. 14, 1740. d. May 31, 1790.

3. Eliphel,	b. Jun. 14, 1742.	d.
4. Jenne,	b. Feb. 20, 1744.	d.
5. Elizabeth,	b. Jun. 12, 1747.	d.

Elizabeth, wife of Jedediah, now dying, he m. 2d, Aug. 11, 1748, Mary Bolles, and had issue :

6. Deborah,	b. May 30, 1749.	d.
7. Simeon,	b. Sep. 14, 1751.	d. young.
8. Phineas,	b. Mch. 15, 1753.	d.
9. Patience,	b. Jan. 21, 1755.	d.
10. Anna,	b. Mch. 28, 1758.	d.
11. Pernall,	b. Apr. 21, 1760.	d.
12. Ruth,	b. Sep. 4. 1764.	d.
13. Jedediah.	b. Jul. 4. 1767.	d.

Of these children, **Jeduthan**[6] died May 31, 1790, and was buried in Middleboro', Mass. **Eliphel**[6] m. Oct. 4, 1764, **Charles Hammond,** son of Archelus. **Jenne**[6] m. at Dartmouth, Mch. —, 1764, John Weston. **Elizabeth**[6] m. at Dartmouth, Apr. 22, 1771, Freeman Ashley. **Phineas**[6] m. at Dartmouth, Jun. 10, 1777, Peace Merrihew. **Patience**[6] m. at Dartmouth, Jun. 10, 1781, Samuel Tupper. **Anna**[6] m. at Dartmouth, Nov. 30, 1780, Jona. Jenney. **Pernall,**[6] or Parnell, m. at Dartmouth, Aug. 12, 1777, Jacob Kenney. Issue : Thomas, Jona., Jacob Jr., and Phineas. [Jacob, Jr., who was born in 1796 and died in 1877, was father of Rachel Bolles, wife of Joshua Bolles, late of Mattapoisett, Mass.], and **Ruth**[6] m. May 22, 1785, Sylvanus Tobey.

†–3–2. **Jeduthan,**[6] who lived in Rochester, Mass., m. Nov. 3, 1764, Mary Jenney, who was born at Dartmouth, May 18, 1749, and died at Rochester about 1826. Issue :

1. Jane : 2. Paul, b. May 20, 1772, d. May 3, 1795 : 3. Elizabeth : 4. Jeduthan : 5. Jedediah ; 6. Mary, b. Oct. 10, 17— : 7. Lydia : 8. Hepsibeth : 9. Lettes, b. Mch. —, 1778, d. Sep. 2, 1852.

Of these children, **Jane**[7] m. 1st, at New Bedford, Sep. 17, 1791, Ephraim Landers. She m. 2d, Obed Griffith.

3. **Elizabeth**[7] married Asa Hacket. **Jeduthan**[7] is said to have married and had three sons, one of whom, Joseph, was a sea captain. Jeduthan, who lived in Dartmouth or Rochester, Mass., died and was buried in the Indian Ocean. **Mary**[7] m. Jun. 30, 1799, Elisha Caswell, and lived at Rochester. Issue : Mary, Gilbert and Sylvia, Elbridge G., Hannah, Rhoda, Tabatha, Martha, Lucy and Cynthia. [Elbridge G. m. Elizabeth Gurney, and had : Mary, Julia, Elbridge G. Jr., Lucy J., Lucinda Ella and Loring.]

7. **Lydia**[7] m. Nov. 6, 1806, Bishop Ashley, a blacksmith, and lived at Rochester.

7. **Hepsibeth**,[7] or Hepsibath, m. Jun. 15, 1806, Stephen Hadley, and lived in what is now the town of Marion, formerly a part of Rochester. Her children were Caroline, Lucy, Mary, Stephen W. and Lydia. [Stephen Wing, who was born Nov. 16, 1812, was a sea captain, and lived at Marion.]

†–3–2–2. **Paul**,[7] oldest son of Jeduthan, and grandson of Jedediah, was a shoemaker, and lived in the old town of Rochester. He m. Oct. 20, 1794, Sarah Edson. Issue :

    1. Paul 2d.   b. May 14, 1795.   d. Jul. 25, 1875.

Sarah Edson was born at Bridgewater or Sandwich, Mass., Mch. 3, 1776, and died at Fairhaven, Mass., Feb. 14, 1861. After Paul Hammond's decease, she m. 2d, a Ryder, and 3d, Joseph Smith, late of Fairhaven, Mass.

†–3–2–2–1. **Paul 2d**,[8] son of Paul, settled at Middletown, Conn., when a very young man, working in North's Gun Factory. About 1828 he kept a store in the suburbs of Middletown, and about 1830 moved to the latter place, and was an Overseer of the Poor one year. He then connected himself with his Uncle Lettes and cousin Joshua in the manufacture of steelyards, locks, etc. In 1834 he moved to Utica, N. Y., and engaged in various mechanical pursuits : in the fall of 1847 he moved to New York city and engaged in like pursuits ; later was agent of the Stephens Manufacturing Company of Cromwell, Conn., makers of iron toys. The last ten years of his life he was an invalid, and died in New York city. Paul 2d m. at Middletown, Conn., May 20, 1819, Abigail Chipman, who was born at Middletown, Conn., June 21, 1796, and died at New York city July 4, 1886, æ. 90, and was a very industrious woman. Issue :

    1. Louisa Maria,   b. Mch. 15, 1822.   d.
    2. Edson Dana,   b. Aug. 12, 1826.   d.
    3. Sarah Amelia,   b. Jul. 17, 1830.   d. Sep. 24, 1832.

1. **Louisa Maria**[9] m. at Utica, N. Y., Jun. 7, 1840, Thomas A. Ashford, who was born at Brightholme, Yorkshire, Eng., Aug. 11, 1814, and died in New York city Apr. 10, 1879. He was a cabinet maker by trade, a skilful mechanic, and for many years worked on piano fortes in New York city. Issue :

    1. Thomas Edson,   b. Jan. 17, 1845.   d. Apr. 28, 1862.

2. Louisa Aug.,   b. Aug. 21, 1848.   d. Nov. 27, 1855.
3. Frances A.,   b. Feb. 3, 1853.
4. Alfred Aug.,   b. Feb. 18, 1856.
5. Chas. Arthur,   b. May 18, 1859.

†–3–2–2–1–2. **Edson Dana,**[9] son of Paul 2d, born at Middletown, Conn., and for two or three years clerk in a store in Utica, N. Y., left there in 1846 and moved to Brooklyn, N. Y.: from 1846 to 1850 was clerk and accountant in a produce, brokerage and commission house; from 1850 to 1856 chief clerk in a stock broker's office; 1856 to 1872 assistant secretary and secretary of the Ohio & Mississippi R. R. in their New York offices; 1872 to 1874 assistant secretary of the Erie R. R. Co.: since July, 1885, clerk in the auditor's office of the Erie Dispatch, New York city. Residence, 54 West 100th Street, New York city. Edson Dana m. 1st, at Franklin, Mass., Oct. 8, 1848, Louise Marion Thurston, who was born at Franklin, Oct. 8, 1829, and died Oct. 1872. Issue:

1. Marion Amelia,   b. Sep. 4, 1850.
2. Annie Brintnall,   ⎱ b. Sep. 24, 1853.
3. Allie Thurston,   ⎰   d. Feb. 17, 1855.
4. Frank Herbert,   b. Nov. 23, 1862.

Edson Dana m. 2d, in New York city, Oct. 31, 1872, Eliza Ann White, née Knapp, who was born at Lowell, Mass., Nov. 7, 1840. Issue by the 2d marriage:

5. Mary Sylvia,   b. Jan. 14, 1874.
6. Gertrude Violet,   b. Jan. 2, 1877.

Of Edson Dana's children, **Marion Amelia**[10] m. in New York city, May 9, 1871, Henry F. Cowles, who was born in North Haven, Conn., May 8, 1839, and died at Colorado Springs, Col., Feb. 9, 1885. They had no issue. Mr. Cowles enlisted in the 16th Connecticut Reg't for three months, and also in the 18th Connecticut Reg't; was a prisoner twenty months—ten months in Libby Prison; was placed under fire at Charleston, S. C., but afterwards made his escape. His widow resides at Colorado Springs, Col.

2. **Annie Brintnall**[10] m. in New York city, Nov. 23, 1873, George W. Southwick, who was born in Brooklyn, Dec. 24, 1851, and resides at Stamford, Conn. Issue:

1. Frank Herbert,   b. Apr. 27, 1879.
2. Arthur Quackenbos,   b. Dec. 6, 1880.
3. Louis Brintnall,   b. Sep. 27, 1883.

G. W. Southwick is a dealer in manufacturers' supplies, New York city; factory at Stamford, Conn.

4. **Frank Herbert,**[10] only son of Edson Dana, at the age of 16 went on the clipper "Black Hawk" as cabin boy, to Australia, China and San Francisco, thence to New York city, doubling both Cape Good Hope and Cape Horn. He afterwards graduated from the schoolship St. Mary's with honor, and then went two voyages on the St. Domingo line of steamers. He was afterwards fireman, and later engineer, on the Erie R. R. He is now engineer on the Myrtle Avenue and Broadway branch of the Brooklyn Elevated R. R. Frank Herbert m. in New York city, Mch. 22, 1881, Annie Kristina Eiler, who was born in Laborg, North Jutland, Denmark, April 14, 1860, and resides at 1378 Broadway, Brooklyn, N. Y. Issue:

1. Louis Edward,	b. Sep. 23, 1881.	
2. George Albert,	b. Aug. 28, 1883.	
3. Henry Clinton,	b. Oct. 23, 1885.	
4. Frank Thurston,	b. Oct. 28, 1887.	
5. Robert Vincent,	b. Oct. 14, 1889.	d. Jul. 9, 1890.
6. Herbert Frederick,	b. Oct. 21, 1890.	

†-3-2-5. **Jedediah,**[7] third son of Jeduthan, m. Nancy Brooks of the State of New York, and lived and died at Farmington, Conn. Issue: Uri, Lettes, Caroline, Annes, Mary, Nancy Catherine, Silas, George and Elizabeth.

Of Jedediah's children, **Uri**[8] left home when a young man and has not since been heard from. **Lettes,**[8] who was a teacher, m. a Miss Bird of Plainville, Conn., and had two daughters, one of whom lives in the West, and the other is Mrs. Granville Bronson of Meriden, Conn.

Caroline[8] m. Thomas Greenfield, a hatter, and dealer in hats, caps, etc., in Middletown, Conn. She had three children: Robert, Caroline and George. The whole family are dead. **Annes,**[8] or **Agnes,** died while a young woman, on the eve of her marriage. **Mary,**[8] born Apr. 11, 1816, and died Feb. 10, 1875, m. Prof. Edmund Longley of Emory and Henry College, Emory, Va. Issue: Selden, Virginia Harriet, Catherine Hammond and Edmund.

Nancy Catherine,[8] who was a music teacher, m. Johnivry M. Sharpe, lives at Nashville, Tenn., and has a large family of children. **Silas,**[8] who was a carpenter, but never married, died at the West Indies, where he went for his health. **George,**[8] who was a printer, m. and had one child, and probably died during the late civil war. **Elizabeth**[8] died in infancy.

3

†–3–2–9. **Lettes Hammond,**[7] fourth son of Jeduthan, learned the trade of gunsmith in the United States Amory at Springfield, Mass., where he resided many years. He then moved to Farmington, Conn., where he carried on the business of gunsmith; from there he moved to Ashford, Conn., where he was engaged in the same business. He afterwards moved to Middletown, Conn., where he resided thirteen years. He invented and manufactured a kind of steel-yards, and died at East Brookfield, Mass. Lettes Hammond married in 1800, Margaret Fosket at Springfield, Mass., who died Apr. 22, 1861. Issue:

1. Jeduthan.	b. Mch. 15, 1802.	d. May 10, 1876.
2. Joshua,	b. Jul. 29, 1805.	d. Sep. —, 1805.
3. Margaret,	b. Mch. 10, 1807.	d. May 11, 1888.
4. Joshua Fosket,	b. Apr. 14, 1810.	d. Apr. 27, 1874.
5. Elizabeth Hacket,	b. Sep. 12, 1813.	d. May 11, 1867.
6. Penelope Keyes,	b. Jul. 14, 1820.	
7. Samuel.	b. Feb. 23, 1823.	d. Sep. 3, 1856.

1. **Jeduthan,**[8] oldest son of Lettes, who manufactured the steel-yards invented by his father, lived and died at East Brookfield, Mass. He m. Oct. 29, 1827, Sophia Bicknell of Ashford, Conn., who d. Jul. 4, 1861. Issue:

1. Caroline,	b. Jul. 28, 1829.	
2. Mary Eliz.,	b. Jun. 20, 1831.	
3. Samuel Edson,	b. May 30, 1834.	d. Oct. 16. 1850.
4. Ellen A.,	b. Aug. 8, 1849.	

Of these children, **Caroline**[9] m. Nov. 8, 1863, Elias H. Bartlett, lived in North Brookfield, Mass., and had a daughter, Mary H. Mr. Bartlett is dead, and his widow lives in East Brookfield, Mass. **Mary Elizabeth**[9] m. Apr. 8, 1858, Alvin S. Moulton, lives at Worcester, Mass., and has: Emma C., Clara A., and Mary L. All dead except Emma, who m. Edwin Marble and lives at Worcester. **Ellen A.**[9] m. Warren R. Upham, lives at East Brookfield, and had one son, George Warren, who d. in infancy.

3. **Margaret,**[9] oldest daughter of Lettes, m. Sep. 23, 1829, Aaron F. Wells of Greenfield, Mass., who d. Dec. 28, 1855. She lived in Middletown, Conn., and had issue: Edward H., Edward Hagain, Samuel Osgood, Ephraim E. Willey, George Eugene, and Francis Henry.

Of Margaret's children: Edward H. d. in infancy; Edward Hagain is a merchant tailor in Middletown, Conn.; Samuel Osgood, also a tailor, was a corporal in the 21st Conn.

Reg't, and died in Confederate Hospital at Upperville, Va.; Ephraim E. Wiley is employed in the manufacture of wringers in Middlefield, Conn.; George Eugene, a farmer, d. at Middletown, Conn.; and Francis Henry, a merchant, also d. at Middletown, Conn.

Margaret [Hammond] Wells, the mother, d. at Middletown, Conn., May 11, 1888.

4. **Joshua Fosket** was a mechanic and inventor at Providence, R. I. He m. Apr. 1, 1832, Eliza Ann Leach, and d. at Providence, R. I., Apr. 27, 1874. Besides three that d. in infancy, his issue were: 1, Edward M.; 2, William Emerson; 3, Charles; 4, Penelope M.; 5, Joshua; 6, Ann Eliza; 7, Henry W.; 8, Julia; and 9, Frank.

Of Joshua Fosket's children: 1. **Edward M.**[9] m. Ann Higgins at Springfield, Mass. Issue: Edward, George and Stella.

2. **William Emerson,**[8] who was b. Mch. 11, 1837, is a metal pattern maker at Meriden, Conn. He m. 1st, May 10, 1861, Irene J. Faulkner in Lynn, Mass., who d. Aug. 23, 1867, without issue. William E. m. 2d, May 19, 1869, Frances Ann Warner at Berlin, Conn., and had issue:

    1. Faith Irene,   b. July 25, 1877.

3. **Charles**[9] d. about 1859, in Lynn, Mass., and **Penelope,**[9] who was a milliner, d. about 1860 in the same city.

5. **Joshua,**[9] who was a carpenter, m. Sarah Corliss at Providence, R. I., and had four or five children.

6. **Ann Eliza**[2] m. 1st, Asa Hendrick of Providence, R. I. She m. 2d, a man by the name of Williams. Eliza left one child, and d. in Providence.

7. **Henry**[9] m. Annie Shepward in Lynn. No issue.

8. **Julia**[9] m. 1st, Lyman Damon of Springfield. She was afterwards divorced, and m. a second time, but had no issue.

5. **Elizabeth Hacket,** second daughter of Lettes, m. Feb. 18, 1839, Ephraim E. Wiley, a graduate of Wesleyan University, Middletown, Conn. Mr. Wiley was afterwards professor and for many years president of Emory and Henry College, Emory, Va., and was a popular Methodist clergyman, residing at Emory, Va., where he d. Mch. 13, 1893. Elizabeth H.

Hammond Wiley d. at Middletown, Conn., May 11, 1867.
Issue:

1. Margaret Ann.	b. Feb. 9, 1840.
2. Frances Elizabeth,	b. Sep. 6, 1841.
3. William Harlow,	b. May 29, 1845.
4. Virginie Watson,	b. Oct. 7. 1847.
5. Olin Fiske.	b. Dec. 28, 1849.
6. George Ephraim.	b. Oct 19, 1851.
7. Charles Sherwood,	b. Oct. 31, 1854. d. Jul. 1, 1855.

Of these children, **Margaret Ann**[9] m. Jun. 29, 1865,
John O. Story, M. D., now residing at Dallas, Tex. Issue:
John E. and Clarence L.

Frances Elizabeth[9] m. Aug. 4, 1859, John L. Buchanan, professor in Randolph Macon College, Ashland, Va.
Issue: Lillian Wiley, William Peters, Margaret Lee, Elizabeth Hammond, Horace Graham, Raymond Wiley, John Lee,
Grace Parker and Frank Emery.

William Harlow[9] m. Helen Parmenter of New York,
and is secretary of the Bromine Arsenic Springs, Crumpler,
Ashe Co., N. C. Issue: Charles Emerson, Harriet Palmer
and Margaret Adaline.

Virginie Watson[9] m. Francis A. Parker, one of the
firm of the Holsteine Woolen Mills. They now reside at
Abingdon, Va., and have issue as follows: Albert, Lillian,
and Virginie.

Olin Fiske,[9] who is a hotel keeper at Knoxville, Tenn.,
m. 1st, Mary Richmond of Va., and had two children. He
m. 2d, Alice McNew and had two more children.

George Ephraim,[9] who is a physician at Abingdon, Va.,
m. Sarah Elizabeth Scarf.

6. **Penelope Keyes,**[5] third daughter of Lettes, formerly
a teacher of music and French in Va., Tenn., and N. C., now
resides at Abingdon, Va. She has never married.

7. **Samuel,**[5] youngest son of Lettes, b. at Ashford, Conn.,
and educated at Wesleyan University, was for many years a
teacher. He m. Feb. 16, 1848, Margaret M. Merrick, lived
at Springfield, Mass., and d. there Apr. 3, 1856. Issue:

1. Adeline L ,	b. Feb. 15, 1849.	d. Sep. 2, 1885.
2. Emma I.,	b. Sep. 6, 1851.	d. Mch. 4, 1887.

Emma[9] m. Dec. 7, 1882, Edward Doton, and lived and
d. at Springfield, Mass. No issue.

4.—SETH 2D, OF DARTMOUTH, MASS.

†-4. **Seth,**[5] third son of Seth, in Nov. 1748, bought of Abraham Russell a farm in that part of East Fairhaven known as "New Boston," then a part of Dartmouth; and in Jan. 1794, gave a life lease of said farm to his son Seth Jr., and after him to his grandson, Caleb Hammond. He m. Aug. 23, 1738, Elizabeth Lombard (or Lumber) of Chatham, Mass., who was b. Apr. 1, 1714. Issue:

1. Adne,	b. May 25, 1739.	d.
2. Lurana,	b. Jun. 3, 1741.	d.
3. Luerriscea,	b Sep. 30, 1743.	d.
4. David,	b. Jan 16, 1746.	d.
5. Seth, Jr.,	b Jul. 4, 1748.	d.
6. Caleb,	b. Jan. 30, 1751.	d.
7. Nathaniel,	b. Jan. 3, 1754	d. at sea, 1781.
8. Jedidah,	b. Jun. 4, 1756.	d.

Of these children, 1. **Adne**[6] m. Nov. 19, 1762, Edward Eldridge at Dartmouth; 2. **Lurana**[6] m. Dec. 17, 1773, Hathaway Randall at Dartmouth; 4. **David**[6] m. Nov. 16, 1766, Abigail Taber at Dartmouth; 8. **Jedidah**[6] m. Jun. 26, 1791, George Handy at Dartmouth; 3. **Luerriscea,**[6] and 6. **Caleb,**[6] probably d. single; 7. **Nathaniel,**[6] probably m. 1st, in 1775, Sarah Stevens; he m. 2d, Dec. 5, 1778, Deborah Bolles at Dartmouth. Issue:

1. Nathaniel,	b. in 1779.	d. Sep. 5, 1802.

Nathaniel,[7] was a sea captain, probably in the merchant service.

†-4-5. **Seth Jr.,**[6] second son of Seth, lived on Wolf Island, Rochester, when his son Caleb was born, but afterwards moved on to his father's farm in New Boston, or East Fairhaven. He m. 1st, Mch. 1, 1773, Mary (or Hannah) Bolles, and had issue:

1. Caleb,	b. about 1774.	d.
2. Deborah, }	b. in 1776.	d Nov. 29, 1849.
3. Jedidah. }		d.
4. Eliza.	b.	d.
5. Elizabeth,	b.	d. Oct. 17, 1797.
6. Anstris,	b.	d. Oct. 20, 1797.

Seth Jr, m. 2d, Jun. 6, 1787, Anstris [Hammond] Jenney, daughter of Elisha Hammond, and granddaughter of Benjamin 2d. Issue:

7. Elisha,	b.	d.
8. Elihu,	b. Sep. 25, 1795.	d. Mch. 26, 1872.
9. Betsey,	b. Apr. 20, 1800.	d. Sep. 7, 1881.

Of these children, 5. **Elizabeth,**[7] and 6. **Anstris,**[7] d. single; 2. **Deborah**[7] m. a Mr. Bracey and d. at Middleboro', Nov. 29, 1849, æ. 73; 3. **Jedidah,**[7] who lived in East Fairhaven, m. Gamaliel Handy, and had issue:

1. Mary,	b. May 21, 1800.	d. Sep. 3, 1888. Single.

4. **Eliza**[7] is said to have m. a Westgate, but nothing further is known of her.

7. **Elisha,**[7] second son of Seth Jr., who was a farmer at East Fairhaven, m. Polly Stevens, but left no issue.

9. **Betsey,**[7] youngest daughter of Seth Jr., lived in Mattapoisett. She m. Dec. 25, 1826, Samuel Purrington, ship-carpenter, who d. Sep. 5, 1847, æ. 66. Issue: Mary E., Phebe, Hattie, Joseph, and Henry W.

Of Betsey's children: Mary E., m. John E. Almy; Phebe m. Jesse Gifford; Hattie m. Edgar S. Silva; and Henry W. m. Sarah O. Hiller.

†–4–5–8. **Elihu,**[7] youngest son of Seth Jr., who was a farmer at East Fairhaven, m. 1st, Phebe Snow, who was b. Jul. 16, 1795. No issue. Elihu m. 2d, Dec. 14, 1822, Almira Snow, who was b. Apr. 18, 1803, and d. Dec. 31, 1891. Issue:

1. Phebe,	b. Jun. 10, 1824.
2. Elizabeth,	b. Jul. 6, 1826.
3. Louisa D.,	b. Oct. 17, 1831.
4. Benjamin,	b. Aug. 24, 1839.

Of these children, **Elizabeth**[7] lives single at Mattapoisett; **Phebe** m. Aug. 22, 1849, Samuel N. Gould of Boston, who was b. in Lisbon, N. H., May 11, 1822. Issue: Sarah E., Mary A., Florence A., and Samuel N. Jr.

3. **Louisa D.,**[7] who lived in the Gelett neighborhood in East Fairhaven, m. Apr. 23, 1849, Edward H. Dillingham, who was b. in New Bedford in 1825. Issue:

1. Salome,	b. Apr. 24, 1849.	d. Sep. 12, 1852.
2. Ebenezer J.,	b. Jan. 10, 1851.	
3. Charles F.,	b. Feb. 10, 1854.	
4. Edward R.,	b. Jan. 10, 1859.	

Edward H. Dillingham served in Co. I, 3d Reg't M. V. M.,

at Newburn, N. C., for 9 months, in 1862–3. He afterwards re-enlisted and died in the service of his country.

4. **Benjamin**[6] resides in Newton Centre, and is senior member of the firm of B. Hammond & Co., flour and grain dealers, Boston. He m. Jun. 25, 1873, Alice D. Wright of Boston. Issue :

1. Alice M.,	b. May 16, 1874.
2. Edward H.,	b. Aug. 29, 1877.
3. Laura P.,	b. Jan. 6, 1884.

†–4–5–1. **Caleb**,[7] oldest son of Seth Jr., was a farmer at East Fairhaven. He m. Oct. 17, 1802, Hannah Barlow, who was b. in 1787, and d. Oct. 23, 1861. Issue :

1. Nathaniel,	b. Sep 18, 1803.	d. Oct. 16, 1887.
2. Amittai,	b. Sep. 4, 1806.	d. Jun. —, 1878.
3. Caroline,	b. Jul. 16, 1810	
4. Frederic P.,	b. Jul. 19, 1813.	d. Jan. —, 1893.
5. Abby,	b. Oct. 22, 1817.	
6. Joseph,	b. Nov. 6, 1821.	
7. Nancy.	b. Oct. 22, 1824.	d. Aug. 21, 1873.

Of these children, 3. **Caroline**[7] m. in 1827, James Stubbs, light-house keeper, who was b. in 1803, and d. in 1862. After the death of her husband, Caroline continued the care of Palmer's Island Light in New Bedford Harbor. Issue : Sarah, Charlotte [m. Jireh W. Clifton of New Bedford], James, Charles, Samuel, John, and Henry.

5. **Abby**,[7] who lives in Taunton, m. Sep. 28, 1834, John Jenkins, who was b. Jun. 7, 1816, and d. May 11, 1865. Issue :

1. Mary Abbie,	b. Nov. 20, 1836.
2. Rebecca Wing,	b. Jul. 31, 1844.

7. **Nancy**[7] m. in 1840, Freeman Snow, and lived in East Fairhaven. Issue : Helen M., Joseph H., Hannah E., John F., Abbie, and Charles M.

†–4–5–1–1. **Nathaniel**,[8] oldest son of Caleb, was a farmer and stone-worker, and lived in New Boston. He m. about 1820, Mary A. Dexter of Mattapoisett, who d. Apr. 14, 1873, æ. 69. Issue :

1. Susan.	b. May 30, 1821.	
2. Celinda,	b. Mch. 15, 1826.	
3. Eliza D.,	b. Dec. 5, 1827.	d. Oct. 26, 1860.
4. George A.,	b. Jan. 26, 1830.	
5. Drusilla M.,	b. Feb. 28, 1832.	d. Dec. 31, 1865.

6. Emila A.,	b. Jan 26, 1834.	
7. Charles W.,	b. Dec. 10, 1835.	d. Oct. 11, 1862.
8. Mary Ann,	b. Mch. 29, 1837.	
9. Albert,	b. Aug. 26, 1839.	d. Aug. —, 1878.
10. Josephine E.,	b. May 30, 1841.	
11. Maria L.,	b. Aug. 4, 1843.	
12. Fannie G.,	b. Aug. 2, 1845.	d. Nov. 9, 1890.
13. Sumner B.,	b. May 30, 1847.	
14. Arabella,	b. Dec. 14, 1849.	

Of Nathaniel's children, 7. **Charles W.**[9] d. single, at sea: and 10. **Josephine**[9] lives at Fairhaven, single.

1. **Susan,**[9] who now lives at Middleboro', m. Sep. 10, 1842, William Shaw of Mattapoisett, who was b. in 1822. Her children, b. at Mattapoisett, are: William Nelson, Henry W., Sarah J., Susan Adelaide, Levi, Eben, Lewis W., and Lillie.

2. **Celinda**[9] m. Mch. 1861, Daniel Dexter, a caulker of Edgartown, Martha's •Vineyard, where they now live. No issue.

3. **Eliza D.**[9] m. Nov. 1852, Daniel Dexter, the present husband of Celinda. Issue: Flora and Mary Lizzie.

4. **George A.**[9] is a shoe manufacturer, and resides at North Middleboro', Mass. He m. Nov. 14, 1848, Sarah J. Bumpus, who d. Apr. 11, 1891. Issue:

1. George Warren,	b. May 28, 1851.	
2. Horace Clifford,	b. May 28, 1854.	d. Feb. 10, 1858.

1. **George Warren,**[10] who is a shoemaker at North Middleboro', m. Dec. 27, 1869, Idella C. Howes. Issue:

1. Horace Clifford.	b. July 12, 1874.

5. **Drusilla M.,**[9] fourth daughter of Nathaniel, m. May 1, 1850, Gilbert Lyon, a shoemaker at Campello, Mass. Issue:

1. Frank M,	b Dec. 24, 1852.
2. Edgar M.,	b. Mch. 8, 1854.

Of Drusilla's children, **Frank M.**[10] is a poultry-raiser and resides at Fairhaven, Mass., on the Noble Gelett place. He m. Dec. 24, 1882, Eliza W. Pattangall. Issue: Laura P., b. Oct. 18, 1883: and Marion, b. Sep. 17, 1892.

Edgar M.[10] is a shoemaker, and resides at Cochesett, West Bridgewater. He m. Sarah Smith, and has Eveline and Bertha, twins, Allie and Della.

6. **Emily A.**[9] m. Sep. 12, 1864, Clarence Bearse, a carpenter, and lives at New Bedford. Issue: Albert and Lottie Hicks.

8. **Mary Ann**[9] m. in 1857, Edward Saunders, a sailor and cooper, and lives at Fairhaven. Issue: Horace and George.

9. **Albert,**[9] who was a shoemaker at New Bedford, m. Dec. 11, 1869, Susan Dexter of Edgartown, Martha's Vineyard. No issue.

11. **Maria L.**[9] m. Feb. 27, 1866, Benjamin F. Austin, a car driver at New Bedford. No issue.

12. **Fannie G.**[9] m. in 1870, John Gelett, a farmer at East Fairhaven, who was b. Nov. 23, 1836. Issue: Lena B., Mary L., Mabel M., John Jr., and Grace E.

13. **Sumner B.,**[9] who is a carpenter at New Bedford, m. Aug. 6, 1874, Emma E. Francis of Fairhaven, who was b. in Apr. 1851. Issue: Sadie, b. in 1875.

14. **Arabelia**[9] m. Oct. 1, 1868, Benjamin Brown, a beltmaker, and lives in Holyoke, Mass. Issue: Minnie Lena.

†–4–5–1–2. **Amittai,**[4] second son of Caleb, was a farmer at Mattapoisett, and afterwards a truckman at New Bedford, where he died. He m. Nov. 1, 1827, Eunice Chandler, who was b. Jan. 2, 1796, and d. Dec. 31, 1876. Issue:

1. Hattie E.,	b. Jun. —, 1828.	d. Apr. 30, 1861.
2. Caleb,	b. Nov. 19, 1829.	
3. Jane W.,	b. Dec. 3, 1832.	
4. Francis W.,	b. Feb. 26, 1836.	
5. Lucy S.,	b. Jan. 27, 1838.	

Of these children, 1. **Harriet E.**[9] m. Nov. 1844, Nelson B. Tinkham, farmer at Mattapoisett. Issue: Adeline, Emma T., Mary F., Allen W., Harris N., and Francis A.

3. **Jane W.**[9] m. Nov. 28, 1850, William W. Wilson, a painter at Fairhaven, who was b. Sep. 12, 1830. Issue: Hattie M., Eunice C., Charles A., Abbie B., Henry L., and Chester B.

5. **Lucy S.**[9] m. Jun. 6, 1857, Latimer S. Blake of New Bedford. Issue: Caleb H., Foster M., Harry M., Inez, Annie I., and Mabel V.

2. **Caleb,**[9] oldest son of Amittai, is an architect and builder at New Bedford. He served as a member of the Common Council five or six years, and of the Board of Aldermen several years, and was also a member of the School Committee. He m. Apr. 25, 1852, Annie T. Hazard, who was b. Oct. 20, 1833. Issue:

    1. Edgar, B.,   b. Mch. 18, 1854.
    2. Henry F.,   b. Oct. 18, 1856.

Of Caleb's children, 1. **Edgar B.,**[10] who is an architect at New Bedford, m. Mch. 26, 1884, Annie V. B. Salsbury, who was b. May 17, 1859. No issue.

2. **Henry F.,**[10] who is a carpenter at New Bedford, m. Apr. 11, 1882, Emma L. Fuller, who was b. Aug. 12, 1862. Issue:

    1. Frank F. T.,   b. Sep. 27, 1882.
    2. Chester B.,   b. Mch. 10, 1886.

4. **Francis W.,**[9] second son of Amittai, who is a carpenter at New Bedford, m. Sep. 1861, Abbie A. Macomber, who was b. Feb. 25, 1843. Issue:

    1. Arthur P.,   b. Aug. 3, 1862.
    2. Gertrude H.,   b. Aug. 7, 1866.
    3. Oscar S.,   b. Mch. 27, 1868.

†–4–5–1–4. **Frederic P.,**' third son of Caleb, was a farmer and laborer at Fairhaven, and has been thrice married. He m. 1st, Nov. 25, 1841, Nancy R. Gifford, who was b. Jun. 10, 1805, and d. Jun. 22, 1854. Issue:

    1. Elijah G.,   b. Aug. 14, 1842.
    2. John S.,   b. Feb. 16, 1845.

Fred m. 2d, Mch. 4, 1855, widow Emeline Tinkham, and had further issue:

    3. Herbert M.,   b. Jun. 9, 1857.

Fred m. 3d, Dec. 25, 1870, Rebecca F. Mendell, who was b. Jan. 23, 1844. Issue:

    4. Alice May,   b May —, 1870.
    5. Fred'c Francis,   b. Jul. 25, 1872.
    6. Susie Leonard,   b. Mch. 7, 1884.

1. **Elijah G.,**[9] oldest son of Frederic, is a painter and paper-hanger at New Bedford. He m. 1st, May 10, 1863, Laura Doane. No issue. He m. 2d, Oct. 19, 1869, Mary Leonard, and had issue:

    1. George L.,   b. Jun. 25, 1872.

2. **John S.,**[9] second son of Fred, is a carpenter and builder, and resides at Mattapoisett. He m. Dec. 26, 1866, Sarah P. Irish, who was b. Feb. 11, 1845. Issue:

1. James L.,	b. Jan. 6, 1868.
2. Charles W.,	b. Jul. 18, 1869.
3. Sarah E.,	b. Dec. 2, 1873.
4. Joseph I., }	b. May 3, 1880.
5. Eugene I., }	
6. Myrtle,	b. Aug. 23, 1885.

3. **Herbert M.,**[9] third son of Fred, who is a milkman at Fairhaven, m. Dec. 25, 1886, Laura E. Curtis, who was b. Feb. 25, 1859. Issue:

1. Chester M.,	b. Sep. 24, 1887.

†–4–5–1–6. **Joseph,**[4] fourth son of Caleb, is a farmer at New Boston, on the old homestead. He m. Jan. 15, 1846, Harriet Macomber, who was b. Apr. 11, 1829. Issue:

1. William,	b. in 1849	
2. Deborah,	b. in 1850.	d. Mch. 10, 1861.
3. Marietta,	b. Mch. 6, 1851.	d. Jan. —, 1874.
4. Arthur C.,	b. Dec. 20, 1852.	
5. Henry W.,	b. in 1854.	
6. Clarence W.,	b. Jan. 21, 1856.	
7. Hattie T.,	b. May 14, 1863.	

Of these children, **Deborah**[9] d. single, and **William**[9] is a laborer at Fairhaven, single.

3. **Marietta**[9] m. Nov. 19, 1868, Martin Snow Jr., of Mattapoisett, and had issue:

1. Ella Martin,	b. Jul. 22, 1869.

4. **Arthur C.,**[9] who is a farmer at Fairhaven, m. Jul. 10, 1884, Janette Pierce, who was b. Nov. 26, 1864. Issue:

1. Leroy C.,	b. Sep. 11, 1885.
2. Clinton P.,	b. Dec. 1, 1887.
3. Everett N.,	b. Dec. 19, 1890.

5. **Henry W.,**[9] who is a laborer at Fairhaven, m. Sep. 17, 1878, Fannie E. Bumpus. Issue:

1. Lewis C.,	b. Jan. —, 1879.
2. Harry C.,	b. Oct. 4, 1881.
3. Marietta F.,	b. Sep. 11, 1884.
4. Ethel E.,	b. May 9, 1889.
5. Lillian T.,	b. Mch. 15, 1891.

6. **Clarence W.,**[9] who is a carpenter at Fairhaven, m. Aug. 8, 1889, Susie L. Mendell. Issue:

1. Ida W.,	b. Aug. 8, 1890.

7. **Hattie T.,**[9] who lives at New Bedford. m. May 7, 1881, Harry N. Tinkham. Issue: Edith and Emma.

II.—SAMUEL HAMMOND 2D, OF ROCHESTER, MASS.

†. **Samuel**[4] **Hammond 2d,** third son of Samuel[3], [Benjamin,[2] William,[1]] probably lived on the West Neck, Mattapoisett, near his father. He m. Nov. 3, 1730, Elizabeth Edmister (possibly Deliverance Admixter), and had issue:

1. Samuel 3d,	b. Nov. 5, 1732.	d.
2. Priscilla,	b. Jul. 18, 1734.	d.
3. Innocent, ⎱ 4. Edminster, ⎰	b. Jan. 5, 1737.	d.
5. Zephahiah,	b. Aug. 18, 1740.	d.
6. Lucy,	b. Aug. 4, 1742.	d.
7 Seth, ⎱ 8. Barnabas, ⎰	b. Sep. 15, 1744.	d.
9. Rose,	b. Feb. —, 1746.	d

Of these children, nothing further is known of Priscilla, Innocent, Zephaniah, Lucy and Rose.

†–4. **Edmister**[5] m. 1st, Nov. 5, 1763, Elizabeth Cornish at Dartmouth. He m. 2d, Apr. 9, 1769, Mary Meigs at Rochester. Issue, if any, unknown.

1.—SAMUEL 3D, OF LAKEVILLE, MASS.

†–1. **Samuel 3d,**[5] oldest son of Samuel 2d, probably lived in the present town of Lakeville, Mass. He m. Jan. 27, 1749, Mary Turner of Dartmouth. Issue:

1. Catherine,	b. May 18, 1749.	d.
2. Mercy,	b. May 9, 1751.	d.
3. Christopher,	b. Nov. 23, 1753.	d. Feb. —. 1824.
4. Almy,	b. Jan. 8, 1758.	d.
5. Anne,	b. about 1760.	d.
6. Molly,	b. about 1762.	d.
7. Freelove,	b.	d.

Of these children, **Mercy**[6] and **Molly**[6] died quite old, single: **Freelove,**[6] called "Lovy," formerly lived at Mattapoisett, also single; and of **Almy**[6] nothing further is known.

1. **Catherine**[6] m. May 10, 1770, Simeon Andrews at Dartmouth, where she probably lived.

5. **Anne**[6] m. Dec. 12, 1781, Joseph Shockley, and lived near "Sampson's Tavern" in Lakeville, Mass., on her father's place. Issue: William, Ephraim, Polly, Esther, and Joseph Jr.

Joseph Jr., m. Sally Alden, and had 15 children, the oldest of whom, Capt. Joseph Shockley, recently d. at New Bedford.

†-1-3. **Christopher,**[6] called Capt. "Kit," was a sea captain, and lived near "Sampson's Tavern" in Lakeville, and d. in Nantucket. He m. 1st, Aug. 15, 1784, Desire Tobey, who was b. in 1758, and d. Nov. 1810, and is buried at the Pond Cemetery, Lakeville. Issue: 1, Rebecca; 2 and 3, Elisha and Samuel, twins, b. 1787; 4, Betsey; 5, Polly; 6, Patience, b. 1794, d. 1859; 7, Thomas; 8, Sally; 9 and 10, Lemuel and Harriet, twins; 11, Catherine, b. 1802, d. 1839.

Christopher m. 2d, a widow Nickerson of Nantucket, where he d. without further issue.

Of the above children, 1. **Rebecca**[7] m. Charles Winant, lived in New York City, and d. in Jersey City, N. J. Issue: Elizabeth, and Emma who m. John Maccabee of Jersey City; 9 and 10, Lemuel and Harriet, twins, d. at two or three years of age.

†-1-3-3. **Samuel**[7] was a sea captain, and lived at "Lund's Corner," Head-of-the-River, New Bedford. He m. 1st, Betsey Spooner, who d. Dec. 8, 1825, æ. 35. Issue: Nancy, Joshua and Lizzie. Of these children, Nancy m. a Shaw; Joshua d. with cholera at 10 or 12 years of age; and Lizzie d. in infancy.

Samuel m. 2d, Lucy Manchester, and moved to Albany, or Utica, N. Y., where he afterwards died, probably without further issue.

4. **Betsey**[7] m. Nov. 2, 1811, Joseph Warren, lived at "Padan Aram," Dartmouth, and had Joseph Warren Jr.

5. **Polly**[7] m. Charles Spooner, lived in Ohio, and had Philip Loring, a lawyer, and other children.

6. **Patience**[7] m. Sep. 13, 1815, Thomas Holmes, who was b. Dec. 7, 1791, and d. May 22, 1866, and was a farmer at New Bedford, where both died. Issue: Betsey, Thomas, Charity, and Mary, b. in Mattapoisett; Eliza, Church, Samuel, and Abby, b. in Woodstock, Vt.

7. **Thomas,**[7] who was a carpenter, in New York City, afterwards moved to Newark, N. J., where he probably died. He married —— ——, and had issue, but nothing further can be learned in regard to his family.

8. **Sally**[7] m. Stephen Snow of Mattapoisett, where were born four children : Serepta, Rebecca, Elisha, and Charles. They then moved to Lowell, and afterwards to Canton, Mass., where both died, and where the following children were born : Olive, Sarah, Lucinda, George, and Mary Ann. Olive m. George Wright of Hyde Park, Mass.

11. **Catherine**[7] m. Aug. 3, 1820, Chandler Carver, who was a ropemaker and lived at Plymouth, Mass., where both died. Issue : Thomas C. of New Bedford, Desire T., Mary A., William H., Edwin E., Samuel, Catherine A., Lucy A., and James M.

†-1-3-2. **Elisha,**[7] oldest son of Christopher, and twin brother of Samuel, was a farmer and lived and d. (May 26, 1858), in the northwesterly part of the old town of Rochester. He m. Apr. 26, 1812, Sally Macomber, and had issue :

| 1. Orrin. | b. in 1815. | d. in 1853. |

†-1-3-2-1. **Orrin**` was a farmer on his father's place in Rochester, but d. at San Francisco, Cal. He m. Nov. 23, 1838, Hannah A. Fisher, who was b. in 1812, and d. in 1872. Issue :

1. Alden M.,	b. in	1840.	d. in	1841.
2. Hattie F.,	b. Dec.	4, 1843.		
3. Sarah E.,	b. Nov.	9, 1845.		
4. Albert A.,	b. in	1847.	d. in	1849.
5. Amelia F.	b. Oct.	12, 1849.		
6. Almira M.,	b. Dec.	9, 1851.	d Mch. 11, 1889.	

Of these children, **Hattie F.**[9] m. Dec. 3, 1867, Frank Harvey, and lives at Lakeville. No issue.

3. **Sarah E.**[9] m. 1st, Apr. 5, 1860, Louis Finney, who d. Apr. 21, 1871. Issue : Mabel Lewis and Cora Hammond. Sarah E. m. 2d, Jun. 23, 1874, Reuben Simmons, who d. Dec. 22, 1884, without issue. Sarah E. resides at Middleboro', Mass.

5. **Amelia F.**[9] m. 1st, Oct. 15, 1857, Isaac Haskins, and had a son, Herbert. Amelia F. m. 2d, Feb. 14, 1878,

Bennajah Hathaway, and lives at Raynham, Mass. Issue:
Emma Hammond, George Orrin, Harold Lewis, and Julia
Francis.

6.   **Almira M.**[9] or Myra, m. Oct. 1867, Henry T. Maxim,
and lived at Taunton, Mass.   Issue: Elbridge and Luella.

--

7.—SETH OF ACUSHNET, MASS.

†–7. **Seth,**[5] fifth son of Samuel 2d, lived near Welden's
Cotton Factory, Acushnet.   He m. Jan. 6, 1773, Mary Bolles,
and had issue: 1. Seth Jr., who d. at the age of 70; and
2. Mercy.
Seth probably had other children, but nothing further is
known.
Of his children, **Mercy**[6] lived at Acushnet, or North New
Bedford, and m. Jul. 18, 1802, Noah Hathaway.   A descendant, Job Hathaway, lives near the Head-of-the-River, Acushnet.

†–7–1. **Seth Jr.**[6] lived near Welden's Factory, Acushnet,
but afterwards moved to New Bedford, where he died.   He m.
Dec. 15, 1796, Elizabeth Randall.   Issue: 1. John Randall,
d. Aug. 23, 1878, æ. 82 : 2. Mercy: 3. Charles; 4. Henry;
5. Polly; 6. Cordelia: 7. Nancy; 8. Susan; 9. Eliza;
10. Seth; 11. Sally.

Of these children, 2. **Mercy,**[7] b. 1801, m. Jabez Gorham
of Mattapoisett, where she d. without issue, Oct. 7, 1874,
æ. 73.

3.   **Charles**[7] was a mariner and lived at Welden's Factory.
He m. Eliza Crocker, and had a son Elbridge, who d. single.

4.   **Henry**[7] d. in New York at the age of 22, single; and
9. **Eliza**[7] d. at New Bedford, single.

5.   **Polly**[7] m. Palmer Haskell, and d. in Rochester, without
issue.

6.   **Cordelia,**[7] b. 1809, m. Edson DeMoranville, and d.
at Long Plain, Acushnet, Apr. 16, 1888.   Issue: Meribah,
Elizabeth, Cordelia, Lucy, Sophronia, and Deborah.

7.   **Nancy**[7] m. 1st, Amos Cushing, and had one son, who
d. at the age of 14.   She m. 2d, William Thatcher, and had

two children, William and Nancy. Of these children, William
d. in the War; and Nancy m. Joseph Reynolds and lived and
d. in New Bedford. Nancy [Hammond] Thatcher is living at
Newport, R. I.

8. **Susan,**[7] who lives in New Bedford, m. Feb. 10, 1845,
William H. Hubbard, and has twin daughters, Mary Elizabeth
and Adeline. Mary Elizabeth d. at the age of 4 years; and
Adeline m. George L. Durfee of New Bedford, and has two
children, William and Susie.

10. **Seth**[7] lived in Acushnet, but afterwards left his family
and went South, perhaps to Florida. He m. Dec. 2, 1846,
Jane M. Orcutt, and had issue:

 1. Emily,   b. Aug. 7, 1847.

11. **Sally,**[7] at the age of 16 or 17, went to Utah, and
lived with the Mormons.

†–7–1–1. **John Randall,**[7] oldest son of Seth Jr., lived
in the Morse neighborhood, Acushnet, where he d. æ. about 80.
He m. 1st, about 1821, Ruth Turner, and had issue:

 1. Charles, b. May 22, 1822.
 2. Henry, b. in 1824.
 3. Ruth A , b. Apr. 7, 1830. d. in 1870.
 4. Job Earl, b. Jul. 19, 1831. d. May 11, 1884.
 5. Calvin, b. Feb. 22, 1837. d. May 27, 1890.

John Randall m. 2d, in 1840, Orpha B. [Hall] Haskins,
and had issue:

 6. Andrew Jackson, b. in 1843. d. Jun. 18, 1885.

Of John Randall's children, 2. **Henry,**[8] who was formerly
a sailor, lives at Cuttyhunk, Mass., single. During the War
he served in the ship Supply, and in the gunboat Sachem, and
was a member of Co. F, 3d Reg't Mass. V. M.

5. **Calvin P.**[8] during the War was a member of Co. B,
3d Reg't. Mass. Heavy Artillery. He was mustered into the
service May 19, 1863, and discharged Jun. 9, 1865. In early
life he was a sailor and telegraph operator; and at the time of
his death, which occurred at Rochester, was a pensioner.

3. **Ruth A.**[8] m. in 1850 George R. Taber, and lived in
New Bedford. Issue: Elizabeth, George L., Susan E., and
Arthur F.

†-7-1-1-1. **Charles,** oldest son of John R., was formerly a whaler and stonemason, but now a grocer in New Bedford. He m. Feb. 2, 1848, Jane C. Gorham, daughter of Jabez Gorham, who d. Sep. 1, 1860. Issue:

1. Charles,	b. in 1850.	d. young.
2. Rebecca J.,	b. Dec. 23, 1852.	
3. Herbert,	b. Oct. —, 1855.	
4. Isabella,	b. in 1858.	d. young.

2. **Rebecca J.,**[9] who lives in New Bedford, m. Nov. 29, 1866, Thomas H. Wall of New Bedford. Issue:

1. Annie B. R.,	b. Oct. 19, 1867.	d. Apr. 15, 1868.
2. Herbert H.,	b. Jan. 1, 1874.	
3. Mary H. D. K.,	b. Sep. 20, 1879.	d. Feb. 17, 1882.

3. **Herbert**[9] is a grocer with his father, Kempton St., New Bedford. He m. Jun. 23, 1889, Mary Kelley of Churchill, N. Y., and has issue:

1. Mary Corrine,	b. Jan. 1, 1891.
2. Son,	b. Feb. 6, 1892.

†-7-1-1-4. **Job Earl,** third son of John R., who was a shoemaker at Fairhaven, m. in 1851 Ruby A. Haskins, and had issue:

1. William H.,	b. Sep. 10, 1851.	
2. John N.,	b. Jul. 11, 1855.	
3. Henrietta F.,	b. Jul. 1, 1858.	d. Jul. 4, 1862.
4. Tott,	b. Jul. 14, 1861.	d. Jun. 28, 1862.
5. Job Herbert,	b. Aug. 5, 1863.	
6. Ruth Alice,	b. Nov. 27, 1866.	
7. Amy Belle,	b. Jun. 16, 1870.	d. Sep. 28, 1872.
8. Emery Walton,	b. Dec. 25, 1872.	
9. Frank Bowers,	b. Jun. 11, 1876.	

Of these children, **William H.,**[9] **Emery,**[9] and **Frank,** live at North New Bedford, single; and **Job Herbert**[9] also single, is a shoemaker at North Middleboro, Mass.

6. **Ruth A.**[9] m. Sep. 8, 1885, James N. Cobb of Marion, and lives in Acushnet. Issue: Roland.

2. **John N.,**[9] second son of Job Earl, who is a laborer and lives in Acushnet, m. Ella F. Reynolds. Issue:

1. Fred Nelson,	b. Apr. 26, 1875.
2. Charles Albert,	b. Aug. 9, 1877.
3. Ethel Francis,	b. May 12, 1880.
4. Harry Allen,	b. Apr. 11, 1882.
5. Edward Clifford,	b. Nov. 28, 1884.
6. Kenneth Roslin,	b. Dec. 18, 1886.
7. Clement Swift,	b. Mch. 20, 1889.

4

†–7–1–1–6. **Andrew Jackson,**[8] youngest son of John Randall, who was a silver polisher, m. 1st, in 1862, Emma J. Slocum of New Bedford. No issue. He m. 2d, Jul. 13, 1870, Annie M. Tripp of New Bedford, who d. in 1880. Issue: One child that d. young.

8.—BARNABAS OF ROCHESTER, MASS.

†–8. **Barnabas,**[5] sixth son of Samuel 2d, m. at Rochester, Dec. 6, 1770, Mary Clark, daughter of David and Maria [Hammond] Clark. He probably had a son:

    1. Seth 3d,   b. in 1773.   d. Jun. 26, 1841.

Barnabas probably had other children, but the records cannot be found.

†–8–1. **Seth Hammond 3d,**[6] probably son of Barnabas, was b. at Fairhaven or Acushnet in 1773, and d. at Marion, Jun. 26, 1841. He was a sea captain, and lived near the Weweantit River, Marion, where all his children were born. He m. 1st, Nov. 19, 1794, Elizabeth Damon of Fairhaven, and had issue:

    1. Catherine,   b. Jul. 30, 1797.   d.
    2. Abigail,   b. in   1800.   d. Aug. 20, 1863.
    3. Charles B.,   b. May 2, 1802.   d. Feb. 14, 1857.
    4. Clement,   b. in   1804.   d. Aug. 6, 1850.
    5. Eliza,   b. Apr. 20, 1806.   d.
    6. Jane,   b. Apr. 7, 1808.   d.
    7. Sarah,   b. Jun. 30, 1810.   d. Jan. 16, 1879.
    8. Leonard,   b. Jan. 22, 1813.   d. in   1856.

Seth 3d m. 2d, Jul. 13, 1818, Elizabeth [Hammond] Blankenship, daughter of Capt. Edward Hammond, and widow of Job Blankenship. No further issue.

Of these children, 1. **Catherine**[7] m. Aug. 8, 1816, Jireh Clifton of Marion. Issue: Fannie, Harriet, Charles, and Joseph.

2. **Abigail**[7] m. in 1825, Charles Damon of Marion. Issue: Charles, Albert, and Helen.

5. **Eliza**[7] m. Oct. 5, 1823, William Haney, or Hana, of Marion, and had issue: Catherine, Sophronia, and William Jr.

6. **Jane**[7] m. Jan. 1, 1832, William Taylor of New York City, and had Virginia, who d. young.

7. **Sarah**[7] m. 1st, Oliver Hunt, and had William H., Sarah M., and Carrie W., who d. young.

Sarah m. 2d, Eleazor Witherspoon, and had Willard W., George F., and Frank E.

8. **Leonard**[7] m. Mch. 1841, Mary Pierce, and d. in California, without issue, in 1856.

†–8–1–3. **Charles B.**[7] was a sea captain and lived at Marion. He m. Ruth A. Nickerson, who was b. Jul. 12, 1801, and d. Dec. 12, 1873. Issue:

1. Betsey D.,	b. Jun. 8, 1826.	d. Dec. 23, 1891.
2 Josiah N.,	b. Jan. 12, 1828.	d.
3. Clement,	b. Jun. 18, 1830.	d. Oct. 7, 1831.
4. Almira Reed,	b. Aug. 8, 1836.	d.
5. Charles A.,	b. Oct. 28, 1838.	

Of these children, 1. **Betsey D.**[8] d. single at Marion.

4. **Almira Reed** m. Jan. 6, 1857, Charles H. Briggs, and lived at Marion. She had one son, Edward.

2. **Josiah N.,**[3] oldest son of Charles B., who was a sailor, lived at Marion until the latter part of his life, when he moved to Fairhaven. He m. Nov. 16, 1861, Elizabeth A. Chase of Fairhaven, and had issue:

1. Herbert E.,	b. Jan. 17, 1865.

1. **Herbert E.,**[9] who resides at South Dartmouth, m. Apr. 22, 1886, Sarah A. Scharves, who was b. in New Bedford, Mch. 20, 1865. Issue:

1. Mabel Elinor,	b. Jun. 6, 1887.
2. Edith Elizabeth,	b. Jan. 7, 1890.

†–8–1–3–5. **Charles A.,**[?] youngest son of Charles B., who is a carpenter at Marion, m. Oct. 21, 1860, Ellen A. Chadwick of Marion. Issue:

1. Hannah Maria,	b. Sep. 10, 1862.
2. Horace Allen,	b. Jun. 20, 1866.
3. Annie C.,	b. Mch. 5, 1872.
4. Ruth E.,	b. Oct. 12, 1873.

1. **Hannah Maria**[9] m. Nov. 29, 1887, William A. Gurney, and resides in Marion. Issue: Elmer Augustus.

2. **Horace Allen**[9] m. Sep. 25, 1890, Mary A. Stowell of North Brookfield, Mass., where they now reside. No issue.

†-8-1-4.   **Clement,**[7] second son of Seth 3d, was a captain in the whaling service, and lived on "Great Neck," Marion. He m. about 1825-6, Charity Allen, and had issue :

1. Seth,	b. Oct. 4, 1827.	d. in 1860-61.
2. Edwy E.,	b. Feb. 27, 1831.	
3. Clement M.,	b. Mch. 22, 1833.	d. Jul. 29, 1874.
4. Mary A.,	b. Mch. 14, 1835.	d. in 1864.
5. Abigail D.,	b. Jan 29, 1837.	b. Sep. 23, 1841.
6. Sarah B.,	b. July 27, 1839.	d. Jul. 27, 1841.
7. Sarah A.,	b. Mch. 11, 1842.	b. Jan. 1, 1849.

Of these children, Mary A. d. single at Marion ; and Abigail D., Sarah B., and Sarah A. d. young.

†-8-1-4-1.   **Seth,**[8] who was a sea captain and lived at Marion, was lost at sea.   He m. about 1850 Emily O. Mendell, and had issue :

1. Ernest,	b. in 1852.	d. May 6, 1873.
2. Oscar Mortimer,	b. Jul. 3, 1854.	d. in 1872.
3. Emily O.,	b. Mch. 20, 1855.	d. in infancy.

Of these children, 1. **Ernest,**[9] who was a sailor, m. Ada Hunt, and d. at Marion without issue.

2.   **Oscar Mortimer**[9] was in the employ of R. H. White, Boston, where he d. single.

†-8-1-4-2.   **Edwy E.**[8] is a retired sea captain, and lives at "Great Neck," Marion.   He m. Sep. 17, 1863, Adeline S. Post of New York City, who was b. Jun. 19, 1831.   No issue.

†-8-1-4-3.   **Clement M.**[8] was a captain in the whaling service, and was lost at sea off the West Indies.   He m. Sep. 8, 1858, Mary S. Babcock, who was b. Aug. 17, 1838.   Issue :

1. Clement Milton,	b. Oct. 15, 1859.	
2. Emma Scott,	b. Jul. 17, 1861.	
3. Amy A.,	b. Apr. 17, 1864.	
4. Agnes M.,		
5. Lydia B.,	b. Aug. 24, 1865.	d. young.
6. Minnie Scott,	b. Apr. 6, 1868.	
7. Seth M.,	b. Jan. 24, 1870.	d. young.
8. Ida P.,		
9. Seth G.,	b. Apr. 28, 1871.	d. young.
10. Anna A.,	b. Jun. 13, 1872.	d. young.

Of these children, 1. **Clement Milton**[9] is business manager of the *New York World*, and resides at Metuchen, N. J.   He m. Jul. 14, 1880, Ada M. Getchel of Mattapoisett. Issue :

1. Milton,   b. Dec. 3, 1881.   d. in 1885.
2. Florence,   b. Jan. 30, 1888.

2. Emma Scott[9] m. Sep. 14, 1880, George A. Hart, and lives at Taunton, Mass. Issue: Emma M., Ida Allen, and George Clement.

3. Amy A.[9] m. Oct. 1888, Jacob B. Savery, and lives at Marion. No issue.

6. Minnie,[9] or **Mary,** m. Feb. 23, 1888, Arthur H., son of Capt. Arthur H. Hammond of Wareham, Mass. Issue: Bethiah H., b. Jul. 31, 1890.

8. Ida P.[9] m. Mch. 1891, Frank Lincoln, and lives at Wareham. No issue.

4. Agnes M.[9] resides with her mother at Wareham, Mass.

III.—THOMAS HAMMOND OF NEW BEDFORD.

†. **Thomas**[4] **Hammond,** fourth son of Samuel[3] [Benj.,[2] William[1]], lived at New Bedford (then a part of Dartmouth). Besides land in Rochester, he received from his father 50 acres of land situated in the town of Wales, Mass. He m. Apr. 6, 1721, Sarah Spooner, and had issue:

1. Benjamin,   b. Mch. 27, 1722.   d.
2. William,   b. Aug. 17, 1724.   d.
3. Abigail,   b. Feb. 6, 1726.   d. May 6, 1739.
4. Maria,   b. May   9, 1729.   d.
5. Samuel,   b. Apr. 29, 1731.   d. May 16, 1801.
6. Lovina,   b. Feb. 9, 1734.   d.
7. Thomas, Jr., b. Nov. 1, 1736.   d.
8. Jabez,   b. July 28, 1738.   d. Sep. 6, 1809.
9. Prince,   b. Jan. 7, 1741.   d.

Of these children, nothing further is known of **Maria** or **Prince.**

6. Lovina[5] m. Jan. 10, 1750–51, John Chase and lived at Dartmouth. Issue: Rhoda, Nathaniel, Elizabeth, Rhoda, Benjamin, Isaac, Meriah, Sarah, Hannah, and John.

†–1. **Benjamin,**[5] oldest son of Thomas, probably lived in New Bedford. He m. Mch. 24, 1742–3, Hannah Gifford at Dartmouth, and had issue:

1. Fear,	b. Apr.	6, 1744.	d.
2. William,	b. Sep.	6, 1745.	d.
3. Zoeth,	b. May	2, 1747.	d.
4. John,)	b. Oct.	10, 1749.	d.
5. Meribah,)			d.
6. Rebecca,	b. Jul.	7, 1750.	d.
7. Andria,	b. Aug.	18, 1752.	d.

Of these children, 1. **Fear**[6] m. Nov. 22, 1774, James Williams at Dartmouth, now New Bedford. Fear probably m. 2d, Jun. 4, 1780, Samuel Gibson at Dartmouth. No issue known.

2. **William**[6] m. Nov. 15, 1769, Dorothy Sherman at Dartmouth. Nothing further known.

3. **Zoeth**[6] m. Mch. 10, 1775, Lois Valler of Plymouth, Mass., and probably went West.

4. **John**[6] m. Oct. 17, 1782, Silvia Eldridge at Dartmouth. Nothing further known.

†–7. **Thomas Jr.,**[5] fourth son of Thomas, lived, and probably died, at that part of Dartmouth which is now New Bedford, Mass. He m. Feb. 17, 1760, Mary Taber, and had issue :

1. Salathiel,	b. Jun.	30, 1761.	d.
2. Thankful,	b. Oct.	19, 1765	d.
3. Prince,	b. May	5, 1769.	d.

Of these children, 1. **Salathiel**[6] m. Oct. 27, 1785, Eunice Young of Dartmouth ; and **Thankful**[6] m. Nov. 1, 1789, John Sanford of Dartmouth.

— — —

2.—WILLIAM HAMMOND OF WALES, MASS., AND NORTHERN NEW YORK.

†. **William,**[5] second son of Thomas[4] [Samuel,[3] Benj.,[2] William[1]], was b. at New Bedford, Aug. 17, 1724. He probably moved first to Wales, Hampden Co., Mass.; and afterwards settled in the northern part of the State of New York, perhaps at or near Pittstown, Rensselaer Co. He m. in 1745 Elizabeth Sheperd, who m. 2d, Archy Macomber. Issue :

1. Benjamin,	b. Apr.	5, 1746.	d.
2. Sarah,	b. Apr.	19, 1748.	d.
3. Paul,	b. Dec.	27, 1757.	d. Aug. 8, 1838.
4. William, Jr ,	b. Jun.	1, 1766.	d. Apr. 4, 1821.

1. **Benjamin**[6] probably m. May 28, 1774, at New Bedford, Hannah Tallman, but the issue, if any, is not known.

- - - - -

(3.)—PAUL OF NORTHAMPTON, AND PENFIELD, N. Y.

†–3. **Paul**,[6*] second son of William, and probably b. at Wales, Hampden Co., Mass., m. at Pittstown, Rensselaer Co., N. Y., and moved to Northampton (Northville), Fulton Co., about 1795, where many of his children were born. About 1815 –20 he moved to Penfield, Monroe Co., afterwards Webster, where he was living at the time of his death. He was a soldier in the Revolutionary War, and afterwards a farmer. He m. in 1780, Mary (called Polly) Fuller, who was b. at Easton, Mass., Dec. 14, 1763, and d. at Concord, Pa., Jul. 9, 1842. Issue:

1. Abner,	b. Jul. 24, 1782.	d. Dec. 22, 1813.
2. Benoni G.,	b. Feb. 16, 1784.	d. Dec. 24, 1866.
3. Elizabeth,	b. May 4, 1786.	d.
4. William,	b. Jul. 27, 1788.	d. Mch. 20, 1860.
5. Charles,	b. Sep. 19, 1790.	d. Feb. 6, 1794.
6. Ruth,	b. Feb. 7, 1792.	d. in 1860.
7. Bartimeus,	b. Mch. 16, 1794.	d. Oct. 23, 1823.
8. Paul, Jr.,	b. Jan 26, 1797.	d. Feb. 8, 1880.
9. Samuel,	b. Feb. 1, 1799.	d. Mch. 4, 1884.
10. Naomi,	b. Mch. 11, 1801.	d. Jan. —, 1892.
11. Sarah,	b. Sep 11, 1803.	d. Jun. 25, 1890.
12. Mahala,	b. Mch. —, 1805.	d. Oct. 25, 1807.
13. Amanda M.,	b. Oct. 30, 1806.	d. Apr. 23, 1891.
14. Mary,	b. Oct. 31, 1810.	d.

Of these children, **Charles**[7] and **Mahala**[7] d. young; **Bartimeus**,[7] who was b. blind, never married; and **Mary**[7]

* There is a tradition and a Bible record that Paul Hammond was born in England, but these may have arisen from the fact that he was probably born in Wales, Mass.

Long before the writer got the record of this branch he had learned from several sources that they were directly related to the Dutchess County branch of Hammonds of New York, whose ancestor came to this country in 1634, they being directly descended from Samuel Hammond[5], [Thomas,[4] Samuel,[3] Benjamin,[2] William[1]], whose wife was Hannah Sheperd.

Jacob Hammond, late of Farmington, N. Y., and a descendant of this Dutchess County family, in his youth knew both Paul and his brother William. Referring to a visit of Paul to his (Jacob's) father in Saratoga Co., after Paul moved to western New York, he says: "I well recollect, on the occasion of Paul's eastern visit at my father's house, of his remarking to father that they were as nearly related as they could be and not be brothers, as their fathers were brothers and their mothers were sisters. This I think effectually disposes of the tradition of English birth."

Andrew B. Hammond of Dutchess Co. and others give corroborative testimony. If the Paul Hammond and Dutchess Co. branches are closely related (and of this there is no reasonable doubt) it is not probable that Paul Hammond was born in England.

is supposed to have gone west with the Mormons at the time of their settlement in Ohio, about 1830–31.

†–3–1. **Abner**[7] was a soldier in the War of 1812, and was killed upon the Niagara Frontier, as western New York was then called. He m. Fela Van Antwerp, and is said to have had five children, of whom nothing is known.

†–3–3. **Elizabeth**[7] m. Caleb Lobdell, and probably lived at or near Watertown, N. Y. Issue: Samuel, John B., Jerusha, and another daughter who probably d. young.

†–3–6. **Ruth,**[7] second daughter of Paul Sr., m. Norman Wadsworth, and lived and d. at Watertown, N. Y. Issue: Paul, Abner, Lloyd, Lemond, Samuel, Sally, and Mahala.

†–3–9. **Samuel,**[7] seventh son of Paul Sr., was for many years a farmer at Webster, Monroe Co., N. Y. In the summer of 1867 he went to California, and finally d. at Hollister, San Benito Co., Mch. 4, 1884. He m. 1823, Clarissa Close, who d. at Webster, Monroe Co., N. Y., Jul. 28, 1828. Issue:

1. Mary Caroline,	b. Dec. 22, 1823.		
2. Corlista,	b. in 1825.	d. in 1830.	
3. Charles Yates,	b. Jul. 18, 1826.	d. Sep. 27, 1884.	

1. **Mary Caroline**[8] m. in 1848, William P. Glover, and lives at Webster, N. Y. Issue: Lewellyn P., Clara, and Eugene A.

†–3–9–2. **Charles Yates**[8] went to California about 1847–8 as a volunteer in the army during the Mexican War, during which service he received injuries which finally resulted in his death, which occurred at Napa City, Sep. 27, 1884. After the Mexican War he settled on "New York" ranch, Amador Co., where he engaged in literary pursuits, and contributed to the leading newspapers of the state. During the late Civil War he was at one time editor of the *Amador Ledger*. He afterwards founded the *Yolo Mail* which he afterwards disposed of on account of failing health, and engaged in farming. He m. Apr. 1853, Maria S. Campbell, née Robinson, who was b. Feb. 8, 1831, at Palmyra, Wayne Co., N. Y., and now resides on the ranch at Mulberry, Cal. Issue:

1. Virginia C.,	b. Jan. 26, 1854.	
2. Charles S.,	b. Apr. 15, 1855.	
3. Kate Elizabeth,	b. Dec. 18, 1856.	d. Nov. 26, 1878.
4. Robinson,	b. Apr. 10, 1859.	d. Feb. 19, 1860.

5. Helen M.,   b. Nov. 22, 1860.
6. Nettie M.,   b. May 1, 1862.
7. Frank Close,   b. Jan. 6. 1865.
8. Grant,   b. Aug. 14, 1868.
9. Ruth,   b. Mch. 6, 1872.   d. Jul. 13, 1872.

Of these children, **Virginia C.**[9] m. Jul. 15, 1871, Sylvester A. Jones, a printer, and resides at San Francisco. Issue: Mary A., Franklin H., Isabel M. and Hattie V., twins, Sarah F., Caroline V., and Helen H.

†–3–9–2–2. **Charles S.**[9] is a printer and lives at San Francisco. He m. Mch. 8, 1885, Phoebe Ellen Gross, who d. Jun. 17, 1887. Issue:

1. Blanche,   b. Dec. 10, 1885.

3. **Kate Elizabeth**[9] m. Dec. 13, 1876, George Theodore Engell, a farmer, and lived and d. at Peach Tree, Monterey Co., Cal. Issue: Charles G., b. Sep. 26, 1877.

5. **Helen M.**[9] m. Dec. 31, 1832, Leo Green at Hollister, Cal. Mr. Green carries on an extensive butchering business at Redwood City, San Mateo Co., Cal. No issue.

6. **Nettie M.**[9] m. Jan. 22, 1885, Barnett Logan Cornwell, a farmer at San Benito, Cal. Issue:

1. James Francis,   b. Feb. 18, 1891.
2. Kate Leverne,   b. Sep. 19, 1892.

7. **Frank,**[9] a farmer, and 8. **Grant,**[9] a musician, both single, reside with their mother at Mulberry, Cal.

†–3–10. **Naomi,** third daughter of Paul Sr., m. 1st, Feb. 22, 1820, James Rouse, and lived at Webster, N. Y. Issue: Hammond, Phœby Ann, Hannah, William, Philander, and Mary Jenette. Naomi m. 2d, Nov. 4, 1839, Peter Randall, and had further issue: Amelia and Catherine Maria.

†–3–11. **Sarah**[7] m. James Close, and lived at Buffalo, N. Y., for many years, but removed to Yellow Springs, O., about 1883–4. Issue: William, Jerome, John, Emery, and Emily.

†–3–13. **Amanda**[7] m. Nov. 24, 1824, Sylvanus Wager, who was b. Jul. 18, 1802, and d. Apr. 27, 1879. He was a farmer, and lived at Webster, Monroe Co., N. Y. Issue: Mahala, Mary Maria, Philetus, Polly E., Lucinda A., and Sylvester.

†–3–2. **Benoni G.,**[7] second son of Paul Sr., was a surveyor and farmer, and lived and d. at Brandt, Erie Co., N. Y. He m. May 1, 1803, Ruth Lobdell, who was b. Feb. 26, 1785, and d. Sep. 17, 1863, at Brandt, N. Y. Issue:

1. Ammon,	b. Dec. 29, 1803.	d. Jul. 21, 1849.
2. John L.,	b Sep. 12, 1805.	d.
3. Charles,	b. Nov. 2, 1807.	d. Jul. 18, 1875.
4. William,	b. Mch. 27, 1810.	d. Oct. 14, 1849.
5. Lany,	b. Mch. 20, 1812.	d.
6. Esther,	b. Apr. 22, 1814.	d. Jul. 20, 1840.
7. J. F. Ellis,	b. Mch. 12, 1816.	
8. George W.,	b. Apr. 21, 1818.	d. May 31, 1841.
9. Samuel D.,	b. Aug. 4, 1820.	d. Mch. 6, 1866.
10. Mary,	b Sep. 29, 1822.	
11. Harry T. W.,	b. Sep 13, 1824.	d. Jul. 24, 1849.
12. Lydia Ann,	b. Sep. 17, 1826.	d. Feb. 17, 1892.
13. Elizabeth J.,	b. Dec. 4, 1830.	

Of these children, **John L.**[8] and **Lany**[8], with their Aunt Mary, are supposed to have gone West with the Mormons about 1830, as they left the State of New York about that time, and have not since been heard from.

†–3–2–8. **George W.,**[8] sixth son of Benoni, studied for a physician with his brother Ammon in Troy, N. Y., and d. there in 1841, unmarried.

†–3–2–11. **Harry T. W.,**[8] who was a school-teacher, also studied for a physician, and d. of the cholera at Troy, N. Y., Jul. 24, 1849, unmarried.

†–3–2–5. **Esther,**[8] second daughter of Benoni, m. in 1835, Orrin Pierce, and lived and d. at Brandt, Erie Co., N. Y. Issue: Marshall, Edgar, and one unnamed. Her husband and children are all dead.

†–3–2–10. **Mary**[8] m. Jan. 2, 1850, John Sly, and lives at Seneca, Kan. Issue: Philo, Elizabeth, and Ruth, all of whom are m. and have families; and three that d. young.

†–3–2–12. **Lydia Ann**[8] Jan. 27, 1847, David Colvin, and lived at Brandt, N. Y. Issue: Edwin, Elizabeth J., Matilda, Emma, Alburn, Mary, Ellis, and Samuel.

†–3–2–13. **Elizabeth J.,**[8] youngest daughter of Benoni, m. Apr. 28, 1853, Charles Skinner, a farmer and carpenter, and lives at Seneca, Kan. No issue.

†–3–2–1. **Ammon,**[3] oldest son of Benoni, and b. at Northampton, Fulton Co., N. Y., received his medical education at Castleton, Vt., and at the medical colleges of New York City. He practiced medicine at Northampton from 1826 to 1830, when he moved to West Troy, N. Y., where he secured and maintained a high position as a physician, and where he d. of cholera, Jul. 21, 1849. He m. 1st, Apr. 30, 1827, Elizabeth Spier, who was b. at Lake Pleasant, Montgomery Co., N. Y., Aug. 2, 1805, and d. at West Troy, Sep. 7, 1845, and was a sister of Joseph F. Spier, late of Northville, Fulton Co., N. Y. Issue :

1. Elmina Eliz.,	b. May 16, 1828.	d. Dec. 5, 1828.	
2. Emma Maria,	b Jan. 21, 1830.		
3. Mary Augusta,	b. Mch. 1, 1833.		
4. Richard Watson,	b. Jan. 19, 1835.	d. Mch. 30, 1835.	
5. Claudius Spier,	b. Jan. 26, 1836.	d. Jul. 20, 1836.	
6. Edwin Fitch,	b. Sep. 3, 1837.	d. ?	
7. Isaac Mark,	b. Dec. 12, 1839.	d. May 16, 1863.	
8. Elizabeth Ann,	b. Aug. 28, 1845.		

Dr. Ammon m. 2d, about 1847, Ann Mark, but had no other issue.

Of his children, **Mark**[9] was killed in battle before Vicksburg, May 16, 1863.

2. **Emma Maria**[9] m. 1st, Feb. 21, 1849, Albertus H. Platt of West Troy. Issue : Laura Belle, b. at Troy, Jun. 21, 1852. Emma m. 2d, Mch. 26, 1860, Hiram Pond Ward of Warrenton, N. C., who was b. at Poultney, Vt., Jun. 24, 1822, and lives at Dubuque, Iowa. Mr. Ward is one of the numerous descendants of William Ward who emigrated from England in 1639 and settled in Massachusetts. No issue by the second marriage.

3. **Mary Augusta**[9] m. John D. Spicer, a lumber dealer at Troy, N. Y. Issue : Lizzie Fitch and Mary Thompson.

6. **Edwin Fitch,**[9] who was in the Army in 1864, went many years ago to St. Paul, Minn., and perhaps d. there. He m. Mch. 1862, Mrs. Helen Hilton Hamilton, who d. in Mch. 1865, without issue.

8. **Elizabeth Ann**[9] m. Dec. 20, 1866, John T. Standring of Deer River, N. Y. Mr. Standring was b. at Lowville, N. Y., Mch. 17, 1840. Issue : Leonard Sydney, Joseph Mark, Elsie, John Henry, William Edward, Lizzie, Fitch Spier, and Benjamin Van Buren.

†-3-2-3. **Charles,** third son of Benoni, was a farmer, and contractor on public works. He lived at Brandt, Erie Co., N. Y., and helped build the Erie Canal. He m. 1st, Aug. 19, 1830, Clarissa Clark, who was b. Dec. 4, 1807, and d. at Brandt, Feb. 12, 1844. Issue :

1. William W.	b. Nov. 4, 1831.	
2. George W.,	b. Oct. 12, 1833.	
3. Marthaline,	b. Apr. 6, 1836.	d. Mch. —, 1892.
4. Sarah Ann,	b. Jun. 13, 1839.	

Charles m. 2d, Jun. 12, 1844, Emeline Rice, who was b. Dec. 25, 1805, and d. Jul. 21, 1877. Issue :

5. Philip Harvey,	b. Jun. 12, 1845.	d. May 21, 1847.
6. Anna Maria,	b. Oct. 5, 1849.	

Of these children, 3. **Marthaline** m. Jan. 1, 1855, Levi Grannis, and lived and d. at Brandt, N. Y. Issue : Clarissa, Hattie H., Amy A., and Maud E.

4. **Sarah Ann** m. Sep. 11, 1859, William W. Stewart, and lives at Washington, Kansas. Issue : Charles H., Flora A., K. Estelle, Wallace H., Martha Lenore, Jessie N., and Clyde H. and Clara H., twins.

6. **Anna Maria** m. in 1865, John Hickey, who was b. May 2, 1844, and lives at Brandt, N. Y. Issue : Franklin H., Harry B., and Emaline.

†-3-2-3-1. **William Wallace,** oldest son of Charles, and b. at Hamburg, Erie Co., N. Y., moved soon after to Brandt, and to Buffalo in 1877. He received his education in the common schools, and at the Academy at Fredonia, N. Y. At the age of 20 he spent a year travelling in the Southern States, and taught two terms of school there. Afterwards, for 12 years, he was engaged in lumbering and in mercantile pursuits. He was County Judge of Erie Co., from 1877 to 1889, having been twice re-elected. In the Spring of 1890, at the close of his term of office, he formed a law partnership at Buffalo, N. Y., now the firm of Hammond, Hatch & Ackerson. During the late Civil War he was Capt. of Co. C, 67th N. Y. National Guard. After General Lee invaded Pennsylvania the regiment was ordered to Harrisburg, Pa., and, after one month's service, was mustered out soon after the battle of Gettysburg. He m. 1st, Sep. 24, 1854, Amy Ann Hurd, who was b. Sep. 24, 1834, and d. Aug. 9, 1860. Issue :

1. Rosabelle A. A., 　　b. Jul. 30, 1860.

WILLIAM W. HAMMOND.

William W. m. 2d, Jul. 21, 1861, Louisa A. Hurd, who was b. Meb. 16, 1844. Issue :

2. Lilly May,	b. Jun. 12, 1869.	
3. Clark Hurd,	b. Feb. 23, 1875.	

Of these children, **Rosabelle A. A.**[10] m. Jan. 7, 1877, Charles Koepka, a farmer, and resides in Brandt, N. Y. Issue : Lloyd W., b. Nov. 5, 1877; Harry D., b. Dec. 2, 1880; Wiley E., b. Jun. 26, 1886; Alice Amy Ann, b. Jun. 21, 1889.

2. **Lilly May**[10] m. Oct. 16, 1888, Edward J. Newell, and resides in Buffalo, N. Y. Mr. Newell is Secretary of the Queen City Bank. No issue.

†–3–2–3–2. **George W.,**[9] second son of Charles, is a farmer, and lives at Brandt, N. Y. He m. 1st, in 1853, Lavina Hoffman, and had issue :

1. Georgiana,	b. Jul. 24, 1856.	

He m. 2d, Dec. 24, 1860, Almira Grannis, and had further issue :

2. Mary E.,	b. in 1861.	d. Sep. —, 1863.
3. Edwin G.,	b. Jul. 10, 1863.	
4. Cora E.,	b. Meb. 24, 1866.	
5. Charles,	b. Jul. 6, 1868.	
6. Luella.	b. Jul. 6, 1871.	
7. Wm. Wallace,	b. Aug. 24, 1873.	
8. Clarissa,	b. Oct. 12, 1875.	
9. John L.,	b. Apr. 10, 1879.	
10. Lester,	b. Nov. 2, 1882.	

Of these children, **Georgiana**[10] m. Feb. 20, 1876, Clark Judson, a farmer, and resides near Buckhorn, Cheboygan Co., Mich. Issue : Mary, George Wallace, Olive, William and Frank.

4. **Cora E.**[10] m. in 1882, Andrew Dugaw, and lives at Brandt with her father. Issue : George, b. in 1882.

3. **Edwin G.**[10] is a farmer, and resides at Brandt, N. Y. He m. Margaret Walters, and had issue :

1. Artemas,	b. in 1885.
2. Charles,	b. in 1887.
3. Seward,	b. in 1889.
4. Vernon,	b. in 1892.

†–3–2–4. **William**[9], fourth son of Benoni, was a lawyer and farmer, and lived at New Buffalo, Berrien Co., Mich., but d. at Brandt, N. Y. He m. about 1831, Betsey Pierce, who d. in 1851. Issue: Ammon, Helen, Maria, Mary, Lydia, Marshall and Matilda.

Of these children, Marshall d. in 1861 in the late War; Ammon in 1880–81 was a conductor on the Michigan Central R. R.; and Helen m. ——— Kelley, and lived for a while at New Buffalo or Three Oaks, Mich. She left the latter place about 1857–8, having at that time two children, Cornelia and Angeline. All attempts to ascertain the whereabouts of William's children have proved entirely fruitless.

†–3–2–7. **J. F. Ellis**,[8] fifth son of Benoni, is a farmer and lives at Saratoga Springs, N. Y. He m. Sep. 16, 1839, Mariette Lewis, who d. at Saratoga, Nov. 8, 1884, æ. 67. Issue:

1. Wm. Jefferson,	b. Sep. 7, 1840.	
2. Adelbert Delos,	b. Sep. 22, 1843.	
3. Homer,	b. Mch. 10, 1846.	d. Aug. 26, 1849.
4. Mary Verona,	b. Aug. 13, 1849.	

Of these children, **Mary V.**[9] m. Jan. 30, 1867, Sumner H. Jennison, and lives at Saratoga Springs, N. Y. Issue: Homer E., Sumner S., Winnie May, Albert E., and Emma L.

†–3–2–7–1. **Wm. Jefferson**[9] is a contractor and builder, and resides at Saratoga Springs. He m. Dec. 30, 1872, Arabelle E. Ward, and had issue:

1. Harry J.,	b. Sep. 7, 1874.
2. Ernest B.,	b. Aug. 11, 1878.
3. Fannie M.,	b. Jun. 1, 1881.
4. Maurice A.,	b. Aug. 30, 1885.
5. Edith W.,	b. Sep. 26, 1888.

†–3–2–7–2. **Adelbert Delos**[9] is a carpenter at Saratoga Springs. He m. Oct. 18, 1876, Helen Bishop, and had issue:

1. May,   b. May 14, 1879.

†–3–2–9. **Samuel D.**,[8] seventh son of Benoni, previous to the Civil War, was a farmer at Three Oaks, Berrien Co., Mich. He was a member of Co. E, 12th Mich. Infantry, from Nov. 13, 1861 to Mch. 5, 1866. He died the day after his discharge at Jackson, Mich., of an injury received on the way home. He m. Sep. 19, 1847, Susan A. Knapp, who d. Apr. 22, 1892, at McKinley, Oscoda Co., Mich. Issue:

1. Harry,	b. Sep. 6, 1848.	
2. Cornelia.	b. May 14, 1850.	
3. Harriet B.,	b. Apr. 9, 1852.	
4. Charles,	b. Apr. 26, 1857.	

Of these children, 2. **Cornelia**[9] m. Sep. 22, 1869, J. Birney Crosby, a farmer, at New Buffalo, Berrien Co., Mich. Issue: Fannie, Nettie, Harry, Fred, John, Hattie, and Henry.

3. **Harriet B.**[9] m. Feb. 24, 1872, Robert T. Farrington, a Methodist clergyman, at McKinley, Mich. Issue: Charles Robert.

1. **Harry**[9] is a sawyer, and lives at Bay City, Mich. He m. Sep. 9, 1875, Mary Higgins at Bay City. Issue:

1. Fred B.,	b. Apr. 14, 1878.	
2. Mable E.,	b. Jun. 20, 1880.	d. Jul. 22, 1881.
3. Earle B.,	b. May 4, 1884.	
4. Glen Martin,	b. Mch. 16, 1885.	
5. Harry Lee,	b. Aug. 26, 1888.	

4. **Charles**[9] is a farmer, and lives at Rose City, Ogemaw Co., Mich. He m. Aug. 14, 1878, Mary Ellsworth of Bancroft, Mich. Issue:

1. Grace Cornelia,	b. Aug. 19, 1879.
2. Ina May,	b. Jan. 30, 1888.

†–3–2–14. **William M.,** son of Benoni G. by a second marriage, is a physician at Kansas City, Mo. He attended medical and dental lectures in Cincinnati, Ohio, and is legally authorized to practice both professions. He formerly lived in northern California, and at one time was located at San Diego. During the late Civil War, he received a lieutenant's commission from Gov. Blair of Michigan, and raised a company of men. In the Summer of 1864 he went with his company to the front, and was attached to the construction corps at Chattanooga, Tenn. He m. 1st, in 1843, Almeda Henry, who d. in 1876. Issue: Francis M. and Melville C., both of whom d. in infancy. He m. 2d, May 15, 1877, Loretta Mann, a graduate of the Women's Medical College of Pennsylvania. Issue:

3. Pansey L.,	b. Feb. 17, 1878.

†–3–4. **William,**[7] third son of Paul Sr., was a mason, and lived and d. at Webster, Monroe Co., N. Y. He m. Apr. 20, 1815, Demaris Osborn, who was b. Jun. 9, 1796, and d. Oct. 20, 1851. Issue:

1. Dewett C.,	b. Jun. 7, 1819.	d Nov. 4, 1864.
2. S. Olmstead,	b. Sep. 20, 1821.	d. Oct. 29, 1837.
3. Stanley,	b. Nov. 6, 1823.	
4. Jane L.,	b. Nov. 27, 1825.	d. Feb. 5. 1853.
5. Marietta,	b. Oct. 7, 1827.	d. May 26, 1866.
6. Asher P.,	b. Dec. 22, 1829.	d. Sep. 9, 1885.
7. William W.,	b. Mch. 29, 1832.	
8. Charles,	b. Jun. 30, 1834.	d. Oct. 21, 1860

Of these children, **Sylvester Omstead**[8] d. at the age of 16 at Webster, N. Y., unmarried; and **Marietta**[5] d. at Worthington, Green Co., Ind., at the age of 38, also single.

4. **Jane L.**[8] m. in 1849, Thomas Jacobs, and lived and d. at Penfield, N. Y. Issue: William, and a daughter, both dead.

†-3-4-8. **Charles,**[8] youngest son of William, was a nurseryman, and lived and d. at Worthington, Green Co., Ind. He never married.

†-3-4-1. **Dewitt C.,**[8] who was a brick-mason at Penfield, N. Y., was in the 8th Reg't, N. Y. Cavalry, and d. at Harper's Ferry, Va., in 1864. He m. in 1844, in Penfield, Monroe Co., N. Y., Parmelia Cheney, who d. Dec. 28, 1880, at Ravenna, Muskegon Co., Mich. Issue:

1. John,	b. May —, 1846.	d. Mch. —, 1848.
2. Abby D.,	b. Nov. 5, 1847.	
3. Nathan K.,	b. Sep. 28, 1849.	
4. J. Dewane,	b. Sep. 19, 1851.	
5. Mary Jane,	b. Sep. 7, 1853.	
6. Delia Maryette,	b. Jun. 9, 1855.	
7. William P.,	b. Aug. 20, 1857.	

Of these children, 2. **Abby D.** [9]m. Mch. 3, 1867, Samuel Morey, who d. Dec. 26, 1875. She lives at Muskegon, and her issue are: Charles B., Lillian D., C. Inza, and Arthur D.

4. **J. Dewane**[9] is a cook, and resides at Bayfield, La Pointe Co., Wis. He m. Aug. 27, 1876, Cecelia Shimmel, but has no issue.

5. **Mary Jane**[9] m. Oct. 11, 1849, William Young, and lives at Muskegon, Mich. Issue: Paschal Cheney, b. Jan. 31, 1879.

6. **Delia Maryette**[9] m. Jul. 4, 1873, Thomas Young, who was b. Nov. 8, 1849. They live at Ravenna, Mich., and their issue are: Hattie, Effie, Gracie, Jessie Earl, Queenie, and Lillian.

3. **Nathan K.**[9] is a sawyer, and resides at Muskegon, Mich. He m. 1st, Sep. 22, 1873, Alice Stowe, who d. May 8, 1874. Issue: Edna A., who d. in infancy. He m. 2d, Apr. 12, 1876, Alice Davis, and had issue:

1. Charles Dewitt,   b. Jan. 17, 1877.
2. Nathan Mark,   b. Nov. 7, 1878.
3. William Dewane,   b. Aug. 15, 1880.
4. Mable Permela,   b. Dec. 2, 1882.

7. **William P.**[9] is a laborer, and lives at Muskegon, Mich. He m. Apr. 17, 1881, Electa Davis, and had issue:

1. Chester Dewitt,   b. Nov. 7, 1882.
2. Claud,   b. Feb. 19, 1888.   d. young.

†–3–4–3. **Stanley,** third son of William, is a farmer, and lives at Fairport, Monroe Co., N. Y. He m. Apr. —, 1850, Jane Turner, who was b. Aug. 30, 1830. Issue:

1. Hattie A ,   b. Dec. 9, 1852.   d. May 31, 1875.
2. John S.,   b. Nov. 20, 1854.
3. James B.,   b. Jan. 17, 1857.   d. Nov. 17, 1858.
4. Charles C.,   b. Feb. 7, 1861.
5. Jeffery,   b. May 6, 1867.

Of these children, **James**[9] d. in infancy; and **Hattie**[9] at the age of 22, single.

5. **Jeffrey,**[9] unmarried, is a conductor on the New York Central & Hudson River R. R., and lives in Buffalo, N. Y.

2. **John S.**[9] is Chief Inspector of the Electric Railway in Rochester, N. Y. He m. 1st, in the Fall of 1876, Hattie Wright, who d. about 1887, without issue. He m. 2d. Anne Roy of Clyde, N. Y., but has no issue.

4. **Charles C.**[9] is a gripman in the employ of the Broadway Cable Railway in New York City. He m. Sep. 9, 1887, Anna Schnell of New York City, who was b. May 22, 1864, in Honesdale, Wayne Co., Penn. Issue:

1. Stanley, Jr.,   b. Jun. 5, 1888.
2. Charles Pollard,   b. May 24, 1890.
3. Helen,   b. Jan. 17, 1892.   d. Jul. 10, 1892.
4. Lulu May,   b. Feb. 22, 1893.

†–3–4–6. **Asher P.** was formerly a farmer at Penfield, N. Y., but moved to Worthington, Green Co., Ind., before the War, and engaged in the nursery business. He served all through the war as Captain of Co. F, 31st Ind. Vols.; was discharged while his regiment was in Texas, and took up his

5

residence at Victoria, Victoria Co., where he was living at the
of his death. He m. 1st, in Penfield, N. Y., Dec. 22, 1852,
Malana Howe, who d. Sep. 26, 1859. Issue :

1. Jerome,	b. Sep. 29, 1853.	d. May 10, 1881.
2. Girard.	b. Jul. 16, 1855.	
3. Clarissa D.,	b. Feb. 26, 1857.	
4. Mary Caroline,	b. about 1859.	d. Oct. 14, 1859.

Asher P. m. 2d, at Macon, Ill., Dec. 18, 1865, Hannah M.
Peter, and had further issue :

4. John D.,	b. Dec. 16, 1869.
5. Charles E.,	b. Feb. 15, 1872.
6. William,	b. Nov. 1, 1874.
7. Rose,	b. Mch. 12, 1877.
8. Catherine,	b. Jul. 29, 1879. d. in infancy.
9. Malana,	b. Jan. 8, 1881.

Of these children, **Clarissa Damorius**[9] m. in 1882–3,
George C. Schermerhorn, P. M. at Penfield, N. Y. Issue :
Fannie J. and Edmond Parmenter.

1. **Jerome**[9] was a brakeman on the Marietta R. R., and
lived in Calhoun Co., Texas. He m. Jul. 12, 1874, Caroline
Robbins, and had issue :

1. Charlotte M.,	b. May 18, 1875.
2. Katie Ann,	b. Feb. 3, 1877.
3. Clara Caroline,	b. Jul. 12, 1879.
4. Ella Jerome,	b. Aug. 20, 1881.

2. **Girard**[9] is a farmer, and lives at De Kalb, Ill. He
m. Jun. 13, 1880, Hattie A. McKee of Macon, Ill., who was
b. Dec. 2, 1856. Issue :

1. Edna May.	b. May 24, 1881.
2. James Albert,	b. Jun. 13, 1882.
3. Jennie Belle,	b. Oct. 29, 1883.
4. Jessie Fern,	b. Apr. 9, 1885.
5. Jerome,	b. Jan 22, 1890.

Asher's children by the second marriage are all single.

†–3–4–7. **William W.,**[5] fifth son of William, is a nurseryman, and lives at Bement, Piatt Co., Ill. He m. Oct. 11,
1866, Alvira Worthing of Penfield, N. Y., and had issue :

1. Lena M.,	b. Jul. 16, 1867.
2. Wilbur A.,	b. Mch. 4, 1870.
3. Winnifred G.,	b. Dec. 28, 1873.
4. Alvira D.,	b. Feb. 14, 1875.
5. Emily J.,	b. Jun. 1, 1877.
6. Carrie M.,	b. Jul. 3, 1879.
7. Stanley C.,	b. Aug. 13, 1886.

The above children of William W. all reside at Bement, Ill., and are all unmarried.

†–3–8. **Paul Jr.,** sixth son of Paul, was a farmer, and lived, during most of his married life, at Webster, Monroe Co., N. Y., and d. at Concord, Erie Co., Penn. He m. about 1818, Abby Sears, and had issue :

1. James D.,	b. Jul. 12, 1819.	
2. Samuel,	b. Jul. 26, 1821.	
3. Harriet,	b. Nov. 27, 1823.	
4. Arnold,	b. Nov. 17, 1825.	
5. Edwin,	b. Oct. 11, 1827.	
6. Sally,	b. May 22, 1830.	
7. Maryette,	b. Apr. 2, 1832.	d. Sep. 27, 1863.
8. Ebenezer P.,	b. Aug. 22, 1834.	
9. Hannah,	b. Oct. 1, 1838.	
10. Wm. Omar,	b. Mch. 28, 1841.	

Of these children, **Harriet** m. Jan. 1, 1848, James Pope, a farmer at Corry, Erie Co., Penn. Issue : Truman and Emma J.

6. **Sally** m. 1st, Oct. 2, 1851, Josiah McCray, a farmer at Concord, Erie Co., Penn., who was b. Nov. 30, 1826, and d. in 1865. Issue : Byron H., Aurilla, Willard D., Chapman B., Hamlin H., William Holt, Cassius F., and Josiah. Sally m. 2d, Mch. 26, 1871, Rev. Samuel McCray, a Methodist clergyman, who afterwards d. in Minnesota. Issue : Minnie B., b. Mch. 21, 1875.

7. **Maryette** m. Jun. 26, 1855, Jasper Fuller, and lived and d. at Sparta, Crawford Co., Penn. Issue : Eva, who m. Frank Hill, and has a daughter Flora, b. Sep. 12, 1883. Frank Hill, who was a hotel keeper, d. at Corry, Penn., Jun. 25, 1892.

9. **Hannah** m. Dec. 26, 1866, George L. Carey, a farmer, at Concord, near Corry, Penn. They have an adopted son Harley, b. May 10, 1875.

†–3–8–1. **James D.,** oldest son of Paul Jr., is a school teacher and farmer, and lives at Corry, Penn. He m. Apr. 30, 1862, Emaline Baxter, who was b. May 2, 1843. Issue :

1. Charles B ,	b. in 1864.	d. Jul. 9, 1884.
2. Willie J.,	b. Jul. 5, 1867.	

2. **Willie J.** is a farmer and stock-dealer, and lives with his father at Corry. He m. Jun. 2, 1892, Lizzie D. Parsons, who was b. Nov. 17, 1867.

†–3–8–2. **Samuel,** second son of Paul Jr., is a farmer and millwright at Corry, Penn. He m. Sep. 10, 1851, Mary Pond, and had issue:

1. Lawson P.,   b. Jun.   6, 1853.   d. Sep.   7, 1854.
2. Florence I.,   b. Jul. 23, 1855.   d. Mch.   8, 1859.
3. Clifford S.,   b. Jan. 19, 1857.   d. Mch.   6, 1859.
4. Clifton L.,   b Dec.   8, 1859.
5. Dor E.,   b. Dec. 14, 1861.
6. S. Bertie,   b. Nov.   5, 1871.

Of these children, **S. Bertie,** a farmer, lives with his parents at Corry, and is not married.

4. **Clifton Leon,** a graduate of the High School of Corry, Penn., class of '88, and of the Iron City College, Pittsburg, Penn., at the age of 22 went to Chester, Wis., where he learned telegraphy, and afterwards entered the service of the Chicago & North-Western R. R., as operator. In 1866, he went to Antigo, Langlade Co., Wis., as cashier for the Milwaukee, Lake Shore & Western R. R., and in 1889 was appointed agent at that station, which position he now holds. He m. Jun. 22, 1887, Carrie Cordelia Cliff of Waupun, Wis., who was b. at Rock River, Wis., May 22, 1864. Issue:

1. Arthur Cliff.   b. Aug. 23, 1890.
2. Harley Vivian.   b. Aug. 15, 1892.

5. **Dor E.** is also a telegraph operator at Antigo. He m. Jan. 4, 1888, Harriet Smith, who d. Jan. 26, 1889, without issue.

†–3–8–4. **Arnold,** third son of Paul Jr., is a farmer and dealer in agricultural implements at Corry, Penn. He m. Nov. 16, 1853, Julia E. Baxter, and had issue:

1. Maylon,   b. Aug. 27, 1854.   d. Dec. 15, 1884.
2. Wiley G.,   b. Nov. 4, 1857.
3. Mary E.,   b. Jun. 2, 1868.

1. **Maylon** was a telegraph operator, and lived at Corry, with his father. He m. Jan. 6, 1878, Mary Travers, and had issue:

1. Walter P.,   b. Mch. 15, 1879.
2. Lillie J.,   b. Oct. 19, 1880.
3. Ray M.,   b. Sep. 10, 1883.

2. **Wiley G.** is a merchant and lives at Corry, Penn. He m. Claire Rockwood, and had issue:

1. Claire Belle,   b. Mch. 5, 1888.

3. **May E.**[9] m. Jun. 26, 1890, Dr. Sidney A. Dunham, and resides at Buffalo, N. Y. Issue: Julia E., b. Sep. 7, 1892.

†–3–8–5. **Edwin,**[8] fourth son of Paul Jr., is a farmer, and lives at Corry, Penn. He m. Jul. 5, 1852, Emaline S. Clark, and had issue:

    1. Ernest Wyatt,   b. Mch 17, 1855.
    2. Clark Edwin,   b. Feb. 15, 1882.

1. **Ernest**[9] is a mechanical engineer, and lives at Lima, Allen Co., Ohio. He m. Dec. 31, 1878, Nellie Bassett at Amherst, Mass. Issue:

    1. Hazel Hiller,   b. Dec. 21, 1883.
    2. Florence Bassett,   b. Mch. 31, 1888.

2. **Clark Edwin**[9] is an artesian-well driller, and resides at Geneva, Ind. He m. Sep. 24, 1892, Minnie Rice.

†–3–8–8. **Ebenezer Paul,**[5] fifth son of Paul Jr., is a teacher and farmer, and lives at Medford, Jackson Co., Oregon. He m. 1st, Jul. 4, 1859, Henrietta L. Preston, who d. in 1870, at Central City, Col. Issue:

    1. Ada Dell Lulu,   b. Aug. 22, 1861.
    2. Maggie Belle J.,   b. Aug. 23, 1862.   d. Dec. 22, 1868.
    3. Viccie Maud,   b. Feb. 29, 1868.

Of these children, **Lulu**[9] m. Jan. 17, 1879, Charles B. Oswald, a farmer, and lives at Express, Baker Co., Ore. Issue: Lottie Maud, Charles Otto, and Blanche Viccie.

3. **Maud**[9] m. Apr. 1, 1888, Asher Otto Sinks, a telegraph operator, and lives at Portland, Ore. Issue: Lenora Dell, and Grover.

Ebenezer Paul m. 2d, Jun. 22, 1871, Annie Pauline Holmes of Georgia, but has no other issue.

†–3–8–10. **Wm. Omar,**[5] youngest son of Paul Jr., a farmer and justice of the peace, lives at Wichita, Kan. He m. Amanda Lyons, and had issue:

    1. Eva J.,   b. Mch. 25, 1880.
    2. Ransom,   b. Apr. 5, 1881.
    3. Annie,   b. Mch. —, 1885.

(4.)—WILLIAM OF NORTHAMPTON, FULTON CO., N. Y.

†–4. **William Jr.,**[6] third son of William, and b. at Wales, Mass., or northern New York, m. at Pittstown, Rensselaer Co., and afterwards moved to Northville, Fulton Co., where he was a teacher and farmer, and where he d. in 1821. He m. Lydia Follett of Pittstown, who was b. May 24, 1771, and d. May 6, 1852, after a second marriage to Daniel Brownell. Issue :

1. Seneca,	b. Jun. 7, 1788.	d. Mch. 3, 1815.
2. Ira,	b. Dec. 3, 1790.	d. Mch. 5, 1845.
3. Mary.	b. Aug. 30, 1792.	d. Oct. 22, 1810.
4. Martha,	b. Oct. 8, 1794.	d. Jun. 1, 1865.

Of these children, **Seneca**[7] d. at the age of 27, unmarried : **Mary**[7] d. at the age of 18, also single ; and **Martha**[7] m. about 1810 Dr. Henry Van Ness, and lived and d. at Northville, N. Y. Issue : William, Seneca, Dr. John, Effie Ann, Dr. Ira Hammond, Lydia, Nancy, Garrett, Mary, and Cornelia Ann.

†–4–2. **Ira**[7] was a farmer, and lived at Northville, N. Y. He m. Wilampey Van Ness, who was b. Nov. 27, 1795, and d. Sep. 30, 1835. Issue :

1. Mary,	b. Jul. 15, 1814.	
2. Lucy,	b. Oct. 23, 1815.	d.
3. Cornelius,	b. Dec. 22, 1817.	
4. Martha,	b. Jan. 23, 1820.	d.
5. Jane Ann,	b. Apr. 1, 1822.	d. young.
6. Lydia Louise,	b. Dec. 24, 1823.	
7. William,	b. Sep. 9, 1826.	d. ?.
8. Senaca,	b. Dec. 11, 1828.	d. Jan. 29, 1868.
9. Patience,	b. May 15, 1831.	

Of these children, **Jane Ann**[8] d. young ; and **William**[8] went to California, on the first discovery of gold, and has not since been heard from.

1. **Mary**[8] m. Nathaniel Pipinger, and lives at Flushing, Genesee Co., Mich. Issue not learned.

2. **Lucy**[8] m. Daniel Russell, and lived in Northampton, Fulton Co., N. Y. Issue : Cornelius and Maria.

4. **Martha**[8] m. Dillon P. Myers, and lived in some part of California. Issue : Delia, Ida, Lizzie, Katie, and Emmie.

6. **Lydia Louise**[8] m. 1st, William Robinson, and had issue: Eliza Ann. She m. 2d, John Gorton, and lives at Flushing, Mich. Issue: Dora, Myra, John, Ira and Dillon.

9. **Patience**[8] m. Jan. 30, 1850, Albert Roe, and lives in Brooklyn, N. Y. Issue: Julia Emma, Millie Louise, Mary Ella, and Albert Fredell.

†-4-2-3. **Cornelius**[8] was a shoemaker and farmer, and lives at Osborn Bridge, Northampton, Fulton Co., N. Y. He m. Sep. 22, 1841, Fanny Potter, who was b. Sep. 29, 1822. Issue:

1. George W.,	b. Dec. 22, 1845.	
2. Mary,	b. Mch. 28, 1849.	d. Nov. 21, 1855.
3. Elsina,	b. Apr. 28, 1854.	d. Oct. 4, 1861.
4. John,	b. Jan. 10, 1862.	
5. Delia,	b. Mch. 10, 1864.	
6. Eugene,	b. Feb. 23, 1867.	

Of these children, **Mary**[9] and **Elsina**[9] d. young: **John**,[9] unmarried, is a foundryman at Syracuse, N. Y.; and **Delia**[9] m. Jul. 4, 1882, Elias H. Ellithorp, and lives at Osborn Bridge, Fulton Co., N. Y. Issue: Clara L., Fannie A., Clark R. and E. Fay.

1. **George W.**[9] is employed in a furniture store in Syracuse, N. Y. He m. Jan. 6, 1866, Mary C. Norris, and had issue:

1. Fred C.,	b. Dec. 20, 1866.	
2. Jessie C.,	b. Dec. 20, 1868.	d. Jan. 2, 1878.
3. George W.,	b. Apr. 5, 1871.	d. Jan. 14, 1878.
4. Lillie M.,	b. Nov. 11, 1873.	d. Jan. 7, 1878.
5. Florence,	b. Aug. 29, 1875.	
6. Frank N.,	b. Apr. 20, 1879.	
7. Grace A.,	b. Jul. 28, 1881.	
8. Alva M.,	b. Sep. 16, 1883.	

1. Fred C. is employed in the same store with his father in Syracuse. He m. Oct. 28, 1890, Carrie Garling? of Clyde, N. Y., who was b. Aug. 28, 1867. Issue:

1. Harold,   b. Oct. 10, 1891.

6. **Eugene**[9] is a glove cutter, and lives at Gloversville, N. Y. He m. Jan. 15, 1888, Grace Winney, and had issue:

1. Maude E.,   b. Dec. 5, 1888.
2. Oneta C. M.,   b. Jul. 1, 1891.

†-4-2-8. **Seneca,**[5] third son of Ira, was a farmer, and lived at Amsterdam, Montgomery Co., N. Y. He m. Feb. 20, 1858, Margaret Thomas, and had issue :

> 1. William J.,   b. Jan.   9, 1859.
> 2. Nicholas D.,   b. Feb. 21, 1863.
> 3. Elmer E.,   b. Mch. 30, 1867.

1. **William**[9] is a butcher and marketman at Amsterdam, in company with his brother Nicholas. He m. Dec. 13, 1882, Emma E. Redway, who d. Jan. 5, 1889. Issue :

> 1. Frank S.,   b. Feb. 29, 1885.
> 2. Edward W.,   b. Dec. 14, 1887.

2. **Nicholas D.,**[9] a butcher and marketman at Amsterdam, m. Apr. 10, 1890, Minnie Hoffman, and had issue :

> 1. Paul,   b. Jan. 15, 1891.

3. **Elmer E.**[9] is foreman in a knitting mill at Mohawk, Herkimer Co., N. Y. He m. Oct. 1, 1867, Rachel Saulwater, and had issue :

> 1. Walter,   b. Feb. 26, 1890.

5.—SAMUEL HAMMOND OF DUTCHESS CO., N. Y.

†. **Samuel Hammond,**[5] third son of Thomas,[4] [Samuel,[3] Benj.,[2] William[1]], was b. at Dartmouth, Mass., Apr. 29, 1731, and was in early life a cooper and whaler at New Bedford. He moved about 1766 to Washington, Dutchess Co., N. Y., where he purchased 200 acres of land, and d. there May 16, 1801. He m. at New Bedford, Jan. 29, 1755, Hannah Sheperd, and had issue :

1. Eliakim,	b.	d.
2. Isaac,	b. Oct. 15, 1756.	d. Sep. 6, 1832.
3. Luthan,	b. Apr. 3, 1758.	d. Oct. 22, 1806.
4. Hannah,	b.	d.
5. Daniel, }	b. Nov. 30, 1764.	d.
6. Thomas, }		d.
7. Mary,	b.	d.
8. Maria,	b.	d.
9. Samuel, Jr.,	b. Aug. 14, 1771.	d. Jul. 9, 1829.
10. Ruth, }	b. Jul. 7, 1774.	d. Mch. 20, 1814.
11. Benjamin, }		d. Sep. 26, 1858.

Of these children, 1. **Eliakim**[6] is said to have lived somewhere in western New York. He m. Margaret Macomber, but his issue, if any, has not been learned.

4. **Hannah**[6] m. Daniel Brownell, and lived in Hope, Hamilton Co., N. Y. Issue: John, Orra, Lewis, Isaac, Cyrus, Mary and Martha.

7. **Mary**[6] m. Thomas Gage, and d. probably young, without issue.

8. **Maria**[6] m. ——— Macomber, and lived in western New York. She d. young, and without issue.

10. **Ruth,**[6] who was b. in Dutchess Co., N. Y., m. about 1800, Titus Palmer, and lived and d. at Poughkeepsie, N. Y. Issue: Samuel, Hannah, Benjamin, Eliza, Emeline, Louiza, and Reuben.

(2.)—ISAAC OF NORTH EAST, DUTCHESS CO, N. Y.

†-2. **Isaac,**[6] second son of Samuel, was a farmer, and settled in North East, Dutchess Co. He m. Feb. 14, 1779, Lois Gardner, who was b. Nov. 20, 1760, and d. Jan. 23, 1850. Issue:

1. Nathaniel,	b. Dec. 2, 1779.	d. Jun. —, 1831.
2. Mary,	b. May 11, 1781.	d.
3. Eunice,	b. Jan. 23, 1784.	d.
4. Ruth,	b. Jan. 18, 1789.	d.
5. Samuel,	b. Dec. 15 1790.	d.
6. Stephen,	b. Apr. 11, 1792.	d.
7. Jemima,	b. May 25, 1794.	d.
8. Zephaniah,	b May 6, 1796.	d. Mch. 20, 1857.
9. Lois,	b. Mch. 9, 1798.	d.
10. Susan,	b. Mch 1, 1802.	d.

Of Isaac's children, **Jemima**[7] d. single on Long Island; and **Susan**[7] d. single at North East.

2. **Mary**[7] m. a Mr. Boice, and died not many years after without issue.

3. **Eunice**[7] m. Jacob Thorne, and lived and d. in western New York near Rochester. Issue: Three sons, and a daughter, names not learned.

4. **Ruth**[7] m. Joseph Haight, settled in Boston, Erie Co., N. Y., and d. without issue.

9. **Lois**[7] m. Richard Grey, lived in North East, and d. there without issue.

†–2–1. **Nathaniel,**[7] oldest son of Isaac, was a carpenter and farmer, and settled in Stillwater, Saratoga Co., N. Y., about 1800. He m. Rhemember Boyce, who d. May 12, 1857, æ. 71. Issue :

1. Daniel,	b. Jun. 10, 1804.	d. Aug. 15, 1878.
2. Nelson,	b. Nov. —, 1807.	d. Sep. 8, 1878.
3. Lewis,	b.	d. in 1872.
4. Jane,	b.	d. in 1866.
5. Samuel,	b.	d. in 1887.
6. Jacob B.,	b. Jan. 1, 1815.	d. Jan. 15, 1885.
7. Alonzo,	b. in 1818.	d. Feb. 21, 1863.

Of these children, **Samuel** was a farmer at Malta, Saratoga Co., where he d. single in 1887.

4. **Jane,** who settled in Clifton Park, Saratoga Co., m. John Lasher of Malta, who d. in 1875. Issue : Priscilla Jane, who m. a Mr. Husted of Clifton Park.

†–2–1–1. **Daniel,**[8] oldest son of Nathaniel, was a farmer, and lived at Stillwater, Saratoga Co. He m. Loretta Parks of Malta, who d. Dec. 28, 1863, æ. 57. Issue :

| 1. George Van R., | b. Mch. 15, 1826. |
| 2. Elizabeth Jane, | b. Jan. 28, 1831. | d. Mch. 15, 1858. |

Of these children, **Elizabeth Jane**[9] d. single at Stillwater at the age of 27.

†–2–1–1–1. **George Van Rensselaer**[9] is a farmer at Stillwater. He m. Feb. 25, 1854, Emily Ann Wait of Malta, and had issue :

1. Reuben Wait,	b. Mch. 5, 1855.
2. George Nath'l,	b. Dec. 14, 1856.	d. Feb. 2, 1882.
3. Albert C.,	b. about 1858.	d. young

1. **Reuben Wait**[10] lives at Fultonville, Montgomery Co., N. Y., and is a book-keeper for the Starin Silk Fabric Co. He m. Nov. 10, 1887, Iva Peckham of Ballston. No issue.

†–2–1–2. **Nelson,** second son of Nathaniel, was a farmer, and lived at Baltimore, Md. He m. Dec. 29, 1842, Sarah Macy of Stillwater, who was b. at Nantucket, Mch. 17, 1818. Issue :

1. John N.,	b. Jan. 24, 1844.
2. Oliver J.,	b. Jan. 9, 1846.	d. Mch. 2, 1846.
3. William A.,	b. Jul. 23, 1847.	d. Jan. 20, 1852.
4. Reed H.,	b. Jun. 11, 1850.	d. Jul. 27, 1851.
5. Sarah J,	b. Oct. 16, 1853.

6. Carrie H.,   b. May 19, 1855.
7. George W.,   b. Oct. 9, 1857.
8. Hattie M.,   b. Jul. 31, 1860.

†-2-1-2-1. **John N.,**[9] oldest son of Nelson, is a steam engineer, and lives at Baltimore. He m. May 13, 1885, Mattie E. Meekins of Baltimore, who was b. Jan. 1, 1858. Issue:

1. George G.,   b. Apr. 10, 1886.
2. Reed A.,   b. Apr. 18, 1888.   d. Jul. 16, 1889.
3. Loris A.,   b. Nov. 6, 1890.

†-2-1-2-5. **Sarah J.,**[9] oldest daughter of Nelson, and b. in Washington, D. C., m. Oct. 23, 1870, Bradford S. McNeil, and lives at Baltimore. Mr. McNeil was b. in Saratoga Co., N. Y., Jul. 19, 1849, and is an engineer on the Baltimore & Ohio R. R. Issue:

1. Allie.   b. Nov. 3, 1871.
1. Wesley A.,   b. Sep. 4, 1873.   d. Jun. 30, 1874.
3. Emmett.   b. May 15, 1875.

Of these children, **Allie**[10] m. Dec. 30, 1891, Joseph Glasgow.

†-2-1-2-6. **Carrie H.,**[9] second daughter of Nelson, m. Feb. 24, 1881, James H. C. Insco, and lives at Baltimore. Mr. Insco, who was b. Jun. 6, 1852, is a tinsmith. Issue:

1. Hattie M.,   b. Sep. 22, 1882.   d. Jul. 17, 1883.
2. James R.,   b. Aug. 16, 1884.

†-2-1-2-7. **George W.,**[9] second son of Nelson, is an ironworker at Baltimore. He m. Jun. 26, 1878, Elanora Minter, who was b. Apr. 29, 1861. Issue:

1. Mamie.   b. Apr. 29, 1880.   d. Dec. 7, 1883.
2. John N.,   b. Aug. 15, 1883.
3. Elanora F.,   b. Aug. 3, 1885.

†-2-1-2-8. **Hattie M.,**[9] youngest daughter of Nelson, m. Mch. 10, 1881, William W. Johnson. Mr. Johnson, who was b. Mch. 5, 1849, is a timekeeper, and lives at Baltimore. Issue:

1. William W.,   b. Oct. 5, 1882.   d. Mch. 21, 1886.
2. Carrie E.,   b. Feb. 13, 1886.
3. Willie H.,   b. Mch. 31, 1891.

†-2-1-3. **Lewis,**[9] third son of Nathaniel, was a farmer, and lived at Chatham, Columbia Co., N. Y. He m. Ann Palmer, who d. in 1870, without issue.

†–2–1–6.　**Jacob B.,**[8] fifth son of Nathaniel, was a farmer, and lived at Ballston, Saratoga Co.　He m. Oct. 28, 1848, Nancy J. Watkins of Stillwater, who was b. Dec. 16, 1829. Issue:

1. Charles J.,	b. Jan.	7. 1849.	
2. George W.,	b. Feb.	5. 1850.	
3. Mary J.,	b. Jun.	13. 1852.	d. Mch. 7, 1878.
4. Frank A.,	b. Mch.	22. 1854.	
5. William W.,	b. Jan.	26. 1856.	
6. Rosa Belle,	b. May	23. 1857.	
7. Jennie E.,	b. May	3. 1859.	
8. Frances S,	b. Jun.	5. 1862.	
9. Grant U.,	b. Jul.	1. 1864.	
10. Lillie A,	b. Jan.	11. 1867.	
11. Daniel N.,	b. Jun.	26. 1869.	
12. Luella J.,	b. May	22. 1871.	
13. Carrie A.,	b. Aug.	7. 1874.	

1.　**Charles,**[9] oldest son of Jacob B., is a farmer at Charlton, N. Y.　He m. Mch. 4, 1881, Eliza Wait, and had issue:

1. Lottie May,	b. Mch.	18. 1883.
2. Clarence,	b. Oct.	1, 1886.

2.　**George W.**[9] is a farmer, and lives at Milton, N. Y. He m. Feb. 1874, Matilda Murry, and had issue:

1. Anna M.,	b. Dec. —,	1875.
2. Lewis H.,	b. Nov. —,	1877.
3. Minnie,	b. Aug. —,	1883.
4. Truman P.,	b. in	1888.

3.　**Mary J.,**[9] oldest daughter of Jacob B., m. Oct. 10, 1871, Henry C. Knox, and lived at Enon, Lawrence Co., Pa. Issue:

1. Joseph H.,	b. Mch. —, 1876.

4.　**Frank A.**[9] is a farmer, and lives at Ballston Spa, N. Y.　He m. Dec. 17, 1879, Ada C. Holmes, and had issue:

1. Edgar L.,	b. Aug.	27. 1882.
2. Leland S.,	b. Nov.	23. 1885.
3. Ethel M.,	b. Jul.	22. 1889.

5.　**William W.**[9] is a farmer, and lives at Birchton, Saratoga Co., N. Y.　He m. Mch. 1883, Sarah Gray, and had issue:

1. Bessie M.,	b. Mch. —, 1886.

6.　**Rosa Belle,**[9] second daughter of Jacob B., m. May 23, 1889, Martin Larable, and lives at Ballston Spa, N. Y. Issue:

1. Carrie M.,	b. Apr. —, 1890.

7. **Jennie E.**[9] m. Aug. 18, 1880, David E. Holmes, and lives at Saratoga Springs, N. Y. Issue:

    1. Arthur J.,   b. May —. 1883.
    2. Eva L.,   b. Mch. —. 1885.

†-2-1-7. **Alonzo,** sixth son of Nathaniel, was a farmer, and lived at Malta, Saratoga Co. He m. Louisa Culver of Malta, who d. in 1869. Issue: Amelia, George N., and Carrie.

†-2-5. **Samuel,**[7] second son of Isaac, inherited the old homestead at North East, Dutchess Co., N. Y., and was also a farmer. He m. Oct. 28, 1834, Lydia Hyde of Connecticut. Issue:

    1. C. Walter,   b. Oct. 11. 1835.   d. Sep. 16, 1875.
    2. Helen A.,   b. Feb. 26, 1837.
    3. Isaac,   b. Nov. 28, 1838.
    4. Frances,   b. Feb.   2, 1841.
    5. Lydia D.,   b. Nov. 27, 1844.
    6. Samuel,   b. Feb. 27, 1847.

Of these children, **Lydia Delphine**[9] resides single at Amenia, Dutchess Co.; and **Samuel**[9] went to Charleston, S. C., in 1879, and engaged in the book business with his brother Isaac.

2. **Helen A.**[9] m. Aug. 17, 1864, Frederick A. Worth, and resides at Amenia. No issue. Mr. Worth was formerly a book-keeper for the New York Gas Light Co., New York City, but was obliged to resign on account of ill health.

3. **Isaac** resides at Charleston, S. C., and is a dealer in books, engravings and etchings, his place being one of the leading literary centres south of Washington. He m. Nov. 18, 1864, Mary Pulver, but has no issue.

4. **Frances**[9] m. Dec. 20, 1877, Charles B. Van Hovenburgh, who d. Jan. 29, 1887. She resides at Amenia, but has no issue.

1. **Cyrus Walter**[9] was a carpenter and miller, and was living at the time of his death at Camden, N. J. He m. Jan. 31, 1860, Mary J. Corbin, whose present residence is at Vineland, N. J. Issue:

    1. Anna B.,   b. Jun. 12, 1862.
    2. Ruth Emma,   b. May   15. 1864.
    3. Charles W.,   b. Sep. 10, 1866.   d. Jan. 23. 1888.

4. Frances,	b. Jul. 26. 1869.	d. Feb. 14. 1870.
5. Arthur W.,	b. Mch. 2. 1871.	d. Feb. 6. 1891.
6. Frederic C.,	b. Aug. 31. 1873.	
7. Herbert L.,	b. Jan. 11. 1876.	

Of these children, **Frances** d. at Syracuse, N. Y.; **Charles** in Charleston, S. C.; and **Arthur** in Riverside, Cal., all single.

1. **Anna B.**[9] is a school teacher in Peekskill, N. Y.; and
2. **Emma**[9] is a dressmaker in Santa Anna, Cal.

7. **Herbert**[9] is a seaman's apprentice on the U. S. S. St. Louis at League Island, to be transferred later to the training ship at Newport, R. I.

6. **Frederic C.,**[9] who is in business at Charleston, S. C., m. Aug. 31, 1891, Emma Phillips.

†–2–6. **Stephen,**[7] third son of Isaac, settled in Skaneateles, Onondaga Co., N. Y., and was a farmer and manufacturer of leather. He m. Phebe Thorne, and had issue:

| 1. Sarah, | b. in 1832. | d. about 1862. |
| 2. Caroline. | b. in 1834. | |

Of these children, **Sarah**[°] d. single; and **Caroline**[°] m. about 1874, Damon H. Hodskins, and lives at Skaneateles. No issue.

†–2–8. **Zephaniah,**[7] fourth son of Isaac, settled in North East, Dutchess Co., N. Y., and was a farmer. He m. Laura Thayer, who was b. Feb. 9, 1794, and d. Mch. 24, 1865. Issue:

1. Nancy,	b. May 25. 1820.	d. May 10, 1824.
2. Maria E .	b. Jan. 12. 1822.	
3. Mary Ann.,	b. Aug. 25. 1823.	
4. Susan Emily,	b. Jun. 6. 1825.	d. May 13. 1859.
5. William H..	b. Aug. 27. 1828.	

Of these children, **Mary Ann**[°] resides single at Pleasantville, Westchester Co., N. Y.

2. **Maria**[°] m. Dec. 8, 1842, John B. Foster, and also resides at Pleasantville, N. Y. Issue: Mary, Browning, William, and Othniel.

4. **Susan Emily**[°] m. Jun. 20, 1846, Myron Hubbell, who d. Nov. 24, 1862. She resided at North East, but d. at Cornwall Bridge, Litchfield Co., Conn. Issue: William H., who d. about 1880.

5. **William Henry,**[6] only son of Zephaniah, is a farmer, and lives at North East, Dutchess Co. He m. Mch. 9, 1859, Catherine A. Tanner, and had issue:

    1. Albert Henry.   b. Mch. 24, 1863.

1. **Albert Henry,**[9] who is a carpenter at Millerton, North East, m. Oct. 29, 1884, Minnie Loucks. No issue.

(3.) — LUTHAN OF FLEMING, CAYUGA CO., N. Y.

†–3. **Luthan,**[6] third son of Samuel, moved from Dutchess Co. to Galway, Saratoga Co., when a young man. In 1806 he moved to Fleming, Cayuga Co., where he died soon after, being a farmer. He m. Mary Rood, or Rude, who was b. Nov. 30, 1757, and d. Oct. 4, 1832, after a second marriage to a Mr. Waddams. Issue:

1. Anna.	b. Feb. 17, 1782.	d.	young.
2. Elizabeth.	b. Jan. 10, 1784.	d.	
3. John.	b. Feb. 10, 1786.	d. Mch. 4, 1865.	
4. Ephraim.	b. Apr. 1, 1788.	d. Jan. 20, 1836.	
5. Hannah.	b. Jul. 11, 1790.	d. Sep. 11, 1853.	
6. Isaac.	b. Apr. 27, 1792.	d.	young.
7. Luther.	b. Mch. 3, 1794.	d.	young.
8. Mary.	b. Mch. 13, 1796.	d. Dec. 15, 1832.	
9. Anna.	b. about 1798.	d.	young.
10. Luthan.	b. May 30, 1799.	d.	
11. Anna.	b. Apr. 17, 1801.	d. Mch. 9, 1869.	
12. Isaac.	b. Nov. 11, 1803.	d. Feb. 27, 1866.	

Of these children, nothing further is known of **Luthan,**[7] he having left home when a young man.

2. **Elizabeth**[7] m. Jun. 23, 1803, Augustus F. Ferris, and lived at Cato, Cayuga Co., N. Y. Issue: Frederic, Eliza Ann, Rosetta, Luthan, Chancey, Sylvanus, Mary Ann, John, Maryett, Melissa, and Elizabeth.

5. **Hannah**[7] m. Eben Gaston, and lived at Castile, Wyoming Co. Issue: Three or four children, names not learned.

8. **Mary**[7] m. Nov. 23, 1814, Nathaniel Close, and lived at Scipio, Cayuga Co. Issue: Mary Ann, Elizabeth, Daphna, Diana, Betsey Ann, and Andrew J., all dead but the last.

11. **Anna**[7] m. Caleb Waddams, a farmer, and lived at Geneva, Ontario Co. Issue: Eliza, Elmina, Mary, and Elizabeth.

†–3–3. **John,**[7] oldest son of Luthan, was a farmer, and lived for many years at Rushford, Alleghany Co., N. Y., but at the time of his death was living near Evansburg, Crawford Co., Pa. He was a soldier in the War of 1812, and a prominent member of the Masonic fraternity, having been at one time, it is said, Grand Master of the Grand Lodge of New York. He m. 1st, about 1810, Hulda Tibbals of Cayuga Co., N. Y., who d. some years after the birth of her only child. Issue :

1. Horatio Nelson.	b. Jun. 34. 1812.	d. Aug. 16. 1864.	

John m. 2d, Eliza Butterfield, who d. Jun. 6, 1880, at Meadville, Crawford Co., Pa. Issue :

2. Lucretia.	b. Jun. 17. 1823.	d. Nov. 13, 1853.	
3 Hannah,	b. Apr. 5. 1825.		
4. Mary.	b. Oct. 4. 1826.		
5. Ruth.	b. Oct. 9. 1829.	d. May 11, 1857.	
6. Luthan.	b. Sep. 29, 1832.		
7. Minerva.	b. Jul. 7. 1834.		
8. Thankful.	b. Jun. 5. 1836.		
9. Elizabeth,	b. Dec. 14. 1840.	d. Mch. 24. 1867.	
10. Thomas Benton.	b. Feb. 9. 1843.	d. Jul. 20. 1880.	

Of these children, **Ruth**[5] and **Elizabeth**[9] d. single at Evansburg, Pa.

2. **Lucretia**[5] m. Oct. —, 1850. Charles Rawson, and lived and d. at Evansburg, Pa. Issue : William Harrison.

3. **Hannah**[5] m. Feb. 3, 1847, Asa Gustavus Nichols, who d. Jan. 10, 1880. Hannah lives at Meadville, Pa. Issue : John, Adaline, Francisca, Wallace, Fred, Eugene, and Nellie.

4. **Mary**[5] m. Nov. 6, 1845, Lyman Sibley, who died Mch. 28, 1891. Mary lives at Le Mars, Iowa, and her issue are : Floid, Ada, Clarence, Eva, Ruth, and Ned.

7. **Minerva**[5] m. Jul. 9, 1857. Thomas Smiley, and lives at Evansburg, Pa. Issue : Ema, Susan, and Edeth.

8. **Thankful**[5] m. about 1862, Athelston Gaston, who is mayor of Meadville, Pa. Issue : Alma, who d. at the age of three years.

†–3–3–1. **Horatio Nelson,**[5] who lived at Rushford, Alleghany Co., N. Y., was a school teacher, land surveyor, and farmer. He m. Sep. 2, 1840, Sophia L. Bennett, who was b. Dec. 8, 1815, and now lives with her son, F. Eugene, at Cuba, N. Y. Issue :

1. Francis Eugene,	b. Jun. 9, 1841.		
2. Hardin Jerome,	b. Nov. 7, 1842.		
3. Floral Annette.	b. Apr. 15, 1844.		
4. Charles De Alton,	b. Mch. 20, 1846.	d. Jan. 27, 1892.	
5. Aurora Sophronia,	b. May 31, 1848.	d. Sep. 23, 1850.	
6. Emma Felicia.			
7. Eva Lucretia.	b. Feb. 20, 1854.		

3. **Flora Annette,**[9] a teacher for many years in Minneapolis, Minn., m. Jun. 1870, Major Wm. D. Hale, postmaster at Minneapolis. Issue: Nellie, Philena, Gertrude Louise and Flossie, twins, Arthur Dinsmore, and Willie Hammond.

6. **Emma Felicia**[9] was formerly a teacher, at Minneapolis. She m. Dec. 29, 1889, C. Elbert Cady, a native of Windsor, Vt., now living at Minneapolis. Issue: Lawrence Hammond, b. Jan. 22, 1891.

7. **Eva Lucretia,**[9] formerly a teacher at Minneapolis, m. Aug. 13, 1884, Walter B. Finch of Jay, Essex Co., N. Y., and also resides at Minneapolis. No issue.

†–3–3–1–1. **Francis Eugene,**[9] oldest son of Horatio Nelson, formerly a teacher and land surveyor, is now engaged in the production of petroleum at Cuba, Alleghany Co., N. Y. He m. Sep. 20, 1867, Emma L. Scott at Pleasantville, Venango Co., Penn. Issue:

1. Victor Hugo,	b. Oct. 25, 1868.	
2. Virgil Scott,	b. Aug. 17, 1870.	d. Dec. 6, 1890.
3. Eugenia Lynn,	b. Nov. 28, 1872.	
4. Cleo Nelson,	b. Mch. 21, 1874.	
5. Haidee Florizel.	b. Jan. 3, 1875.	
6. Halley Waldo,	b. Jun. 19, 1882.	
7. Evangeline.	b. Sep. 2, 1887.	

Of these children, **Virgil Scott**[10] was quite proficient in music, especially on the violin; **Eugenia Lynn,**[10] **Cleo Nelson,**[10] and **Haidee Florizel,**[10] all educated at the Geneseo State Normal School, N. Y., are teachers.

1. **Victor Hugo,**[10] b. at Shamburg, Venango Co., Pa., is a teacher and supervisor at West Clarksville, N. Y. He m. Aug. 28, 1891, Mary R. Congdon, and had issue:

1. Maude Ione. b. Aug. 9, 1892.

†–3–3–1–2. **Hardin Jerome,**[9] second son of Horatio Nelson, is a lawyer at Minneapolis, Minn., making a speciality of land titles and rights of way for railroads. He m. Oct. 19,

1870, Susie E. Hendy, who was b. May 12, 1848, at Elmira, N. Y. Issue:

1. Agnes,   b. Sep. 7. 1871.
2. Alice,   b. Jun. 1. 1876.
3. Grace,   b. Oct. 29. 1879.
4. Flora,   b. Oct. 18, 1884.

†–3–3–1–4. **Charles De Alton,**[9] third son of Horatio Nelson, in his younger days a teacher, was later a dealer in lumber and real estate at Minneapolis, where he died in 1892. He m. Oct. 5, 1870, Laura D. Farewell, who was b. Dec. 26, 1846. Issue:

1. John Bertrand,   b. Nov. 13, 1872.
2. Florenstein,   b. Sep. 3, 1879.

†–3–3–6. **Luthan,**[8] second son of John, is a lumber merchant, and resides at Corry, Erie Co., Penn. He m. Mch. 26, 1857, at Sadsbury, Crawford Co., Penn., Caroline Brown, who was b. Jul. 10, 1841. Issue:

1. Ruth Alice,   b. Aug. 22. 1858.
2. Clara B.,   b. Jul. 15. 1861.
3. Clarence R.,   b. Aug. 24. 1864.
4. John Pierson,   b. Sep. 12. 1868.
5. Le Roy Gilford,   b. Jun. 19. 1874.
6. Douglas L.,   b. Jun. 21. 1880.

Of these children, **Ruth Alice**[9] m. Feb. 21, 1891, John W. Saunders, a jeweler at Corry, Penn. No living issue.

2. **Clara R.**[9] m. Jun. 14, 1887, Percival White, a teacher at Buffalo, N. Y. Mr. White was formerly dean and professor of mathematics in Wesleyan University located at Fort Worth, Texas. Issue: Alice, b. Sep. 27, 1891.

3. **Clarence Russell**[9] is book-keeper and general manager of the lumber-yard at Barberton, O. He is not married.

4. **John P.,**[9] engaged in the lumber business with his father, lives at Washington, Penn. He m. 1st, Nov. 15, 1887, Jennie E. Briggs, who d. Oct. 5, 1888. Issue:

1. Clinton L.,   b. Sep. 28, 1888.

He m. 2d, Dec. 23, 1890, Emma Hathaway of Garland, Warren Co., Penn., who was b. Dec. 21, 1872. Issue:

2. Cashus Russell,   b. Nov. 26, 1892.

†–3–3–10. **Thomas Benton,**[8] youngest son of John, was a farmer and lumberman. After living some years in the

West, he returned to Pennsylvania and was living at the time of his death at Meadville, Crawford Co. He m. Jul. 3, 1867, Sarah S. Brown at Ontario, Iowa. Issue:

1. Maude L.,	b. May 28, 1870.
2. Ralph K.,	b. Nov. 19, 1871.
3. Lawrence K.,	b. May 5, 1876.
4. Grace,	b. Dec. 1, 1877.

Of the above children, **Ralph[9]** is in partnership with his uncle, Athelston Gaston, in the lumber business, at Meadville, Penn.

1. **Maude L.**[9] m. Jun. 20, 1888, Charles Joseph Swift of Corry, Penn. Mr. Swift is manager of electrical works, and resides with his family at Cleveland, O. Maude L. graduated at sixteen at the Corry High School, and afterwards studied at the State Normal School at Oswego, N. Y. She is noted for her fine elocutionary talents. Issue: Alice Ophelia; and Marion, who d. in infancy.

†–3–4. **Ephraim,**[7] second son of Luthan, was a farmer and surveyor; justice of the peace most of his life; was in the State Assembly two sessions; and supervisor, town of Aurelius, when Aurelius, Auburn, and Fleming were one town; d. in Aurelius in 1836. He m. Jan. 31, 1811, Ruth Goodrich, who was b. Dec. 8, 1792, and d. Jul. 18, 1839. Issue:

1. Angelina,	b. Oct. 24, 1811.	d. Jan. 25, 1872.
2. Eliza Ann,	b. Feb. 25, 1813.	d. Jan. 29, 1872.
3. Harriet,	b. Jan. 26, 1815.	d. Nov. —, 1890.
4. Lucius G ,	b. Jun. 15, 1816.	d. in 1887–8.
5. Emily,	b. May 3, 1818.	
6. John,	b. Oct. 12, 1820.	d. Feb. 22, 1865.
7. Luthan,	b. May 25, 1823.	d. Jun. 4, 1864.
8. Daniel,	b. Mch. 5, 1825.	
9. Julia Ann,	b. Jan. 25, 1827.	d.

Of Ephraim's children, **Angelina**[8] m. Nov. 2, 1831, Daniel Gould, and lived at Owosso, Shiawassee Co., Mich. Issue: Henry, Amos, Ephraim, Ebenezer, Adelaide, and Emily Louise.

2. **Eliza Ann,**[8] m. 1st, Nov. 25, 1835, Nicholas H. Storing of Jorden, and lived at Little Falls, Herkimer Co., N. Y. Issue: Homer H. and Mary Emily. She m. 2d, Nov. 25, 1848, Jacob Shaw, and lived at Red Creek, Wayne Co. Issue: Edwin B., who lives at Red Creek.

3. **Harriet**[8] m. May 25, 1839, Alexander Kerr, and

lived and d. at Ann Arbor, Mich. Issue: Ruthette, Emily, Alice, Mary, Theodore, John, Minerva, Cornelia, William, Harriet, and Alexander.

5. **Emily**[8] m. Sep. 5, 1848, Winfield S. Ament, and lives at Owosso, Mich. Issue: Claribel, William S., Clarence, Edward, and Harriet Eliza, all dead except William.

9. **Julia Ann**[8] m. 1st, Feb. 11, 1850, George W. Barnum, and had issue: Lucius L. and Georgiana. She m. 2d, John N. Ingersoll, and lived and d. at Corunna, Shiawassee Co., Mich. Issue: Ward and Nell, both dead.

†–3–4–4. **Lucius G.**,[8] oldest son of Ephraim, was a mechanic, after his return from the Army, and lived at Kirksville, Adair Co., Mo. He m. May 3, 1842, Anna Maria Sumner, and had issue: Charles G. and three others that d. young.

1. **Charles G.**,[9] the last known of him, was a station agent near Mosby, Mo. He is married and has several children.

†–3–4–6. **John**,[8] second son of Ephraim, was a farmer, and lived at Fleming, Cayuga Co., N. Y. He m. Feb. 20, 1849, Phila Austen, who was b. Dec. 22, 1826. Issue:

1. Mary E.,	b. Jan. 26, 1850.
2. Augusta,	b. Oct. 29, 1852.
3. Ephraim,	b. Feb. 14, 1855.
4. Ruth Anna,	b. Jun. 24, 1857.
5. Grace E.,	b. Feb. 1, 1864.

Of these children, **Augusta**[9] is a school teacher at Fleming, unmarried.

1. **Mary E.**[9] m. Dec. 21, 1870, Titus W. Cuykendall, and lives at Owasco, Cayuga Co. Issue, if any, not learned.

3. **Ephraim**[9] is a copyist in an art gallery in Auburn, N. Y. He m. Oct. 17, 1877, Georgia Hadsell, and had issue:

1. Howard E.,   b. Aug. 18, 1878.

4. **Ruth Anna**[9] m. Dec. 24, 1878, J. P. Nye, and lives at Auburn. Issue: Mable E., Walter, and Clarabell.

5. **Grace E.**[9] m. Jun. 27, 1883, Edwin L. Hamilton, and lives at Cincinnati, Ohio. Issue: Earl, Lula May, and Robert.

†–3–4–7. **Luthan,**[8] third son of Ephraim, was a physician and surgeon, and lived at Hartford Centre, Van Buren Co., Mich. He studied medicine at Pittsfield, Mass., under old Dr. Childs, and graduated at Woodstock, Vt., in 1844. During our late War he was a member of Co. D, 66th Ill. Vols. At the time of his death he was assistant surgeon in a hospital in Mo., was taken sick, and d. at Decatur, Mich., on his way home. He m. Dec. 25, 1845, Marietta Cook, and had issue:

    1. Henry M.,   b. Jan. 12, 1847.   d. May 11, 1865.
    2. Mina J.,   b. Nov. 23, 1855.

    1. **Henry M.**[9] was a member of Co. K, 1st Mich. Cavalry, and d. of wounds received at or near Yellow Tavern, Va.

    2. **Mina J.**[9] m. Oct. 25, 1877, Alpheus S. Anderson, and lives at Kalamazoo, Mich. No issue.

†–3–4–8. **Daniel,**[8] fourth son of Ephraim, is a farmer at Venice Centre, Cayuga Co., N. Y. He m. Feb. 1, 1854, Lucina Whitten, and had issue:

    1. Luthan W.,   b. Jan. 14, 1855.
    2. Emma E.,   b. Jul. 21, 1856.
    3. Ezra D.,   b. Nov. 15, 1858.

Of Daniel's children, **Luthan**[9] and **Emma**[9] reside at home; **Ezra**[9] is a Baptist minister at Rome, Bradford Co., Penn. All are single.

†–3–12. **Isaac,**[7] youngest son of Luthan, was a farmer, and lived at Le Roy, Genesee Co., N. Y. He m. Jan. 5, 1836, Amanda Dunning, who was b. Feb. 20, 1808, and d. Apr. 28, 1892. Issue:

    1. Mary Josephine,   b. Oct. 6, 1836.   d. May 17, 1861.
    2. Lydia Amelia,   b. Jan. 11, 1838.   d. Aug. 28, 1890.
    3. Flora Tryphena,   b. Jul. 22, 1839.
    4. Phebe Cornelia,   b. May 9, 1841.
    5. Felicia Anna,   b. Apr. 26, 1843.
    6. Elmina Amanda,   b. Mch. 1, 1845.
    7. Caroline Cynthia,   b. Mch. 29, 1847.

Of Isaac's children, **Lydia Amelia**[8] d. single: **Felicia Anna**[8] lives at Le Roy: and **Phebe Cornelia**[8] and **Elmina Amanda**[8] are artists at Le Roy.

    1. **Mary Josephine**[8] m. May 13, 1857, Alexander Van Pelt, and lived at La Porte, Ind. Issue:

    1. Clayton H'd,   b. May 6, 1858.   d. Sep. 7, 1859.
    2. Julia Amanda,   b. Feb. 19, 1860.   d. Aug. 31, 1870.

3. **Flora Tryphena**[5] m. Oct. 22, 1861, M. R. Forney, a builder and contractor, and lives at La Porte, Ind. Issue: Katherine Hammond, b. Apr. 14, 1870.

7. **Caroline Cynthia**[9] m. Jun. 23, 1870, George Gallup, and lives at Blue Rapids, Kan. Issue: Elmina A., Stella C., and Alfred Hammond and Ralph Forney, twins.

†–5. **Daniel,**[6] fourth son of Samuel, was a blacksmith and farmer, and settled in Washington, Dutchess Co., N. Y. He m. Amy Green, who was b. Apr. 5, 1764. Issue:

1. Elizabeth,	b. Oct. 25, 1788.	d. Sep. 6, 1869.
2. Hannah,	b. Dec. 19, 1790.	d. Mch. 10, 1845.
3. George,	b. Dec. 17, 1792.	d.
4. Mary,	b. Dec. 14, 1794.	d. Jul. 11, 1862.
5. Joseph,	b. May 2, 1797.	d. Nov. 30, 1853.
6. Benjamin,	b. May 13, 1799.	d. Dec. 24, 1843.
7. Henry,	b. Sep. 28, 1801.	d Nov. 28, 1872.
8. Caroline,	b. Apr. 6, 1806.	d. Nov. 28, 1853.
9. Emma,	b. Apr. 10, 1808.	d. Mch. —, 1826.

Of the above children, Elizabeth, Hannah, and Joseph d. single at Bethel, Clermont Co., Ohio; and Emma d. single at Washington, N. Y.

4. **Mary**[7] m. Joseph W. Lockwood, and lived in New York city, until after the death of her husband, when she moved to Bethel, Ohio, where she died. Issue: Daniel H., Sarah, and Walter. Daniel H. lived at Loveland, Clermont Co., Ohio, where he d. Jun. 2, 1892.

†–5–3. **George,**[7] oldest son of Daniel, was a hatter and farmer, and settled in Oneonta, Otsego Co., N. Y. He m. Hannah Coons, and had issue: Daniel, George Henry, and Myra who d. young.

Of George's children, 1. **Daniel**[8] was a merchant in California, but whether married or single, is not known.

2. **George Henry**[8] m. at Oneonta and had several children. He afterwards left Oneonta, and about 1870–72 was living at Crete, Saline Co., Neb. Nothing further can be learned in regard to his whereabouts, his wife, or his children.

†–5–6. **Benjamin,**[7] third son of Daniel, was a carpenter and builder, and lived in Dayton, Ohio. He m. ——— ———, and d. at Dayton, Ohio, without issue.

†–5–7. **Henry**[7] was a farmer, and lived at Bethel, Ohio.

He m. Emma Hitch, daughter of Benjamin Hitch, and d. at Bethel, without issue.

8. **Caroline**[7] m. Nelson A. Hitch, and d. at Bethel, Ohio, without issue.

†–6. **Thomas,**[6] fifth son of Samuel, was a farmer, and lived at Washington, Dutchess Co., N. Y. He m. Abigail ————, and had issue : Charles, Milton, Jane, and Phebe who was b. in 1815, and d. Jun. 18, 1878.

Of Thomas's children, **Charles**[7] and **Jane**[7] d. single at Washington, N. Y.; **Milton**[7] settled in Ohio, and nothing further is known of him; and **Phebe**[7] m. 1st, Esek Dunkin, and lived at Washington. Issue : Jane A. and Isaac H. She m. 2d, Samuel Bishop, and had further issue : Hannah, Franklin, George and Delia.

†–9. **Samuel Jr.,**[6] sixth son of Samuel, was a farmer, and settled in Stillwater, Saratoga Co., N. Y. He m. Apr. 8, 1797, Polly Green of Pawlings, and sister of Daniel's wife. Issue :

1. Amy,	b. Jun. 2, 1802.	d. Apr. 17, 1885.
2. Hannah,	b. Aug. 25, 1804.	d. Dec. 17, 1882.
3. Dorus,	b. Jul. 20, 1808.	d. Jul. 1, 1869.
4. Jenetty,	b. Mch. 5, 1810.	d. Aug. 10, 1835.
5. Louisa,	b. Jan. 9, 1812.	d. Mch. 11, 1872.
6. Jacob,	b Aug. 16, 1814.	d. Feb. 20, 1893.

Of these children, **Amy,**[7] **Dorus,**[7] **Louisa,**[7] and **Jacob**[7] never married. All four first settled in Stillwater, Saratoga Co., but left there in 1868 and moved to Farmington, Ontario Co., where they finally died.

Dorus and his brother **Jacob** were men of high character, who commanded the esteem and respect of men of all parties and sects. Dorus, though living in a strongly Democratic town, was repeatedly elected to various town offices. Jacob, who died but recently, the author found to be a remarkably reliable and trustworthy correspondent.

2. **Hannah**[7] m. Dec. 11, 1822, Ebenezer Carey, and lived at Halfmoon, but died at Farmington, N. Y. Issue : Maria, Amy H., Lydia C., Mary S., Samuel, and Ruth H.

4. **Jenetty**[7] m. Dec. 29, 1830, William P. Barbour, and lived and d. at Northumberland, N. Y. Issue : Parmelia, who m. John Rowe of New York city.

†-11. **Benjamin,**[6] seventh son of Samuel, also lived in Washington, Dutchess Co., and was a farmer, having received 100 acres of land from his father by bequest. He m. about 1800 Anna Fitch, and had issue:

1. Lydia,	b. Jan.	10, 1801.	d. Jan.	31, 1864.
2. Maria,	b. Dec.	25, 1802.	d. Apr.	18, 1817.
3. Cyrus,	b. Oct.	25, 1805.	d. Dec.	17, 1884.
4. Isaac,	b. Nov.	15, 1807.	d. Jun.	1, 1867.
5. James,	b. Jan.	22, 1810.	d. Jun.	6, 1867.
6. Amy,	b. Mch.	2, 1812.	d. Oct.	15, 1816.
7. Emmor,	b. Jan.	16, 1815.	d. Oct.	7, 1816.
8. John,	b. Nov.	13, 1817.	d. Mch.	1, 1881.
9. Andrew B.,	b. Dec.	22, 1822.		

Of these children, Maria, Amy, and Emmor d. young; and **Isaac,**[7] who was a saddler at Dover, d. single at the age of 60.

†-11-1. **Lydia**[7] m. Nathaniel Lockwood, a farmer, and lived at Washington, Dutchess Co. Issue: John F., Anna, and Lydia.

†-11-3. **Cyrus,**[7] oldest son of Benjamin, was a farmer, and lived in Washington, Dutchess Co. He m. in 1837-8 Caroline Sutherland, and had issue:

1. David S.,	b. Aug.	3, 1840.
2. Frederick A.,	b. Aug.	23, 1848.

2. **Frederic A.,**[8] who is a bachelor, is proprietor of the Plaza Hotel, New York city.

1. **David S.**[8] is proprietor of Murray Hill Hotel, New York city. He m. Lydia Lockwood, who d. in 1870. Issue: Caroline.

Caroline[9] m. Robert W. Gibson, an architect in New York city.

†-11-5. **James,**[7] third son of Benjamin, was a farmer, and lived at North East, Dutchess Co. He served his district in the New York legislature during the years 1846-7, and in 1858 was elected sheriff of Dutchess Co. for three years. He m. Nov. 7, 1837, Lucinda Washburn, and had issue:

1. Anna Melinda,	b. Nov.	10, 1840.	
2. Henry Clay,	b. Aug.	6, 1842.	b. Nov. 17, 1872.
3. James Edwin,	b. May	18, 1844.	
4. John Lockwood,	b. Aug.	7, 1850.	

DAVID S. HAMMOND.

Of these children, **Henry,**[8] who was a farmer, d. single at the age of 32.

1. **Anna**[8] m. Oct. 12, 1864, Calvin C. Brayan of North East. Issue: Elizabeth, Ellen, Elihu, Clara, and Henry, all residing in North East.

3. **James Edwin,**[7] a farmer at Stanford, m. Oct. 25, 1871, Clarinda Thompson of that town. No issue.

4. **John L.,**[8] a farmer at Washington, Dutchess Co., m. Oct. 11, 1877, Josephine M. Bertine of Amenia, Dutchess Co. Issue:

    1. James Edwin,   b. Apr. 16, 1879.
    2. Robert Bertine,   b. Feb. 3, 1883.

†–11–8. **John,**[7] fifth son of Benjamin, was a farmer, and lived at Newfane, Niagara Co., N. Y. He m. May 26, 1842, Maria L. Washburn of Boston, Erie Co., who was b. May 30, 1824. Issue:

    1. Melinda,   b. Sep. 23, 1843.
    2. Amy M.,   b. Jun. 26, 1850.   d. Jun. 17, 1864.
    3. James M.,   b. Nov. 18, 1862.   d. Apr. 7, 1864.

1. **Melinda**[8] m. Oct. 6, 1874, Stephen C. Hoag, and lives in Newfane, Niagara Co. No issue.

†–11–9. **Andrew B.,**[7] sixth son of Benjamin, is a farmer at Washington, Dutchess Co., and lives on the old homestead of his father and grandfather. He has been a valuable correspondent to the writer. He m. in 1856 Sarah E. Conklin, and has issue:

    1. Anna,   b. Oct. 31, 1856.
    2. George,   b. Sep. 3, 1858.
    3. Conklin,   b. Jul. 26, 1860.   d. Jan. 1, 1892.
    4. Isaac B.,   b. Jul. 22, 1862.
    5. Andrew B., Jr., b. Jul. 12, 1866.   d. Oct. 16, 1877.

Of these children, Anna and Isaac B., both single, reside with their parents.

2. **George**[8] is a butcher, and lives in Washington, Dutchess Co. He m. Dec. 11, 1889, Caroline Hicks of Stanford, Dutchess Co. No issue.

8.—JABEZ OF NEW BEDFORD.

†–8. **Jabez**[5] fifth son of Thomas, lived at New Bedford,
and was admitted to the Friends Society in May 1806. He
m. Feb. 16, 1760, Zilpha Merrihew, who d. May 29, 1817,
æ. 77. Issue :

1. Luke,	b.	d. Apr. 21, 1807.
2. Jabez, Jr.,	b. Jul. 31, 1769.	d. Dec. 31, 1821.
3. Maria,	b. in 1771.	d. Aug. 29, 1837.
4. Thomas,	b. in 1776.	d. Sep. 29, 1799.

Of these children, **Maria**[6] lived at New Bedford, and m.
May 5, 1795, Jehaziel Jenne, who d. Nov. 13, 1843, æ. 73.
Issue : Abigail, Zilpha, Rebecca, Silvia C., and Alice.

1. **Luke**[6] was a master mariner in the merchant service
sailing from New Bedford. Capt. Luke m. Jul. 26, 1789,
Rebecca Nye, and had issue :

1. Mary,   b. Mch. 1, 1872.   d. Sep. —, 1865.

Mary,[7] who was b. in China, m. Jan. 1816, Jashub Wing
of New Bedford. Issue : Eleanor H., Charles, Leonard,
William, David C., and Rebecca. Of these children, Eleanor
H. m. Henry N. Dean, blacksmith, and lives in New Bedford.

†–8–2. **Jabez Jr.**[6] was a ship-carpenter at New Bedford,
and a deacon in the Congregational Church. He m. Apr. 14,
1792, Abigail Hathaway, daughter of E. A. Hathaway, who
d. Dec. 9, 1829, æ. 57. Issue :

1. Susan,	b. Sep. 22, 1793.	d. Dec. 14, 1831.
2. Thomas W.,	b. Apr. 1, 1795.	d. Mch. 23, 1838.
3. Maria,	b. Mch. 14, 1797.	d. Dec. 31, 1817.
4. Alice,	b. Apr. 8, 1801.	d. May 31, 1804.
5. Loring,	b. Nov. 14, 1803.	d. Dec. 9, 1803.
6. David,	b. Jun. 19, 1808.	d. Sep. 22, 1808.
7. Abigail,	b. Feb. 29, 1810.	d. Apr. 4, 1810.
8. Charles E.,	b. Jun. 9, 1814.	d. Apr. 19, 1842.

Of these children, Alice, Loring, David, and Abigail, d.
young : and Maria d. single at New Bedford at the age of 21.

1. **Susan**[7] m. Jan. 5, 1823, George Shorkley, a sailmaker
at New Bedford. Issue : Abigail, who m. 1st a Gifford of
New Bedford, and 2d, Hiram Snow of Mattapoisett. Abigail
lives at New Bedford, but has no issue.

8. **Charles**[7] in early life, was a cooper, in the whaling
service from New Bedford. 1838–9, he went to Galena, Ill.

and carried on the business of cooper with his uncle, Abraham
Hathaway, where he d. single, Apr. 19, 1842.

†–8–2–2. **Thomas W.,**[7] oldest son of Dea. Jabez Jr.,
was a sea captain in the merchant service, trading at West
Indian and South American ports. He lived for many years at
New Bedford, but afterwards moved to New York, where he d.
Mch. 23, 1838. He m. Oct. 8, 1817, Betsey Davis, neice
of Perry Davis, who d. Sep. 14, 1840, æ. 45. Issue:

1. Maria,	b. Jul. 16, 1818.	
2. Abigail,	b. Feb. 10, 1820.	d. Feb. 27, 1823.
3. Thomas C.,	b. Oct. 8, 1821.	
4. George S.,	b. Dec. 19, 1824.	d. Apr. 7, 1861.
5. Susan,	b. Feb. 5, 1827.	d. Sep. 17, 1818.
6. Henry C.,	b. Sep. 6, 1828.	d. Nov. 2, 1829.
7. Abigail,	b. Mch. 21, 1829.	d. Sep. —, 1829.
8. Charles E.,	b. Apr. 3, 1834.	

Of these children, the two Abigails and Henry d. young;
and Susan d. at the age of 21, single.

1. **Maria**[9] m. in 1845 Stephen Green, and lived some
years ago at Boulder, Col. Issue: George, Phebe, Julia,
Charles, and Abigail.

†–8–2–2–3. **Thomas C.**[8] went to Pullman, Wis., and
was employed as a carpenter by the Pullman Car Co., during
which time he invented and patented a wrench. He m. at
Platteville, Wis., ——— ———, and afterwards moved to
California. Issue: Two sons, names not known.

†–8–2–2–4. **George S.**[8] went to Platteville, Wis., where
he became a dry goods dealer, firm of Baylies & Hammond.
He m. Apr. 8, 1852, Jane Matthew Penberthy of Penzance,
Cornwall, Eng., who was b. Dec. 25, 1833. Issue:

1. Thomas C.,	b. Dec. 26, 1852.	d. Oct. 1, 1870.
2. Jane M.,	b. Jan. 27, 1856.	
3. Walter F.,	b. Dec. 2, 1857.	
4. George S.,	b. Dec. 27, 1863.	

Of the above children, all b. in Platteville, Wis., Thomas
Clemence d. single, Oct. 1, 1870.

2. **Jane Maria**[9] lives at Tiverton, R. I., and m. Dec. 27,
1876, Samuel West Hathaway, who was b. Sep. 25, 1854.
Issue:

1. George West,	b. Jan. 28, 1879.
2. William Edgar,	b. Jul. 7, 1881.
3. Charles E.,	b. Sep. 24, 1883.

3. **Walter Ford**[9] is a merchant in the clothing line, and resides at Grinnell, Iowa. He m. Jul. 1878, Hattie Childs, and had issue:

    1. Russell Childs,   b. Feb. 4, 1882.
    2. Martha,   b. Feb. 15, 1883.   d. Jul. 31, 1883.
    3. Walter Jona.,   b. Mch. 5, 1888.
    4. Arthur George,   b. May   7, 1890.

4. **George Snockley**[9] is agent for Bell & Provost, men's clothing, and resides at Waterloo, Iowa. He m. Jun. 8, 1889, Ruby Alice, who was b. Jan. 3, 1863, and daughter of Charles and Arvilla Hoag. Issue:

    1. Ruby.   b. Dec. 22, 1890.

†–8–2–2–8. **Charles Edwin,**[8] youngest son of Thomas W., is a farmer, and resides in either Oregon or Washington. He m. Sep. 15, 1862, Sylvia, daughter of Alanson and Nancy Noble, and has issue: Frank, Maria, and another daughter, name unknown.

†–8–4. **Thomas,**[6] third son of Jabez, was a sea captain living at New Bedford, and d. while in port at Wilmington, N. C., Sep. 29, 1799. He m. Dec. 3, 1795, Hearty Church, daughter of Charles and Elizabeth Church, who d. May 7, 1838, æ. 71. Issue:

    1. Eliza,   b. Sep. 5, 1797.   d. May 7, 1816.
    2. Thomas, Jr.,   b. Dec. 3, 1799.   d. Jul. 27, 1847.

†–8–4–2. **Thomas Jr.**[7] was also a sea captain, living at and sailing from New Bedford. He m. Jan. 1835, Cynthia Kirby, who was b. in Dartmouth, Jul. 24, 1810. After Capt. Hammond's death she m. 2d, John M. Taber, also deceased, and resides with her daughter at New Bedford. By Capt. Thomas Jr. she had issue:

    1. Thomas Henry,   b. Jan. 30, 1840.   d. Apr. 3, 1881.
    2. Hannah Eliza,   b. Jan. 4, 1845.

Of these children, **Hannah**[8] has never married, and lives with her mother in New Bedford.

Thomas Henry,[8] during the late Civil War, was a corporal in Co. G, 3d Reg't, M. V. M. In early life he was a book-keeper, and later a wholesale dealer in oils in New Bedford. He never married.

IV.—JEDEDIAH HAMMOND OF SCITUATE, MASS.

†. **Jedediah[4] Hammond,** fifth son of Samuel,[3] [Benjamin,[2] William[1]], went from Rochester to Scituate, and was first of the name in that town. His residence was west of the North Meeting-House, near the Four Corners. He received land from his father in the town of Mattapoisett, near the salt water, which is still pointed out as the "Diah Place." He m. at Scituate, Nov. 5, 1712, Elizabeth, daughter of Joseph Parker. Issue:

1. Agatha,	b. Sep. 13, 1713.	d
2. Joseph,	b. Dec. 1, 1714.	d.
3. Benjamin,	b. Jul. 28, 1718.	d.
4. Joanna,	b. Mch. 9. 1721.	d.

1. **Agatha[5]** m. 1st, Jan. 15, 173–, Thomas Pincin. She m. 2d, Mch. 31, 1803, William Damon. Issue not known.

†-2. **Joseph,[5]** who lived at Scituate Harbor, m. Nov. 11, 1736, Thankful Damon, and had issue:

1. Thankful,	b. Aug. 13, 1738.	d.
2. Lettice,	b. Apr. 14, 1740.	d. in 1803.
3. Seth,	b. Mch. —, 1743.	d.
4. Joanna,	b. Apr. 11, 1746.	d.
5. Joseph,	b. Nov. 24, 1748.	d. Apr. 9, 1819.
6. Lucy,	b. Apr. 17, 1750.	d.
7. David,	b. Sep. 4, 1753.	d. Feb. 10. 1786.
8. Bela,	b. Jan. 29, 1756.	d. before 1794.
9. Experience,	b. Dec. 17. 1757.	d. Aug. 6, 1825.
10. William,	b. Aug. 26, 1760.	d.
11. Frederick,	b. Nov. 10, 1761.	d. Dec. 25, 1794.
12. Agatha,	b. Aug. 15, 1764.	d.

Of these children, **Lucy[6]** and **Fred[6]** probably never married, and Lucy very likely d. young: 1. **Thankful[6]** m. 1st, Joseph Nash, and 2d, in 1755, a Bailey. Issue not known.

2. **Lettice[6]** d. at Scituate of consumption, æ. 63. She m. about 1756, Joseph Hayden, Jr., who was a sailor, and was b. at Scituate in 1725. He enlisted as a soldier in the Revolutionary War, was stationed at Roxbury, Mass., where he d. at the age of 50. Issue: Abigail, who m. John Coggeshall, and d. in New Bedford; Lettice, who m. Prince Jenney; Pamelia, who m. Samuel Jones; Fanny, who m. Elisha Dunbar, and lived at New Bedford; Lucy, who m. Elijah Kempton of New Bedford; Temperance, who m. Asa Sherman; Esther, who m. John Mack; and Elizabeth, who m. Isaac Collier.

3. **Seth⁶** m. Feb. 17, 1763, Mary Buck of Scituate, and is said to have left a family.

4. **Joanna⁶** m. Jan. 23, 1765, Nehemiah Curtis at Scituate. Issue, if any, not known.

8. **Bela⁶** m. at Scituate, Jan. 16, 1779, Jennie Staples, who d. in 1794, a widow. No further record.

10. **William⁶** moved to Thibodeaux, La Fourche, Interior Parish, La., where he became, it is said, very wealthy. He m. Margaret Delonnay, who was of French descent, but had no issue.

12. **Agatha⁶** m. in 1784, Moses Gardner, lived first in Hingham, and afterwards in Chesterfield, N. H. Has descendants in Hartford, Conn.

5.—JOSEPH OF HINGHAM, MASS.

†-2-5. **Joseph,⁶** second son of Joseph, was a ship-carpenter and joiner, and resided at Hingham, Mass. He m. 1st, Jan. 2, 1774, Anna Barnes, who d. Dec. 29, 1782. Issue:

1. Anna,	b. Apr. 14, 1774.	d. Mch. 8, 1778.
2. Joseph, Jr.,	b. Aug. 14, 1776.	d. Jan. 25, 1835.
3. Anna 2d,	b. Apr. 27, 1779.	d.

Joseph m. 2d, Dec. 30, 1781, Susanna Loring, who d. Sep. 10, 1815, æ. 69, and had further issue:

4 Benjamin,	b. Sep. 29, 1782.	d. Dec. 29, 1782.
5. Benjamin,	b. Nov. 10, 1783.	d. Aug. 7, 1859.
6. Loring,	b. Sep. 5, 1785.	d. Oct. 4, 1864.

Of these children, the 1st Anna and the 1st Benjamin d. young. 3. **Anna⁷** sometimes called Nancy, m. Oct. 5, 1800, John Young of Union River, Me. They lived first at Hingham, but moved in 1802 to Union River. No further record.

5. **Benjamin,⁷** in 1799, went to Boston and learned the trade of silversmith of David Tyler of that city. He afterwards became demented, and d. single at Hingham, Aug. 7, 1859.

6. **Loring,⁷** who was a carpenter and ship-joiner at Hingham, m. May 15, 1836, Sophia Ewell, who d. Mch. 2, 1856. He died at Hingham, without issue.

†-2-5-2. **Joseph Jr.,**[7] who was a ship-carpenter at Hingham, m. 1st, Jun. 4, 1797, Abigail Clapp, who d. Feb. 26, 1800. Issue:

1. William, }
2. Joseph. } twins; both d. young.   d. May 17, 1800.

Joseph Jr. m. 2d, Jan. 4, 1801, Elizabeth Lincoln, who was b. Sep. 15, 1772, and d. Sep. 15, 1848. Issue:

3. Joseph Lincoln.   b. Oct. 24, 1801.   d. Mch. 19, 1855.
4. Elizabeth Lisle,   b. Jan. 17, 1804.   d. Jan. 11, 1886.
5. Anna Barnes,   b. Oct. 10, 1806.   d. Oct. 8, 1881.
6. Grace Lincoln,   b. Jul. 24, 1809.   d.
7. William,   b. Oct. 17, 1814.   d. about 1837.

Of these children, 4. **Elizabeth L.**[s] m. Oct. 27, 1828, Oliver Cushing of Hingham, and had issue: Oliver, William, and Elizabeth.

5. **Anna B.**[s] m. Dec. 1, 1831, Samuel Sprague of Hingham, and had issue: Samuel, Grace L., Anna B., Caroline, and Sarah Gardner.

6. **Grace Lincoln**[s] never married; and 7. **William,** who was a sailor, d. at Charleston, S. C., of yellow fever about 1837, never having married.

†-2-5-2-3. **Joseph Lincoln,**[s] who was a clerk at Hingham, and afterwards a cashier in Dorchester, moved to Philadelphia in 1851. He m. Aug. 25, 1824, Sarah Elizabeth Hooper of Boston, who d. Jun. 10, 1880, in Philadelphia. Issue:

1. Joseph Henry.   b. Sep. 29, 1824.
2. Charlotte Lincoln, b. Nov. 4, 1830.
3. Jane Frances.   b. Nov. 4, 1836.
4. Sarah Elizabeth,   b. Jun. 25, 1838.
5. John Sewall.   b. May 15, 1839.
6. Louisa Hooper,   b. Aug. 21, 1841.

Of these children, the first four were b. in Boston, and the last two in Dorchester. Besides the above there were a number of others, who d. in infancy.

2. **Charlotte Lincoln**[9] m. Feb. 3, 1853, William Means, resides at Philadelphia, and had issue: Edith Lincoln, Grace Burroughs, and Laura Hammond, all married. Edith and Laura live at Philadelphia, and Grace at Pottsville, Pa.

3. **Jane Frances**[9] m. Jan. 31, 1873, Samuel McLauren,

who was an artist, in Philadelphia, and d. Apr. 2, 1879. No issue.

4. **Sarah Elizabeth**[9] m. Oct. 28, 1858, Martin Hayward of Philadelphia, broker, who d. Sep. 19, 1879. Issue: Amy, Albert, Martin, and Mary M.

5. **John Sewall**,[9] a broker at Philadelphia, m. May 17, 1860, Sadie Hill, who was b. Apr. 1837. Issue:

    1. Josephine Stafford,   b. in 1861.

Josephine S.[10] m. Apr. 1887, James S. Van Frocken, pay clerk in the Navy, and resides at Portsmouth, Va.

6. **Louisa Hooper**[9] m. Apr. 8, 1869, George T. Deiss, an attorney at Philadelphia. Issue:

    1. Mabel Wolbert,   b. Jan. 26. 1870.
    2. Joseph Allison,   b. Aug. 9. 1872.   d. Nov. 2, 1881.
    3. Newlin Fell,   b. May 13, 1877.   d. Nov. 5, 1881.
    4. Arthur Lincoln,   b. Sep. 18, 1883.

†–2–5–2–3–1. **Joseph Henry**,[9] who is a shoe and leather dealer, commenced business in 1840 at Blackstone St., Boston, where he continued until the Spring of 1847; then moved to New York, carrying on the same business; afterwards moved to Newton in 1870, where he resided 13 years; he then moved to Corona, Long Island, and later to Brooklyn, N. Y., his present residence. He m. Nov. 26. 1850, Mary Louisa Robins of New York, and has issue as follows:

    1. Sarah Ann.   b. Aug. 13. 1851.
    2. William Henry,   b. Feb. 16, 1853.   d. Jul. 3, 1887.
    3. Benjamin Conly.   b. Jan. 11, 1854.
    4. Mary Ellen,   b. Mch. 24. 1860.
    5. Frances Louisa,   b. Jan. 4, 1865.
    6. Lillian Augusta,   b. Aug. 28. 1869.
    7. Elizabeth Jackson,   b. Feb. 28. 1873.

Besides the above, five children d. in infancy.

Of these children of Joseph Henry, 1. **Sarah Ann**[10] m. May 10, 1869, Edwin Willis Clark of New York City, and had: Joseph Edwin, Maud Elenor, Florence Ethel, Willis Provost, Clarence, Harry Clifford, and three that d. young.

2. **William Henry**,[10] a book-keeper at Newton, L. I., m. Oct. 29, 1879, Addie Devoe Van Wickell of Newtown, L. I., and had issue:

    1. Charlotte Louisa,   b. Sep. 11, 1880.   d. Nov. 4, 1885.
    2. Edith Leslie,   b. Jul. 24, 1882.   d. Jun. 6, 1883.

3. Grace Whitman,   b. Aug. 4, 1884.
4. Whitman White,   b. May 29, 1886.
5. Willetta Henry,   b. Oct. 26, 1887.

3. **Benjamin Conly**[10] is connected with Reilly & Woods's Circus, as chief property clerk, and resides at Brooklyn, N. Y., when at home. He is not married.

4. **Mary Ellen**[10] m. Apr. 24, 1889, Warren G. Hamilton, lives at Flushing, L. I., and has issue: Warren Alexander, b. Dec. 2, 1889. Warren G. Hamilton, formerly a solicitor of advertisements, is preparing a work on silks.

5. **Frances Louisa**[10] m. Apr. 23, 1891, Wm. Harrison Shell, a machinist in Brooklyn, who was b. Dec. 2, 1862. No issue.

6. **Lillian Augusta**[10] m. Jun. 1, 1891, Joseph G. Eno, a compositor, and lives at Brooklyn. No issue.

7.—DAVID OF HINGHAM, MASS.

†-2-7. **David Hammond**,[6] third son of Joseph, lived at Hingham, and is said to have been drowned in the harbor there, Feb. 10, 1786. He m. Elizabeth ———, who d. Oct. 6, 1793, at Hingham. Issue:

1. Betsey,   b. Jun. 13, 1779.   d.
2. David 2d,   b. Oct. 30, 1781.   d.
3. Francis,   b. Jul. 19, 1784.   d.
4. George,   b. Oct. 15, 1786.   d.

Of these children, 1. **Betsey**,[7] or **Elizabeth**, m. Dec. 12, 1798, Charles Otis of Scituate. Issue unknown.

†-2-7-2. **David 2d**,[7] who was a blacksmith at Pembroke, Mass., m. 1st, Apr. 13, 1808, Betsey Mann Nash of Pembroke, who d. Mch. 10, 1823. Issue:

1. David.   b. Mch. 11, 1809.   d. Jan. 10, 1810.
2. David 3d,   b. Jan. 5, 1811.   d. May 14, 1891.
3. Clement,   b. Mch. 18, 1813.   d. Aug. 14, 1823.
4. Betsey M.,   b. Mch. 1, 1815.   d. in 1883.
5. Charlotte N.,   b. Dec. 5, 1817.   d. in 1848.
6. Chas. Fred,   b. Nov. 25, 1821.
7. Thos. Edw.,   b. Jan. 13, 1823.   d. Jul. 7, 1823.

David 2d m. 2d, Mch. 8, 1825, Judith Cook, and had further issue:

7

8. Asa C.,   b. Apr. 19, 1826.
9. Judith R.,   b. Nov. 20, 1827.   d. Jun. 12, 1853.

Of these children, 4. **Betsey** m. Apr. 1844, Joseph Dunn, lived in Rockland, Mass., where she d. in 1883. Issue: John, Fred, Joseph, and Betsey.

5. **Charlotte** m. about 1844, Albert Poole, lived in Rockland, and d. there in 1848, without issue.

6. **Charles Fred,** who is a shoemaker at Rockland, m. Feb. 25, 1865, Isannah Hodge of Maine. Issue:

1. Frank B.,   b. Sep. 2, 1874.
2. Edna M.,   b. May 25, 1880.

†-2-7-2-2. **David 3d,** who was a farmer and shoemaker at Rockland, m. Sep. 1834, Celia Hatch, and had issue:

1. Mary,   b. in   1835.   d. in 1840.
2. Charlotte, b. Feb. 4, 1837.
3. Celia,   b. in   1839   d. in 1842.
4. Mary,   b. Aug. —. 1843.   d. in 1843.

Of these children, **Charlotte,** who is strongly in favor of temperance and Woman's Rights, m. Dec. 25, 1863, Josiah Mann, foreman of a shoe factory in Rockland. Issue: Paul Grayson, who d. at birth, and Gordon who is a member of the medical department of Boston University.

Judith [Cook] Hammond with Asa C. and Judith R., her children, moved to Kingston about 1837.

9. **Judith R.,** m. about 1850, Horace Bradford of Kingston, and d. there Jun. 12, 1853, without issue.

†-2-7-2-8. **Asa C.,** a carpenter at Kingston, Mass., m. Nov. 4, 1849, Amanda Clark, who was b. Aug. 23, 1827, at Plympton, Mass. Issue:

1. Eugene H.,   b. Nov. 9, 1850.
2. Walter C.,   b. May 17, 1852.
3. Isabella A.,   b. Mch. 12, 1856.
4. Chester E.,   b. Dec. 19, 1860.

Of these children, **Eugene H.,** a graduate of Cornell University, class of '87, is an architect in New York City. He has never married.

Isabelle is a teacher and dressmaker in Kingston; and **Chester** is a contractor and builder in the same town.

2. **Walter C.,**[9] contractor and builder at Kingston, Mass., m. Jun. 15, 1879, Eliza H. Chandler of Kingston, and has issue as follows:

1. Lester G., b. Nov. 11, 1880.
2. James C., b. Apr. 29, 1882.
3. Helen A., b. Jul. 24, 1883.
4. Elizabeth Penn, b. Apr. 18, 1886.
5. Walter C., Jr., b. Dec. 27, 1890.
6. Asa C., b. Dec. 24, 1891.

†-2-7-3. **Francis,**[7] the second of David, a laborer at Pembroke, Mass., m. 1st, Feb. 22, 1807, Lois Ramsdell, and had issue as follows:

1. George, b. in 1807. d. in 1869.
2. Harriet, b. Feb. 15, 1808. d. Apr. 23, 1890.
3. Franklin, b. d.
4. Freeman, b. in 1813. d. Aug. 5, 1850.
5. Lucinda, b. in 1815. d. Aug. 16, 1872.
6. William, b. d.
7. Elizabeth, b. Oct. 10, 1818. d. Mch. 21, 1878.
8. Henry M., b. Feb. 3, 1825.
9. Mary, b. in 1827. d. Aug. —, 1846.
10. Sarah B., b. Nov. 13, 1829.
11. Joseph, b. in 1834.
12. Charles A. b. d. at 3½ years of age.

Of these children, 1. **George,**[7] who was a furnaceman at Baltimore, Md., m. Julia Divoll, and had among other issue: George, Julia, Sarah, Elizabeth, etc.

2. **Harriet**[7] m. Mch. 17, 1831, Albert Southworth of Stoughton, Mass., a carpenter. Issue: Albert L., Jedediah, George, Louisa, and Cordelia.

3. **Franklin**[8] lived in Florida during the Seminole War, and served as a soldier in that war. His house being burned by the Indians while he was on duty, his wife, who was an English woman, succeeded in making her escape. He afterwards was a teamster in New Orleans, where he d. more than thirty years ago, without issue.

4. **Freeman,**[8] who was a shoemaker, went to Franklin, N. H., and m. Alice B. Robertson, and d. there without issue.

5. **Lucinda**[8] m. at Newton, Mass., Charles F. N. Hard, and lived and d. at Lowell. Issue: Charles F., Josephine, William H., Alice E., and Walter.

6. **William,**[8] a furnaceman, went first to Pennsylvania,

and then to Grafton, Va., where he was living at the time of his death. He m. Mary ——— , and had three sons : William, George, and ———, one of whom d. at Andersonville Prison.

7. **Elizabeth**[5] m. Daniel M. Robertson of Franklin, N. H. She lived at Manchester, N. H., and d. at East Boston. Issue : Daniel F., William F., and Ida Lucinda.

8. **Henry,**[8] laborer and farmer at Hanover, Mass., m. Jul. 18, 1854, Rebecca Johnson. Issue :

1. Elizabeth J.,	b. Sep. 17, 1857.	
2. Joseph H.,	b. Aug. 13, 1859.	d. Jan. 15, 1866.
3. Mary J.,	b. Dec. 16, 1860.	
4. Florence E.,	b. Apr. 18, 1879.	

Of these children, 1. **Lizzie**[9] m. Aug. 30, 1874, John Frank Hollis, and lives in South Weymouth, Mass. Issue : Charles, Grace, Willie, Everett, and Mary.

9. **Mary,**[8] fourth daughter of Francis, m. John Studley Jr., of Bridgewater, Mass., and lived at Hanover and Lowell, Mass. She had a daughter, Sarah, who d. young. Mary d. at Lowell, Mass., Aug. 1846.

10. **Sarah**[8] m. Jun. 20, 1846, Charles W. Rowell of Manchester, N. H., where she now resides. Her children were : Charles W. Jr., Herbert S., Clara L., Lois Alma, Grace L., James F., and Henry I.

11. **Joseph,**[8] a laborer and farmer at Hanover, Mass., m. Oct. 4, 1863, Ellen C. Barrell. Issue :

1. Loyd Frank,	b. Mch. 1, 1864.
2. Seth Oscar,	b. Oct. 26, 1865.
3. Charles F.,	b. Jan. 24, 1868.
4. George H.,	b. Apr. 1, 1870.
5. Charlotte,	b. Mch. 31, 1872.
6. Benjamin,	b. Mch. 17, 1874.
7. Herbert F.,	b. Mch. 17, 1876.
8. Lizzie E.,	b. Jul. 29, 1878.
9. Nellie M.,	b. Sep. 26, 1881.
10. Willie,	b. Jan. 19, 1884.

1. **Frank,**[9] who is a farmer at Norwell, Mass., m. Nov. 1881, Lettie Sylvester, and had a son Sylvanus, who d. when a few weeks old. Frank is Noble Grand of North River Lodge, 167, I. O. O. F., at Hanover, Mass.

2. **Seth Oscar,**[9] who is a book-keeper in Boston, m.

Dec. 15, 1886, Lizzie Osborne, and has a daughter, name not learned.

4. **George H.,**[9] m. Mch. 2, 1890, Nellie E. Doherty, lives at South Weymouth, Mass., and is a shoemaker.

9.—EXPERIENCE OF SCITUATE, MASS.

†-2-9. **Experience,**[6] fifth son of Joseph Hammond, lived at Scituate Harbor, Mass. He m. Jun. 18, 1780, Lettice Wilder at Hingham, and had issue:

1. Polly,	b. Feb. 26, 1781.	d. Aug. —, 1878.
2. William,	b. Feb. 18, 1783.	d. Dec. 15, 1865.
3. Thomas.	b. Jan. 15, 1785.	d. May 11, 1847.
4. Experience, Jr., ⎫	b. Aug. 11, 1789.	d.
5. John. ⎭		d. at sea.
6. Sarah,	b. Jan. 25, 1793.	d. Aug. —, 1842.
7. Frederick,	b. Jul. 28, 1795.	d. Oct. 5, 1874.
8. Olive,	b. Jul. 22, 1798.	d. Aug. 1, 1811.
9. Joseph,	b. Dec. 10, 1800.	d. Aug. 12, 1827.

Experience Hammond m. 2d, in 1820, Elsie Coleman. No issue by this marriage.

Of the above children, 1. **Polly**[7] m. 1st, Oct. 27, 1800, Ezra Vinal of Scituate, a sea captain, who d. at sea, Aug. 16, 1821. Issue: 1. Mary Ann: 2. Abigail C.; 3. Adeline; 4. Olive H.; 5. Ezra. 1. **Mary Ann**[8] m. 1st, John S. Vinal, and had issue: John T., Mary Ann, Ezra, Adeline, Betsey Capen, and Sarah Curtis. Mary Ann m. 2d, John D. Torrey, and had further issue: Mary Ann, Mercy, and Walter. 2. **Abigail C.**[8] m. Martin T. Peaks of North Scituate, and had: Walter S. 3. **Adeline**[8] m. James Hyde, who d. Feb. 1878, æ. 59. Issue: Annie E., Addie V., George E., and James A. Annie E. m. Henry E. Johnson, and with her mother resides at Dorchester, Mass. 4. **Olive H.**[8] m. Henry Hyland of Scituate, Mass. Issue: Olive, Georgiana, Abbie Carrol, and Henry Puffer. 5. **Ezra**[8] m. Ann Collins, and had issue: Mary M., Ezra, Lettice, Abbie, James, Martha, Charlotte, Henry, and Samuel.

Polly m. 2d, about 1825-6, Walter Wall, a farmer, and d. Aug. 1878, without further issue.

4. **Experience Jr.**[7] probably died young; 5. **John**[7] never married, and was lost at sea; 9. **Joseph,**[7] who was a

sailor, contracted yellow fever from which he partially recovered, and d. at home; *8. Olive*[7] d. in childhood; and *7. Fred,*[7] who was a farmer at Scituate, m. about 1814-5 Polly Coleman, who d. Jun. 11, 1879, æ. 82, without issue.

6. **Sarah**[7] m. Sep. 15, 1814, Gideon Vinal, a captain of militia, living at Scituate, who d. Jun. 17, 1840. Issue: 1. **Carolina A.,**[8] who m. James Elleman, who was b. at Birmingham, Eng., and is now a manufacturer of electroplates and galvanic batteries at Providence, R. I., and has no issue. 2. **Sarah,**[8] who m. Perry Brownell and lives at New Bedford, and had Gideon, William, John F. (who m. Sarah Dunham of Mattapoisett), Susan A., Mary, etc. 3. **Col. John Frederic**[8] b. Jan. 28, 1820, captain and major 41st Mass. Vol. Inf., and major and lieutenant colonel 3d Mass. Cavalry, was in the service from Aug. '62 to Aug. '65, and was wounded in the thigh by a ball. He is now pension attorney at Washington, D. C., practising before all the departments. He m. Lydia G. Cory, but has no issue. 4. **William,**[8] who m. Lavina A. T. Lavare, and had Augusta, William, Charles, Lillie, and Florence. 5. **Gideon,**[8] proprietor of a hotel in Albany, N. Y., m. Margaret ——, and had Sarah, Carrie, Frederick, William, John, Lavinia, and Florence. Two other children of Sarah Vinal, **Joseph**[8] and **Malinda,**[8] d. in infancy.

†-2-9-2. **William Hammond,**[7] oldest son of Experience, was a ship-joiner, and deacon of the Congregationl Church at New Bedford, Mass. He m. Mch. 3, 1805, Abigail Carroll, who was b. at Salem, Mass., Jan. 4, 1782, and d. at New Bedford, Dec. 17, 1861, æ. 80. Issue:

1. Abigail.	b. Aug. 10, 1805.	d. Oct. 16, 1888.
2. Hannah B.,	b. Nov. 19, 1807.	d. Feb. 4, 1886.
3. Elizabeth,	b. Dec. 24 1809.	
4. Juliette L.,	b. Jan. 2, 1812.	d. about 1883.
5. Priscilla,	b. May 9, 1815.	
6. Malinda,	b. Jul. 9, 1817.	d. in 1875.
7. William, Jr.,	b. Sep. 30, 1820.	d. Jan. 9, 1891.
8. Margaret, ⎱	b. Sep. 1, 1822.	d. about 1855.
9. Charlotte, ⎰		d. Oct. —, 1822.

Of these children, 1. **Abigail,**[8] b. in Salem, lived at New Bedford. She m. Nov. 10, 1835, Capt. Stephen Christian, who was in the whaling business. Issue: Stephen Jr., who was killed in battle in the late Civil War.

2. **Hannah Beckett**[5] was b. at South Boston, and lived and d. in Salem, Mass. She m. May 20, 1832, Capt. John Goldsmith of that city, who d. May 21, 1888, æ. 80, and was a captain in the merchant service. Issue: John Henry Jr., b. at Salem, Feb. 18, 1833.

3. **Elizabeth**,[5] who lives at Scipioville, Cayuga Co., N. Y., m. Nov. 21, 1826, Francis Bowman of Falmouth, Mass., a carpenter. Issue: Francis Jr., Elizabeth, Harriet, Mary, Daniel, Sarah, etc.

4. **Juliette**,[5] was b. in South Boston, and d. in Providence, R. I. She m. Nov. 29, 1832, John T. Stall of New Bedford, and had: Sarah, Juliette, and Emma.

5. **Priscilla**,[5] was b. in Charlestown, and is living at New Bedford, Mass. She m. 1st, Nov. 9, 1835, Alden Gifford, and had: Stephen C., William, George P., and Isabella. Priscilla [Hammond] Gifford m. 2d, Feb. 14, 1871, Eben Ryder of New Bedford. No issue by the second marriage.

Of Priscilla's children, **Stephen**[9] was in the 2d Mass. Heavy Artillery; and **William**[9] was in Co. C, 2d Mass. Cavalry, was discharged for disability, and re-enlisted in Co. E, 58th M. V. Inf. **George P.**,[9] who was formerly in the whaling service, was appointed mate in the U. S. Navy, Feb. 1864, and was ordered to report to Rear Admiral D. G. Farragut; was detailed to duty on the U. S. S. Octovana, and participated in the following battles: Mobile Bay, Aug. 5, 1864, capturing Forts Morgan and Gaines, and causing the evacuation of Fort Powell; captured the ram Tennessee, the gunboat Selma, and caused the destruction of the Gaines; also participated in the bombardment and capture of Fort Huger and the Spanish fort, and was in the first gunboat to arrive at Mobile City; and remained in the service until 1870. He joined the G. A. R., May 22, 1867; was Commander of Logan Rodman Post, No 1, 1888–89–90; was Councillor of the Cumberland Association of Naval Veterans; and was an aid-de-camp on the Staff of the Commanders-in-Chief Warner and Veazey.

6. **Malinda**[9] was b. at Charlestown and lived at New Bedford. She m. Nov. 23, 1837, Horace S. Tower, and had: Abbie, Louis and Charles, Lucy, Malinda, and William.

8. **Margaret,**[8] who was b. and lived in New Bedford, m. Apr. 5, 1845, William Hinckley, and had: Margaret, who d. in infancy.

7. **William Jr.,**[8] who was b. at Fairhaven, was a naval architect and ship-joiner at New Bedford. He m. 1st, Jul. 19, 1840, Susan B. King, and had issue:

1. James C.,	b. Sep. 16, 1842.	d. Jul. 19, 1872.
2. Lizzie Imbert,	b. Jun. 16, 1846.	d. May 16, 1886.

William Jr., went to San Francisco about 1854, and amassed quite a fortune, having had a contract with the U. S. Government to convey Government stores up the Colorado River to Salt Lake, and building a steamer for this purpose. While re-visiting New Bedford the steamer was blown up, causing the loss of a greater part of his fortune. In 1859, he came to Seattle, Puget Sound District, and built the first steamer of any dimensions on the Sound; from 1870 to 1881, he held the office of Local Inspector of Steam Vessels of the Puget Sound District. After 1882 he retired from business, his health not permitting active labor. He m. 2d, Jul. 2, 1867, Eliza Ann Fearer, who was b. in Rock Island City, Ill., Feb. 6, 1844. Issue by the second marriage:

3. Lolila Margueret,	b. Dec. 11, 1869.
4. Catherine Abigail,	b. Sep. 23, 1871.

Of the above children of William Hammond Jr., 1. **James C.**[9] enlisted in May 1861, in the 31st Reg't M. V. M., and was honorably discharged; re-enlisted in Co. G, Mass. Heavy Artillery, and served until the close of the war. He again enlisted, Sep. 25, 1865, in Co. C, 3d Heavy Artillery, U. S. Army, and was discharged at Omaha Barracks, Dec. 25, 1868. He afterwards entered the employ of the Fitchburg R. R. Co., and made his residence in Charlestown, Mass., where his wife d. Jan. 6, 1871. He d. at Nantucket, Jul. 19, 1872. James C. m. Jun. 1871, Emily F. Dow of Nantucket. Issue:

1. Sadie H.,	b. Jan. 6, 1871.	d. Jan. 6, 1871.

2. **Lizzie I.**[9] lived and m. in Boston, Apr. 1863, George W. Gould of that city, who d. Mch. 11, 1891. Issue: Susie I., Carrie Gibson, Annie M., Lizzie L., Sadie H., George W., and Willie James.

3. **Lolila M.**[9] m. Dec. 21, 1886, Harry Harkins, lives at Seattle, Wash., and has two children: William Hammond and Marjorie.

4. **Catherine A.**[9] m. Oct. 23, 1889, Frank W. Cotterill, resides at Seattle, and has one son : Charles Phillip.

†-2-9-3. **Thomas,**[7] second son of Experience Hammond, was a ship-builder, and lived, until after the birth of his children, at South Boston. He built a residence at the base of Washington Heights, 70 years ago, where it still remains without impairing the grandeur of more modern and more imposing dwellings. He was a Deacon in the Congregational Church, Superintendent of the Sabbath School, and a temperate and devout man, much respected for his wisdom and integrity of character. After his second marriage he purchased a farm at Fitchburg Hill, where he was living at the time of his death. He m. 1st, Nov. 5, 1809, Betsey Lovell, who d. May 27, 1832. Issue :

1. Thomas, Jr.,	b. Nov. 13, 1810.	d. Apr. 8, 1879.
2. John,	b. Nov. 8, 1811.	d. May 9, 1882.
3. Elizabeth Ann,	b. Jul. 24, 1814.	
4. Mary Lovell,	b. Nov. 28, 1816.	d. May 12, 1873.
5. William,	b. Dec. 14, 1819.	d. Dec. 21, 1883.
6. Zephaniah W.,	b. Jul. 10, 1823.	d. Feb. 26, 1891.
7. Joseph,	b. May 24, 1826.	d. Jun. 4, 1826.
8. Sarah Jane,	b. Feb. 13, 1828.	d. Jul. 17, 1833.
9. Benjamin F ,	b. Oct. 7, 1830.	d. Oct. 25, 1830.
10. Frederick,	b. Feb. 27, 1832.	d. Apr. 29, 1832.

Thomas Hammond m. 2d, Aug. 15, 1833, Nancy Pierce Dodge, who d. Nov. 14, 1845. He m. 3d, May 20, 1846, Mary Bates. No issue by the second and third marriages.

Of these children, 3. **Elizabeth Ann,**[8] b. in South Boston, taught in the schools there and later opened a private school in New Bedford. She afterwards was a teacher, and later principal of Plaquemine Female Seminary, Plaquemine, La. After her marriage she moved with her husband to Beulah Plains, La., where they resided thirteen years. Their plantation was three-fourths of a mile from Port Hudson, which surrendered after Vicksburg fell, and their buildings were burned on the first assault, May 27, 1863. About the close of the war, she came to Boston, remaining two years, and returned to find her plantation pre-empted, which was only regained after a three years lawsuit. She m. Jul. 1, 1849, Frederick Steinman Ernst, who was b. in Easton, Penn., Feb. 2, 1810. After his graduation at Yale in 1832, Mr. Ernst studied theology at Princeton, N. J., and commenced his ministerial labors at Natchez, Miss., where he labored several years. He afterwards received a call to Beulah Plains, near Baton Rouge,

La., where he remained until the time of his death. It is said
of him, "He was an earnest pastor, his sermons heart-reaching
and impressive, his character strong, unselfish and true, and as
a man he was greatly beloved." Issue :

    1. Anna M. Dickinson,   b. Nov. 24, 1850.   d. Jun. 26, 1861.
    2. Frederick W.,   b. Jun. 28, 1853.

Frederick,[9] b. in East Feliciana Parish, La., was educated at Covington and Danville, Ky., graduated at Dartmouth,
N. H., in '76, at the Yale Divinity School in '79, and in '83
accepted a Congregational pastorate at South Hartford, N. Y.,
where he remained about five years. His health demanding
a change, he went to Europe, and upon his return was called
to organize Dow Academy, Franconia, N. H., of which institution he is still Principal. He m. Mch. 18, 1880, Hattie E.
Holt, of New Haven, and has two sons and two daughters:
Clara L., Gertrude S., Clayton H., and Frederic S.

    4. **Mary Lovell**[3] m. Jan. 19, 1837, George Bradford,
who was b. in Boston, Jul. 15, 1814, and moved to San Francisco, Cal., about 1850-52. Mr. Bradford, who was a lumber
dealer, and one of the city fathers, d. Jul. 5, 1888. Mary,
his wife, d. May 12, 1873. Issue: Elizabeth Lewis, Daniel
Lewis, Thomas Hammond, Joseph Franklin, Eveline, George,
Lovell, Mary Eva, Charles Aug., William G., and Edward
Winslow. Elizabeth L. m. George B. Hawley and lives at
Oakland, Cal.

    5. **William,**[8] who was a house-carpenter, at New Bed-
ford, m. Sep. 15, 1844, Lydia P. Carr of Nantucket, who d.
at Campello, Mass., Oct. 25, 1887, æ. 66. William d. at
New Bedford, Dec. 21, 1883, without issue.

†-2-9-3-1. **Thomas Jr.,**[8] eldest son of Thomas, was a
deacon of the Congregational Church, and a clothing manufacturer, Broadway, South Boston. He m. May 13, 1835, Harriet W. Trow, and had issue as follows :

    1. William A.,   b. Jun. 19, 1837.
    2. James B.,   b. Apr. 23, 1839.
    3. Hattie W.,   b. Jan. 22, 1841.
    4. Martha Ann,   b. Nov. 14, 1843.
    5. John T.,   b. Sep. 16, 1845.
    6. Henry W.,   b. Apr. 30, 1847.
    7. Jennie S.,   b. Jul. 25, 1849.
    8. Thomas F.,   b. Feb. 22, 1852.
    9. Mary Elizabeth,   b. Sep. 3, 1854.
    10. George F.,   b. Apr. 9, 1857.   d. Jan. 18, 1883.
    11. Charles N ,   b. May 3, 1859.

JAMES B. HAMMOND

Of these children, 1. **William Augustus,**[9] who is a patternmaker in New York City, m. Feb. 16, 1875, Sarah Fowler of South Boston. No issue.

2. **James Bartlett**[9] was b. Apr. 23, 1839, in South Boston, where he remained until his thirteenth year; entered successively the Boston High School and Latin School; finished preparation for college at Phillips Academy, Andover; graduated from the University of Vermont in '61, and was a member of the Phi Beta Kappa Society; entered the Union Theological Seminary, Schenectady, N. Y., the next year, and graduated four years later; army correspondent of the *New York Tribune*; reported Beecher's sermons for the *Boston Traveller*; collaborator American edition Lange's Commentary; compiled a volume of Psalms, published by Chas. Scribner; student at University of Halle, Germany; teacher at Dedham, Mass.; inventor Hammond typewriter; president Hammond Typewriter Co., and resident of New York City. James B. has never married.

3. **Hattie Walker**[9] b. at Weymouth, Mass., m. Dec. 24, 1867, William S. Phipps of Hyde Park, and resides in New York City. Mr. Phipps is general manager and book-keeper of the Hammond Typewriter office, New York City. Their only daughter, Mabel E., b. Dec. 17, 1869, is very talented in music.

4. **Martha Ann**[9] m. May 13, 1870, Capt. John J. Raynes, who was b. at Deer Isle, Me., Jul. 5, 1823, and resides at Hyde Park, Mass. Her children are: Marion Trow, John Charles, Joseph Francis, and William Augustus.

5. **John Trow,**[9] who was in the late War, has never married. He is at present superintendent of the Capital Park, Sacramento, Cal.

6. **Henry W.,**[9] who is a carpenter, resides at Taunton, Mass.

7. **Jennie Swan**[9] is a teacher at Hyde Park, Mass., living with her mother.

8. **Thomas Francis,**[9] who is general agent of the Hammond Typewriter for Pennsylvania, New Jersey, Delaware and West Virginia, resides at Philadelphia. He m. Nov. 14, 1874, Lucy Elizabeth Waters, and had issue:

1. Richard Ralph,	b. Jun. 19, 1878.
2. Percy Waters,	b May 4, 1886.
3. Edith,	b. May 26, 1889.

9. **Mary Elizabeth**[9] m. Mch. 1870, Rev. Edmund Hardy, and resides at Buffalo, N. Y. Issue: Gertrude, Alice Cary, Eddie J., Jennie Hammond and Fred Hammond.

10. **George Frederic,**[9] who was a salesman, was on the ill-fated steamer City of Columbus, which was wrecked at Gay Head, Mass, Jan. 18, 1883. He clung to the rigging of the doomed vessel, and just after being rescued died of exhaustion.

11. **Charles Nash,**[9] who is a salesman, in the Boston office of the Hammond Typewriter Co., resides at Boston. He m. Oct. 1. 1889, Myra Belle Libby, and has a son:

1. James Bartlett, 2d,   b. Dec. 10, 1890.

†–2–9–3–2. **John Hammond,**[8] second son of Thomas, was a ship-joiner and house-carpenter, and lived at South Boston, Fitchburg, and Ashburnham, and d. at Detroit, Mich., May 9, 1882. He m. Nov. 8, 1834, Sarah Huston, who was b. in Wells, Me., Mch. 21, 1809, and d. in Turner's Falls, Mass., Jul. 23, 1880. Issue:

1. John L.,	b. Nov. 3, 1835.	d. Jul. 27, 1864.
2. Sarah J. F.,	b. May 18, 1836.	d. Jun. 19, 1855.
3. George Henry,	b. May 5, 1838.	d. Dec. 29, 1886.
4. Leaffie A.,	b. Mch. 9, 1840.	
5. Martha H.,	b Jan. 17, 1841.	
6. Thomas,	b. Feb. 27, 1843.	
7. Walter,	b. Mch. 21, 1846.	d. Feb. 5, 1847.
8. Frederic,	b. Feb. 27, 1847.	
9. Henry,	b. Jul. 30, 1848.	d. Dec. 7, 1888.
10. Albert,	b Sep. 26, 1850.	d. Sep. 24, 1873.
11. Juliet,	b. Oct. 26, 1852.	
12. Herbert,	b. Mch. 16, 1854.	d. Aug. 1, 1855.

Of these children, **Walter**[9] and **Herbert**[9] d. in infancy; **Sarah**[9] was b. in South Boston, and d. in Ashburnham, Mass., single; and **Albert,**[9] who was b. in Ashburnham, d. near Kansas City, Mo., also single.

1. **John L.,**[9] who was b. at South Boston, was a mechanic at Detroit, and d. at East Saginaw, Mich. He m. Aug. 1, 1857, Jane L. Howe of Ashburnham, and had one son:

1. Herbert H., 2d,   b. Jun. 6, 1858.

Herbert H.,[10] who is single, is a hardware merchant at Baldwinsville, Mass.

4. **Leaflie A.,**[9] who was b. in Fitchburg, m. Jan. 24, 1865, Granville Hosmer, who is a machinist at Fitchburg, Mass. Issue:

1. Birdie,	b. Oct. 21, 1872.	d. Nov. 3, 1872.
2. Julia H.,	b. Apr. 12, 1874.	d. Jul. 14, 1874.

5. **Martha H.,**[9] who was b. at Fitchburg, m. Sep. 22, 1863, Gilbert L. Rist, who is a merchant at Turner's Falls, Montague, Mass. Issue:

1. Albert H.,	b. Sep. 5, 1865.
2. Walter J.,	b. Sep. 1, 1869.
3. G. Frank,	b. Aug. 23, 1871.
4. George H.,	b. Dec. 12, 1875.

6. **Thomas,**[9] who was b. at Westminster, Mass., resides at Hammond, Ind. of which city he was recently mayor. He is superintendent of that branch of the George H. Hammond Beef Shipping Co., which is located in that city. He is also a member of the 53d Congress. He m. Oct. 31, 1866, Helen E. Potter of Leominster, Mass., and had issue:

1. Lizzie,	b. Dec. 4, 1869.
2. Carrie,	b. Feb. 11, 1872.
3. Walter,	b. Oct. 27, 1873.
4. Frank,	b. May 15, 1875.
5. Edith,	b. Dec. 8, 1878.

8. **Frederic,**[9] who was b. in Ashburnham and now resides at Allston, was for twenty years connected with the New England Branch of the George H. Hammond Beef Shipping Co. He enlisted, Aug. 23, 1864, in Co. H, 4th Reg't Mass. Heavy Artillery, and was mustered out Jun. 17, 1865; lived in Detroit from '65 to '82, and in Allston since the latter date; member of the Allston Club, and dealer in real estate. He m. Jan. 29, 1879, Ada Savanac at Detroit, Mich., who was b. Sep. 9, 1850. Issue:

1. Merrill Mills,	b Nov. 18, 1879.	
2. Wesley Likins,	b. Jul. 22, 1881.	d. Aug. 11, 1881.
3. Marie Louise,	b. Feb. 22, 1883.	

9. **Henry,**[9] who was b. at Ashburnham, Mass., and d. at Detroit, Mich., was connected with the Detroit Branch of the George H. Hammond Beef Shipping Co. He m. 1st, in 1873-4 Hattie Wise, and had issue:

1. Hattie,	who lived in the West.

Henry m. 2d, Nov. 25, 1882, Ella Fowles of Detroit, and had further issue:

    2. Raymond,   b. Sep. 11, 1883.
    3. Norman Henry,   b. Feb.   3, 1886.

11.   **Juliet,**[9] who was b. in Ashburnham, m. Dec. 9, 1875, George H. Goddard, who is a farmer at Montague, Mass. Issue:

    1. Cora Leaffie,   b. Jan. 19, 1877.   d. Feb. 13, 1878.
    2. Hattie May,   b. Feb.   3, 1882.
    3. Sarah H.,   b. Dec.   9, 1886.

†–2–9–3–2–3.   **George Henry,**[9] second son of John and Sarah [Huston] Hammond, and for years one of the most extensive dealers of dressed beef in the world, was b. at Fitchburg, Mass., May 5, 1838. Leaving school at the early age of ten years, he began making leather pocket-books for a Mr. Barrett of Ashburnham, Mass., and afterwards carried on the business for himself, employing twelve girls and doing a profitable business. Leather pocket-books being now superseded by steel-clasp pocket-books, he, for the next three years, worked at Fitchburg, in the mattress and palm-leaf hat factory of Milton Frost. At the age of fifteen he purchased the business of his former employer, but at the end of six months sold it out and went to Detroit, Mich., arriving there in 1854. Here for two years and a half, he carried on a mattress and furniture factory. When only nineteen, his establishment was destroyed by fire, and left him with but few dollars in cash. With this small amount, he opened a meat store at the corner of Howard and Third Streets, which became an immediate success, and in 1860 he erected a brick building to meet the demands of his increasing trade. In 1865, the business, now removed to Michigan Grand Avenue, had become a large and prosperous one. In the mean time, he engaged extensively in beef and pork packing, forming in 1872 a partnership with J. D. Standish and S. D. Dixon, under the firm name of Hammond, Standish & Co. The firm erected large packing-houses on Twentieth Street, and the business grew to such proportions that for several years preceding Mr. Hammond's death they did the largest business of the kind in the city.

Although substantial success followed Mr. Hammond's exertions in his regular line of trade, it is chiefly in connection with the transportation of dressed beef that he exhibited the largest business capacity. From the incipiency of the undertaking until the method of carrying on the beef trade of the United States had undergone complete revolution, his energy was the chief factor in the undertaking. The problem of how to preserve meats, fruits, and like perishable products, for any length of time in transportation, without affecting their quality of flavor, had been practically unsolved until 1868, when William Davis of Detroit tried in vain to induce capitalists to take hold of the invention. Finally Mr. Hammond had a car fitted up expressly for carrying dressed beef to Eastern markets. The experimental trip was made in May 1869, from Detroit to Boston, and was a complete success. Mr. Hammond, with characteristic boldness and far-seeing business sagacity, soon after purchased the right to the exclusive use of the invention, and with Caleb Ives formed the Dressed Beef Transportation Company of Hammond, Ives & Co., which a few years after was changed to the firm name of George H. Hammond & Co. Commencing with one car the business steadily increased until at the time of Mr. Hammond's death, 800 cars were in constant use in their fresh meat trade with the Atlantic Coast, and they sent three ship-loads weekly to trans-Atlantic ports. They established slaughter-houses at Hammond, Ind., and Omaha, Neb., actually founding and building the first named city, which now has a large population, and is a thriving city. At this immense establishment, 1500 to 2000 head of cattle are killed each day, the business transacted reaching the sum of $12,000,000 to to $15,000,000 annually. The creation of this business was almost entirely due to the enterprise and sagacity of Mr. Hammond, and the results accomplished have been of great benefit to the commercial world.

In many respects Mr. Hammond was a remarkable man. He scarcely had a boyhood. Beginning life's battles when ten years old, before he was twenty he carried upon his shoulders the responsibilities that would have tested the powers of most mature men. A course of study in Goldsmith's Commercial College while in his teens, begun and completed in the evening, gave him a knowledge of accounts, that supplemented his business training and his practical experience. He was shrewd and careful, but clear business perception gave him courage and boldness. At forty-eight he had not only become one of the wealthiest men of Detroit, but one of the best business men in the United States, and the central figure in a gigantic system of operations of which few people in Detroit realized the extent, and which revolutionized the beef trade of the country and made his name well-known and respected in commercial circles, in Chicago, New York, and Boston. He was a large real estate owner, in and near Detroit, and realized so fully that his success was gained here, that he desired that the city should reap the advantage due to his success. He was vice-president of The Commercial National Bank, a director in the Michigan Savings Bank, and in the Detroit Fire & Marine Insurance Company, and in many ways was a reliable factor in the prosperity of Detroit.

In the full tide of his success, when wealth and honor had rewarded his efforts, and when seemingly he could illy be spared from the management of the great interests his genius had developed, the end came suddenly and unexpectedly. Naturally of a strong and robust physique, the hard work and unremitting toil of many years appeared to fall lightly upon him, but disease of the heart, baffling medical skill, terminated his life Dec. 29, 1886.

His death caused deep and genuine sorrow wherever he was known, and the community in which he had long lived mourned the loss of one whose name was a synonym of business honor, whose private life was unexceptionable, and whose future promised so much.

He was not a member of any church, but made liberal gifts to church enterprises, and his contributions to charitable and benevolent objects were many but unostentatious. He was reserved in manner, and gave his confidence only to a few, whom he implicitly trusted, and in whom he created unbounded faith. His chief pleasures were found in the domestic circle, and he was able to leave the perplexing, and annoying cares of business outside of his home, where he was the ideal father and husband.

He was fond of travel, going twice to Europe with part of his family, visiting also California and the South, and frequently visited, for business or pleasure, various parts of the United States.

Dying in the prime of life, he left the impress of his work upon the commercial history of his generation, and to his family the rich legacy of a spotless reputation.

George H. Hammond m. in 1857, Ellen Barry of Detroit, who was b. Jan. 20, 1838, and had eleven children, seven of whom are living. Issue:

1. Annie Jennie,   b. Mch. 15, 1859.
2. George Henry, Jr.,   b. Feb. 2, 1861.

GEORGE H. HAMMOND.

3. Sarah Agnes,	b. Mch. 31, 1863.	d. Oct. —, 1892.
4. Mary Leallie,	b. Jan. 12, 1866.	d. Feb. 20, 1868.
5. Charles Frederic,	b. Jan. 31, 1868.	
6. John William,	b. Oct. 24, 1870.	
7. Ellen.	b. Apr. 8, 1872.	d. Nov. 17, 1873.
8. Herbert H.,	b. Nov. 11, 1874.	d. Apr. 19, 1875.
9. Florence Pauline,	b. Dec. 2, 1877.	
10. Ethel Kate.	b. Jun. 10, 1880.	
11. Edward Percy,	b. Aug. 3, 1884.	

Of these children, 1. **Annie Jennie**[10] m. Feb. 25, 1886, Charles William Casgrain, who was b. May 24, 1859, and is a lawyer at Detroit. Issue:

1. Charlotte Marie Chase,   b. Oct. 1, 1887.

2. **George Henry Jr.**[10] is president of the firm of Hammond, Standish & Co., and resides at Detroit. He m. Jul. 18, 1882, Francis Belle Perkins, who was b. Aug. 10, 1861. No issue.

3. **Sarah Agnes**[10] m. Jun. 1885, Gilbert Wilson Lee, who was b. Mch. 28, 1861. Mr. Lee is senior partner of a large and extensive wholesale firm, dealing in canned goods and fancy groceries, at Detroit. Issue: George Hammond.

5. **Charles Frederic**,[10] educated in the schools of Detroit, and a graduate of the Institute of Technology, Boston, class of '91, resides at Detroit.

6. **John William**,[10] after being educated at Detroit, made a tour around the world, and is now a student at Detroit.

†-2-9-3-6. **Zephaniah Woods**,[8] fourth son of Thomas, b. at South Boston, was a farmer and gardener, and lived and d. in Fitchburg, Mass. He m. 1st, Jun. 8, 1846, Mary Bates, who was b. at Cohasset, Aug. 6, 1830, and d. at Fitchburg, Jan. 30, 1867. He m. 2d, May 8, 1868, Martha L. Lawrence, who was b. in Leominster, Jun. 11, 1838, and survives him. Issue by the first marriage:

1. Elizabeth Ann,	b. Feb. 14, 1848.	
2. Fannie Bates.	b. Sep. 28, 1851.	d. Jun. 24, 1891.
3. Frederick Herbert,	b. Sep. 15, 1853.	d. Jun. 3, 1878.
4. William Hiram,	b. Sep. 6, 1858.	

Of these children, 1. **Elizabeth Ann**[9] m. Nov. 1868, George Francis Burrage, who was b. in Leominster, Sep. 14, 1838, and was an officer in the Civil War. The Burrages

resided first at Boston, where the first three children were born,
later at Denver, and now live at Redcliffe, Col. Issue:

1. Frank Sumner,	b. Oct. 23, 1872.	
2. Mary Catherine,	b. Nov. 18, 1874.	d. Apr. 23, 1875.
3. Louise Minott,	b. Mch. 3, 1877.	
4. Marion Elizabeth,	b. Nov. 22, 1887.	

2. **Fannie Bates**[9] m. Jun. 20, 1876, Walter C. Colby,
who was b. in Charlestown, Mch. 9, 1844, and is a gate-tender
at Everett, Mass. Issue:

1. Edith M.,	b. Nov. 25, 1877.	
2. Mabel E.,	b. Jan. 17, 1879.	d. Jul. 12, 1888.
3. William A.,	b. Jun. 29, 1887.	d. Jul. 2, 1887.
4. Mary A.,	b. Oct. 7, 1888.	

3. **Frederic Herbert**,[9] who was b. at Fitchburg and d.
at Leominster, Mass., was assistant keeper of the Boston Light-
house for several years, and was keeper of the Narrows Light at
the time of his death. He never married.

4. **William Hiram**,[9] who is a rancher at Brush Creek,
Col., m. Aug. 20, 1890, Laura Lobb, and has a daughter:

1. Helen Bates,	b. Jun. 23, 1891.

V.—JOSIAH HAMMOND OF ROCHESTER, MASS.

†. **Josiah**[4] **Hammond**, sixth son of Samuel[3] [Benja-
min,[2] William[1]], lived first on the southeast part of his father's
farm, the house standing quite near the waters of Buzzard's
Bay. He afterwards sold this farm near the salt water, to his
son Josiah 2d, and received land to the north of his father's
place, where he built a second house. Although the house
has disappeared, the place is still pointed out as the "Siah"
place. He m. Mary Barlow, and had issue:

1. Nathan 3d,	b. Apr. 27, 1716.	d.
2. Charity,	b. Jun. 5, 1718.	d.
3. Josiah 2d,	b. Jun. 17, 1729.	d. May 21, 1816.
4. Bethiah,	b. Jul. 3, 1731.	d.
5. Hannah,	b. May 26, 1733.	d.
6. Abner,	b. Jun. 10, 1735.	d.
7. Mary,	b. May 20, 1737.	d.
8. Deborah P.,	b. in 1741.	d.

Of these children, nothing further is known of Bethiah and
Deborah P.

2. **Charity**[5]* m. Apr. 15, 1744, Roger Hammond, son of Benjamin 2d, and lived in Hammondtown. Issue: Olive, Deborah, Anna, Benjamin, Thankful, and Roger Jr.

5. **Hannah**[5] probably m. Jan. 15, 1764, Jona. Wing, and perhaps lived in the Wing neighborhood, Acushnet, Mass. Issue unknown.

7. **Mary**[5] probably m. Joseph Briggs, and lived in Rochester. Issue: Lucy, and perhaps a son Ebenezer. After Mary's death, Joseph Briggs m. 2d, Rose Hammond, daughter of Nathan 3d, and a neice of his first wife.

1.—NATHAN 3d, OF ROCHESTER, MASS.

†-1. **Nathan 3d,**[5] oldest son of Josiah, probably lived in that part of the old town of Rochester which adjoined the town of Wareham. He m. Mary Barlow at Rochester, and had issue :

1. Bathsheba,	b. Aug. 23, 1740.	d. Apr. 1, 1767.
2. Beulah,	b Apr. 13, 1742.	d.
3. Aaron,	b. May 23, 1744.	d. Nov. 30, 1833.
4. Barlow,	b. Nov. 7, 1745.	d.
5. Experience,	b. Sep. 13, 1747.	d. Sep. 24, 1747.
6. Rose,	b. Mch 5, 1749.	d. Dec. 21, 1826.
7. Shubael,	b. May 17, 1750.	d. Jul. 1, 1835.
8. Josiah,	b. Dec. 30, 17. 2.	d. Dec. 12, 1809.
9. Thankful,	b. Mch. 22, 1755.	d.

Of Nathan's children, nothing further is known of Barlow and Thankful, and they very likely d. young.

1. **Bathsheba**[6] m. Dec. 23, 1762, Bezaliel Washburne, and probably lived at Rochester. Issue not learned.

2. **Beulah**[6] m. Apr. 1, 1767, John Briggs Jr. at Rochester, but her issue is not known.

6. **Rose**[6] m. Joseph Briggs, and the family afterwards moved to Vermont, perhaps near Barnard, where Joseph d. Jul. 15, 1819, æ. 76. Issue: Joseph, Mary, Peleg, Florina, and Abigail. Florina m. Dr. Thomas Swift of Barnard, and had a daughter Mary A., who m. George C. Hammond of Barnard. This George C. was a grandson of Jabez Hammond 2d, who settled at Woodstock, Vt.

* For further record of Charity, see Genealogy of Roger Hammond, Part V.

8. **Josiah,**[6] who was a sailor, was lost at sea near Charleston, S. C., Dec. 12, 1809.

†-1-3. **Aaron,**[6] oldest son of Nathan 3d, lived near the old Friends' Meeting House, Marion, and perhaps a part of the time near Blackmore's Pond, Wareham. He was thrice married. He m. 1st, Aug. 24, 1769, Abigail Weston, and had issue:

1. Anna,	b. Oct.	30, 1770.	d.
2. Aaron, Jr.,	b. May	10, 1772.	d.
3. Mary,	b. May	29, 1775.	d.
4. Barlow,	b. Jul.	9, 1777.	d.
5. Lettes,	b. Feb.	21, 1779.	d.
6. Isaac W.,	b. Oct.	13, 1782.	d.
7. Bathsheba,	b.		d.

Aaron m. 2d, Dec. 23, 1784, Jedida White, and had further issue:

8. Elijah,	b. Jul.	7, 1782.	d. Feb. 16, 1830.
9. John,	b. Dec.	27, 1790.	d. in 1848.
10. Abigail,	b.		d.

Aaron m. 3d, May, 8, 1794, Hannah Benson, but had no other issue.

Of these children, nothing further is known of Anna, Aaron Jr., Mary, Lettes, and Isaac W. Probably most of them d. young.

4. **Barlow**[7] m. a Miss Skiff of Rochester, and had issue: Celista, and Polly who d. at the age of 10. Celista m. May 4, 1823, Jabez Benson of Rochester, and had issue: William, Benjamin, Charity, Mercy, Jabez, and Mary.

7. **Bathsheba**[7] m. Stephen Briggs of Rochester. Issue: Stephen, Daniel and Weston.

10. **Abigail,**[7] daughter of Aaron, m. in 1814 Benjamin Rogers at Wareham.

†-1-3-8. **Elijah,**[7] fifth son of Aaron, was a farmer, and lived first near Blackmore's Pond, Wareham, and afterwards on the farm now occupied by Stephen Hammond Jr., between Rochester Centre and the Marion R. R. Station. He had three wives. He m. 1st, in 1813, Sally Hathaway, who d. about 1816. Issue:

1. Arthur H.,	b. Jul.	20, 1814.	
2. Delia,	b. Oct.	25, 1815.	d.

Elijah m. 2d, Apr. 13, 1817, Nancy [Clifton] Hammond, widow of William Hammond, who d. Mch. 29, 1818. Issue:

   3 Sarah,   b. Feb. 15, 1818.   d. Sep. 8. 1873.

Elijah m. 3d, Sep. 6, 1818, Beulah [Delano] Richmond, who was b. in 1787, and d. May 1, 1837. Issue:

   4. Nancy Clifton,   b. May 15, 1819.   d. Apr. 4, 1867.
   5. Job Delano,   b. Nov. 9, 1820.
   6. Nathan Mendell,   b. Jun. 21, 1822.   d.

Of the above children, **Nathan Mendell,**[8] who was captain of a coasting vessel, d. single, at Baltimore, Md., at the age of 35. **Delia**[8] m. Horace Lovell of Sandwich, and had issue: Horace, James, and Sarah. **Sarah**[8] m. 1st, George B. Folger of Nantucket, who d. in Dec. 1849. Issue: Lydia Winslow and Mary Russell, both dying young and unmarried. Sarah m. 2d, Apr. 23, 1872, Anthony K. Whittemore, but had no other issue.

   4. **Nancy Clifton**[8] m. Dec. 4, 1849, John Gould Luce of Marion, and had issue:

     1. John Frank,   b. Oct. 11. 1851.   Single, at Marion.

   †–1–3–8–1. **Arthur H.,**[7] oldest son of Elijah, is a farmer, and lives in Wareham, Mass., near the Marion line. He m. 1st, Nov. 10, 1834, Bethiah T. Crapo, who was b. in 1801, and d. Jan. 15, 1882. Issue:

     1. Arthur H.. Jr.,   b. Jan. 15, 1836.
     2. Philander,   b. about   1838.   d.   young.
     3. Lucy,   b. in   1840.   d. May —, 1887.

Arthur H. m. 2d, Mrs. Catherine Louisa Pratt, widow of Winslow Pratt. No other issue.

   3. **Lucy**[9] m. 1st, Paul Briggs, but had no issue. She m. 2d, Warren T. Crapo, and moved to North East, Erie Co., Pa., where she died. Issue: Delia, Carrie, and Alonzo.

   1. **Arthur H. Jr.**[9] was for many years a sea captain in the whaling service, but is now a farmer at Wareham, Mass. He m. Mch. 30, 1859, Sophia M. Savery, who was b. Mch. 5, 1838. Issue:

     1. Arthur H. 3d,   b. Sep. 18, 1869.
     2. Sophia,   b. Jun. 27, 1875.

   2. **Sophia**[10] was lately in the Preparatory School connected with Oberlin College, Oberlin, Ohio.

1. **Arthur H. 3d,**[10] who resides at Wareham, m. Feb. 23, 1888, Mary S. Hammond, daughter of Capt. Clement Hammond, late of Marion, Mass. Issue:

    1. Bethiah H.,   b. Jul. 31, 1890.

†–1–3–8–5. **Job Delano,**[8] second son of Elijah, is a farmer at East Wareham, Mass., Point Independence having been originally a part of his farm. He m. Apr. 4, 1846, Mary E. Swift of Wareham, and had issue:

1. Obed Warren,	b. Jun. 2, 1847.	d. Feb. 27, 1866.
2. James Henry,	b. Aug. 3, 1849.	d. Jun. 13, 1886.
3. Mary Elizabeth.	b. Oct. 30, 1851.	
4. Job Delano 2d,	b. Feb. 2, 1854.	
5. Nellie Blossom,	b. Dec. 27, 1855.	d. Dec. 19, 1865.
6. Susan Bennett,	b. Mch. 15, 1858.	d. Dec. 17, 1883.
7. Chas. Edward,	b. Feb. 27, 1861.	
8. Irvin Carleton,	b. Oct. 27, 1864.	
9. Arthur Burton,	b. Sep. 9, 1867.	
10. Lillie Richmond.	b. Jan. 13, 1873.	

Of the above children, 1. **Obed Warren**[9] and 5. **Nellie Blossom**[9] d. single, at East Wareham; 3. **Mary Elizabeth,**[9] a teacher, 4. **Job Delano 2d,**[9] a farmer, and 10. **Lillie Richmond,**[9] are all single and all reside at East Wareham.

2. **James Henry**[9] a seaman living at East Wareham, m. Aug. 2, 1879, Minnie Westgate, and had issue:

    1. Merle Kimball,   b. Aug. 2, 1880.

6. **Susan Bennett**[9] m. Jan. 15, 1881, Fred. Davis of Falmouth, Mass., where they resided. No issue to live.

7. **Charles Edward**[9] is a fisherman and lives at East Wareham. He m. Jan. 9, 1885, Ella M. [Tobey] Perry of Falmouth. No issue.

8. **Irvin Carleton**[9] is a real estate broker at East Wareham. He m. Oct. 7, 1889, Laura Gunther of Louisville, Ky. Issue:

    1. Carlton D.,   b. Oct. 2, 1890.

9. **Arthur B.,**[9] who is a clerk at East Wareham, m. Sep. 1891, Minnie Hall of Bourne, Mass.

†–1–3–9. **John,**[7] sixth son of Aaron, was a whaler, and lived at Wareham, but d. at Fall River, Mass. He m. May 4,

1817, Susan Green of Rochester, who was b. Aug. 16, 1795.
Issue:

1. Susan,	b. in	1820.	d. Sep. 6, 1886.
2. John, Jr.,	b. Mch. 25, 1823.		
3. Elijah G.,	b. Feb. 29, 1825.		d. Jul. 4, 1838.
4. Elisha Clark,	b. Oct. 10, 1827.		d. Oct. 8, 1856.
5. Isaac D.,	b. Jun. 1, 1829.		d.

Of these children, **Elijah G.**[8] was drowned at Fall River,
Jul. 4, 1838.

1. **Susan**[8] m. 1st, Russell T. Lawton, who lived at Fall
River, and d. there May 16, 1851. She m. 2d, about 1853,
Walter Perry of Acushnet, where she afterwards lived and
died, near Mason Taber's Corner. No issue.

2. **John Jr.,**[8] who was formerly a sea captain, is the
oldest pilot in the employ of the Fall River & New York Steamboat Co., and lives in Fall River. He m. Jan. 24, 1855,
Clarissa A. Battey of Fall River, who was b. Jul. 1, 1833.
Issue:

1. Adeline.	} b. May 20, 1857.	
2. Clara Eliza,		d. Feb. 12, 1863.

Adeline[9] is a teacher in the public schools of Fall River.

4. **Elisha Clark,**[8] a machinist, lived at Taunton, but
was buried in Middleboro', Mass. He m. Louisa Sherman,
who d. Oct. 29, 1856. Issue: Isadore and Clarence, both of
whom d. young.

5. **Isaac D.**[8] was a carpenter, and lived and d. in Fall
River. He m. Mary Nichols, and had issue:

1. Clarence, b. in 1855.

Clarence[9] is a grocer, and lives in Somerset, Mass. He
m. Francis Marble, but has no issue.

†-1-7. **Shubael,**[6] fourth son of Nathan 3d, was a farmer,
and lived in the northeasterly part of Rochester. He m. Oct.
17, 1773, Anna Barden, who was b. in 1755. Issue:

1. Nathan,	b. Jul. 18, 1775.	d.
2. Josiah,	b. Jan. 15, 1778.	d. Oct. 5, 1799.
3. Stephen,	b. Apr. 25, 1780.	d. Feb. 3, 1828.
4. Olive,	b. Oct. 16, 1782.	d.
5. Anna,	b. Mch. 22, 1785.	d.
6. Noah,	b. Jan. 7, 1788.	d.
7. Shubael, Jr.,	b. Jan. 22, 1790.	d.

8. Waitstill,	b. Oct. 15, 1792.	d.
9. Rosanna,	b. May 22, 1795.	d.
10. Charity.	b. Sep. 28, 1798.	d. Sep. 9. 1861.

Of the above children, nothing further is known of **Nathan**[7]; **Josiah**[7] d. single, at the age of 21 ; and **Anna**[7] is said to have lived in some part of Connecticut.

4. **Olive**[7] m. in 1803, Eliphalet Hall, and lived in some part of Connecticut.

7. **Shubael Jr.**[7] m. Mch. 6, 1806, Patty Shurtleff, and lived in Middleboro'. Nothing further known.

9. **Rosanna**[7] m. Richard Doty, and lived in Middleboro', Rochester, etc. Issue : Harrison, Almira, Lucinda, Maria, Rufus, Eliza, and Nathan.

8. **Waitstill**[7] m. David Shurtleff of Carver, and lived in South Carver. Issue : Harriet, b. 1813 ; Martha, b. 1815 ; David W., b. 1817 ; Mercy A., b. 1819 ; Jared, b. 1821 ; Anna, b. 1823 ; Nathan, b. 1825 ; Stephen, b. 1827 ; Lorenzo, b. 1829 ; and Lousia, b. 1834.

10. **Charity**[7] m. in 1815 Eldredge Lovell of Yarmouth, Mass., where she lived and died. Issue :

1. Shubael,	b. Dec. 7. 1816.	d. Dec. 26. 1817.
2. Mary A.,	b. Nov. 28, 1818.	d. Nov. 28, 1820.
3. Mary A.,	b. Aug. 31, 1820.	d. Dec. 8, 1821.
4. Lewis E .	b. Sep. 11, 1821.	
5. George,	b. Aug. 24. 1823.	d. Dec. 6, 1860.
6. Noah H'd,	b. Feb. 12. 1826.	
7. Sarah A.,	b. Jan. 26, 1828.	d. Sep. 12. 1854.
8. Martha,	b. Oct. 31, 1830.	d. Mch. 11, 1832.
9. Benjamin,	b. Aug. 9, 1832.	
10. Oliver,	b. Nov. 8. 1834.	d. in 1880.
11. Nelson,	b. Mch. 14, 1842.	d. Oct. 17, 1843.

†-1-7-3. **Stephen**,[7] third son of Shubael, was a nailer, and lived at Wareham. He m. Martha Shurtleff, and had issue :

1. Abiel S.,	b. Dec. 22, 1818.	d. Jun. 14, 1885.
2. Otis M.,	b.	d.

2. **Otis M.,**[7] who was an ensign in the State Militia from 1837 to 1840, was a nailer, and lived at West Wareham. He m. in 1835 Nancy Jackson, and had : Nancy Malvina, who m. Jun. 30, 1855, R. Whitney Studley of Boston.

†-1-7-3-1. **Abiel S.,**[9] who was a nailer at Wareham, served in the 32d Mass. Reg't during the Civil War. He m. Permelia Westgate, who was b. Oct. 25, 1825. Issue:

1. Abiel S., Jr.,	b. Mch. 20, 1843.	d. May 22, 1845.
2. George W.,	b. Jun. 22. 1845.	
3. Augustus S.,	b. Oct. 2, 1848.	d. Sep. 23, 1849.
4. Martha,	b. Oct. 25, 1850.	d
5. John C.,	b. Nov. 24, 1853.	d.

4. **Martha**[8] m. William H. H. Deardon, and lives at Somerset, Mass. No issue.

2. **George W.**[8] is a nailer, and has resided at Plymouth and Somerset, Mass., but now lives at West Wareham. He m. Sarah Ellis of Marion, and had issue:

1. William W.,	b. Aug. 30, 1870.
2. Mattie Wing,	b. Dec. 27, 1871.
3. Nellie C.,	b. Nov. 3, 1873.
4. Susie Ellis,	b. Mch. 7, 1884.
5. George Abiel,	b. Feb. 1, 1886.
6. Ellis D.,	b. Jul. 24, 1889.

5. **John C.**[9] is a nailer, and lives at West Wareham. He m. Minnie A. Pierce, and had issue:

1. Clifford A.,	b. Sep 24, 1883.
2. Chester H.,	b. Mch. 18, 1885.
3. Thurman C.,	b. May 12, 1888.
4. John Franklin,	b. May 7, 1889.

†-1-7-6. **Noah,**[7] fourth son of Shubael, was a moulder, and lived first at Middleboro', but afterwards moved to Pocassett, Mass., where he died. He m. Zilpha Maxim, and had issue:

1. Noah, Jr.,	b. in 1814.	
2. Zilpha,	b. in 1816.	
3. Lucy,	b. in 1818.	d. in 1883.
4. Jesse,	b. in 1824.	d. in 1855.
5. Ann,	b. in 1827.	d. in 1868.
6. Robert C.,	b. in 1831.	
7. Eliza,	b. in 1834.	
8. Luther,	b. in 1836.	d. in 1863.

2. **Zilpha**[8] m. in 1834 Stillman Wright, and lives at Pocassett, Mass. Issue: Rose, Loretta, Martha, Zilpha, Anderson, Noah, Preston, William, Bradford, and Stillman Jr.

3. **Lucy**[8] m. in 1838, Gardner Hathaway, resided at Tremont, Mass. for many years, but finally moved to Pocassett, where she died. Issue: Lavina, Mary, Mercy, Gardner, and Robert.

4. **Jesse**[6] was a moulder, and lived at Pocassett, Mass. He m. in 1853 Ann Raymond, and had issue :

    1. Lucy,   b. in 1854.

5. **Ann**[8] m. in 1841 Anderson Wright, and lived at Pocassett. Issue : Harriet, Ira, Jesse, Mabel, and Clara.

6. **Robert C.**[8] is a moulder, and resides at Pocassett. He m. in 1851 Cordelia Bennett, and had issue :

    1. Harry B.,   b. in 1866.
    2. Charles F.,   b. in 1868.

1. **Harry B.**[9] m. Feb. 24, 1892, May A. Bowman of West Falmouth, and resides at Monument Beach, Mass.

7. **Eliza**[8] m. in 1855 Asa Adams, and resides at Taunton, Mass. Issue : Estelle R. and Lizzie N.

8. **Luther**[8] was a moulder, and lived at Pocassett. He enlisted in Co I, 40th Reg't M. V. M., and d. in the Hospital at Beaufort, S. C. He never married.

†–1–7–6. **Noah Jr.**[8] was formerly a moulder at Pocassett, Mass. In 1859 he moved to and now lives on the Dolores River, La Plata Co., Col. He m. 1st, Feb. 10, 1842, Rosetta Taylor, and had issue :

    1. Joanna,   b. Jul. 7, 1843.
    2. Nahum W.,   b. Jun. 8, 1847.
    3. Mary E.,   b. Apr. 22, 1850.
    4. Eliza L.,   b. Jul. 26, 1854.
    5. Jesse,   b. Jun. 29, 1859.
    6. Etta, }
    7. Effie. }   b. May 13, 1862.
    8. Robert C.,   b. May 12, 1865.

Noah Jr. m. 2d, in 1888, Mrs. Almyra Pratt, but had no further issue.

1. **Joanna**[9] m. Jul. 7, 1864 , Edgar G. Bates, a ranchman of Denver, Col., and lives at Pine River, La Plata Co., Col. Issue : Laura E., Rosetta, Martin, Norman, William, Everett, Grace, Bertha, Myrtle, and Huldah.

2. **Nahum W.**[9] is a blacksmith and wagonmaker, and resides at Durango, Col. He m. Mch. 6, 1883, Anna M. Little, daughter of Orrin G. Little of New Albany, Ind. Issue :

    1. Owen C.,   b Feb. 18, 1884.
    2. Gilbert N.,   b. Jul. 15, 1888.

At 17, Nahum W. was enrolled in Co. E, 3d Reg't Col. Vol.
Cavalry, for 100 days, and was mustered out at Denver,
Dec. 28, 1864.

3. **Mary E.**⁹ m. Apr. 23, 1865, Johnson Gibson of Denver, and resides at Hamburg, Fremont Co., Iowa. Issue:
James, Jennie, Robert, Oscar, and Effie.

4. **Eliza L.**⁹ m. 1st, Aug. 3, 1871, Simon Graves of
Denver, and resides at Dolores. Issue: Herbert, Lillie, and
Frank. Eliza m. 2d, Jun. 1882, Samuel Johnson of Pine
River. Issue: Hattie, John, and Myrl. Mr. Johnson is a
stock-raiser on Dolores River, Col.

5. **Jesse**⁹ is a lumberman, and resides at Pine River.
He m. Jun. 27, 1883, Renie W. Little, sister of Nahum's
wife. Issue:

    1. Clyde R ,   b. May 17, 1884.
    2. Amy B.,   b. Apr. 12, 1886.
    3. Roscoe C.,   b. May 18, 1888.
    4. Lola M.,   b Sep. 20, 1890.

6. **Etta**⁹ m. Nov. 15, 1880, Oswald C. Sommers, a ranchman of Pine River, Col., where they reside. Issue: Earl,
Minnie, Raymond, Bessie, and Miles.

7. **Effie**⁹ m. Aug. 3, 1879, Y. C. Salabar, a ranchman of
Pine River, where they now reside. Issue: Florence, Tylean,
Raymus, Earnest, and Albert.

8. **Robert C.**⁹ is a sawyer and resides at Pine River.
He m. Dec. 24, 1887, Elsie N. Little, sister of Nahum's wife.
Issue:

    1. Myron N.,   b. Oct. 23, 1890.

3.—JOSIAH 2d, OF ROCHESTER, MASS.

†-3. **Josiah 2d,**⁵ second son of Josiah, and a sea-faring
man, bought of his father and lived on the first "Siah" place
near the waters of Buzzard's Bay, in the extreme southwestly
part of the old town of Rochester. He m. 1st, Jan. 10, 1750,
Rebecca Hammond, daughter of Capt. Jabez Hammond, who
was b. Feb. 14, 1731, and d. Dec. 29, 1767. Issue:

    1. Elnathan,   b. Nov. 19, 1751.   d. Jul. 19, 1831.

2. Anstris,	b. Oct. 11, 1753.	d.
3. Richard,	b. Jan. 1, 1756.	d.
4. Eunice,	b. Jan. 22, 1758.	d. Feb. 15, 1785.
5. Priscilla,	b. in 1760.	d.
6. Lothrop,	b. Apr. 3, 1762.	d.
7. Mary,	b. Apr. 2, 1764.	d.
8. Nathan,	b. Feb. 26, 1766.	d. Apr. 8, 1802.

Josiah 2d m. 2d, Jul. 7, 1771, Mary Barlow, who d. Feb. 11, 1805, æ. 75. No further issue.

Of the above children, nothing further is known of Anstris, Priscilla, and Lothrop.

4. **Eunice**[6] m. May 31, 1777, Noah Hammond, son of Israel, and grandson of Benjamin 2d. Issue: Rebecca, Elizabeth, and Priscilla.

7. **Mary**[6] probably m. Jan. 24, 1785, Job Neal of Rochester. Issue: Josiah, Nathan, Abigail, and Nathaniel Hammond.

†–3–3. **Richard**,[6] who lived in Fairhaven, Mass., m. Mch. 30, 1784, Rebecca Stetson. Issue: Rebecca, Richard, Josiah, Fanny, and Eliza.

Of these children, nothing further is known, except that **Rebecca** m. A. French Taber, and lived at Fairhaven, Mass.

†–3–1. **Elnathan**,[6] oldest son of Josiah 2d, who was a captain of militia, lived on what is known as the William Bowles place in Hammondtown, Mattapoisett. He m. 1st, Oct. 3, 1776, Temperance Clark, who d. Oct. 7, 1816, æ. 64. Issue :

1. Ansel,	b. in 1779.	d. in 1805.
2. Alice,	b. in 1782.	d. Feb. 13, 1860.
3. Lothrop,	b. in 1783.	d. Dec. 2, 1854.
4. Abigail,	b.	d. Jan. 16, 1847.
5. Eunice,	b. Aug. 5, 1790.	d. Jun. 11, 1815.
6. Wyatt,	b.	d. Apr. 20, 1853.

Elnathan m. 2d, Elizabeth Allen of Chilmark, who d. Jun. 17, 1845, æ. 85. No other issue.

Of the above children, **Ansel**,[7] who was a sea captain, is supposed to have been captured at sea by pirates in 1805; and **Lothrop**[7] d. single, at Mattapoisett.

2. **Alice**,[7] or **Elsie**, m. 1st, in 1805, Nathaniel Cushing, and lived at Mattapoisett. Issue: Capt. Elnathan, Eunice, Charles Henry, Elizabeth, and Mary Ann.

Alice m. 2d, Josiah Sparrow of Rochester, but had no other issue.

4. **Abigail**[7] m. in 1805 Alfred Kendrick of New Bedford, and had issue: Ansel, Hulda, Frank, Caroline, Eliza, Abby, Emily, John, Henry, George, and Ann Eliza.

5. **Eunice**[7] m. in 1810, Dr. Seth Haskell of Rochester, and had issue: David, Caroline, Lucy, William, and Maria.

†–3–1–6. **Wyatt**[7] was a house-carpenter, and lived at Mattapoisett. He m. Mch. 12, 1810, Mary LeBaron of Plymouth, who d. Jul. 19, 1833. Issue:

1. William LeBaron,	b. May 27, 1813.	d.	
2. Mary Allen,	b. Sep. 26, 1816.	b. in 1836.	
3. Ansel,	b. May 9, 1822.	d.	

Of these children, 1. **William LeBaron**[5] was lost at sea, and 3. **Ansel**[5] d. at sea, both single.

2. **Mary Allen**[8] m. Oct. 27, 1834, Hallett M. Cannon, a ship-carpenter at Mattapoisett. No issue.

†–3–8. **Nathan,**[6] fourth son of Josiah 2d, was a sea captain, and lived and d. at Mattapoisett, Mass. He m. Oct. 18, 1789, Mehitable Barlow, who was b. May 27, 1765, and d. Mch. 14, 1835, at Poughkeepsie, N. Y. Issue:

1. Anstis,	b. Sep. 3, 1791.	d. Jun. 24, 1811.	
2. Nathan, Jr.,	b. Mch. 13, 1793.	d. Sep. 5, 1800.	
3 Thomas,	b. Feb. 28, 1794.	d. May 24, 1880.	
4. Sally,	b. Sep. 18, 1796.	d. Sep. 11, 1800.	
5. Charlotte,	b. Jul. 14, 1798.	d.	

Mehitable with three children, Anstis, Thomas, and Charlotte, after the death of her husband, moved from Rochester, Mass., to Amenia, Dutchess Co., N. Y., about 1803–5.

Of the above children, Anstis, Nathan Jr., and Sally d. young; and **Charlotte**[7] m. Theodorus Gregory, lived at Poughkeepsie, N. Y., and had three children: Clarissa, Thomas, and Mariette, all dead.

†–3–8–3. **Thomas,**[7] second son of Nathan, was a physician and surgeon, and lived at Dover, Dutchess Co., N. Y., from 1824 to 1865, and d. at Port Huron, Mich. He m. Jan. 7, 1814, Clarissa Barlow, daughter of Thomas and Amy [Delano] Barlow, who was b. Nov. 25, 1794, and d. Feb. 27, 1859. Issue:

1. Anstis.	b. Dec. 9. 1815.	d. Dec. 29, 1834.
2. Haviland.	b. Feb. 19, 1818.	d. Jun. —. 1866.
3. Nathan.	b. Jun. 14, 1820.	d. Jun. 20, 1839.
4. Thomas, Jr.,	b. Dec. 17, 1822.	
5. Theodore,	b. Jun. 7, 1825.	d. Apr. 5, 1857.
6 Charles,	b. Jun. 23, 1826.	
7. Harriet,	b. Jul. 31, 1830.	d. in 1887.
8. Edwin, }	b. Nov. 18. 1838.	d. Mch. 21, 1859.
9. Edward. }		d. Dec. 21, 1838.

2. **Haviland,**[8] who was a gunsmith, served during the Civil War, in a N. Y. Reg't of Heavy Artillery. He m. Kate Maney of St. John, N. B., now deceased. Issue: Clara, who died at the age of 10 or 12.

5. **Theodore**[8] was a wheelwright at Dover, Dutchess Co., N. Y. He never married.

6. **Charles**[8] is a railroad conductor, and lives at Babylon, Long Island. He m. Sep. 1849, Hannah McKoy, and had issue: Charles Edward and Clarissa, both dying young.

7. **Harriet**[8] m. Jun. 17, 1858, Asa Wright, and lived at Port Huron, Mich. Issue: Bertha and Harry.

†–3–8–3–4. **Thomas Jr.,**[8] third son of Thomas, is a physician and resides at Dover Plains, Dutchess Co., N. Y. He graduated in medicine at the University of New York in 1846; and was a member of the New York State Assembly in 1876–7. He m. 1st, May 18, 1854, Rachel Burton, who was b. May 26, 1825, and d. Oct 27, 1873. Issue:

1. Burton.	b. Oct. 18, 1856.
2. Charles,	b. Mch. 11, 1862.

Dr. Hammond m. 2d, Aug. 29, 1877, Harriet A. Burton, a relative of his first wife. No further issue.

1. **Burton**[9] is an attorney-at-law, and resides at Lyons, Wayne Co., N. Y. He m. Nov. 14, 1878, Sophie Van Marter, and had issue:

1. Clara Dorsey,	b. Apr. 13, 1881.
2. Rachel Burton.	b. Jan. 30, 1884.
3. Helen Cline,	b. Apr. 13, 1887.
4. Mary Ellen,	b. Jul. 14, 1889.

2. **Charles**[9] is a clerk in the War Department at Washington, D. C. He m. in 1885 Etta Adams, daughter of Allan Adams of Richmond, Va., where she d. Nov. 16, 1892, without issue.

†–6. **Abner,**[5] third son of Josiah, lived to the north of the first "Siah" place, West Mattapoisett Neck. He m. in 1760 Huldah Hammond, and had issue :

1. Roger,	b. Jan. 16, 1761.	d.
2. Jeduthan,	b. Sep. 27, 1762.	d.
3. Charity,	bap. in 1770.	d
4. Elizabeth,	bap. in 1772.	d.
5. Ruth,	bap. in 1774.	d.
6. Abner, Jr.,	bap. in 1776.	d.

Of these children, nothing further is known of Jeduthan, Charity, Elizabeth, Ruth, and Abner Jr. Probably some or all of them died young.

†–6–1. **Roger,**[6] who lived in Rochester, Mass., m. 1st, Oct. 1, 1780, Lydia Jenney, who was b. in 1759, and d. Nov. 27, 1796, and was buried at Acushnet. She was a daughter of Nathaniel and Mercy Jenney. Roger probably m. 2d, Oct. 1792, Olive Hovey, and is said to have moved to Portland, Me. Nothing further is known of him.

VI.—BARNABAS HAMMOND OF ROCHESTER, MASS.

†. **Barnabas**[4] **Hammond,** seventh son of Samuel,[3] [Benjamin,[2] William[1]], was a farmer, and lived on the old homestead of his father. The old house built by him in 1767 is still standing, fairly well preserved. He m. Mch. 14, 1722, Susannah Hammond, his cousin, and daughter of Nathan Hammond [V. Part IV.], who was b. Mch. 24, 1701. Issue :

1. Elizabeth,	b. Jan. 29, 1722	d. Sep. 16. 1796.
2. James,	b. about 1725.	d. in 1780.
3. Mary,	bap. 7, 11, 1742.	d.
4. Ellis,	bap. 7, 11, 1742.	d.

Of these children, nothing further is known of Elizabeth, Mary, and Ellis.

†–2. **James**[5] was a farmer, inheriting his father's farm. He m. Apr. 3, 1753, Hannah Barlow, and had issue :

1. Gideon,	b. Jun. 2, 1754.	d. Mch. 21, 1849.
2. Barnabas 2d,	b. in 1756.	d.
3. Susannah,	b. Aug. 21, 1758.	d.
4. James, Jr.,	b. Jan. 25, 1763.	d. Jan. 29, 1826.
5. Jesse,	b. Apr. 24, 1765.	d. Aug. 29, 1844.

Of these children, **Susannah**[6] m. Jun. 1803, Harper Delano, and lived on Great Neck, Marion. No issue.

1.—GIDEON OF ROCHESTER, MASS.

†–2–1. **Gideon,**[6] oldest son of James, was a sergeant in Capt. Clapp's Company, Col. Cotton's Regiment, in 1775. During the Revolutionary War, he was a captain in the Regular Army, and did good service in the field, being with Gen. Washington at Medford, Mass., at one time. He was afterwards a farmer, having the old homestead as an inheritance from his father. He m. Nov. 7, 1793, Mary Norton, who was b. Sep. 14, 1756, and d. Apr. 5, 1839. Issue :

1. James.	b. Dec. 11, 1795.	d. Oct. 23, 1857.
2. Priscilla.	b. Sep. 8, 1799.	d. Feb. 9, 1884.
3. Waitstill,	b. Oct. 2, 1801.	d. May 17, 1826.

Of these children, **Waity**[7] d. at the age of 24, and **Priscilla**[7] at the age of 84, both single.

†–2–1–1. **James,**[7] only son of Gideon, was a schoolteacher and a farmer on his father's place. He m. 1st, May 12, 1836, Hannah [Morgan] Cowell, who was b. Nov. 1805, and d. Aug. 6, 1846. Issue :

1. John M.,	b. Mch. 22, 1837.	
2. Edwin,	b. Nov. 10, 1838.	d. Aug. 21, 1891.
3. Mary Eliza,	b. Apr. 5, 1841.	*d. Dec. 18, 1905.*

James m. 2d, Mary [Hammond] Davis, daughter of Timothy Hammond, and widow of Moses Davis. No further issue.

†–2–1–1–1. **John M.,**[8] who in early life was a shoemaker, afterwards bought out the other heirs, and lived on his father's place a number of years after his marriage. He afterwards sold the old homestead, and moved to New Bedford, where he is now working as a carpenter. He m. Nov. 27, 1858, Mary Ann Shaw of Fairhaven, who was b. Apr. 20, 1842. Issue :

1. Joanna P.,	b. Aug. 29, 1859.	d. Feb. 4, 1874.
2. Eloise M.,	b. Aug. 9, 1861.	d. Dec. 23, 1886.
3. Edwin F.,	b. Jul. 14, 1863.	

3. **Edwin F.,**[9] who is a carpenter at New Bedford, m. Jan. 5, 1886, Augusta L. Escher. Issue :

1. Leroy E.,	b. Jan. 31, 1887.

†–2–1–1–2. **Edwin,**[8] when a young man, went to Sacramento, Cal., where he was in business for many years, but died at Los Angeles. He m. Sep. 1870 Annie France, and had issue :

1. John Edwin,	b. about	1873.	d.	young.
2. Edna,	b. in	1876.	d. May —, 1891.
3. Etola,	b. Dec. —,	1878.	d. Sep. —. 1879.
4. Edwin, Jr.,	b. about	1880.		

Mrs. Hammond, with her son Edwin Jr., resides at Sacramento.

†–2–1–1–3. **Mary Elizabeth,**[6] a graduate of the Normal School at Bridgewater, Mass., was for a number of years a teacher in the public schools in Mass. She m. Sep. 7, 1866, Lemuel Pitts, who was b. Aug. 22, 1841, and lives in Quincy, Mass. Issue :

1. Annie Hollywood,	b. Nov.	1, 1867.
2. Clara Belle,	b. Aug.	21, 1869.
3. Ralph Shaw,	b. Jul.	8, 1873.
4. Marian Hammond,	b. Apr.	26, 1877.
5. Mary Eva Thayer,	b. Sep.	8, 1878.
6. Lemuel, Jr.,	b. May	4, 1881.

2.—BARNABAS 2D, OF FAIRHAVEN, MASS.

†–2–2. **Barnabas 2d,**[6] second son of James, was a rigger, sailmaker, and ship owner, and lived in Fairhaven, Mass. He m. in 1780 Hulda Hillman of Gay Head, Martha's Vineyard. Issue :

1. Daniel,	b. about	1782.	d.	
2. James,	b. in	1784.	d. Oct.	4, 1858.
3. Barney,	b. in	1787.	d. Sep.	11, 1864.
4. Susan,	b. Jan.	14, 1788.	d. Jan.	11, 1850.
5. Freelove,	b. Jul.	31, 1789.	d May	26, 1831.
6. Polly,	b. in	1790.	d.	
7. Wilson,	b. Feb.	17, 1791.	b. Dec.	15, 1871.
8. Freeman,	b.		d.	

Of these children, **Daniel**[7] d. single at Fairhaven ; **Susan**[7] m. Feb. 14, 1805, Tripp Taber, and lived at Fairhaven. Issue : Harriet, Francis, Daniel Hammond, Enoch, Granville, and Emily. **Freelove**[7] m. in 1801 Anthony Allen, who was b. Apr. 21, 1777, and d. Apr. 27, 1857. She lived at Fairhaven, and had issue : Eliza F., Charles C., and William W. **Polly**[7] m. Selick Osborn, and lived at Fairhaven. Issue : Nathaniel and Mary.

8. **Freeman**[7] was a sailor, and lived at Fairhaven. He m. Ruby Blankenship of Marion, but had no issue.

9

†–2–2–2. **James[7]** was a rigger and sailmaker, and lived at Fairhaven. He m. 1st, Sep. 27, 1807, Catherine Blankenship of Marion. Issue :

1. Eliza B.,	b. in	1811.
2. Susan,	b. in	1814. d. Aug. 22, 1843.
3. Francis,	b. Jun. 12, 1817.	

James m. 2d, Ruth Sherman, but by her had no issue. He m. 3d, Lydia Howard, and had further issue :

4. James, Jr.,	b. Mch. 4, 1828.	
5. Charles A.,	b. in	1829. d. Oct. 8, 1863.
6. George L ,	b. about	1831. d. young.
7. Catherine,	b. Dec. 6, 1833.	

Of James's children, **Susan[8]** died at Fairhaven, single : **Eliza B.[8]** m. in 1830 Abner Brownell, and lived in Little Compton, R. I. Issue : George Morgan, Ann Eliza, Henry Grinnell, and Susan Augusta. **Catherine[8]** m. Jan. 1, 1857, James Lewis, and lives at Fairhaven. Issue : Charles W., b. Mch. 22, 1865, who lives single at Fairhaven.

†–2–2–2–3. **Francis,[8]** oldest son of James, is a laborer, and lives at Fairhaven. He m. 1840, Sally Eldredge, and had issue :

1. Charles E.,	b. Nov. 24, 1844.	
2. Francis, Jr.,	b. Apr. 24, 1846.	
3. John,	b. Nov. 14, 1847.	d. young.
4. Georgianna,	b. Aug. 22, 1849.	
5. Sarah E.,	b. Nov. 1, 1858.	d. Jun. —, 1887.

Of these children, 4. **Georgiana,[9]** who lives in Fairhaven, m. Jul. 4, 1866, James M. Hall Jr., who was b. in 1845. Issue : Charles F., b. 1870 ; James M. Jr., b. 1874.

5. **Sarah E.[9]** m. Charles Thomas, and lives at Fairhaven. Issue : Albert, Thomas, Ellery, and Bertha.

1. **Charles E.[9]** is a laborer, and lives at Fairhaven. He m. Feb. 7, 1866, Louise [Macomber] West, who was b. Sep. 26, 1842. Issue :

1. Helen Mar,	b. Feb. 4, 1868.	
2. Mary,	b. about 1871.	d. young.
3. William,	b. about 1874.	d. young.
4. Charles W.,	b. Jul. 22, 1878.	

Of these children, **Helen Mar,[10]** who lives at Fairhaven, m. Jun. 25, 1889, Audelle W. Monk, who was b. Feb. 9, 1870. Issue : Louise E. Monk, b. Feb. 27, 1890.

2. **Francis Jr.**[9] is a laborer, and lives at Fairhaven. He m. Jul. 3, 1870, Esther Davis, and had issue :

    1. Lydia,   b. Sep. 12, 1871.
    2. Henry,   b. Apr. 10, 1873.

†-2-2-2-4. **James Jr.,**[9] who is a caulker at Fairhaven, m. in 1853 Parmelia Howard. Issue :

    1. Adelaide N.,   b. Nov. 30, 1856.   d. Oct. 8, 1884.
    2. Marcia D.,   b. Sep. 30, 1860.

Of these children, **Adelaide N.**[9] d. at Fairhaven, single : and **Marcia D.**[9] m. Jul. 23, 1885, Frederick H. Wood of Fairhaven. No issue.

†-2-2-2-5. **Charles A.,**[9] who was also a caulker at Fairhaven, m. Oct. 28, 1855, Marcia T. Davis. Issue :

    1. George,   b. Sep. 1, 1858.

1. **George**[9] is a druggist in New Bedford, firm of Church & Hammond, and lives at Fairhaven. He m. Nov. 4, 1882, Edvina A. Stowell. No issue.

†-2-2-3. **Barney,**[7] third son of Barnabas 2d, was a rigger and sailmaker at Fairhaven. He m. 1812 Sally P. Delano, who was b. in 1786, and d. in 1863. Issue :

    1. David Delano,   b. in 1812.   d. in 1866.

†-2-2-3-1. **David Delano**[8] was a cooper at Fairhaven, and was thrice married. He m. 1st, in 1834 Sarah Hodges, who was b. in 1817, and d. in 1838. Issue :

    1. Julia A. Bates,   b. Aug. 16, 1836.
    2. George F.,   b. in   1838.   d. in 1850.

David D. m. 2d, May 22, 1839, Sarah [Brown] Paine, who was b. Nov. 5, 1801, and d. in 1851. Issue :

    3. Sarah Thomas,   b. Aug. 6, 1841.

David D. m. 3d, Dec. 30, 1854, Mrs. Betsey P. Hattlestone (or Huddlestone), but had no further issue. Of David's children, 3. **Sarah Thomas**[9] resides, single, at Boston ; and **Julia A. Bates**[9] m. Jun. 21, 1870, Capt. Aaron C. Sergeant, and lives at Melrose, Mass. Capt. Sergeant, who was formerly in business in Boston, d. Apr. 4, 1890. No issue.

†-2-2-7. **Wilson,**[7] fourth son of Barnabas 2d, was a

rigger and a sailmaker at Fairhaven. He m. Nov. 2, 1811,
Harriet Blankenship of Marion, who was b. in 1790, and d.
Nov. 13, 1834. Issue :

1. William B.,	b. Jun. 12, 1812.	*d. Sept. 1900*
2. Lydia Parker,	b. Oct. 17, 1816.	d. Oct. 15, 1823.
3. Harriet,	b. Jan. 25, 1818.	
4. Elizabeth H.,	b. Feb. 9, 1821.	
5. Henry,	b. May 11, 1828.	d. Jul. 18, 1884.
6. Jane Hiller,	b. Oct. 28, 1833.	

Wilson m. 2d, Jun. 7, 1840, Cloe Phillips, who was b. in
1801, and d. Dec. 18, 1870. No further issue.

Of Wilson's children, **Henry**[5] was a painter at Fairhaven,
where he d. single at the age of 56.

3. **Harriet**[8] m. about 1836, Edwin R. Almy, and lived
at Fairhaven. Issue : Edwin R., Harriet, Frank, William,
Nathaniel, and George.

4. **Elizabeth H.**[8] m. Jul. 6, 1839, Samuel Rand of
Fairhaven, who d. in 1858. Issue :

1. Mary,	b. Feb. 15, 1844.
2. Deborah,	b. Jun. 3, 1849.
3. Frank A.,	b. Feb. 17, 1854.

6. **Jane Hiller**[8] m. in 1853 Charles L. Wrightington,
and lives in Wilmington, Del. Issue : Susan, Ida Frances,
Luella, and Hattie Almy.

†–2–2–7–1. **William Blankenship**,[5] oldest son of Wilson, educated in the common schools, in early life was a grocer's
clerk, and then a cooper at Fairhaven. In 1832 the Congregational Church at Fairhaven, appreciating young Hammond's
earnestness of purpose, and devotion to the cause of Chris-
tianity, determined to prepare him for the ministry. Accord-
ingly he was fitted for college at Bangor Seminary, Maine ;
graduated at Amherst College, class of '40; and at the
Andover Theological Seminary in '43 ; was ordained at Canton,
Mass., as a Congregational clergyman, Jun. 5, 1844 ; installed
at South Braintree in 1849 ; was agent for the Mass. Sabbath
School Society in 1856 ; preached at Morrisville, N. Y., seven
years, and at Lenox, N. Y., seven more ; in 1870 was installed
pastor of the Congregational Church in Acushnet, Mass. ; and
in 1878 in Rome, N. Y., where he now lives, a retired clergyman. He is an honest man, of positive ideas, and an accepta-
ble preacher, full of many years and good works. He m.

Rev. William B. Hammond.

Mch. 18, 1844, Louise M. Pond of Clinton, N. Y., who was
b. Oct. 9, 1818, and d. Jun. 24, 1880, at Rome, N.Y. Issue:

1. Sarah B.,	b. Jan. 1, 1845.	
2. William F.,	b. Sep. 1, 1848.	d. Sep. 30, 1852.
3. Julius W.,	b. Sep. 1, 1855.	d. Oct. 20, 1856.
4. Eddie L.,	b. Jun. 14, 1858.	d. Jul. 28, 1862.

Sarah Bachelder[9] resides with her father at Rome, N. Y.,
never having married.

4.—JAMES JR. OF ROCHESTER, MASS.

†–2–4. **James Jr.,**[6] third son of James, was a farmer,
and lived on the West Neck, Mattapoisett, in the southwesterly
part of the old town of Rochester. He m. May 10, 1786,
Deborah Snow, who was b. in 1765, and d. Dec. 3, 1843.
Issue:

1. Nancy,	b. Sep. 17, 1786.	d. Apr. 10, 1874.
2. Gideon 2d,	b. in 1791.	d. Jun. 3, 1848.
3. Bruce F.,	b. in 1798.	d. Oct. 18, 1854.
4. Deborah.	b. May 13, 1800.	d. Feb. 8, 1867.

†–2–4–1. **Nancy**[7] m. about 1806 Seth Bradford, and
lived in what is now Acushnet, Mass. Seth was a farmer in
Acushnet, and was b. at Plympton, Mass., Dec. 22, 1783.
Issue: James H., Henry A., Sarah A., Melvin Otis, Deborah,
Aaron, Philip A., and Josiah.

†–2–4–3. **Bruce F.**[7] was a ship-carpenter, and lived in
the village of Mattapoisett. He m. 1st, Lydia Blossom, who
was b. Oct. 18, 1796, and d. Aug. 12, 1848. Issue:

1. Horace Bruce.	b. in 1825.	d. Nov. 26, 1848.

Bruce F. m. 2d, Sapphira Peckham, who d. Sep. 19, 1853,
but had no other issue.

†–2–4–4. **Deborah,**[7] who lived in Mattapoisett Village,
m. 1st, Mch. 31, 1822, Luther Avery. She m. 2d, Jul. 31,
1837, Wyatt Snow of Mattapoisett. No issue by either husband.

†–2–4–2. **Gideon 2d,**[7] oldest son of James Jr., inher-
ited and lived on his father's farm. He m. about 1810 Rebecca
Blossom, who was b. Aug. 31, 1792, and d. May 7, 1872.
Issue:

1. Joseph J.,	b. Aug. 11, 1812.

2. Adeline J ,	b. Nov. 13, 1814.	d. Mch. 18, 1878.
3. Amelia L.,	b. Jan. 26, 1815.	d. May 14, 1887.
4. Frederic A.,	b. Nov. 2, 1817.	
5. Mary B..	b. Jan. 25, 1821.	d. Mch. 3, 1843.
6. Sylvia R.,	b. Oct. 6, 1832.	d. Mch. 19, 1884.

2. **Adeline J.,**[8] who lived at Fairhaven, m. in 1830, Edward Simmons, who was b. at Middleboro', Mass., and d. in California. Issue:

1. Eliza A.,   b. Dec. 14, 1834.
2. Edward W.,   b. Jul. 12, 1839.

Of these children, **Eliza A.**[9] m. Jun. 20, 1866, Robert Bennett of Fairhaven. No issue. **Edward W.**[9] m. S. Helen Wilcox. Issue: Walter E., b. Feb. 18, 1874.

3. **Amelia L.,**[8] second daughter of Gideon 2d, who also lived in Fairhaven, m. Feb. 13, 1834, Peleg W. Gifford, who was b. Jul. 10, 1805. Peleg Gifford was a captain in the whale fishery, sailing from Fairhaven, where he d. Sep. 27, 1888. Issue:

1. Sarah Eliz.,   b. Apr. 25, 1839.
2. Abbie Palmer,   b. Jan. 20, 1841.

Of these children, **Sarah E.**[9] m. Feb. 7, 1861, Cornelius Grinnell, and lives at Brooklyn, N. Y. Issue: Mary Arnold, Henry Rogers, Lizzie Winslow, and Leslie Clark.

Abbie[9] m. Nov. 17, 1862, Henry H. Rogers, and lives in New York City. Mr. Rogers, who is a member of the Standard Oil Co., is giving his native village, Fairhaven, many substantial tokens of his regard in the form of public buildings, etc. Issue: Annie S., Cara Leland, Millicent Gifford, Mary Huddlestone, and Henry Huddlestone Jr.

5. **Mary Blossom,**[8] who lived and died on the old homestead, m. James Allen who was born in New Bedford. Issue: Mary, who died young.

6. **Sylvia R.**[8] lived first in Fairhaven, and afterwards lived and d. in Brooklyn, N. Y. She m. Daniel Ripley, who was b. in New Bedford. Issue: Willie, who d. in infancy.

†-2-4-2-1. **Joseph J.,**[8] oldest son of Gideon 2d, was a farmer and lived on the old homestead, West Neck, Mattapoisett. He m. Dec. 23, 1835, Nancy Allen of Acushnet, who was b. Apr. 4, 1814, and d. Sep. 26, 1870. Issue:

1. Mary A.,   b. Jul. 29, 1838.   d. May 15, 1864.
2. Rebecca H.,   b. Dec. 18, 1840.   d. Mch. 5, 1886.

| 3. Amelia L., | b. Apr. 18, 1843. | d. May 9, 1883. |
| 4. James A., | b. Aug. 8, 1846. | |

Of these children, **Mary A.**[9] and **Rebecca H.**[9] d. at Mattapoisett, single.

3. **Amelia L.**[9] m. Nov. 13, 1866, Benjamin F. Robinson, and lived at Mattapoisett. Issue:

| 1. Harry L., | b. Oct. 6, 1867. | d. Mch. 8, 1886. |

4. **James A.**[9] is a shoemaker, and lives at Brockton, Mass. He m. Jan. 6, 1869, Hattie Burrell of Falmouth, Mass., who was b. Jan. 26, 1841. Issue:

| 1. Horace Bruce, | b. Feb. 9, 1880. |

Joseph J. now resides, with his son James, at Brockton, Mass.

†-2-4-2-4. **Frederic A.,**[8] second son of Gideon 2d, is a rancher at Los Angeles, Cal. He m. Sep. 12, 1844, Rebecca [Gelett] Bly, who d. Feb. 10, 1892. Issue:

1. Andrew R.,	b. Jul. 31, 1845.	
2. Thomas B.,	b. Oct. 4, 1847.	d. Sep. 1, 1876.
3. Mary,	b. in 1849.	d. in 1849.
4. Sylvia,	b. in 1850.	d. in 1852.
5. George S.,	b. Mch. 20, 1857.	d. Aug. 18, 1888.

Of these children, who were b. at Buffalo, N. Y., **Mary**[9] and **Sylvia**[9] d. young: **Thomas B.**[9] was killed by the Apaches at Globe City, Ariz., in 1876; and **George S.**[9] d. single, at Los Angeles, in 1888.

1. **Andrew Robinson**[9] is a broker, and lives in New York City. He m. 1st, Della ———, and had issue:

| 1. Alice, | b. Mch. 15, 1877. |

He m. 2d, Kate Wame, but has no further issue.

5.—JESSE OF ROCHESTER, MASS.

†-2-5. **Jesse,**[6] fourth son of James, was a house-carpenter, and lived in Mattapoisett Village. He m. 1st, Susannah Shaw of East Fairhaven, daughter of William Shaw, who was b. in 1776, and d. Aug. 14, 1811. Issue:

1. Hannah,	b. Jun. 19, 1795.	d. Nov. 3, 1879.
2. Sophia,	b. Nov. —, 1796.	d. Dec. 19, 1859.
3. Mary,	b. Sep. 25, 1800.	d. Feb. 20, 1865.
4. Susan,	b. about 1802.	d. young.

5. Lucy,	b. in	1803.	d. Feb. 6, 1879.
6. Roger Wing,	b. in	1807.	d. Dec. —, 1849.
7. Sarah Shaw,	b. in	1809.	d. Jan. —, 1812.

Jesse m. 2d, Mch. 20, 1813, Charity Winslow, who was b. in 1773, and d. Jun. 13, 1849. Issue :

8. Joseph W.,	b. Dec. 27, 1813.	
9. Sarah W.,	b. Nov. 22. 1817.	d. Jan. 1, 1827.
10. Jesse, Jr.,	b. Feb. 7, 1820.	
11. Susan,	b. Jan. 13, 1822.	
12. William,	b. Feb. 2, 1825.	d. Aug. 25, 1825.

Of Jesse's children, the two **Sarahs**, the first **Susan**, and **William** d. young ; and **Jesse Jr.**[7] resides at Stockton, Cal., single.

†–2–5–1. **Hannah**[7] lived in the southwesterly part of Bridgewater, Mass., near the Middleboro' line. She m. in 1815 David Hall, who was b. Mch. 5, 1784, and d. Nov. 16, 1865. Issue : Susan, Henry C., David, David 2d, William, Stephen P., Sophia C., Abbie Leach, Sylvia L., and Mary.

†–2–5–2. **Sophia,**[7] who lived in New Bedford, m. Jan. 1818, Henry Cannon, who was b. Jul. 4, 1796, and d. Oct. 4, 1863. No issue.

†–2–5–3. **Mary,**[7] who lived in New Bedford, m. Nov. 13, 1821, Stephen Potter, who was b. Aug. 17, 1799, and d. May 31, 1834. Issue : John Kempton, Gideon Hammond, Southward 2d, Sophia Cannon, and Gideon Hammond 2d, Southward 2d was for many years a noted accountant in New Bedford.

†–2–5–5. **Lucy**[7] lived first at New Bedford and afterwards at Bridgewater, Mass. She m. Sep. 1, 1826, Thomas Cottle Briggs, who was b. in Freetown, Mass., Jul. 6, 1806, and d. Jan. 21, 1861. Issue : Mary Durfee, Susan Delano, John Burbank, Charles Peirce, Ruth Burbank, Sophia Cannon, William Taber, Isaac Stackhouse, Jesse Hammond, and George Durfee.

†–2–5–11. **Susan**[7] m. Nov. 4, 1854, Charles H. Smith, and resides at Norton, Mass. No issue.

†–2–5–6. **Roger Wing,**[7] known as Wing, moved to Bridgewater and lived near the Raynham line, where he died. He m. 1st, in 1832, Jane Leach, who d. Apr. 3, 1838. Issue :

1. Isaac,   b. Sep. 13, 1834.
2. Jane,   b. Aug. 13, 1836.

Wing m. 2d, Marriet Susan King, who was b. in 1814. No other issue.

Of Wing's children, 2. **Jane,**[8] who lives in Taunton, Mass., m. Aug. 1852 George E. Leonard, who was b. in 1832, and d. in 1864. Issue: George Edward, b. Jul. 1855; Jesse Hammond, b. 1857 and d. 1862; Ella Jane, b. 1860; and Harry Ellsworth, b. 1862.

†-2-5-6-1. **Isaac**[5] lives at Raynham, and formerly kept a livery stable in Taunton. He m. 1st, Jane Leonard, who was b. in 1836, and d. Oct. 1862. Issue:

1. Nellie,   b. Sep. 14, 1857.
2. Jennie,   b. Aug. 3, 1860.

Isaac m. 2d, in 1865, Maria J. Williams, who was b. in 1849. Issue:

3. Fannie W.,   b. Jun. 7, 1867.
4. Herbert,   b. Feb. 22, 1870.
5. Frank,   b. Jan. 14, 1872.
6. Emma King,   b. Mch. 1, 1873.

Of Isaac's children, **Nellie**[9] m. Apr. 1, 1876, Martin L. Sturtevant, and lives at South Braintree, Mass. Issue: Harry P., Embert, and Jennie and Fannie, twins.

2. **Jennie,**[9] who lives at Bridgewater, Mass., m. Feb. 3, 1892, Harry Amos Clark, a jeweler, who was b. Mch. 11, 1861. Issue: Amy Hammond, b. Apr. 12, 1893.

3. **Fannie Williams**[9] m. Aug. 2, 1885, Edwin Vial, and lives in Raynham, Mass. Issue: Lena Hammond and Marion Frances.

4. **Herbert**[9] lives in Taunton and at present is a hack-driver. He m. May 19, 1892, Hattie Jane Field, but has no issue.

5. **Frank,**[9] who is a butcher and unmarried, lives at Raynham; 6. **Emma King,**[9] also unmarried, lives at Raynham.

†-2-5-8. **Joseph Winslow,**[7] who was formerly a captain on the river steamers in California, resides at Stockton, Cal. He m. Oct. 12, 1842, Sophia Wing Southworth, who was b. at Mattapoisett, Jan. 12, 1817. Issue:

1. Sarah Winslow,   b. Dec. 7, 1845.

1. **Sarah Winslow,**[8] who was b. at Mattapoisett, m. Jun. 24, 1862, Willard J. Belding, who was b. Apr. 9, 1828, at Barre Centre, Orleans Co., N. Y. Issue: Sophie, b. Apr. 10, 1863, at Stockton, Cal. Sophie m. Mch. 15, 1888, Charles O. Bennett, who was b. in Knowlesville, Orleans Co., N. Y., May 19, 1856.

VII.—JOHN HAMMOND OF FALMOUTH, MASS.

†. **John**[4] **Hammond,** eighth son of Samuel[3] [Benjamin,[2] William[1]], went to Falmouth, Mass., and m. Jan. 23, 1728, Marah [Maria] Green. He was chosen town clerk in 1736, and selectman and assessor in 1739, and was a pew-holder in 1756. Issue:

1. Phela [Phebe],	b. Nov. 2, 1729.	d.
2. Lydia,	b. Feb. 25, 1731.	d.
3. John, Jr.,	b. Apr. 17, 1734.	d.
4. Mary,	b. Nov. 4, 1735.	d. Nov. 13, 1736.
5. Jeduthan,	b. Dec. 25, 1737.	d.
6. Paul,	b. Apr. 29, 1740.	d.
7. Marah,	b. May 23, 1742.	d.
8. Barnabas,	b.	d.

Of these children, 1. **Phebe**[5] m. Sep. 6, 1750, Reuben Gifford of Falmouth. Issue unknown.

2. **Lydia**[5] m. Mch. 28, 1754, Jabez Weeks of Falmouth. Issue, if any, not learned.

5. **Jeduthan**[5] m. Dec. 27, 1759, Fear Gifford of Falmouth. Issue, if any, not known.

6. **Paul**[5] m. Feb. 27, 1766, Anna Davis Jr. of Falmouth. Issue: Perhaps a son Abner, who d. in the West Indies.

3.—JOHN Jr. OF FALMOUTH, MASS.

†-3. **John Jr.,**[5] who lived at "Quissett," so called, in Falmouth, m. Dec. 1761, Rebecca Nye, and had issue:

1. Silvanus,	b. Feb. 14, 1764.	d. Feb. 16, 1850.
2. Nathaniel,	b. Feb. 14, 1766.	d. Dec. 24, 1851.
3. Hannah,	b. Mch. 19, 1768.	d. Apr. 24, 1851.
4. Lydia,	b. Oct. 15, 1769.	d. May 23, 1791-2.
5. Huldah,	b. Apr. 8, 1772.	d.

6. Lucy,	b. May 14. 1775.	d. Feb. 26, 1848.
7. Isaiah,	b. Apr. 9, 1777.	d. Mch. 20. 1817.
8. Jeduthan,	b. Mch. 11, 1780.	d. Sep. 17, 1798.
9. Samuel.	b. Aug. 15, 1783.	d. Jun. 5, 1863.

Of these children, **Silvanus,**[6] who was a mariner, **Hannah,**[6] **Lydia,**[6] and **Lucy,**[6] were all single, and lived and d. at Quissett, Falmouth; and **Jeduthan**[6] d. a young man.

†–3–2. **Nathaniel**[6] who was on the State Valuation in 1811, and was a mariner, lived at Quissettt. He m. Jun. 27, 1806, Thankful Meigs, and had issue:

| 1. Lydia, | b. Sep. 17, 1807. | d. Mar. 16, 1834. |

Nathaniel m. 2d, Betsey Rowley, but had no further issue.

†–3–5. **Huldah**[6] m. Barnabas Chadwick Jr., lived at Quissett, and had issue: John, Joseph, Samuel, and William. All dead, except Samuel, who resides at Quissett.

†–3–7. **Isaiah,**[6] who was a master mariner, m. Oct. 11, 1804, Ruth Hatch, and d. at Martinique, West Indies, without issue. His widow m. in 1818 Timothy Parker.

†–3–9. **Samuel**[6] was a farmer at Quissett. In the War of 1812, he was one of a company of 32 men, who under the command of Capt. Weston Jenkins, went in a wood coaster and captured an English privateer, called the Retaliation, lying at anchor in Taupoline Cove. It was a bold enterprise, but was done without losing a man. He m. his cousin, Eunice Hammond, daughter of Barnabas, and d. without issue.

8.—BARNABAS OF FALMOUTH, MASS.

†–8. **Barnabas**[5] was repeatedly elected to various minor offices in the town of Falmouth, and was on the State Valuation in 1811. He m. Oct. 20, 1782, Joanna Hatch, and had issue:

1. Eunice,	b. May 12. 1783.	d. Dec. 30, 1866.
2. Robert,	b. Dec. 11, 1785.	d. Apr. 30, 1859.
3. Elizabeth,	b. May 19, 1788.	d.
4. Joanna,	b. Sep. 4, 1791.	d.

1. **Eunice**[6] m. Samuel Hammond of Falmouth, as stated above, and d. without issue.

2. **Robert,**[6] who was a sea captain and master rigger at Woods Holl, Falmouth, m. Rebecca Hatch, and d. leaving no issue.

4. **Joanna,**[6] the youngest of the other two sisters, m. Andrew Y. Davis of Woods Holl, and lived but a few months, dying without issue. Andrew Y. Davis afterwards m. 3. **Elizabeth**[6] and had two children: Prince A. and Joanna Elizabeth.

Of these children, Prince A. d. in California in 1850; and Joanna Elizabeth m. Louis C. Swift, and has two sons: Prince D. and John P., both living. The older son, Prince D., who lives at Woods Holl, m. Charlotte O. Field of Middleboro', and has two daughters. The younger son, John P., m. Jennie E. Hannaford of South Boston, and has no issue.

Deed of King Philip and Monjoham to Hugh Cole.

Know all men by these Presents, that I, Philip, Chief Sachem of Porhanlett [Pokanoket], & Monjoham of Mattapoisett, Do acknowledge that for and in Consideration of the Summ of five Pounds & ten Shillings to us in hand Paid by Hugh Cole of ye Town of Swansey, in the Jurisdiction of Plymouth in New England, Ship Wright, wherewith We Do acknowledge our Selves to be fully Satisfied, Contented and fully Paid, and thereof & of every Part & Parcell thereof Do Exonerate, acquit & Discharge the s⁴ Hugh Cole Ile, his Heirs, Exec⁰ˢ & Admin⁰ˢ forever, by these Presents Have Bargained, alienated & Sold, Enfeoffed & Confirmed, and by these Presents Do Bargain, Alienate, Sell, Enfeoffe & Confirm, from us the s⁴ Philip & Monjoham & our Heirs, to Him, the s⁴ Hugh Cole & his Heirs & assigns forever, A certain Parcell of Land lying & being near a Place called Acushenah in the Township of Dartmouth in ye Jurisdiction of Plymouth afores⁴, Being Bounded on the Southwest Corner with a Stake by the Water Side, which is on the Southeast Corner of Dartmouth afores⁴, & so runs to the Eastward to a red oak tree marked, and from the red oak to the Water Side on a South Point, and northerly to a Pine tree marked on four Sides, and from the s⁴ Pine to ye Westward to Dartmouth Bounds to a Small red oak tree with Stones about it, With free Liberty to cut Wood & Timber on ye Commons adjacent.

To Have & to Hold all the s⁴ Tract or Parcell of Land bounded as afores⁴ With the Liberty of Cutting Wood & Timber on ye Commons. The which s⁴ Tract or Parcell of Land was likewise granted unto ye s^d Hugh Cole by the Court of Plymouth, unto Him the s^d Hugh Cole, To Him & his Heirs & Assigns forever. The s^d Premises with all & Singular the appurtenances, Profits, Benefits, Priviledges & Immunityes belonging thereunto With all our Rights, Title & Interest of and into ye Same or any Part thereof, With the Liberty of Cutting Wood or Timber on ye Commons adjacent as afores^d.

To appertain unto the only proper use and Behoof of him, the s^d Hugh Cole, him, his Heirs and assigns forever, free & clear, & clearly acquitted of & from all other & former Gifts, Grants, Bargains & Sales whatsoever. To be Holden of his majesty, Charles King of England, as of his manors of East Greenwich in the County of Kent in the Realm of England, in free & common Souage & not in Capite, nor by Knight Service, nor by the Rents & Services thereof & thereby due & of Right accustomed, With Warranty against all Persons that by our Right & Title of or into the s^d Premises or any Part or Parcell thereof. Giving & hereby Granting Liberty unto the s^d Hugh Cole, either by Himself or his attorney to Record or Enroll these Presents, Or to Cause them to be Recorded or Enrolled in his majesties Court of New Plymouth afores^d, Or in any other Place of Publick Records, according to yousual manner of Recording & Enrolling Deeds and Evidences of Lands made & Provided.

In Witness whereof We, the s^d Philip & Monjoham, have hereunto Set our hands & Seals this third day of November, One thousand, Six hundred, Seventy & one, 1671—

Signed, Sealed & D'd	The Mark ⌐⌐ of Philip,
In ye Presence of	the Sachem, & of his [Seal]
William Harvey,	The Mark ∿ Monjoham,
Thomas Leonard.	and his [Seal]

This deed of Sale was acknowledged Before me, Constant Southworth, assistant, this third Day of November 1671—

Copy as of Record Exm^d by Josiah Cotton, Clerk & keeper of the Colony Records.

— —

Will of Samuel Hammond.

In the name of God, Amen :

This twelveth day of July, 1728, in the first year of the reign of our Lord King George II, I, Samuel Hammond of Rochester, in the county of Plymouth, in the Province of Massachusetts-Bay in New England, yeoman, being of a disposing mind and memory and desirous to set my house in order before I die, do make this my last will and testament. 1st, I give my soul to God and my body to the ground after my decease in hopes of a glorious resurrection, and as touching such worldly estate as hath pleased God to bless me withal, I give and dispose of the same in the following manner and form :—

Imprimis: I give and bequeath to my beloved wife, Mary, all the estate both out and indoors, wherever it is or may be found during her continuing my widow, and then after her decease to be disposed of to my children as hereafter in my will I shall order.

Item 2nd, I give to my son Thomas, besides what I have already given him, fifty acres of land and three parts of the ten acres of meadow land I have in the town of Wales, and 20 acres of land in Rochester not yet laid out, which land I lent to my brother Nathan Hammond, to go to his heirs and assigns forever.

Item 3d, I give to my son Jedediah, 50 acres of land and three parts of the 10 acres, a lot of fresh meadow that I have in Rochester and the ½ of the share of land in Rochester, not yet laid out, to be to him and his heirs and assigns forever.

Item 4th, I give to my son John, 50 acres of land, and the three parts of my 10 acre lot of meadow that lays aforesaid, and a certain piece of land lying to the south of my homestead, as it has already been bounded out to go to him, and his heirs and assigns forever ; likewise I give to my son John, ½ of my land and meadow lying on Branch Island.

Item 5th, I give to my grandson, Archelus Hammond, 50 acres of land to him his heirs and assigns forever.

Item 6th, I give to my grandson, Peter Spooner, 50 acres of land lying in Wales aforesaid, to him his heirs and assigns forever.

Item 7th, I give to my daughter, Mariah Clark, 50 acres of land, in the town of Wales, to her her heirs and assigns forever.

Item 8th, I give to my son Samuel Hammond 10 acres of land whereon he now liveth, to him his heirs and assigns forever.

Item 9th, I give to my son Josiah the lot of land where his house now stands, together with the meadow at the foot of it, and 4 acres of meadow in Cook's meadow, and ¼ of a share of Cedar swamp together with ½ of all my lands in Rochester, and 1 farrow cow which he heth already I give to his heirs and assigns forever.

Likewise I also constitute my son Josiah and my son John to be joint executors of this my last will and testament.

Item 10th, I give to my son Barnabas 3 acres of land in Cook's meadow, and the remaining part of said meadow I give to my son Seth with what I have given him.

Item 11th, I give to my granddaughter Abigail one featherbed and bedding.

Item 12th, I give to my granddaughter Elizabeth Spooner 15 sheep when she shall come to the age of 18 years, to be paid to her by the executors of my movable estates.

Item 13th, I give to my granddaughter Rose Spooner 15 sheep as above.

Item 14th, I give to my 6 grandchildren Jeduthan, Benjamin, John, Thomas, Hobbs, and Mary Spooner, 5 shillings apiece to be paid to them by my executors after my decease.

Item 15th, I give to my wife my best featherbed and bedding, to be all hers and her assigns.

Item 16th. I give to my daughters Mariah and Jedidah all of my movables both within and out of doors after my wife's decease.

My will is that my executors pay all my debts out of the money that shall be due me at my decease so far as that will go, and the remainder if any there be out of my personal estate.

In witness whereof I have hereunto set my hand and seal this day and year above written.

SAMUEL HAMMOND.

Signed, Sealed, Published and pronounced by Samuel Hammond as his last will and testament in presence of us.

Thos. Clarke.
Joshua Coggshall.
Nath'l Delano.

Sept. the 20th 1728.

The within named Thos. Clarke, Josh. Coggshall and Nath'l Delano made oath that they saw the within named Samuel Hammond, late of Rochester county of Plymouth deceased, sign, seal and heard him declare the within written on to be his last will and testament.

Isaac Winslow, Judge of Probate.

[Probate Records, Plymouth, Mass., Vol. 5, Page 477.]

PART III.

JOHN HAMMOND, SECOND SON OF BENJAMIN.

---

†. **John² Hammond,** [second son of Benjamin,² William¹], was b. at Sandwich, Mass., Nov. 30, 1663, came to Rochester, Mass., with his brother Samuel about 1680, and d. there Apr. 19, 1749, O. S. He settled in the southwesterly part of the present town of Mattapoisett, where about the year 1700 he built the "Old Hammond House," known at the present time as the "Howes House." It is the oldest dwelling-house in the town, and is well preserved. It stands on the west bank of the Mattapoisett River, in a picturesque location, and is one of the old landmarks of the town.

John Hammond was a noted man of his time: was selectman and assessor three years; member of the State legislature two years; a lieutenant of militia, and a justice of the peace. He was also one of the founders, and a prominent member of the first Congregational Church in Rochester. He m. in 1691 Mary Arnold, eldest daughter of the Rev. Samuel Arnold, first minister of the gospel that was settled in Rochester. Mary Arnold was b. May 1672, and d. Aug. 3, 1756, and had seven sons and four daughters. Issue to grow to maturity and marry were :

1. Bethiah,	b. Aug. 11, 1693.	d. Mch. 17, 1757.
2. Sarah,	b. Dec. 23, 1695.	d.
3. Jabez,	b. Feb. 26, 1699.	d. Feb. —, 1786.
4. Elnathan,	b. Mch. 7, 1703.	d. May 24, 1793.
5. Benjamin,	b. Dec. 1, 1704.	d. Jul. 19, 1758.
6. Rowland,	b. Oct. 30, 1706.	d. Jun. 16, 1788.
7. Elizabeth,	b. Jan. 5, 1709.	d.
8. Abigail,	b. Mch. 27, 1714.	d. May 16, 1753.
9. John, Jr.,	b. Sep. 4, 1716.	d. Dec. 20, 1785.

10

Of these children, 1. **Bethiah**[4] m. Joseph Haskell of Rochester, and had many children that grew to maturity and married. Issue: Nathaniel, Jean, Sary, Joseph, Mary, Elnathan, John, Nathaniel, Bethiah, Abigail, and Hannah.

2. **Sarah**[4] m. Apr. 26, 1722, Noah Sprague of Rochester, son of Samuel Sprague. She had sons and daughters, whom she lived to see married and dead. Issue: Joshua, Alden, Allathia, Elizabeth, Samuel, Mary, Samuel, Noah, Elizabeth, and John.

7. **Elizabeth**[4] m. Oct. 13, 1731, Ebenezer, son of Capt. Hope Lothrop of Falmouth, and had two sons and three daughters. They moved to New Township, Ga., where he purchased a farm, built a comfortable dwelling-house, and died soon after. His widow and five small children were afterwards attacked by the Indians, and she was obliged to leave at an hour's warning, carrying nothing with her but her children and one bed. The Indians burnt her house and destroyed all her stock of cattle and household goods. Through the assistance of friends she was enabled to get back to Oblong, Dutchess Co., N. Y., where with the aid of her friends in Rochester she made a comfortable living. After some years she m. Dea. Wilcox, a man of property, who died a few years after with a cancer. After that she lived with her two sons in New York, perhaps at Oblong.

8. **Abigail**[4] m. Feb. 11, 1750, Ebenezer Perry of Rochester, and had one son Nathan, who d. at the age of 40.

I.—JABEZ HAMMOND OF ROCHESTER AND NEW BEDFORD, MASS.

†. **Jabez**[4] **Hammond 1st,** oldest son of John,[3] [Benjamin,[2] William[1]], was b. at Rochester, Mass., Feb. 27, 1699, moved to Dartmouth, afterwards New Bedford, Mass., probably about the first of Dec. 1765, and, with his son John, went to South Woodstock, Vt., in 1782, where he d. Feb. 1786, æ. 87. Jabez Hammond was a prominent man in his day, and is said to have held a commission as captain from the King of England. After the birth of his children, probably May 17, 1765, he wrote out a Family Record, giving the births, marriages and deaths, and the names of his father and mother, himself, his

John Hammond House. (Old Howes House.)

wives and children, up to the date of writing. This ancient paper, somewhat impaired by time, is still in existence, and is a rare and remarkable document.* Jabez Hammond was twice married, and was the father of 18 children. He m. 1st, Apr. 14, 1725, Sarah, daughter of Hope Lothrop of Falmouth, who d. Nov. 9, 1734. Issue:

1. Joshua,	b. Apr. 1, 1726.	d. Jan. 2, 1727.
2. Hannah,	b. Jul. 20, 1727.	d. Jun. 9, 1730.
3. Zilpha,	b. Aug. 10, 1729.	d. Jun. 18, 1730.
4. Rebecca,	b. Feb. 14, 1731.	d. Dec. 29, 1767.
5. Lothrop,	b. Apr. 24, 1733.	d. Nov. 26, 1756.
6. Sarah,	b. Oct. 15, 1734.	d. Dec. 8, 1734.

Jabez Hammond m. 2d, May 12, 1736, Abigail Faunce, who d. at the age of 84. She was a daughter of Rev. Mr. Faunce from England, minister at Plymouth, Mass., and granddaughter of Thomas Faunce of England. Issue:

7. Faunce,	b. May 20, 1737.	d. Feb. 8, 1813.
8. Sarah,	b. Mch. 24, 1739.	d.
9. Jabez 2d,	b. Jun. 9, 1741.	d. May 2, 1807.
10. Luther,	b. Apr. 8, 1744.	d. young.
11. Calvin,	b. Dec. 29, 1745.	d.
12. Rhoda,	b. Nov. 16, 1747.	d.
13. John,	b. Jan. 20, 1750.	d. Aug. —, 1814.
14. Elijah,	b. Mch. 4, 1751.	d. Apr. 20, 1815.
15. George,	b. Aug. 19, 1754.	d. about 1800.
16. Caleb,	b. Dec. 3, 1757.	d.
17. Ruth,	b. Sep. —, 1759.	d. Dec. 11, 1761.
18. Abigail,	b. Jun. 26, 1762.	d. about 1812.

Of these children, Joshua, Hannah, Zilpha, Sarah, Luther and Ruth d. young; **Lothrop**[5] d. single at Jamaica, West Indies; and **George**[5] and **Caleb**[5] d. single at Woodstock, Vt.

4. **Rebecca**[5] m. Jan. 10, 1750, Josiah Hammond Jr., her second cousin, grandson of Samuel Hammond. She lived in what is now Mattapoisett, and was the mother of eight children: Elnathan, Austris, Richard, Eunice, Priscilla, Lothrop, Mary, and Nathan.†

8. **Sarah**[5] m. in 1761 Enoch Winslow of Rochester, and moved to Woodstock, Vt., about 1789. Issue: Two daughters, and a son Noah, who left a large family, and d. at Pembrook, N. Y., when about 40 years old.

12. **Rhoda**[5] m. Aug. 2, 1774, Calvin Washburn of Dartmouth, and lived and d. in Pawtucket, R. I. Issue: Mary and Nancy.

* See end of Part III.
† For further record of Rebecca's children, see Genealogy of Josiah Jr., p. 107.

18. **Abigail**[5] m. Enoch Leonard, and moved to Pomfret, Vt., about 1790-95, where she d. at the age of about 80. Issue: Three sons and three daughters.

7.—FAUNCE HAMMOND OF NEW BEDFORD, AND READING, VT.

†. **Faunce**[5] **Hammond,** son of Jabez 1st,[4] [John,[3] Benjamin,[2] William[1]], was b. at Rochester, Mass., May 20, 1737, moved to Dartmouth, now New Bedford, about the year 1777, and to Reading, Vt., Nov. 1787, where he d. Feb. 8, 1813. He m. Dec. 3, 1761, Mary Holmes of Plymouth, Mass., who d. Feb. 1, 1813. Issue:

1. Nathaniel,	b. Feb. 6, 1763.	d. Aug. 19, 1834.
2. Stephen,	b. Feb. 17, 1765.	d. Sep. 23, 1806.
3. Ruth,	b. Mch. 2, 1767.	d. May 9, 1857.
4. Luther,	b. May 28, 1769.	d. Jun. 6, 1771.
5. Sally,	b. Mch. 31, 1771.	d.
6. Jabez Holmes,	b. May 1, 1773.	d. Oct. 25, 1841.
7. Mary Clark,	b. Jul. 13, 1775.	d.
8. Jiry,	b. Sep. 25, 1778.	d. Jun. 9, 1834.
9. Luther,	b May 5, 1781.	d. Feb. 27, 1871.
10. Thomas Faunce,	b. Dec. 17, 1783.	d. Dec. 24, 1865.

Of these children, 3. **Ruth,**[6] oldest daughter of Faunce, was b. in Rochester, Mass., Mch. 2, 1767, and moved to Reading, Vt., Nov. 1788. She m. Nov. 10, 1786, Mitchell Pope of Dartmouth, Mass., who d. Jan. 23, 1849. She had 13 children: Elnathan, Nathaniel, Mary, Sally, Jabez, Reuben, Ruth, Mitchell Jr., Cynthia, Luther Ralph, Thomas Faunce, Lutina, and Andrew.

In Mch. 1856 Ruth moved to Wisconsin with her son Thomas Faunce, where she d. May 9, 1857, æ. 90. It is said that none of her children are living.

5. **Sally,**[6] second daughter of Faunce, was b. at Rochester, Mass., and probably lived and d. at Middlebury, Vt. She m. 1st, Feb. 25, 1790, Henry Carlton, who d. May 20, 1812, æ. 51. She m. 2d, Oct. 12, 1813, Harvey Monger, and probably d. without issue. Both marriages occurred in Reading, Vt., but Harvey Monger, her second husband, was a resident of Middlebury.

7. **Mary Clark,**[6] third daughter of Faunce, was b. at Dartmouth, Jul. 13, 1775, lived at Woodstock, Vt., and d. there previous to Nov. 1824. She m. David Kendall, who d. Mch. 1857, after a second mariage in Nov. 1824. No issue known.

(1.)—NATHANIEL HAMMOND OF SOUTH WOOD-STOCK, VT.

†. **Nathaniel**[6] **Hammond,** oldest son of Faunce,[5] [Jabez,[4] John,[3] Benjamin,[2] William[1]], who was a shoemaker, lived at South Woodstock, and d. at Reading, Vt., with his son David. He m. about 1785 Mary Adams, who was b. in 1755, and d. Oct. 29, 1821. Issue :

1. Nathaniel, Jr.,	b. Nov. 2, 1786.	d. Feb. 2, 1874.
2. Abram,	b. in 1788.	d. Mch. 18, 1812.
3. Mary,	b. in 1790.	d. in 1821.
4. David,	b. in 1792.	d. Oct. 29, 1851.
5. George,	b. about 1794.	d. about 1829.
6. Henry Clinton,	b. Aug. 20, 1797.	d. Jun. —, 1844.
7. John G.,	b. Apr. 8, 1800.	d. Jul. 8, 1876.

Of these children, 2. **Abram**[7] d. at the age of 24, and probably never married; 3. **Mary**[7] m. a Mr. Proctor of Vermont, and had several children; and 5. **George**[7] was b. at Woodstock, Vt., and d. at Brookville, Ind. He m. 1st, Sally Hawley, who was b. in Massachusetts. He m. 2d, Mary ————. No issue.

†-1. **Nathaniel Jr.,**[7] b. in the Blue Hills, Me., at six years of age moved with his father to Vermont, and in 1820 to Indiana, where he d. at Rensselaer, Jasper Co., Feb. 2, 1874. He at first studied law, but afterwards studied and successfully practiced medicine for a number of years in Franklin and Bartholomew Cos., Ind. But being troubled with deafness, which increased with his years, he afterwards devoted his time to agricultural pursuits. He was a devout Christian, a great reader, and one of the best informed men of his time. He was thrice married. He m. 1st, Oct. 9, 1811, Patty Ball at Hartford, Vt., who was b. at Weston, Mass., Apr. 17, 1790, and d. at Brookville, Ind., Jun. 14, 1822. Issue :

1. Nath'l Allen,	b. Nov. 9, 1811.	d. Jun. 15, 1822.
2. Abram Adams,	b. Mch. 21, 1814.	d. Aug. 27, 1874.

3.	Sarah Ball,	b.	Aug.	9, 1816.	d.	Jun.	8, 1838.
4.	William Penn,	b.	Oct.	25, 1818.,	d.	Feb.	19, 1875.
5.	John Arnold,	b.	Oct.	14, 1821.	d.	Aug.	1, 1822.

Nathaniel m. 2d, Aug. 29, 1822, Hannah Van Meter, who was b. in Virginia, Jun. 29, 1794, and d. Sep. 21, 1831. Issue :

6.	George W.,	b.	Sep.	4, 1823.	d. Oct.	10, 1879.
7.	Martha Ann,	b.	Oct.	31, 1825.	d. May	24, 1890.
8.	David,	b.	Oct.	14, 1827.	d. Feb.	2, 1854.
9.	Mary,	b.	Jan.	8, 1830.		

Nathaniel m. 3d, May 29, 1832, Hannah H. Serring, who was b. Aug. 11, 1803, and d. in Rensselaer, Ind., Mch. 14, 1885. Issue :

10.	Henry,	b. Jul.	13, 1833.	d. Jul.	31, 1833.
11.	Ellen H.,	b. Aug.	30, 1834.	d. Sep.	19, 1834.
12.	Edwin Pollok,	b. Nov.	26, 1835.		
13.	Sarah L.,	b. Apr.	30, 1838.	d. May	1, 1874.
14.	Jane,	b. Feb.	26, 1840.		
15.	Elizabeth,	b. Mch.	1, 1842.	d. Jan.	15, 1885.
16.	Samuel,	b. May	26, 1845.	d.	young.

Of these children, Nath'l Allen was b. at Hartford, Vt. ; Abram Adams at Brattleboro', Vt. ; Sarah Ball and William Penn at Middlebury, Vt. ; and the others at Brookville, Franklin Co., Ind. Nath'l Allen, John Arnold, Henry, Ellen H., and Samuel d. young ; and Sarah Ball at the age of 22, single.

13. **Sarah L.,**[8] fifth daughter of Nathaniel Jr., m. Feb. 2, 1859, John Miller of Rensselaer, who d. there Mch. 18, 1878, æ. 50. Issue : May, Edith A., Halleck H., Jennie L., Albion, and Mary S.

14. **Jane**[8] m. 1st, Aug. 29, 1861, James G. Sale, who d. while in the Army at Bowling Green, Ky., Dec. 7, 1862. Issue : Frank G. Jane m. 2d, Apr. 24, 1870, Thomas E. Antrim, and resides in Norton, Kan. Issue : Charles Dickens.

†-1-15. **Elizabeth**[8] m. Sep. 27, 1865, Mordecai F. Chilcote, one of the leading attorneys-at-law at Rensselaer, Ind. Mr. Chilcote is a graduate of Olivette College, Michigan, and was a captain in the 42d Indiana Regiment, serving in the Departments of Tennessee and Virginia. Issue : Fred L. and Gaylord H.

†-1-2. **Abram Adams Hammond,**[8] second son of Nathaniel Jr., was b. at Brattleboro', Vt., Mch. 21, 1814.

Gov. Abram A. Hammond

He came to Indiana when six years old, and was raised at Brookville, where he studied law with John Ryman, a lawyer of note of that place. In 1835 he commenced the practice of law in Greenfield, Hancock Co. He afterwards was in partnership with various eminent lawyers, — including John H. Bradley, Hugh O'Neal, a celebrated criminal lawyer of his day, and Hon. Thomas H. Nelson, — and in various parts of the State of Indiana. He filled the position of Prosecuting Attorney while at Columbus with decided ability. In 1850 he was elected first Judge of the Court of Common Pleas for Marion Co. In 1855 he removed from San Francisco, Cal., where he had previously moved, to Terre Haute, Ind. In 1856 Mr. Hammond was nominated for Lieut.-Governor by the Democrats, he having gone over to that party after the dissolution of the Whig party in 1852. He made an active canvas and was elected Lieut.-Governor of Indiana, having given Mr. Douglas a weak support, not caring to follow the Breckenridge movement.

Gov. Willard d. at St. Paul, Minn., Oct. 5, 1860, and Mr. Hammond became Governor, serving until the inauguration of Gov. Lane, Jan. 14, 1861. His only message to the Legislature was an able and timely one. His recommendations were favorably received and acted upon by the Legislature.

In the election of 1860, Col. Henry S. Lane was elected Governor, and Oliver P. Morton Lieut.-Governor of Indiana. Five days after the delivery of Gov. Hammond's message Lieut.-Governor Morton became Governor by reason of the resignation of Governor Lane, who had been elected to the United States Senate.

About this time rheumatism fastened itself upon Gov. Hammond and never let go its hold; he even had to walk on crutches. He tried all manner of remedies but got no relief. After a while asthma attacked him, and in the Summer of 1874 he went to Colorado, hoping to be benefited by its climate, but the dry mountain air failed to work a cure. He d. at Denver, Aug. 27, 1874, and was buried in Indianapolis, Ind.

Gov. Hammond was not a showy man, but he was an able one, much abler than the public gave him credit for. He had a logical mind, and was remarkably clear in stating his positions and drawing his conclusions. He had not great learning, but he was a close observer of events, and during his life gathered a large mass of information; neither was he particularly well read in law, but he was a good lawyer, for he comprehended principles and was able to apply them in practice.

Gov. Hammond's residence was at Indianapolis, though he made several changes in the location of his business. He was a man that would have succeeded anywhere, for in ability he was far above most of his competitors at the bar.

Gov. Hammond was an unusually fine specimen of physical manhood. He walked with a spring, and moved with the agility of an athlete. He was of medium height, compactly built, and of dark complexion. His head was large and well-shaped. While the expression of his countenance was kind and gentle, it never betrayed passion or emotion. He was cool, deliberate and self-possessed, keeping his temper and feelings under perfect control. He was frank in his manners, honorable in his dealings, and dignified in his deportment. Although not one of the most learned Governors of Indiana, he was, by nature, one of the ablest.

Gov. Hammond m. Apr. 5, 1838, at Greenfield, Ind., Mary B. Amsden, who, after the death of her husband, resided at Denver, Col., with her daughter Mrs. Sweeney, and where she d. Feb. 4, 1890. Issue:

1. George,	b. Jun.	2, 1852.	
2. Mary,	b. in	1855.	d. in 1866.

1. **George,**[9] a girl, m. May 30, 1876, Anthony Sweeney, a fire insurance and real estate broker at Denver. No issue.

†-1-4. **William Penn,**[8] third son of Nathaniel Jr., was b. at Middlebury, Vt., Oct. 25, 1818: practiced law at Greenfield, Ind., from 1841 to 1843, and from the latter date to 1852 in Martinsville, Ind.: was in the Indiana Legislature about 1848; moved to Keokuk, Iowa, in 1852, and thence, about 1857, to Albia, Iowa, where he d. Feb. 19, 1875.

He m. Nov. 3, 1841, at Greenfield, Ind., Sarah J. Wooster, who was b. Mch. 10, 1824, and now resides at Los Angeles, Cal. Issue:

1. Mattie M.,	b. Oct.	29, 1842.	
2. Albert Hugh,	b. Nov.	29, 1844.	
3 Georgia C.,	b. Mch.	29, 1847.	d. May 20, 1870.
4. Mary E.,	b. Mch.	18, 1850.	
5. Colypso H.,	b. May	11, 1853.	d. Jul. 30, 1853.
6. Nathaniel,	b. Jun.	16, 1854.	d. Jun. 16, 1854.
7. Thomas Bell,	b. Sep.	5, 1856.	
8. Charles J.,	b. Feb.	13, 1861.	d. Jul. 11, 1862.
9. William E.,	b. Aug.	4, 1862.	d. Apr. 20, 1884.
10. Katie Y.,	b. Jul.	20, 1864.	

Mattie was b. at Greenfield, and Albert, Georgia, and Mary

WILLIAM PENN HAMMOND.

at Martinsville, Ind.; Colypso, Nathaniel, and Thomas at Keokuk, and William, Charles, and Katie at Albia, Iowa.

Of these children, **Thomas Bell**[9] is a book-keeper and stenographer, and resides at Los Angeles, Cal. He has never married.

1. **Mattie M.**[9] m. Jan. 1, 1860, Samuel L. Cramer, and lives at Ballard, Wash. Issue: Charles, George, and William Penn.

2. **Albert H.**[9] is a harnessmaker at East Los Angeles, Cal. He m. Oct. 14, 1887, Frances L. Gessler, but has no issue.

3. **Georgia C.**[9] m. Mch. 14, 1867, Harry L. Waterman, lived at Albia, and d. at Ottumwa, Wapello Co., Iowa. Issue: Philip, b. Mch. 14, 1868.

4. **Mary E.**[9] m. Jan. 14, 1868, Thomas W. Milburn, and lives at Raven Wood, Mo. Issue: Edwin P., Albert P., Pearl A., Edwin Fred., Roy, Earl, and Clifford.

10. **Katie Y.**[9] m. Aug. 18, 1880, Frank Humphreys, and resides at Los Angeles. Issue: George H.

†-1-6. **George W.**,[9] fifth son of Nathaniel Jr., was a farmer, and lived and d. near Alexandria, Madison Co., Ind. He m. Apr. 7, 1842, Rebecca A. Manering, who now resides at Alexandria, Monroe Township, Ind. Issue:

1. Nathaniel,	b. Mch. 25, 1843.	d. Aug. 4, 1843.
2. Ambrose M.,	b. Sep. 21, 1845.	
3. Mary J.,	b. May 29, 1848.	d. Oct. 8, 1890.
4. William T.,	b. Dec. 30, 1850.	d. Feb. 15, 1851.
5. Nancy C.,	b. Jan. 14, 1852.	d. Sep. 16, 1871.
6. George H.,	b. Sep. 12, 1854.	
7. Jessie C.,	b. Mch. 11, 1857.	
8. Charles,	b. Dec. 31, 1859.	d. Aug. 31, 1860.
9. Elmer E.,	b. Mch. 12, 1860.	
10. Richard G.,	b. Nov. 11, 1864.	
11. Lucy,	b. Jun. 13, 1867.	d. Jul. 6, 1867.

Of these children, **Jessie C.**,[9] single, resides with her mother at Alexandria, Madison Co., Ind.

2. **Ambrose M.**[9] is a carpenter, and lives at Alexandria. He m. Feb. 16, 1881, Almyra Lloyd, and had issue:

1. Cora E.,	b. Oct. 3, 1882.	
2. Georgia,	b. Apr. 27, 1885.	
3. Guy,	b. Jul. 16, 1889.	d. June 28, 1890.

3.   **Mary J.**[9] m. Aug. 24, 1866, Henry Babbitt, and lived at Newton, Harvey Co., Kan.   Issue: Charles H., b. Jun. 20, 1879.

6.   **George H.**[9] is a farmer in Monroe Township, Madison Co., Ind.   He m. Oct. 5, 1874, Eliza J. LaRue, and had issue:

1. Lillie M.,	b. May 1, 1875.	
2. Gertrude,	b. Sep. 8, 1879.	

9.   **Elmer E.**[9] is also a farmer in Monroe Township, Ind. He m. Aug. 8, 1886, Laura A. Foland, and had issue:

1. Jessie M.,	b. Jun. 14, 1887.	
2. Mary M.,	b. Nov. 14, 1889.	d. Feb. 7, 1890.

10.   **Richard G.**[9] is a clergyman in the Methodist Episcopal Church, and is now located at Plainfield, Hendricks Co., Ind.   He m. Mch. 31, 1889, Hortense A. Riggs, but has no issue.

†–1–7.   **Martha Ann,**[8] second daughter of Nathaniel Jr., m. 1st, Feb. 16, 1842, in Franklin Co., Ind., James M. Alley, who d. Oct. 5, 1842.   Issue:

1. Jennie,	b. Jan. 15, 1843.	d. Jan. 26, 1873.

Martha Ann m. 2d, Apr. 13, 1847, William Potts, who was b. Mch. 21, 1825, at Laurel, Ind.   He is a farmer, and lives near Greenfield, Ind.   Issue:

2. James K.,	b. Mch. 11, 1848.	d. Apr. 12, 1865.
3. George W.,	b. May 14, 1850.	
4. Mary E.,	b. Nov. 1, 1852.	
5. Edwin H.,	b. Dec. 17, 1854.	d. Nov. 18, 1889.
6. John W.,	b. Feb. 1, 1857.	
7. Belle H.,	b. Jul. 9, 1859.	
8. Alice,	b. Jan. 1, 1862.	
9. Lucy J.,	b. Mch. 5, 1864.	

Of these children, **Mary E.**[9] m. Oct. 2, 1872, Kepler Boyd; **John W.**[9] m. Mch. 12, 1881, Rebecca Elsbury; and **Belle H.**[9] m. Aug. 18, 1889, Prof. Alpheus Reynolds.

†–1–8.   **David,**[8] sixth son of Nathaniel Jr., was killed by the accidental discharge of a gun Feb. 2, 1864, in Jasper Co., Ind.   He m. Oct. 10, 1849, Nancy J. Sherwood, who d. about 1863.   Issue:

1. William E.,	b. Oct. 17, 1850.	d. Oct. 23, 1871.
2. John Edwin,	b. Feb. 11, 1853.	d. Apr. 19, 1870.

†-1-9. **Mary,**[3] third daughter of Nathaniel Jr., lives at Alexandria, Madison Co., Ind. She m. Dec. 25, 1845, James H. Manering, a farmer, who was b. in Kent Co., Del., Dec. 9, 1823. Issue:

1. Nathaniel H.,	b. Sep. 19, 1847.	
2. Ambrose A.,	b. Sep. 21, 1850.	
3. Martha C.,	b. Dec. 17, 1852.	
4. Sarah L.,	b. May 18, 1855.	d. May 19, 1855.
5. James W.,	b. Jun. 1, 1857.	
6. Elizabeth J.,	b. Mch. 18, 1859.	d. Mch. 19, 1859.
7. Ella N.,	b. Aug. 24, 1860.	
8. Edwin B.,	b. Jun. 30, 1863.	
9. Hannah B.,	b. Sep. 1, 1865.	d. Oct. 13, 1865.

Of these children, **Nathaniel H.**[9] is a physician residing in Grant Co., Ind.

†-1-12. **Edwin Pollok Hammond,**[8] eighth son of Nathaniel Jr., was b. at Brookville, Franklin Co., Ind., Nov. 26, 1835. Mr. Hammond in early life had fair school advantages, and with diligent application obtained a good education. In 1855 he studied law in the office of his half brother, Abram A. Hammond, in Terre Haute; and in 1856–7 was admitted to the senior law class of Asbury University at Greene Castle, and graduated with the degree of Bachelor of Laws. In 1858 he located at Rensselaer, Jasper Co., Ind., and opened a law office.

Upon the breaking out of the Rebellion Mr. Hammond enlisted in Co. G, 9th Ind. Volunteers, and was commissioned 2d, and afterwards 1st, Lieutenant, and served in the Three Months' Campaign, in West Virginia. He was with the force that surprised the Rebel Camp at Philippi, and in the engagement at Carrick's Ford, in which the Confederate General Garnett was killed. Returning to his home in Rensselaer, he resumed the practice of law. In 1861, he was elected as Representative in the Legislature from the Counties of Newton, Jasper and Pulaski. In 1862, he helped organize Co. A, 87th Ind. Volunteers, and was commissioned as Captain of the Company. He was promoted, Mch. 22, 1863, to the rank of Major, and Nov. 21, 1863, to that of Lieut. Colonel. The Regiment lost heavily in killed and wounded, in the battle of Chickamauga. Col. Newell Gleason, having been placed in charge of the brigade, Lieut.-Col. Hammond commanded the Regiment during the last year of the War. They were at Chattanooga, and at the siege of Atlanta, and with Sherman on his march to the sea.

Mr. Hammond enjoyed the respect and good-will of the officers and men under his command, and the confidence of his superior officers. At the close of the War, for gallant and meritorious services, he was appointed by the President to the Brevet rank of Colonel in the United States Volunteers. Col. Hammond again entered the practice of law in Rensselaer, and at once had a large business.

In March, 1873, Gov. Hendricks appointed Col. Hammond to be Judge of the 30th Judicial Circuit, which was ratified by the people at the next October election. In October, 1878, the Judge was unamiously re-elected. May 14, 1883, he was appointed Judge of the Supreme Court from the Fifth District, by Gov. A. G. Porter, to fill a vacancy. Judge Hammond is a Republican, and was a delegate to the National Convention in 1872, which nominated General Grant for his second term. In 1884, he was defeated for Judge of the Supreme Court, but received 5000 more votes than Blaine and others on the same ticket.

At the November election of 1890 he was elected Judge of the 30th Judicial Circuit for the term of six years. In August, 1892, he resigned the office of Circuit Judge, and formed a law partnership with Charles B. and William V. Stuart, under the firm name of Stuart Bros. and Hammond, with headquarters at Lafayette, Ind., where the Judge now resides. In June, 1892, Judge Hammond received the Degree of LL.D. from Wabash College, Indiana.

Judge Hammond m. 1st, Aug. 8, 1861, Lucy J. Sayler, who d. Jan. 3, 1863, æ. 22, without issue. He m. 2d, Mch. 1, 1864, Mary V. Spitler, who was b. at Rensselaer, Ind., Mch. 12, 1843. Mrs. Hammond is an able and accomplished lady, and highly cultivated in vocal and instrumental music. She was also one of the Board of Managers of the World's Fair, Women's Department for Indiana.   Issue :

1.	Louie,	b. Nov. 18, 1864.	
2.	Maude,	b. Apr. 16, 1868.	d. Sep. 6, 1869.
3	Mary A.,	b. Jul. 19, 1870.	
4.	Edwin P., Jr.,	b. Mch. 2, 1873.	
5.	Jean,	b. Aug. 16, 1875.	
6.	Nina Van R.,	b. Feb. 29, 1880.	

Of these children, 1. **Louie**[9] m. Nov. 7, 1882, William B. Austen, who was b. at Rensselaer, Ind., Apr. 21, 1860. Mr. Austen graduated at Wabash College, Indiana, Jun. 22, 1881, and is an attorney-at-law at Rensselaer. Issue : Virginia, b. Aug. 25, 1883.

COL. EDWIN P. HAMMOND.

†–4. **David,**[7] third son of Nathaniel Sr., b. at Woodstock, Vt., moved to Reading, and became a prominent man in the town. He was extensively engaged in the manufacture of shoes, and was also interested in farming. He was afterwards interested in the manufacture of shoes at Windsor, Vt., although he resided at Reading, and d. there Oct. 20, 1854, æ. 62. He m. Alice Stone, who was b. in 1793, and d. Jan. 7, 1864, æ. 71. Issue:

1. George A.,	b. Aug. —, 1816.	d. Feb. 18, 1817.
2. George Augustus,	b. Sep. 28, 1818.	d. Mch. 29, 1819.
3. Augusta,	b. Apr. 16, 1820.	d. May 18, 1850.
4. Mary,	b. Oct. 16, 1822.	d. Nov. 12, 1891.
5. Samuel Albro,	b. Aug. 16, 1825.	
6. Edmund Stone,	b. Apr. 16, 1828.	
7. Oliver Bailey,	b. Apr. 20, 1830.	d. Sep. 26, 1852.
8. Frederic C.,	b. Apr. —, 1833.	d. Jan. 18, 1861.
9. George Henry,	b. Apr. 9, 1837.	

Of these children, Mary and Oliver Bailey d. single, at Reading.

3. **Augusta**[8] m. Oct. 2, 1838, James Lawrence Hartwell of Reading, Vt., and lived at Windsor, Vt. Issue: Alice Augusta, Mary Ellen, Charles Gale, James Lawrence Jr., Frank, and Alice Augusta 2d. These children all d. young, except **Mary Ellen,**[9] who m. Nov. 13, 1867, Theodore H. Sayre, and lives in New York City.

†–4–8. **Frederic C.,**[8] sixth son of David, was a hotel-keeper, and lived at Belvidere, Ill. He m. Susan Downer of of Weathersfield, Vt., and d. without issue.

†–4–5. **Samuel Albro,**[8] third son of David, is a farmer and stock-raiser, and lives at Le Mars, Plymouth Co., Iowa. He m. 1st, Nov. 10, 1851, Mary Louisa Hapgood, who was b. Jul. 30, 1827, and d. Apr. 28, 1857. Issue:

1 David,	b. Mch. 21, 1855.

Samuel A. m. 2d, Nov. 1863, Salome F. Hapgood, a cousin of his first wife, who was b. Dec. 9, 1826, and d. Dec. 28, 1876. He m. 3d, Sep. 25, 1878, Mrs. S. J. Benton, who was b. in Wethersfield, Conn., Apr. 28, 1831. No issue by the second and third marriages.

†–4–5–1. **David,**[9] son of Samuel A., is a farmer and stock-raiser with his father at Le Mars. He m. Apr. 7, 1881, Lizzie M. Benton, who was b. Dec. 24, 1861, and d. Apr. 15, 1887. Issue:

1. Mabel B.,	b. Sep. 19, 1882.	
2. Chester H.,	b. Jun. 3, 1884.	
3. Louise S. H.,	b. Aug. 16, 1886.	

†–4–6. **Edmund Stone,**[8] fourth son of David, lives at Reading, Vt., and is one of the most extensive farmers in town, and has been largely engaged in the breeding of Merino sheep. He was for several years one of the selectmen of the town of Reading. He m. Feb. 26, 1852, Jane Mandana Shedd, who was b. Apr. 16, 1833. Issue:

1. Oliver Guy,	b. Oct. 26, 1855.	d. Jun. 29, 1878.
2. Dwight S.,	b. Mch. 8, 1859.	

Of these children, **Oliver Guy**[9] d. single at Reading.

2. **Dwight S.,**[9] is a farmer, and lives at Felchville, Vt. He m. Sep. 9, 1880, Ida J. Barnes. No issue.

†–4–9. **George Henry,**[8] seventh son of David, is a butcher, and resides at Springfield, Vt. He m. in 1862, Ann Eliza Clark, and had issue:

1. Fred Collamer,	b. Mch. 24. 1863.	
2. John Nathaniel,	b. Mch. 11, 1865.	

1. **Fred Collamer**[9] is a machinist, and resides at Reading. He m. Jan. 5, 1883, Carrie Ellen Slade of Springfield, Vt., and had issue:

1. George Allan,	b. May 30, 1887.	
2. Ruth,	b. Dec. 10, 1890.	

2. **John Nathaniel**[9] is a butcher with his father at Springfield. He m. Nov. 8, 1882, Emma Safford of Springfield, and had issue: Alice Stone and Georgia Anna, both of whom d. young.

†–6. **Henry Clinton,**[7] fifth son of Nathaniel Sr., b. in Woodstock, Vt., was an eminent lawyer in Indiana, and d. at Wappelo, Iowa, Jun. 1844. He m. in 1820, Mehetable B. Thomas, who was b. in Pennsylvania, Feb. 27, 1798, and d. in Milford, Butler Co., Ohio, Jun. 11, 1841. Issue:

1. Mary Adams,	b. Nov. 19, 1821.	d. Aug. 14, 1839.
2. Elvira Thomas,	b. Jul. 5, 1823.	
3. John Q. Adams,	b Apr. 13, 1825.	d. Nov. 15, 1850.
4. George Clinton,	b. May 20. 1827.	d. Mch. 3, 1875.
5. Eveline Tredway,	b. Jul. 8, 1829.	
6. Thomas Harrison G.,	b. Sep. 16, 1831.	
7. Augustus Adelia,	b. Dec. 27. 1833.	d. Dec. 16, 1856.
8. Aurelia Teresa,	b. Jun. 9, 1839.	d. Sep. 18, 1839.

Of these children, born in Brownsville, Union Co., Ind.. **Mary Adams**[8] d. single, and **Aurelia Teresa**[8] d. young.

†–6–3. **John Q. Adams,**[8] oldest son of Henry Clinton, in 1845 moved from Wappelo, Iowa, to Waukegan, Ill. In 1849 he went to California, and, while returning, d. on board ship Nov. 15, 1850, and was buried at sea.

†–6–2. **Elvira Thomas,**[8] m. in Milford, Ohio, Apr. 2, 1845, Thomas H. Boone, who was b. in County Derry, Ireland, Mch. 14, 1823, and d. at Dousman, Waukesha Co., Wis., Jun. 28, 1890, and was a Protestant of Scotch descent. Mrs. Boone, soon after her marriage, moved with her father and remaining family to Wappelo, Louisa Co., Iowa, and afterwards to Dousman, Wis., where all her children were born except the oldest. Issue :

1. Alice J.,	b. Dec. 17, 1845.	
2. George H.,	b. Jan. 28, 1856.	
3. Eva J.,	b. Apr. 21, 1858.	d. May 29, 1890.
4. Gussie E.,	b. Dec. 31, 1859.	
5. Mary A.,	b. Dec. 26, 1861.	
6. Lizzie L.,	b. Jan. 27, 1866.	

Of these children, **Alice J.**[9] m. Apr. 5, 1871, William M. Jacques, and lives in West Olive, Mich. No issue.

2. **George H.**[9] m. Oct. 17, 1884, Nellie M. Doe in Big Rapids, Mich., and lives in Waukesha, Wis. No issue.

3. **Eva J.**[9] m. in 1882, Thomas Edmonds, and d. at Jeffersonville, Ind., May 29, 1890. Issue : Evelyn Elvira.

5. **Mary A.,**[9] or Mamie, m. Nov. 26, 1885, Henry D. Howell, and lives at Waukesha. No issue.

6. **Lizzie L.**[9] m. Sep. 4, 1889, Warren Wheeler, and lives in Waukesha. Issue : Dora May. **Gussie**[9] lives at home with her mother.

†–6–4. **George Clinton,**[8] second son of Henry Clinton, was a carriagemaker, and lived in Dayton, Ohio, till 1855, when he returned to Janesville, Wis., where he died. He m. in 1851, Martha Gosling, and had issue :

1. Nellie Laura,	b. Mch. 27, 1858.
2. George S.,	b. Jun. 9, 1865.
3. Edith Bird,	b. Jun. 10. 1870.

Of these children, **George S.**[9] is agent for a tobacco firm with headquarters at St. Paul, Minn.: and **Edith Bird**[9] lives with her sister in Chicago, both single.

1. **Nellie Laura,**[9] oldest daughter of George C., m. at Watertown, Wis., May 18, 1882, Newton Partridge, who was b. Mch. 23, 1852, and is a lawyer at Chicago. Mr. Partridge has recently been elected professor in the legal department of the North Western University, Chicago. Issue:

> 1. Edith Alice,   b. Aug. 24, 1883.
> 2. Edgar Hammond,   b. Nov. 6, 1885.
> 3. Newton Lyman,   b. Dec. 10, 1890.

†-6-5. **Eveline Treadway**[8] m. Mch. 7, 1850, Samuel Stewart, a Protestant of Scotch descent, who d. Apr. 15, 1892, and resides at Ottowa, Wis., near her sister Mrs. Boone. Issue: Lizzie M., Hettie J., Gussie A., Ella E., Clinton D., Lucy A., Harrison J., Charles S. and Arthur W.

Of these children, **Gussie A.**[9] m. Adelbert Tuthill, and has two daughters: Lela and ———; **Lizzie**[9] m. Jos. Kennedy, and had: Eva, Lottie and Wilbur; **Hettie**[9] m. Andrew Kennedy, and had: Clifford and Lucy. **Ella E.**[9] m. Walter Jones, and has a daughter: Edith Eveline; **Lucy A.**[9] m. Dec. 1889, Rev. T. D. Williams, and has a son: Samuel Stewart; **Harry**[9] is in Chicago; and **Clinton**[9] and **Charles**[9] are at home.

†-6-6. **Thomas Harrison,**[8] third son of Henry Clinton, was formerly a carriage-trimmer, and resided at Dayton, Ohio. In 1856 he moved from Dayton to Janesville, Wis., and after several years to Oshkosh. A few years later he moved on to a ranch at Redlands, Cal., where he is now a fruit-grower. He m. at Madison, Wis., in 1858, Emily Fergason, and had issue:

> 1. Ella A.,   b. Sep. 9, 1860.
> 2. Lottie,   b. Dec. 16, 1868.

1. **Ella Augusta**[9] m. Sep. 17, 1890, Edward Glover Judson, an enterprising business man, and at present Mayor of Redlands. Issue:

> 1. Henry Hammond,   b. Jan. 1, 1892.

2. **Lottie**[9] m. Apr. 1887, Francis Townsend of Redlands, and now resides at Los Angeles. Issue:

> 1. Mabel,   b. Jun. 1, 1888.

†–6–7. **Augusta Adelia,**[8] fourth daughter of Henry Clinton, m. Dec. 16, 1854, Charles West, and d. in Venice, Ohio, Dec. 16, 1858. Issue:

1. Emma A.,   b. Mch. 11, 1856.
2. Addie R.,   b. Jun. 18, 1857.

Of these children, **Addie R.**[9] lives single at Bushnell, Ill., and **Emma A.**[9] m. in 1876, John Chapman at Big Rapids, Mich., where they lived several years. They afterwards moved to Knoxville, Tenn., and thence to Albany, Ore., where they now reside. Issue: Holley West and Altha Emma.

†–7. **John G.,**[7] sixth son of Nathaniel Sr., was b. at Woodstock, Vt., Apr. 8, 1800, and d. at Brookville, Ind., Jul. 8, 1876. While a soldier in the Florida War, he was wounded, and after returning home drew a pension. He afterwards settled down to steady life, and spent a portion of his time in farming at Brookville. He m. Mch. 15, 1840, Charlotte Davies, who was b. in 1806, and is still living, at Metamora, Franklin Co., Ind. Issue:

1. Nathaniel R.,   b. Aug. 22, 1841.   d. Feb. 10. 1862.
2. Abram,   b. May 17, 1842.
3. William Penn, b Feb. 6, 1844.
4. Sarah A.,   b. Jan. 10, 1846.
5. John,   b. Jun. 29, 1848.
6. Robert M.,   b. Jun. 1, 1852.
7. Augusta,   b. Jan. 1, 1856.

The above children were b. at Brookville, except Augusta, who was b. at Metamora.

†–7–2. **Abram,**[8] second son of John G., is a farmer, and lives at Muncie, Delaware Co., Ind. He m. Mch. 1, 1868, Charlotte Mathews, and had issue:

1. William E.,   b. Dec. 12, 1868.
2. David,   b. Oct. 4, 1870.
3. Samuel,   b. Dec. 11, 1877.
4. Mary C.,   b. Jan. 10, 1879.

†–7–3. **William Penn,**[8] third son of John G., is a farmer, and resides near Metamora. He m. Sep. 21, 1865, Elizabeth Lacy, and had issue:

1. Kattie,   b. Sep. 2, 1866.
2. William H., b. Jan. 29, 1868.
3. John G.,   b. May 17, 1871.

11

†-7-4. **Sarah A.,**[8] oldest daughter of John G., m. Mch. 9, 1862, N. P. Force of Metamora, and resides at Oak Forest, Franklin Co., Ind. Issue :

    1. Alice C.,   b. Aug. 18, 1865.
    2. Albert J.,   b. Dec. 17, 1870.

†-7-5. **John,**[8] fourth son of John G., is an extensive farmer, and resides at Metamora. He m. Feb. 1, 1869, Maria Matthews, and had issue :

    1. Marshall,   b. Sep. 8, 1871.   d. Jul. 4, 1891.
    2. Kate,   b. Jul. 4, 1873.
    3. Ellen,   b. Jun. 5, 1875.
    4. Cora,   b. Sep. 26, 1877.
    5. Mary,   b. Apr. 22, 1879.

†-7-6. **Robert M.,**[8] fifth son of John G., is a farmer, and lived recently at Delena, Ark. He m. Sep. 20, 1878, Mary Bright, and had issue :

    1. Nathaniel L.,   b. Dec. 28, 1879.
    2. Blanche,   b. Jul. 20, 1881.

†-7-7, **Augusta,**[8] second daughter of John G., m. Feb. 14, 1878, Henry Lacy, and lives at Metamora. Issue :

    1. Mabel,   b. Dec. 13, 1878.
    2. Otis,   b. Feb. 5, 1879.
    3. Flora,   b. Jan. 10, 1881.
    4. Alice,   b. Feb. 20, 1883.

(2.)—STEPHEN HAMMOND OF HARDWICK, MASS.

†. **Stephen,**[6] second son of Faunce,[5] [Jabez,[4] John,[3] Benjamin,[2] William[1]], who was b. in Rochester, Mass., and lived and d. in Hardwick, Mass., was a manufacturer and seller of boots and shoes. He m. about 1790 Hannah Stone, who was b. in 1766, and d. Oct. 1848, in Copenhagen, N. Y. Issue :

    1. Submit,   b. Mch 7, 1791.   d. May —, 1879.
    2. Hannah,   b. Mch. 23, 1792.   d. Nov. 7, 1885.
    3. Larissa,   b. May —, 1793.   d. in   1878.
    4. Stephen, Jr.,   b. Jun. 16, 1797.   d. Mch. 20, 1883.
    5. Elias,   b. Jun. 28, 1799.   d. Dec. 12, 1837.
    6. Mary,   b. Sep. —, 1801.   d. in   1840.
    7. Eliza,   b. Aug. 12, 1803.   d. Jun. 28, 1873.
    8. Sarah S.,   b. Sep. 23, 1806.   d. Feb. 18, 1892.

†–1. **Submit,**[7] who lived at Copenhagen, N. Y., m. 1st, Jun. 1834, Jared Knapp, who d. Mch. 27, 1859. She m. 2d, in 1861, Levi Robbins, and d. at Copenhagen, May 1879. No issue.

†–2. **Hannah,**[7] who lived and d. at Windsor, Vt., m. Mch. 3, 1814, James Wardner, who was b. May 12, 1791. Issue: Frederic, Fanny, Laura, Mary, Frank Homer, Charles, James Sullivan, George Waldo, Eliza, Shubael and Byron Ferdinand.

†–3. **Larissa**[7] lived at Colerain, Mass., and d. at Brattleboro', Vt. She m. Ignatius Perkins of Colerain, and had issue: Larissa, James, Maria, Mary, George, Caroline, Charles, Elias and Sarah.

†–6. **Mary,**[7] who lived and d. at Hardwick, Mass., m. Timothy Fay, and left six children: James, Maria, Stephen, Rhoda J., Larissa and Augusta.

†–7. **Eliza,**[7] who lived and d. at Watertown, N. Y., m. Feb. 1830, Darius Sherwin, who was b. Jan. 29, 1831. Issue: Mary E., b. May 4, 1833. Mary E. m. ——— Keyes, and resides at Petoskey, Mich.

†–8. **Sarah S.**[7] m. Feb. 19, 1824, Gilbert Stafford, and lived and d. at Ceres, Cal. Issue: Larissa H., William G., Franklin, Aurelia and Aureeta, twins, Sarah E., Mary S., Ignatius P., and Submit L.

†–4. **Stephen Jr.,**[7] oldest son of Stephen, was a blacksmith, and lived and d. at Copenhagen, N. Y. He m. 1st, in 1828, Harriet Bledgett, who d. in the Fall of 1851. Issue:

1. William M., b. Jul. 6, 1829. d. Nov. 23, 1882.
2. Irene, b. Jun. —, 1832.

Of these children, **Irene** resides, single, at Copenhagen.

1. **William M.**[8] was a woolen merchant, and lived in New York. He m. Jul. 24, 1860, Emily L. Sikes, and had two sons, one of whom d. in infancy. Issue:

1. Fred S., b. Mch. 17, 1862.

Fred S.,[9] who is a life insurance agent, m. Jul. 9, 1881, Mary Tazer, and had one daughter, who d. young.

Stephen Jr. m. 2d, in 1853, Linda Munger, and had issue:

3. Ida H.,   b. Jan. 19, 1854.
4. Frank H., ⎫
5. Fred H., ⎬   b. Jul. 4, 1856.
6. Linda H.,   b. Sep. 25, 1858.

After the death of their mother, which occurred soon after Linda's birth, Ida was adopted by her uncle Nelson Munger, and took the name of Ida Munger; Frank was adopted by his mother's cousin, Josiah Rich, and his name became Frank H. Rich; a family by the name of Perkins adopted Fred and Linda, and they took the name of Perkins.

3. **Ida H.,**[8] second daughter of Stephen Jr., was b. at Adams, Jefferson Co., N. Y., and resides at Watertown. She m. Jun. 10, 1874, Charles E. Holbrook, a printer. Issue: Henry M., Charles W., and Raymond H.

4. **Frank H.**[8] keeps a livery stable, and resides at Lowville, Lewis Co., N. Y. He m. Apr. 25, 1877, Lucinda Chamberlain, and had issue:

1. Floyd,   b. Mch. 30, 1879.

5. **Fred H.**[8] is pastor of the Methodist Episcopal Church at Williamsport, Penn. He m. Nov. 23, 1876, Elizabeth McIntrye. No issue.

6. **Linda H.**[8] m. Feb. 16, 1875, William Smart, a farmer at Rose, Wayne Co., N. Y. Issue:

1. Nellie,   b. Jun. 1, 1876

†–5. **Elias,**[7] second son of Stephen, was a tanner and shoemaker, and lived and d. at Leroy, N. Y. He m. at Shelburne, Mass., Sep. 20, 1825, Mercy Allen, who was b. Feb. 24, 1802, and d. Jan. 14, 1892. Issue:

1. Martha Ann,   b. May 8, 1827.
2. Maria,   b. Jul. 3, 1831.
3. Stephen H.,   b. Apr. 5, 1834.

After the death of Elias, the family returned to Shelburne, Mass.

1. **Martha Ann**[8] m. 1st, George Roberts, and lived at Colerain. Issue: Charles, Clifford, Stephen, Noah, Porter, Martha, and Fidelia.
Martha m. 2d, about 1886, William R. Whittaker of East Wilmington, Vt., where they now reside. No further issue.

LEWIS M. HAMMOND.

2. **Maria**[3] m. Henry Baldwin, and lives in Cleveland, Ohio. Issue: Lillie, Jennie, and George.

3. **Stephen H.**[3] is a boot and shoe dealer at Springfield, Mass. He m. 1st, Jun. 10, 1869, Caroline James of Providence, R. I., who d. in 1873. He m. 2d, Feb. 14, 1877, Louise Warren of Leicester, Mass., who d. about 1884. He m. 3d, Oct. 13, 1888, Mrs. J. F. Baker of Springfield, who d. Jan. 10, 1890. No issue by either marriage.

(6.)—JABEZ HOLMES HAMMOND OF WINDSOR, VT.

†. **Jabez Holmes**,[6] fourth son of Faunce,[5] [Jabez,[4] John,[3] Benjamin,[2] William[1]], was b. at Rochester, Mass., May 1, 1773, moved to Windsor, Vt., and d. at West Windsor, Oct. 25, 1841. He m. about 1796 Mary Rowe, who was b. Apr. 22, 1773, and d. Aug. 30, 1839. Issue:

1. Faunce,	b. Jan. 8, 1797.	d. Dec. 10, 1874.
2. Celia,	b. Apr. 23, 1798.	d Oct. 18, 1813.
3 Calvin,	b. Feb. 16, 1800.	d. Mch. 4, 1871.
4. Stephen,	b. Jun. 14, 1801.	d. Oct. 14, 1875.
5. Jiry,	b. Nov. 14, 1802.	d. Nov. 26, 1868.
6. Dudley,	b. Feb. 21, 1804.	d. Feb. 26, 1804.
7. Jabez,	b. Jan. 31, 1805.	d. Nov. 29, 1813.
8. Holmes,	b. Jan. 17, 1807.	d. Jan. 25, 1892.
9. James,	b. Aug. 18, 1808.	d. Apr. 27, 1872.
10. Elon Oscar,	b. Mch. 25. 1811.	d. Mch. 20, 1872.
11. Daniel.	b. Jul. 14, 1812.	d. Apr. 13, 1882.
12. Jabez 2d.	b. Jun. 15, 1815.	d. Aug. 12, 1893.

Of these children, Celia, Faunce and Calvin were b. at Windsor, Vt.; Stephen and Jiry at Woodstock; Dudley at Reading; and the remaining children at West Windsor.

†-1. **Faunce**,[7] oldest son of Jabez Holmes, was a shoemaker at Windsor and Woodstock, and d. at Greensborough, Vt. He m. Jul. 20, 1818, Clarissa Thompson, who was b. Nov. 29, 1795, and d. at Lowell, Mass., Feb. 11, 1883. Issue:

1. Stephen Frederic,	b. Mch. 30, 1820.	d. Nov. 21, 1844.
2. Celia Francis,	b. May 28, 1821.	d. Jan. 30, 1881.
3. Clara Sulia,	b. Dec. 13, 1822.	d. Jun. 4, 1889.
4. Mary Jane,	b. Nov. 20, 1824.	
5. Elon Oscar Eells,	b. May 19, 1826.	
6. Susanna Artemisa,	b. Jul. 15, 1828.	
7. Jabez Faunce,	b. May 17, 1831.	
8. John Melville.	b. Mch. 30, 1834.	
9. Zacheus Dudley,	b. Nov. 24, 1836.	d. Jan. 18, 1843.

Of these children, **Clara Sulia**[8] m. Jan. 1, 1846, Philip D. Badger, and d. at Greensborough, Vt., without issue. **Stephen F.**[8] d. single, at Greensborough, Vt.

†-1-2. **Celia Francis**[8] m. Jan. 7, 1857, Eugene Allen Fisher of St. Albans, Vt. She lived at Greensborough, Vt., West Broome and Sweetsburg, Que., and d. at Dunboro, P. Q. Issue:

1. Henrietta,	b. Sep. 18, 1859.	
2. George Edward,	b. May 16, 1861.	
3. Eugene Allen,	b. May 2, 1862.	d. Jun. 18, 1866.
4. Geo. Wash. Wilson, Jr.,	b. Feb. 14, 1868.	

†-1-4. **Mary Jane**[8] m. Jan. 17, 1854, Stephen Foster Collier, and lives in Greensborough, Vt. Issue:

1. Stephen Fred'c,	b. Nov. 14, 1854.	d. Dec. 8, 1880.
2. Frank Foster,	b. Mch. 13, 1856.	d. Nov. 18, 1869.
3. Minnie Ellwya.	b. Feb. 21, 1858.	
4. Thomas Faunce H'd,	b. Oct. 24, 1859.	d. Jul. 16, 1818.
5. Clarissa Jane,	b. May 17, 1861.	
6. Mary Elsie Kezia,	b Sep. 1, 1862.	d. May 3, 1885.
7. Hattie Ameda.	b. Oct. 23, 1864.	

Of these children, **Minnie E.**[9] m. May 7, 1891, John A. Campbell.

†-1-5. **Elon Oscar Eells**[8] is a carpenter, and lives at West Derby, Vt. He m. Nov. 12, 1849, Martha Ann Cole, who was b. at Salem, Vt., Dec. 15, 1826. Issue:

1. Leona Adella,	b. Aug. 10, 1851.	
2. Lilla Ophelia,	b. Jun. 14, 1854.	d. Aug. 30, 1854.
3. Dora Inez.	b. Jun. 22, 1857.	
4. Fred Bertrum,	b. Oct. 12, 1859.	
5. Willie Palmer,	b. Nov. 7, 1861.	
6. Elon Alanthus,	b. Jul. 12, 1869.	

1. **Leona A.**[9] m. Mch. 15, 1867, Frank Wheelock, and had issue: Burnice and Hattie.

3. **Dora Inez**[9] m. Jan. 1, 1878, Clarence Charles Tower of Rochester, Vt., and lives at West Derby, Vt. Issue: Alton, Ines, Theodore, and Benjamin.

4. **Fred Bertrum**[9] is a merchant, and lives at South Troy, Vt. He m. May 1, 1884, Frances A. Chandler, who was b. Oct. 8, 1865. Issue:

1. Arline H.,	b. Nov. 3, 1886.

5. **Willie Palmer**⁹ is a travelling salesman for the Lovell M'f'g Co., and lives at Milwaukee, Wis. He m. Jan. 16, 1886, Nellie Conner, who was b. in Plymouth, Ind., Nov. 10, 1863. Issue:

1. Harry Grover, b. Sep. 6, 1888.
2. Ethel May, b. Oct. 31, 1890.

6. **Elon A.**⁹ is a carpenter, and lives at Barre, Vt. He m. Jan. 1, 1890, Ella Marrett, and had issue:

1. Lucretia P., b. Jul. 25, 1891.

†-1-6. **Susanna Artemisa,**⁷ fourth daughter of Faunce, lives at Highlands, Col. She m. at Lowell, Mass., Oct. 15, 1854, Joel Washington Chaffee, who was b. at Roxbury, Vt., Aug. 25, 1834. Issue:

1. Namena Silvene, b. Jul. 24, 1859.
2. Onia F. W., b. Mch. 2, 1861.
3. Clarissa Abigail, b. Mch. 7, 1863.
4. Philip H., b. May 11, 1881. d. Jun. 13, 1887.

Of these children, **Namena Silvene**⁹ m. Jan. 11, 1884, Amos L. Parker of St. Johnsbury, Vt.; and **Onia F. W.**⁹ m. Nov. 21, 1884, Laura Maria D'Rosia of North Adams, Mass. Issue: Bessie and Milt.

†-1-7. **Jabez Faunce,**⁷ third son of Faunce, is a farmer, and resides at Coplin, Me. He m. at Lowell, Mass., Feb. 1, 1857, Mary F. W. Hinds, daughter of Lisdale L. Hinds of Kingfield, Me. Issue:

1. Inez Adelaide, b. Jun. 21, 1858. d. Jan. 10, 1863.
2. Charles Henry, b. Aug. 31, 1859.
3. Etta Susie, b. Jan. 22, 1862.
4. Lamont Faunce, b. Mch. 23, 1864.
5. Nellie Cutler, b. Aug. 24, 1866.
6. Elon Bartlett, b. Apr. 1, 1869.

2. **Charles Henry,**⁹ is a farmer at Coplin, Me. He m. at Coplin, Oct. 31, 1885, Ellie S. Taylor. Issue:

1. Nellie Blanche, b. Apr. 16, 1886.
2. Nora May, b. May 10, 1888.
3. Dau., b. Oct. 20, 1891. d. Jan. 22, 1892.

3. **Etta Susie**⁹, who lives at Flagstaff, Me., m. Jan. 1, 1885, John R. Viles, son of Asa Viles of Madison, Me. Issue:

1. Harry L., b. Sep. 2, 1886. d. May 13, 1888.
2. Glenn R., b. Oct. 21, 1888.
3. Leah Verna, b. Mch. 29, 1891.

4. **Lamont Faunce**[9] is a lumberman and farmer at Flagstaff, Me. He m. May 7, 1888, Nira M. Viles of Flagstaff, Me. Issue:

    1. Hugh Faunce,   b. Mch. 29, 1890.

†-1-8. **John Melville**,[8] fourth son of Faunce, is a clergyman, and resides at Brownsdale, Minn. He m. 1st, Aug. 15, 1859, Helen G. Fairbrother of Brownington, Vt. Issue:

    1. Annie L.,   b. Sep. —, 1859.   d. Apr. —, 1869.
    2. George Herbert.   b. Jul. 21, 1865.
    3. Leora Belle,   b. Jan. 8, 1868.
    4. Gertrude L.,   b. Nov. 20, 1872.   d.

John M., having obtained a divorce from his first wife, m. 2d, Dec. 15, 1879, Mrs. Mary S. Leroy at Lowell, Mass. Issue:

    5. Fred Elwyn,   b. Apr. 26, 1881.

Of these children, Annie L. was b. at Coventry, George Herbert at Craftsbury, and Leora B. and Gertrude L. at Barton Landing, Vt.; and Fred Elwyn at Lowell, Mass.

†-3. **Calvin Hammond**,[7] second son of Jabez Holmes, was a farmer and laborer, and was born, lived and died at West Windsor, Vt. He m. Jan. 1, 1829, Lucy McGrath, who was b. Mch. 31, 1810, and d. Oct. 16, 1873. Issue:

    1. Henry Holmes,   b. Sep. 5, 1830.
    2. Lucy Ann,   b. Nov. 9, 1832.   d. Nov. 28, 1881.
    3 Sarah Lovina,   b. Apr. 30, 1837.
    4. Melissa Sophia.   b. Apr. 22, 1839.
    5. Augusta Melinda,   b. Feb. 11, 1848.

Of these children,

†-3-1. **Henry Holmes**,[6] who is a farmer and carpenter at West Windsor, Vt., m. Aug. 31, 1863, Caroline F. Bellows, who was b. Apr. 3, 1849. Issue:

    1. Henry Foster,   b. May 15, 1865.
    2. Clarence Arthur,   b. May 9, 1869.   d. Mch. 17, 1885.
    3. Carl Wade,   b. Sep. 9, 1871.

†-3-2. **Lucy Ann**[8] m. in 1854 Hiram Soule, and had: Charles, Alma, Cora, and Mary.

†-3-3. **Sarah Lovina**[8] m. Nov. 4, 1854, David G. Gardner, who was b. Jul. 14, 1838, and d. Jan. 22, 1884. Issue: D. Clinton, Lindon E., Ida M., and Frank L.

CARR LYALL HAMMOND.

†–3–4. **Melissa Sophia** m. Nov. 28, 1856, Allen Gardner, and had: Juliette E., Henrietta, George and Henry, twins, Lucy Emma, and Mabel Melissa.

†–3–5. **Augusta Melinda** m. Jan. 1, 1875, Lewis McGrath. No issue.

All the children of Calvin Hammond resided at West Windsor, Vt.

†–4. **Stephen,** third son of Jabez Holmes, was b. at Woodstock, Vt., Jun. 14, 1801, and d. at Clinton Junction, Rock Co., Wis., Oct. 14, 1875. In 1835 he moved to Lawrence, St. Lawrence Co., N. Y., where he carried on farming principally, but was a builder to some extent. In Jun. 1854, he removed to Clinton Junction, and pursued the calling of a farmer until failing health compelled him to abandon labor about 1865. He acquired a competence, and lived in comparative quiet during the evening of his life. He was a consistent Christian and prominent in Church work, being for nearly fifty years a member of the Baptist Church.

His widow, living at Chicago at the age of 86 with her son Lewis M. Hammond, enjoys good health, reads the finest print without the aid of spectacles, and devotes her days to doing all in her power to alleviate the unfortunate, — a grand, noble woman, full of many years and good works.* Stephen Hammond m. Jun. 14, 1824, Lovina McGrath at Windsor, Vt. Issue :

1. George Washington,	b. Mch. 22, 1825.
2. Lewis Morelle,	b. Dec. 12, 1835.
3. Stephen Ford,	b. Jan. 20, 1843.

†–4–1. **George Washington,** b. at Windsor, Vt., at 21 was employed in the foundry of Hammond & Draper at Windsor, Vt. In 1854 he moved first to Wisconsin, and afterwards to Iowa, where he bought a large tract of land near Maquoketa. In 1857 he moved to Lyons, Iowa, and for about 15 years dealt in merchandise, after which he retired to his beautiful fruit farm about a mile from the city, where he now resides. He m. Jul. 4, 1849, Mary Adams at Lawrence, N. Y. Issue :

1. Emma,	b. May 3, 1853.	
2. Frank,	b. Mch. 12, 1864.	d. Feb. 23, 1867.

* She d. Dec. 4, 1892, and was buried at Clinton, Wis.

1. **Emma**[9] m. Oct. 22, 1890, D. B. Bishop at Lyons, Iowa, and resides at North Williston, Vt.

†-4-2. **Lewis Morelle,**[8] second son of Stephen, b. in Lawrence, St. Lawrence Co., N. Y., lived there, and in Potsdam, N. Y., until the Spring of 1853, when he removed to Clinton, Wis., where he remained the next ten years. In 1868 he moved to Janesville, and was engaged in the Internal Revenue Dept. until Nov. 1873; then moved to Milwaukee and engaged in life insurance; in 1880 removed to Chicago, where he has since resided, having been for the last seven years a coal shipper. Business and pleasure trips have taken him to nearly every State and Territory in the Union. In the Summer of 1888 he took a trip through Continental Europe, returning to business in the Fall of that year.

Lewis Morelle m. Apr. 27, 1858, Esther L. Willis at Clinton Junction, Wis., who d. Jan. 10, 1888, at Chicago. Issue:

1. Carr Lyall,	b. Jan. 24, 1861.	d. Mch. 22, 1888.
2. Rollin Gage,	b. Oct. 11, 1862.	d. Apr. 10, 1863.
3. Theodore Morelle,	b. Sep. 16, 1864.	
4. Ray Benson,	b. Feb. 24, 1871.	

4. **Ray Benson,**[9] fourth son of Lewis Morelle, and b. at Janesville, Wis., is at present engaged in the coal business with his father in Chicago. He m. Sep. 28, 1891, Lizzie Graham of Chicago. Issue:

1. Esther Louise,   b. May 27, 1893.

1. **Carr Lyall,**[9] oldest son of Lewis Morelle, and b. at Clinton, Wis., d. at Las Vegas, New Mexico, Mch. 22, 1888. After receiving a liberal education, he settled at Sioux City, Iowa, where he was Capt. of Co. H, 3d Iowa National Guard. His health failing, he removed to Chicago in Apr. 1887. In Mch. 1888 he started with his father for California, and while resting at Las Vegas, d. of hæmorrhage of the lungs. Thus this noble man, fitted to vie with any, as a scholar, as a gentleman, and as a business man, — with his wife and two little ones,—all passed away in a few months. He m. at Milwaukee, Jan. 1, 1884, Maude Cunningham, who d. at Chicago, Feb. 3, 1888. Issue:

1. Theodora May,	b. Sep. 20, 1885.	d. Jul. 20, 1886.
2. Fannie Maude,	b. Aug. 6, 1887.	d. Jul 24, 1888.

†-4-2-3. **Theodore Morelle**[9] Hammond, second son of Lewis M., was b. at Clinton Junction, Rock Co., Wis.,

THEODORE M. HAMMOND.

Sep. 16, 1864. He removed with his parents to Janesville, Wis., in 1867, and to Milwaukee, in 1874. In Jul. 1880 he removed to Chicago, and took the Latin Scientific Course in the old University of Chicago. He graduated in '85 with the Degree of B. S., winning the Anderson English Essay prize, and enjoying the title of class poet.

In the Fall of 1885 he was chosen Principal of the City High School at Sandwich, Ill., where he remained during the school year. He then abandoned teaching, and soon afterwards engaged in the coal business in Chicago, where he now resides. Besides the coal business, he engages to some extent in newspaper correspondence, and in literary and social work, being President of the Plymouth Club, composed of young men.

At its organization, Mr. Hammond was chosen by the Trustees to be University Factor, — the Business Department, — of the new University of Chicago, and entered upon the responsible duties thereof Aug. 1, 1892.

He m. at Milwaukee, Wis., Jun. 14, 1888, Fannie Loring Merrick, daughter of Lewis Merrick, formerly of Worcester and Monson, Mass. Issue :

    1. Lewis Merrick,   b. Apr. 11, 1889.
    2. Ralph Perry,   b. Nov. 28, 1891.

†–4–3. **Stephen Ford,** third son of Stephen, was b. at Lawrence, N. Y., and moved with his parents to Wisconsin in 1851; was in the Army one year, Co. D, 10th Reg't, and served as Dept. Commander of Wisconsin in 1878; was freight agent of Wisconsin Central R. R. at Milwaukee for nine years, and station agent for several years. In Mch. 1880 he settled in Ashton, Spink Co., South Dak., and engaged in farming and in handling merchandise; was for four years Register of Deeds in Spink Co.; was also President of the Bank of Ashton; and in 1888 was Div. Commander of the G. A. R. of Dakota; was afterwards real estate broker at Duluth, Minn.; and moved to Minneapolis, Minn., May 1, 1891, where he is now a broker. He m. Jun. 3, 1863, Ida Mendenhall of Janesville, Wis. Issue :

    1. Arden Ford,   b. Mch. 21, 1867.
    2. Ida May,   b. Jan. 17, 1879.

    1. **Arden Ford** is Assistant Manager of the *Duluth News*, and resides at Duluth, Minn. He m. Jul. 8, 1891, Nellie Foster at Yankton Indian Agency, [Greenwood], S. D. Issue :

    1. Esther Nyle,   b. Jun. 16, 1892.

2. **Ida May**[9] lives with her father at Minneapolis, Minn.

†–5. **Jiry,**[7] fourth son of Jabez Holmes, b. at Woodstock, was a farmer at Windsor, Vt. He m. Nov. 19, 1824, Hulda Davis, who was b. Oct. 17, 1804, and d. at Hartland, Vt., Mch. 25, 1889, æ. 84. Issue:

1. Hulda.	b. Mch. 6, 1826.	d. young.
2. Lucinda Marie.	b. Jan. 16, 1830.	
3. Rasselas Wait,	b. Jun. 25, 1832.	
4. Erasmus Winslow,	b. Dec. 5, 1837.	

2. **Lucinda Marie**[8] m. Apr. 15, 1856, Thomas S. Luce, a farmer, and resides at Stowe, Vt. No issue.

4. **Erasmus W.**[8] never married, and is night watchman, at the Windsor Prison, Windsor, Vt.

†–5–3. **Rasselas Wait**[8] is a laborer, and lives in Lake City, Calhoun Co., Iowa. He m. Sep. 14, 1856, Eliza McGeorge, who was b. in Licking Co., Ohio, Jan. 7, 1832. Her grandfather McGregor, who was a Scotchman and participated in the Scottish Rebellion, was an eminent physician, and with his family came to New York. Issue:

1. William Henry,	b. Oct. 3, 1857.
2. George Washington,	b. May 17, 1860.
3. Emma Lucinda,	b. Feb. 6, 1870.

1. **William Henry,**[9] oldest son of Rasselas W., is in the mercantile business at Bloomfield, Neb. He m. Mch. 19, 1882, Malana Elizabeth Stevens, who was b. Sep. 6, 1861. Issue:

1. Mabel Rose,	b. Dec. 10, 1882.
2. Jessie Fullmer,	b. Aug. 26, 1884.
3. Edith Irene,	b. Jun. 25, 1888.
4. A. V.,	b. Jun. 21, 1890.
5. Son,	b. Feb. 16, 1892.

2. **George W.,**[9] second son of Rasselas W., resides at Bloomfield, Neb., and is engaged in boring wells. He m. Nov. 23, 1884, Eliza Jennie Worth of Michigan. Issue:

1. Maggie May,	b. Sep. 14, 1888.

3. **Emma Lucinda,**[9] only daughter of Rasselas, m. Jul. 6, 1887, Gideon D. Thompson, and resides at Lake City, Calhoun Co., Iowa. Issue:

1. Nellie Kathleen,	b. Sep. 20, 1888.
2. Vivian Deloss.	b. Mch. 22, 1889.
3. Charles Rinaldo,	b. Feb. 13, 1892.

HOLMES HAMMOND.

†–8. **Holmes,**[7] seventh son of Jabez Holmes, was b. at Windsor, Vt., Jan. 17, 1807. He followed the occupation of mason at Windsor until 1843, when he removed to Milwaukee, Wis., where he engaged in farming. In 1857 he removed to Clinton, where he d. Jan. 25, 1892.

Holmes m. 1st, at Windsor, Vt., Mch. 8, 1832, Sarah Marcy, daughter of Prosper Marcy, who d. at Janesville, Wis., Jul. 16, 1873, æ. 68. Issue:

1. Carrie,	b. May 17, 1833.	d. Aug. 1, 1891.
2. Marcia,	b. Dec. 24, 1834.	
3. Emma Sarah.	b. Jul. 18, 1842.	d. Oct. 17, 1871.

Holmes m. 2d, at Beloit, Wis., Jul. 21, 1874, Caroline Winkler. No further issue.

1. **Carrie,**[8] b. at Ludlow, Vt., m. at Clinton, Wis., Dec. 25, 1860, Thomas W. Williams. They moved to Whitewater, Wis., in 1860, and to Milwaukee in 1870, where she d. Aug. 1, 1891. Issue:

1. Clarence Holmes,   b. Sep. 2, 1864.

Clarence Holmes[9] is manager of the Northwestern Collection Co. at Milwaukee. He m. Oct. 22, 1885, Libbie Germaine at Milwaukee. Issue:

1. Reginald Germaine,   b. Sep. 27, 1890.

2. **Marcia,**[8] b. at West Windsor, Vt., formerly lived at Milton, Wis., but now resides at Janesville. She m. Oct. 15, 1856, A. Webster Baldwin, attorney, of Milton, who d. May 29, 1885, at Janesville. Issue:

1. Carrie May,	b. May 17, 1858.	
2. Emma Eliza,	b. Feb. 2, 1861.	
3. Bertie,	b. Apr. 22, 1872.	d. Jun. 3, 1872.

Of these children, **Carrie May**[9] m. Apr. 28, 1891, Robert J. Rogan, a train dispatcher, and lives at Louisville, Ky. Issue: Marcia May, b. Jun. 12, 1892.

2. **Emma Eliza**[9] m. Jun. 2, 1887, Frank E. Clark, real estate broker, and lives at Chicago. Issue:

1. Maurice James,   b. Sep. 9, 1890.

3. **Emma Sarah,**[8] third daughter of Holmes, b. at West Windsor, Vt., m. Dec. 25, 1868, J. Willard Hartshorn at Clinton, Wis., where she d. without issue Oct. 17, 1871.

†–9. **James,**[7] eighth son of Jabez Holmes, was a farmer, and lived in various places. He m. Feb. 5, 1831, Lucy B. Flanders of Warner, N. H., who was b. Nov. 3, 1812. In 1831 he moved to Lawrence, N. Y., where he had the following issue :

  1. John F. C.,   b. Jan. 30, 1833.
  2. Adelaide H.,   b. Dec. 5, 1834.   d. Mch. 22, 1858.

James then moved back to Windsor, and had further issue :

  3. Harrison James,   b. May 29, 1838.   d. Oct. 21, 1888.
  4. Laura A.,   b. Nov. 4. 1842.   d. Jan. 18. 1864.

He moved to Calais, Vt., in 1845, and had two more children :

  5. Charles W.,   b. Feb. 19, 1847.   d. Mch. —, 1852.
  6. Ella H.,   b. Feb. 5, 1850.

James remained in Calais until 1867, and then went to Shopiere, Rock Co., Wis., where he d. Apr. 27, 1872. His widow, Lucy B., is now living at East Calais, Vt. Adelaide d. single.

†–9–1. **John F. C.,**[8] oldest son of James, during the late Civil War was a sergeant in Co. A. 6th Reg't Vt. Vols. He is now a farmer at East Calais, Vt. He m. May 9, 1854, Martha Long of Waitsfield, Vt., and had issue :

  1. Cora Adelaide,   b. Aug. 28, 1857.   d. Oct. 18. 1872.
  2. Lucy Jane,   b. Jul. 26, 1860.
  3. Hannah Gertrude,   b. Sep. 2. 1866.

Of these children, **Lucy Jane**[9] is single, East Calais ; and **Hannah Gertrude**[9] m. Mch. 19, 1890, Edson J. Sparrow, and lives at Calais, Vt.

†–9–3. **Harrison J.,**[8] second son of James, graduated from the Medical College at Cleveland, Ohio, in '69 or '70, and engaged in the practice of medicine and surgery. He located successively in Wisconsin, Texas, and Florida. He was City Physician of Prairie-du-Chien, Wis. ; assistant surgeon and medical director of recruits, in the Cow-boy War on the Rio Grande in Texas ; and the first mayor of Orange City, Volusia Co., Fla., where he resided 12 years. He was a Mason, and a Knight Templar of high rank, and a devoted member of the Fraternity. For many years a sufferer from asthma, his disease finally assumed the form of consumption, and he died of hœmorrhage, Oct. 21, 1888, while on a visit to his former

home at East Calais, Vt. He m. 1st, Sep. 1, 1890, Mary J. Dickinson of Cambridge, Vt., who d. Feb. 22, 1866, at Clinton, Vt. Issue:

    1. Mary J.,   b. Feb. 16, 1866.

Dr. Hammond m. 2d, Nov. 27, 1866, Libbie J. Scott of Emerald Grove, Wis. Issue:

    2. Kate Luella,   b Sep. 15, 1874.

1. Mary J.,[9] b. at Clinton, Wis., m. at Orange City, Fla., Jan. 4, 1888, William P. Liffler, and resides at St. Augustine, Fla. No issue.

2. Kate Luella,[9] b. at Austin, Tex., resides with her mother in Orange City, Fla.

†–9–4. Laura A.,[8] second daughter of James, m. Mch. 11, 1860, W. C. Bugbee at Calais, Vt., where they resided. Issue:

    1. Mary A.,   b. Apr. 4, 1861.   d. Dec. 25, 1863.
    2. Minnie G.,   b. May 17, 1863.

2. Minnie G.[9] m. Dec. 28, 1886, Fred J. Robbins, and resides at Barre, Vt. Issue:

    1. Clarence,   b. Jul 24, 1888.

†–9–6. Ella H.,[8] third daughter of James, m. Mch. 27, 1838, Clarence R. Dwinell, who is a merchant at East Calais, their place of residence. No issue.

†–10. Elon Oscar,[7] ninth son of Jabez Holmes, was a farmer at East Montpelier, Vt., and d. at Wolcott, Vt., Mch. 20, 1872. He m. 1st, in 1830, Fanny Burnham, and had issue:

    1. Helen,   b. May 10, 1832.
    2. Jane,   b. Oct. 13, 1833.

1. Helen[8] m. Jan. 13, 1852, D. Willard Dudley, and lives at Montpelier, Vt. Issue:

    1. Fanny Hammond.   b. Feb. 21, 1854.

2. Jane[8] m. 1st, Jul. 1, 1853, Charles Austin Tabor, who d. Sep. 21, 1879, æ. 47, and lived at East Montpelier, Vt. Issue:

    1. Diana Foster,   b. Feb. 22, 1855.
    2. Helen Frances,   b.

Jane m. 2d, Oct. 14, 1890, Hon. Albert Dwinell, and lives at East Calais, Vt. No issue.

Elon Oscar m. 2d, Jul. 4, 1847, Mrs. Parmelia Harrington, who d. Oct. 10, 1865. No issue. He m. 3d, Feb. 5, 1866, Wid. Hannah S. Randall, and had issue:

3. Olie E. H., } b. Dec. 4, 1866.
4. Elon Oscar, }   d. Jan. 14, 1872.

The son died in childhood; and **Olie**[9] m. Apr. 2, 1889, Norton W. Jipson, M. D., of Chicago, where she with her mother now reside. Issue: Lucy Hannah, b. Feb. 20, 1891.

†-11. **Daniel**[7] **Hammond,** tenth son of Jabez Holmes, b. at West Windsor, Vt., Jul. 14, 1812, m. Apr. 17, 1834, Mary Sawin, who was b. Jan. 28, 1815, and d. Feb. 20, 1885. Daniel lived at West Windsor, where he d. Apr. 13, 1882. They had eight children, six now living, viz:

1. Ira Mallory,   b. Feb. 7, 1835.
2. Stephen F.,   b. May 14, 1836.
3. Ulysses Haller,   b. Feb. 18, 1839.
4. Jabez Holmes,   b. Feb. 20, 1842.
5. Sarah Lovina,   b. Apr. 28, 1843.   d. May 28, 1864.
6. Mary Delight,   b. Mch. 10, 1846.   d. Sep. 16, 1847.
7. Elwin Elverton,   b. Nov. 4, 1848.
8. Ernest Mark,   b. Jul. 30, 1852.

Of these children, 5. **Sarah Lovina,** by an early marriage, had Guy P., who afterwards took his mother's maiden name, Hammond.

1. **Guy P.,**[9] who is a farmer at Windsor, Vt., m. Sep. 13, 1887, Hattie E. Spaulding. Issue:

1. Edith Maude,   b. Jan. 1, 1891.

†-11-1. **Ira Mallory**[8] lives at Cornish, N. H., and is managing a farm for the Hon. Wm. M. Evarts. He served nine months in Co. A, 12th Vt. Vols. He m. Sep. 1863, Ellen F. Kendall, and had issue:

1. Abbie,   b. Jun. 2, 1866.
2. Mary,   b. May —, 1875.

†-11-2. **Stephen F.**[8] is a mechanic and carpenter and lives at Brownsville, Vt. He was 1st Sergeant of Co. A, 12th Vt. Vols., and was promoted to 2d Lieutenant. He m. 1st, Feb. 2, 1864, Helen Perkins, who was b. Dec. 24, 1839, and d. Oct. 1881. Issue:

    1. George C.,   b May 23, 1865.
    2. Forest,   b. Jan. 28, 1867.

Stephen F. m. 2d, May 11, 1885, Eliza M. Backus, but had no issue by the second wife.

1. George C.[9] is a brakeman and lives at Windsor, Vt. He m. Sep. 12, 1885, Jennie Hastings, and had issue:

    1. Helen Forest,   b. Mch. 4, 1888.

2. Forest,[9] who is a shoemaker at Lebanon, N. H., m. Jun. 9, 1888, Jennie A. Brooks. Issue:

    1. George Luman.   b. Apr. 7, 1889.
    2. Susie Claribel.   b. Sep. 27, 1890.

†–11–3. **Ulysses H.**[8] resides at Middlesex, Vt., and has had the contracts for sawing the wood for the Vermont Central R. R. He served nine months in the army in the same company as his brothers. He m. Mch. 19, 1865, Lauraette Winn, and has one daughter living:

    1. Addie Mary.   b. Nov. 16, 1866.

†–11–4. **Jabez Holmes**[8] resides in West Windsor and is a farmer and jobber. He served nine months in Co. A. 12th Vt. Vols., being promoted from Corporal to Sergeant. He m. Aug. 24, 1865, Julia Ann Blanchard, who was b. Nov. 3, 1846. Issue:

    1. Dwight,   b. Apr. 1, 1867.
    2. Charles C.,   b. Aug. 29, 1869.
    3. Fred A.,   b. Aug. 2, 1874.
    4. Addie M.,   b. Dec. 15, 1877.   d. May 8, 1889.
    5. Luther J.,   b. Jun. 22, 1881.
    6. Duane D.,   b. Jan. 19, 1886.
    7. Maxwell H.,   b. Jul. 19, 1887.

1. Dwight,[9] who lives at West Windsor, m. Apr. 3, 1888, Lucy J. Spaulding of that town. Issue:

    1. Gladys,   b. Aug. 19, 1890.

†–11–7. **Elwyn E.**[8] lives at West Windsor on his father's place, and is a farmer. He m. Aug. 15, 1888, Mrs. Mary E. Hale. No issue.

†–11–8. **Ernest Mark**[8] resides at Turner's Falls, Mass., and is a machinist in a cotton mill. He m. 1st, Sep. 1875, Nellie Blood, who was b. May 1853, and d. Jul. 1879. Issue:

    1. Elmer Clinton,   b. Oct. 2, 1876.
    2. Martha Lovina,   b. Mch. 14, 1878.
    3. Nellie,   b. May —, 1879.

12

162 HAMMOND GENEALOLY.

Mark m. 2d, Sep. 24, 1883, Mary Blood, sister of his first wife. They have one child:

4. Clara Belle, b. Jul. 14, 1884.

†–12. Jabez 2d,[7] eleventh son of Jabez Holmes, was a tinsmith and hardware dealer, and resided at Perkinsville, Vt., but died with his daughter at South Royalston, Vt. He m. May 2, 1841, Adaline Rogers of Claremont, N. H. Issue:

1. Juliette, b. Sep. —, 1841.
2. Edward H., b. Mch. 2. 1844.
3. Charles W., b. Feb. 11, 1846. d. Aug. 16, 1849.
4. Millard F., b. Nov. —, 1848.

Of these children, 1. **Juliette**[3] m. in 1866, Albert Sargeant, and lives at South Royalton, Vt. Issue: Edward W.

4. Millard F.,[8] the last known of him, was assistant postmaster at Northport, N. Y. He m. Jul. 19, 1874, Harriet E. Shepard, who was b. in Alstead, Cheshire Co., N. H., Mch. 22, 1848. Issue:

1. Gertrude Mina, b. Apr. 4, 1875.

Gertrude Mina,[9] b. in Worcester, Mass., is employed in a store in Boston, Mass.

†–12–2. Edward W.[8] is a repairing and jobbing machinist at Worcester, Mass. He m. 1st, Jul. 30, 1865, Ellen L. Wellington, and had issue:

1. Adeline Lucy, b. May 22, 1866.
2. Charles Lewis, b. Feb. 21, 1868.
3. Alice Louise, b. Aug. 16, 1869.
4. Carrie, b. Apr. —, 1872. d.
5. Francenia W., b. May 8, 1873. d. Sep. 18. 1873.
6. Edward E., b. Aug. 27, 1874.
7. Harry. b. Jan. 13, 1877.

Edward W. m. 2d, in 1879, Rosette L. Morse. No further issue.

Of these children, **Edward**[9] and **Harry**[9] live with their father at Worcester.

1. **Adeline Lucy**[9] m. Apr. 10, 1892, Walter A. Waite, and resides at East Northfield, Mass.

2. **Charles Lewis,**[9] b. at Greenfield, Mass., is a lumber salesman, and resides at Holyoke, Mass. He m. Sep. 17, 1890, Flora Ella, daughter of William B. and Mary Miles, and b. at Springfield, Mass., Apr. 2, 1860. No issue.

3. **Alice Louise**[9] m. at Holyoke, Sep. 5, 1891, Martin Lemuel Shufelt, who was b. at Montreal, Apr. 8, 1859. No issue.

(8.)—JIRY HAMMOND OF WINDSOR, VT.

†. **Jiry**[6] **Hammond**, fifth son of Faunce,[5] [Jabez,[4] John,[3] Benjamin,[2] William[1]], was b. at Dartmouth, Mass., Sep. 25, 1778, and d. at Windsor, Vt., Jun. 9, 1834. He moved to Reading, Vt., in Nov. 1787, and thence to Windsor, Vt., where he lived, and where his chief occupation was that of a foundryman. He m. Oct. 7, 1804, Huldah Morton, who was b. at Windsor, Feb. 12, 1777, and d. Mch. 26, 1857, at Jacksonville, Ill. Issue:

1. Lathrop,	b. May 27, 1805.	d. Aug. 1, 1867.
2. Drusilla,	b. Sep. 22, 1806.	d. Sep. 27, 1807.
3. Sally Carlton,	b. Jun. 20, 1808.	d. Nov. 6, 1886.
4. Sophronia,	b. Feb. 8, 1810.	d. Mar. 31, 1811.
5. Joab,	b. Aug. 18, 1811.	d. Nov. 27, 1811.
6. Jiry, Jr.,	b. Sep. 16, 1813.	d. Aug. —, 1837.
7. Sylvanus, }	b. Aug. 24, 1815.	d. Jun. 2, 1816.
8. Sylvester. }		d. Sep. 16, 1815.
9. Aaron,	b. Jun. 30, 1817.	d. Dec. 21, 1888.

Of these children, Drusilla, Sophronia, Joab, Sylvanus, and Sylvester d. young; and Sally Carlton and Jiry Jr. d. single at Jacksonville, Ill.

†-1. **Lathrop**,[7] or Lothrop, was a mechanic, and worked a great deal in stone masonry. He lived in Windsor Co., Vt., until 1850, when he emigrated to Jacksonville, Ill. Here he lived three years, and in 1853 moved to Mercer Co., Mo. He then went back to Illinois, bought a lease at Oak Ridge, near Petersburg, and engaged in mining coal. His death occurred in a very tragic and unknown manner, his lifeless body having been found at the bottom of the coal shaft more than 150 ft. deep. He m. Oct. 18, 1840, Sarah Adams Craigue, who was b. Mch. 3, 1816, and d. Jan. 27, 1883. Issue:

1. Eliza,	b. Aug. 3, 1841.	
2. Ellen,	b. Jan. 8, 1843.	d. Apr. 16, 1883.
3. Wellington,	b. May 8, 1845.	
4. Emma,	b. Jan. 27, 1847.	
5. Aaron,	b. Feb. 9, 1849.	
6. Elmina Esther,	b. Apr. 17, 1851.	
7. William Jiry,	b. Aug. 2, 1854.	

Of Lathrop's children, 2. **Ellen**[8] was a teacher from 18 years of age, and d. single at Jacksonville.

†–1–1. **Eliza,**[8] was a teacher for 36 years, and is a writer and poetess, and resides at Harris, Sullivan Co., Mo. She m. Jul. 27, 1862, Walter H. Odneal, who is an attorney-at-law and member of Legislature. Issue : William Grant, S. Ellen, and Walter Sherman.

2. **S. Ellen**[8] m. Apr. 17, 1887, F. M. Clobb, and was a teacher for 23 years, dying at the age of 41.

†–1–4. **Emma**[8] was also a teacher and resides at Blandinsville, Ill. She m. Nov. 1, 1874, William G. Short, who is a farmer. Issue : Louie, John, Charles, Joseph, and Elmina.

†–1–6. **Elmina Esther**[8] was a school-teacher, and resides at Oakland, Pottawattomie Co., Iowa. She m. Aug. 2, 1883, William H. Davis, a farmer. Issue : Floyd, Emma, and a son.

†–1–3. **Wellington,**[8] oldest son of Lothrop, served three years in the Union Army under Sherman, being a member of the 23d Missouri Reg't. He was formerly a farmer in Mercer Co., Mo., but in Feb. 1889 moved to Ilwaco, Pacific Co., Wash. He m. 1st, Sep. 14, 1873, Catherine Ann Hunter, and had issue :

1. Susan Cora.	b. Dec. 11, 1875.
2. Sarah Daisy,	b. Nov. 15, 1878.
3. John Wellington.	b. Aug. 20, 1881.
4. Missouri.	b. Feb. 18, 1885.

Wellington m. 2d, Oct. 18, 1885, Susan Gregory, and had further issue :

5. Lelia.	b. Aug. 21, 1886.
6. Tenia.	b. Oct. 19, 1887.
7. William Glen.	b. Nov. 10, 1889.

†–1–5. **Aaron**[8] is a farmer and stock dealer at Topsey, Mercer Co., Mo. He m. Feb. 4, 1877, Jemima Horn, and had issue :

1. Ellen,	b. Mch. 9, 1878.	
2. Elza.	b. Oct. 26, 1879.	
3. Carl,	b. May 3, 1881.	d. Sep. 25, 1882.
4. Eli,	b. Jan. 28, 1883.	
5. Wm. Jesse.	b. Jul. 19, 1888.	d. Jul. 21, 1888.
6. Elbert,	b. Dec. 23, 1889.	
7. Elmer.	b. Aug. 31, 1891.	

†-1-7. **William Jiry**[8] is a rancher and stock raiser, and resides at Challis, Custer Co., Idaho. He m. Feb. 2, 1882, Jane Horn, and had issue:

1. John Lathrop.   b. Nov. 11, 1882.
2. Frank Edgar.   b. Nov. 13, 1884.
3. George Bertie,   b. Mch. 17, 1888.
4. Catherine Vuelta,   b. Jul. 13, 1889.

†-9. **Aaron,**[7] sixth son of Jiry, and b. at Windsor, Vt., was a foundryman and locater of minerals, and resided the most of his life at Jacksonville, Ill. He m. 1st, Aug. 2, 1843, Laura Russell, who was b. at Reading, Vt., Aug. 24, 1813, and d. at Jacksonville, Mch. 24, 1855. Issue:

1. Sarah Huldah,   b Jul. 4, 1846.   d. Aug. 11, 1847.
2. Homer Alonzo, }
3. Georgia Ella, }   b. Jun. 8, 1849.   d. Aug. 27, 1849.

Aaron m. 2d, Mch. 15, 1856, Lucy Minerva Headle, who was b. at Plymouth, Vt., Aug. 15, 1827. Issue:

4. Hattie Elvira,   b. Sep. 29, 1857.   d. Aug. 17, 1888.
5. Son.   b. Sep. 27, 1859.   d. Oct. 7, 1859.
6. Henry Joseph.   b. Apr. 19, 1861.
7. Geo. Clarence.   b. Feb. 24, 1863.
8. Laura M.,   b. Aug. 27, 1865.
9. Eva S. E.,   b. Oct. 9, 1867.

Of these children, **George Clarence**` is a blacksmith, and resides at Jacksonville; and **Laura**` and **Eva**` are teachers at Jacksonville.

†-9-4. **Hattie Elvira**` m. Apr. 26, 1887, George M. Savage, an attorney, and lived and d. at Olympia, Wash. No issue.

†-9-6. **Henry Joseph**[8] was recently Assistant Secretary of the Y. M. C. A., and resides at Jacksonville. He m. Dec. 6, 1888, Amanda Moore, but has no living issue.

(9.)—LUTHER HAMMOND OF CORNISH, N. H.

†. **Luther**[6] **Hammond**, sixth son of Faunce,[5] [Jabez,[4] John,[3] Benjamin,[2] William[1]], was b. in Dartmouth, Mass., May 5, 1781, and d. at Cornish, N. H., Feb. 27, 1871, æ. 90. He moved from Dartmouth to Cornish previous to his marriage in 1809, as all his children were born in the latter place. He

m. Sep. 6, 1809, Abigail Hall of Cornish, who was b. Feb. 24, 1788, and d. Apr. 26, 1874, æ. 86.   Issue :

1. Luther, Jr.,	b. Jan. 17, 1811.	
2. Marcia,	b. Jan. 9. 1813.	d. Jan. 22, 1836.
3. Adin Hall.	b. Sep. 20. 1814.	d. May 26, 1874.

Of these children, **Marcia** d. single at Cornish.

†–1. **Luther Jr.**[7] is a farmer, and lives at Amsden, Vt. He m. 1st, Dec. 17, 1838, Amanda H. Currier, who d. Oct. 13, 1848.   Issue :

1. Marcia,	b. Sep. 7, 1839.

Luther m. 2d, Sep. 25, 1849, Sophia Smith, who d. Jul. 25, 1851.   No issue.
He m. 3d, Sep. 25, 1851, Mary M. Farwell.   Issue :

2. Adin Luther,	b. Dec. 21, 1858.	d. Aug. 29, 1862.
3. Mary Maria.	b. Dec. 16, 1860.	d. Aug. 28, 1862.

1. **Marcia**[8] m. Jan. 1, 1861, Jarvis Walker of Langdon, N. H., and now resides at Alstead, N. H. Issue : Mary Abbie and Della Caroline.   Della Caroline d. Sep. 13, 1889.

†–3. **Adin Hall,**[7] second son of Luther, was a graduate of the Eclectic Med. College at Cincinnati, O., and a noted specialist in midwifery and in thoracic diseases.   He practised medicine for many years in Oneida Co., N. Y., and while a resident of Stowe, Vt., had a large and successful practice. He had a fine physique, a kind heart, and was much esteemed both by patients and by the profession.   He died and was buried at Stowe in May 1874.   He m. in 1840 Betsey Ann Randall of Woodstock, Vt., who was b. May 15, 1814, and d. Oct. 2, 1891, at Saratoga, N. Y.   Mrs. Hammond studied medicine with her husband, and was for many years a prosperous and successful nurse.   Issue :

1. Thomas Ogilvie,	b. in 1841.	d. young.
2. Haller D.,	b.	d. young.
3. Joseph Volney,	b. Feb. 8, 1855.	
4. Elizabeth Marie,	b. Feb. 12, 1858.	

Of these children, **Thomas**[8] and **Haller**[8] d. young; and **Joseph**[8] left home at the age of 21, and nothing further is known of him.

4. **Elizabeth Marie,**[8] only daughter of Dr. Adin Hammond, and b. in Oneida Co., N. Y., was educated at the State Normal School at Brockport, N. Y., and at the Academy at

Waterbury, Vt. She graduated from the Boston Cooking
School in '85, and for two years was Principal of the second
incorporated Cooking School in America. Her health requiring
a dry atmosphere, she moved to Colorado and now resides at
Denver in that State, still pursuing her chosen vocation. She
has never married.

(10.)—THOMAS FAUNCE HAMMOND OF READING AND WEST WINDSOR, VT.

†. **Thomas Faunce,**[6*] youngest son of Faunce[5] [Jabez,[4]
John,[3] Benjamin,[2] William[1]], was b. in Dartmouth, Mass.,
and went with his father to Reading, Vt., in 1787, where he
was a Justice of the Peace and Judge of Probate. He lived
in Reading until 1836, when he removed to what is now West
Windsor, Vt. In the Spring of 1864 he removed to Chester,
Vt., where he d. Dec. 24, 1865, æ. 82. He m. 1st, Jan. 25,
1808, Betsey Bishop, who was b. Jan. 25, 1783, and d.
Apr. 9, 1844. Their children, all born in Reading, were:

1.	Achilles Volney,	b. Apr. 12, 1809.	d. Dec. 6, 1845.
2	Homer Hamilton,	b. Mch. 16, 1811.	d. Dec. 12, 1872.
3.	Alexander Hanson,	b. Nov. 3, 1812.	d. Oct. 6, 1866.
4.	Ulysses Haller,	b. Nov. 25, 1814.	d. Dec. 21, 1890.
5.	Elizabeth,	b. Feb. 12, 1817.	d. Sep. 13, 1869.
6.	Lycurgus Claxton,	b. May 10, 1819.	d. Feb. 18, 1890.
7.	Mary,	b. Aug. 16, 1821.	d. Jun. 23, 1845.
8.	Levi Carver,	b. Mch. 17, 1824.	d. May 13, 1872.
9.	Henry Clay,	b. Apr. 15, 1828.	d. May 26, 1859.

Thomas Faunce m. 2d, Jul. 1, 1845, Betsey Sargeant, who
d. Jun. 28, 1848. He m. 3d, Nov. 22, 1848, Anna Henry,
with whom he lived until his death. No issue by second and
third wives.

Of these children, **Mary**[7] d. single, at the age of 24, at
West Windsor; and **Henry Clay**[7] went to California in
1851, where he d. May 26, 1859, never having married.

†-1. **Achilles Volney**[7] engaged in early life in mercantile pursuits, and was for a time located in Chester, Vt., and
later in New York City. In 1845 he went to Savannah, Ga.,
with a cargo of merchandise, and was stricken with the yellow
fever and died within a few days. He m. Jun. 4, 1833, Mary
Elizabeth Pomeroy, who was b. Dec. 8, 1816. Issue:

* See end of Part III. for obligation to parents.

1. George Pomeroy.   b. Mch. 24, 1834.   d. Aug. 13, 1834.
2. Bishop Pomeroy,   b. Oct. 10, 1835.   d Jan. 24, 1837.
3. Mary Elizabeth,   b. Feb. 11, 1838.   d. Nov. 1, 1841.
4. William Haller.   b. Oct. 31, 1840.   d. Dec. 8, 1840.
5. Henry Clay,   b. Oct. 31, 1842.

†-1-5. **Henry Clay,**[6] son of Achilles Volney, enlisted at Brockport, Apr. 26, 1861, as private, Co. K, 13th N. Y. Vol. Inf. for two years, and was discharged as Sergeant, May 3, 1863. He was engaged in eleven battles: 1st Bull Run, Yorktown, Williamsburg, Hanover Court House, Mechanicsville, Gaine's Mill, Savage Station, Malvern Hill, 2d Bull Run, Antietam, and Fredericksburg. He re-enlisted Feb. 24, 1864, as Q. M. Serg't, in Co. C, 22d N. Y. Vol. Calvary, at Brockport, for three years. Under this enlistment he was engaged in the following battles: Wilderness, White Oak Swamp, Seven Days Raid [Wilson's], and Stony Creek. At the latter place he was taken prisoner of war, on the 28th of June 1864, and confined in Salisbury, N. C., Andersonville, Ga., and Florence, S. C., prisons for eight months, exchanged at Wilmington, N. C., Feb. 28, 1865, and re-joined the army at Winchester, Va., in May 1865. He was discharged from the service at Winchester in August, 1865, by reason of general orders mustering out prisoners of war. Henry C. resides at Brockport, Monroe Co., N. Y. He m. May 3, 1870, Helen A. Richards, and had issue:

1. Mary Lucy,   b. Jun. 21, 1871.
2. Henry Clay, Jr.,   b. May 19, 1887.

†-2. **Homer Hamilton,**[7] second son of Thomas Faunce, lived in Reading, Vt., with the exception of a few years spent in Massachusetts, while learning the carriage-maker's trade. He manufactured carriages and sleighs in his native town for a number of years, and later worked as carpenter and builder. He was a Justice of the Peace for a number of years, and was serving his tenth year as Town Clerk at the time of his death. He m. Sep. 22, 1844, Nancy Maria Goddard, who was b. Apr. 27, 1817, and d. Jan. 28, 1846. They had one daughter:

1. Mary Elizabeth,   b. Jan. 23, 1846.   d. May 2, 1865, single.

He m. 2d, Jan. 25, 1848, Eliza Goddard, a sister of his former wife, who was b. Nov. 4, 1808, and d. Dec. 3, 1886. They had two children:

2. Volney Homer,   b. Jul. 17, 1849.
3. Jane Amelia,   b. Nov. 11, 1852.   d. Aug. 18, 1863.

' †-2-2. Volney Homer⁶ resides at Windsor, Vt., and is a lawyer. He m. Nov. 2, 1886, Mrs. Sarah D. Waite. No issue.

†-3. Alexander H.,⁷ third son of Thomas Faunce, was a bachelor and lived in many different places. He was living at Reading, Vt., at the time of his death, but died at Weathersfield, Vt.

†-4. Ulysses Haller,⁷ bachelor, was a teacher of penmanship, &c., and was at one time engaged in some of the departments at Washington, as clerk. He went to California in 1854, where he d. in Dec. of 1890. He served his country in the War of '61-'65.

†-5. Elizabeth,⁷ oldest daughter of Thomas Faunce, resided at Dodge's Corners, Waukesha Co., Wis., where she died. She m. Sep. 9, 1841, Royal L. Bayley, and had six children: James Austin, Haller Hammond, James Luther, Thomas Faunce, Mary Elizabeth, and John Dodge.

†-6. Lycurgus C.⁷ engaged in early life in the foundry business and in the manufacture of iron. He lived in West Windsor, and Windsor, Vt., until 1852-3, when he went to California, where he has since remained. He m. Jan. 22, 1850, Arvilla Draper, who d. May 15, 1851. No issue.

†-8. Levi Carver,⁷ sixth son of Thomas Faunce, was a farmer, and settled at Lone Rock, Richland Co., Wis. He m. Oct. 5, 1845, Susan M. Lanphier, who was b. Mch. 28, 1823. Issue:

<ol>
<li>Ida Ann, b. Sep. 12, 1846.</li>
<li>Rasselas Alstine, b. Jul. 20, 1848.</li>
<li>Florence Rosina, b. Sep. 7, 1852.</li>
<li>Levi Carver, Jr., b. Apr. 28, 1857.</li>
</ol>

1. Ida Ann⁸ m. Jan. 1, 1866, Robert Clement, a farmer, and resides in Richland Centre, Wis. Issue:

<ol>
<li>Dora, b. Oct. 14, 1866. d. Sep. 23, 1867.</li>
<li>Scott, b. Jun. 23, 1869.</li>
</ol>

2. Rasselas Alstine,⁸ who is a farmer at Sextonville, m. Sep. 13, 1868, Ida Cleveland. Issue:

<ol>
<li>Frank J., b. Mch. 31, 1870.</li>
<li>Elmer E., b. Aug. 10, 1871.</li>
<li>Charles, b. Nov. 29, 1873. d. Sep. 28, 1875.</li>
<li>Carl S., b. Dec. 18, 1875.</li>
</ol>

5. Lillie F.,   b. Sep. 22, 1876.
6. Susie,   b. Mch. 27, 1879.
7. Benjamin H ,   b. Dec. 19, 1888.

3. **Florence Rosina**[5] m. Apr. 20, 1874, Philip Rolfe, a farmer, and resides at Viola, Wis. Issue :

1. Leota Irene,   b. Feb. 24, 1875.

4. **Levi C. Jr.**[5] m. Aug. 28, 1879, Hattie L. Andrews, and is a farmer at Lone Rock, Wis. Issue :

1. Dora M.,   b. Oct. 10, 1881.
2. Glenn W.,   b. Sep. 8, 1884.
3. Jennie,   b. Dec. 1, 1886.

9.—JABEZ HAMMOND 2D, OF WOODSTOCK, VT.

†. **Jabez**[5] **Hammond 2d**, second son of Jabez[4], [John,[3] Benjamin,[2] William[1]], was b. at Rochester, Mass., Jan. 16, 1741, and d. at South Woodstock, Vt., May 2, 1807. He lived first at Rochester, Mass., afterwards at New Bedford, and moved to Woodstock about 1775–80, where he bought a farm of 50 acres of Thomas Cottle. He m. Dec. 19, 1764, Priscilla Delano, who d. Mch. 11, 1810, and was a descendant of a celebrated French Huguenot family, De La Nois. Issue :

1. Philip,   b. Jul. 19, 1765.   d. Jul.   2, 1854.
2. Mary,   b about   1768.   d.
3. Rhoda,   b. Apr. 27, 1771.   d. Aug. 27, 1849.
4. Rebecca,   b. Mch. 7, 1772.   d. Sep. 28, 1855.
5. Abigail,   b. in   1774.   d. in   1825.
6. Jabez D.,   b. Aug. 2, 1778.   d. Aug. 18, 1855.
7. Priscilla,   b. in   1782.   d. May   6, 1819.
8. George C.,   b. Jul. 16, 1783.   d. Oct. 16, 1849.
9. Thankful,   b. about   1785.   d. in   infancy.

In addition to the above there was probably a son **Caleb**,[6] b. in 1776, and d. in 1795, single.

Of these children, **Abigail**[6] never married, and lived with her sister Priscilla at Barnard, Vt.

†–1. **Philip**,[6] oldest son of Jabez 2d, was a farmer, and at the age of 30 moved to Bridgewater, Vt., where he lived and died. He m. 1st, Dec. 2, 1792, Lydia Green, who was b. Sep. 1, 1770, and d. Jan. 29, 1825. Issue :

1. Caleb,   b. May 19, 1794.   d. Apr. 16, 1821.
2. Lucia A.,   b. Apr. 3, 1796.   d.
3. Ruby,   b. Jun. 4, 1798.   d. Mch. 13, 1832.
4. Lydia,   b. Jul. 14, 1802.   d. Mch. 24, 1812.
5. Jabez M.,   b. May 21, 1805.   d. Apr. 3, 1841.

REV. PHILIP DELANO HAMMOND.

Philip m. 2d, Jan. 30, 1826, Mary [Knapp] Potter of Onondaga, N. Y., who was b. Jan. 14, 1794, and d. Jul. 2, 1854. Issue:

6. Philip Delano,	b. Jan. 1, 1827.	d. Dec. 21, 1884.
7. Lydia Green,	b. Jun. 24, 1828.	d. Sep. 28, 1829.
8. Charles G.,	b. Jan. 26, 1831.	d. Aug. 5, 1831.
9. Calvin F.,	b. Dec. 5, 1832.	d. Jul 31, 1833.
10. Mary M.,	b. Feb 18, 1835.	
11. Amasa B.,	b. Jul. 12, 1836.	d. Aug. 13, 1841.

Of these children, the two Lydias, Charles, Calvin, and Amasa d. young; **Lucia A.**[7] m. Joel Tucker of Barnard, Vt., and had two children: Lucia Ann and Jane Ann, who d. in infancy; **Ruby**[7] m. Abiel Tripp, and d. without issue; and **Jabez M.**[7] m. Mariette Hancock of Michigan, and also d. without issue. Lucia A. is said to have d. in Michigan.

†-1-1. **Caleb,**[7] oldest son of Philip, was one of the pioneer physicians of Rochester, N. Y., a very cultivated man, and very active in educational matters. He m. Sep. 1820 Jane Ann Stillson of Rochester, N. Y., who d. Nov. 14, 1869. Issue:

1. Caleb Holton.	b. Aug. 14, 1821.	d. Apr. 22, 1883.

†-1-1-1. **Caleb Holton,**[8] born and educated in Rochester, N. Y., graduated from the Geneva Medical College in 1845, being a student with Dr. Frank H. Hamilton of New York City, and also his surgical assistant in college for two years. In 1846 he commenced practice in West Henrietta, Monroe Co., N. Y., moved in the Spring of 1854 to East Rush, and in 1877 he removed to Ionia, Mich., where he d. Apr. 22, 1883, of disease of the heart.

He m. 1st, Oct. 10, 1848, Susan Cutler of Lima, Livingston Co., N. Y., who d. Sep. 4, 1865. Issue:

1. Joanna Dean,	b. Mch. 16, 1851.	d. Jan. 21, 1862.
2. Eliz Fairbanks,	b. Sep. 11, 1853.	
3. Susan Cutler,	b. Sep. 3, 1855.	
4. Alice,	b. Nov. 16, 1857.	
5. Jabez Dean,	b. Jul. 29, 1860.	
6. Caleb Stillson,	b. Nov. 27, 1862.	

Caleb Holton m. 2d, Oct. 1866, Mrs. Louisa Green, who d. Dec. 23, 1867. He m. 3d, Aug. 9, 1871, Mrs. Ann E. Bunnell of East Rush. No issue by the second and third marriages.

Of Dr. Hammond's children, 2. **Elizabeth F.**[9] m. Jun.

21, 1883, John H. Bird, M. D., of Rochester, N. Y., and now resides in New York City. Dr. Bird is a graduate of the College of Physicians and Surgeons, Chicago, and represents the Eastern branch of the house of Park, Davis & Co. No issue.

3. **Susan Cutler**[9] m. Aug. 7, 1883, Frank L. Stillson, and resides at Craig, Neb. Issue:

1. Harriet Alice.	b. May 7, 1884.
2. Frank Benj..	b. Feb. 13, 1887.
3. Gracie Eliz..	b. Mch. 13, 1891.

4. **Alice**[9] m. Jan. 25, 1882, Frank H. Harter, and resides at Ionia, Mich. No issue.

5. **Jabez Dean**[9] graduated from the Rush Medical College, Chicago, in Feb. 1884; has never married, and is practising medicine in Chicago.

6. **Caleb Stillson**[9] resides in East Orange, N. J., and is the Eastern Manager of the publishing house of Rand, McNally & Co. of Chicago. He m. Jun. 7, 1886, Grace Simms of Lincoln, Ill., and had issue:

1. Caleb Dean.	b. Mch. 25, 1887.
2. Helen,	b. Sep. 22, 1889.

†-1-6. **Philip Delano,**[7] third son of Philip, was b. at Bridgewater, Vt., May 18, 1794, and d. at Minneapolis, Minn., Dec. 24, 1884. He was a teacher of more than ordinary merit, beginning the work at 16, and continuing it until the age of 35. He graduated from Wesleyan University, Middletown, Conn., in the Fall '50, and in the Spring of '57 became Principal of the Seminary at Danville, Ill. Soon after leaving college, he was ordained a minister of the Methodist Episcopal Church, and in '61 was elected Chaplain of the 35th Reg't Ill. Vols., and was a pensioner for the last ten years of his life. He now connected himself with journalism, was a fine editorial writer, and was constantly on the staff of some of our best newspapers. He was a ready and pleasing writer, and a good speaker from either pulpit or platform. He removed to Harrisburg, Dak., in the Spring of '85. He m. Nov. 23, 1854, Pauline C. Whitman, and had issue:

1. William Bowen,	b. Aug. 28, 1855.
2. Linnie Pauline.	b. Jun. 21, 1857.
3. Venora E.,	b. May 14, 1860.
4. Stella.	b. Dec. 24, 1861.
5. Dean Whitman,	b. May 18, 1866.

PAULINE HAMMOND CLARK.

Of these children, 5. **Dean Whitman**[8] resides with his mother at Lakota, North Dak.

†–1–6–1. **William Bowen**[8] is a printer, and lives at Minneapolis. He m. May 31, 1878, Maggie L. Higgins of Zionville, Ind., who was b. Nov. 15, 1856. Issue :

1. Arthur Delano.	b. Mch. 4, 1879.	d. Jun. 29, 1879.
2. Bertha Kate.	b. Sep. 27, 1880.	
3. Albert Carlos.	b. Oct. —, 1882.	
4. Alfred Percy,	b. Jul. 4, 1884.	
5. Jessie,	b. Jun. 30, 1889.	

2. **Pauline**[8] who is a fine contralto singer, was Manager of the Telephone Exchange at Roxbury for 13 years. She m. Apr. 11, 1893, William Tilden Clark of the Peason Cordage Co., and resides at Roxbury, Mass.

3. **Venora E.**[8] m. May 23, 1883, Charles F. Robbins, an attorney, and resides at Indianapolis, Ind. Issue :

1. Charles F., Jr.,   b. Jul. 6, 1886.

4. **Stella**[8] m. Jun. 4, 1884, Franz Untersee, an architect, and resides at Brookline, Mass. Issue : Franz Joseph, Carl Roland, Emie, and Marie.

†–1–10. **Mary M.,**[7] youngest daughter of Philip, taught in the public schools from the age of 16 until she entered Danville Seminary, as a teacher, with her brother Philip, where she taught a full 20 years. She afterwards taught in Hedding College, Abingdon, Ill. ; Female College, Jacksonville, Ill. ; and Baker University, Baldwin, Kan. She also taught drawing and painting, and gave some years to painting portraits in India ink and crayon. For some years she has been connected with the Women's Foreign Missions, and other charitable institutions of Kansas, her residence being at Baldwin.

†–2. **Mary,**[6] oldest daughter of Jabez 2d, lived at Woodstock, Vt., and was twice married. She m. 1st, Ebed M. Burke, and had two sons : Albert and Ebed M. Jr. **Albert**[7] lived at Lodi, N. Y., and died while a member of the New York senate. He is said to have married, and to have left a daughter Nellie. Mary m. 2d, Noah Winslow, but had no other issue. After her second marriage, she moved to the State of New York, where she afterwards died.

†–3. **Rhoda,**[6] second daughter of Jabez 2d, m. Dec. 31,

1801, Nathaniel Dean of Barnard, Vt., who was b. Apr. 11, 1761, and d. Feb. 11, 1851. They resided at Albany, N. Y., and had issue: Amos, Mary, Minerva, Priscilla D., and Nathaniel W.

Of Rhoda's children, **Mary,**[7] **Minerva,**[7] and **Priscilla**[7] all d. single at Albany.

5. **Nathaniel W.**[7] m. Mary B. Dean, and d. at Glenwood, Iowa, in 1879. Issue: Maria, Albert, Amos, and William G.

1. **Amos Dean,**[7] b. Jan. 16, 1803, became an eminent lawyer, and was afterwards elected President of the Albany Law School. He was celebrated for his great abilities as a jurist, and was the author of several volumes on legal subjects. He m. Eliza J. Davis, and had issue: Amos Hammond, b. Jun. 16, 1845, Frederick Augustine, Josephine Davis, and Joanna Armsby. Of these children, **Amos Hammond,**[8] who is a clergyman at Monmouth, Ill., m. Jun. 1870 Sarah J. Treadwell. Issue: Ellen Edwards, Fred Porter, Edna, Mary, Alice, and Ethel. **Frederic Augustine**[8] resides single at Albany. **Josephine**[8] m. Theodore D. Palmer, resides at Newark, N. J., and has two children: Josephine Eudora and Amos Dean. **Joanna**[8] m. Fred M. Cameron, and resides at Albany. No issue.

†-4. **Rebecca,**[6] third daughter of Jabez 2d, m. in 1800 Samuel Laird, who was b. in 1770, and d. in 1838. She lived at Warren, Vt. until after the birth of her children, and in 1820 the family all moved to North Madison, Ind., where Mrs. Laird and her husband lived, and afterwards died. After removing to Indiana, Mr. Laird engaged in farming, while his wife became a teacher of the classics. Mrs. Laird was an intelligent and educated woman for her time, and was quite a poetess. She wrote a number of volumes of poems, several of which were published. Issue: Julia, Samuel, Horatio Nelson, and Charles K., all dead except the last.

Of these children, **Julia**[7] m. a James Hammond, lineage not known, and had issue: John, Jabez, Maria, and James Jr.

2. **Samuel**[7] was a merchant and steamboat owner at Natchez, Miss. He m. Margaret S. Bright, sister of J. D. Bright, late U. S. senator. Issue: Juliet, Louisiana, and Margaret Antoinette.

3. **Horatio Nelson**[7] was a farmer in Kansas, and d. in 1886. He m. 1st, Hannah Stonemetz, and had issue: Julia Walton, and Mary who d. young. He m. 2d, Eliza A. Waldsmith. No other issue.

4. **Charles K.**[7] was engaged in mercantile pursuits for 35 years, during which he travelled through many parts of the United States. He is now a retired merchant, living at North Madison, Ind., enjoying the fruits of his labors, having been a very successful business man. He m. 1st, Jane Dinwiddie, and had issue: Margaret, Caroline, and Josephine. He m. 2d, Sarah Zenor, and had further issue: Brooke, Flora Rhea, Mariamine, and Graham Bright.

†–6. **Jabez Delano,**[6] second son of Jabez 2d, author and statesman, was b. in New Bedford, Mass., Aug. 2, 1778, and d. in Cherry Valley, N. Y., Aug. 18, 1855. With a limited education he taught school at 15, was admitted to the bar in 1805, and settled in Cherry Valley, N. Y. He was elected to Congress as a Democrat, serving from Dec. 4, 1815, till Mch. 3, 1817; was State senator from 1817 to 1821; and in 1822 removed to Albany, where he practised his profession until 1830. From 1825 till 1826 he served as a commissioner to settle the claims of New York against the Federal government; and was at one time a member of the Council of Appointment, consisting of three members, who had the distribution of the State patronage. In 1831 he visited Europe for his health, and on his return again settled in Cherry Valley. In 1838 he was chosen County Judge, and from 1845 until his death was one of the Regents of the University of New York. He received the Degree of LL.D. from Hamilton College in 1845. Failing health compelled him to retire from public life, and he then devoted his time to writing various works, among which are "The Political History of New York," in three volumes: "Life and Opinions of John Melbourn": "Life of Silas Wright"; and "Evidence, Independent of Written Revelation, of the Immortality of the Soul." He was of a kind and sympathetic nature, and, remembering his own struggles in early life, gave kindly assistance and advice to many young men just beginning life's battles.*

He m. 1st, probably about 1810, Miranda Stoddard of Woodstock, Vt., who d. in 1832. Issue:

* Taken mainly from Appleton's "Cyclopedia of American Biography," by permission.

1. Maria B.,	b. Oct. 31, 1811.	d. Oct. 19, 1818.
2. Wells Stoddard.	b. Dec. 15, 1814.	d. Jan. 28, 1849.
3. Jabez.	b. about 1816.	d. at the age of 10.

These children were all born at Cherry Valley, and all died single, Maria and Jabez when young.

2. **Wells S.,**[7] a very able man, was, at the time of his death, a lawyer of considerable note at Cherry Valley, N. Y.

Judge Hammond m. 2d. in 1834–5, Laura Williams of Woodstock, Vt., who d. Jul. 9, 1853, without issue.

†–7. **Priscilla,**[6] fifth daughter of Jabez 2d, m. John S. Bicknell, and lived and d. at Barnard, Vt. Mr. Bicknell, who was a captain in the regular army in the War of 1812, was a farmer at Barnard, and a man of note in his day. Issue: Fannie, Abigail, John Starks Jr., and Jabez H.

Of Priscilla's children, **Fannie**[7] d. single at the age of 20; **Abigail**[7] m. Orrin Gambell, and had a daughter Fannie and a son Orrin Jr. who is a lawyer at Albany, N. Y. Abigail and her husband died some years ago.

John Starks Jr.,[7] who was b. in 1814, and d. in 1864, was a farmer at Barnard. He m. Helen [Dyer] Bicknell, his brother's widow, and had: Abbie Elizabeth, Frank Dean, and Olin Dyer. Frank d. at the age of 20; Abbie m. J. Wylie and lives in California; and Olin is a lawyer at Morrisville, Vt.

Jabez H.[7] who was b. in 1816, and d. in 1846, was a physician of some eminence, and practised medicine in Bridport, Vt. He m. Helen L. Dyer, and had: Stark John and Hammond Jabez. Hammond d. at the age of 5 years; and Stark lives at Johnson, Vt.

†–8. **George C.,**[6] third son of Jabez 2d, who was a schoolmaster and farmer, lived some 30 years in Pomfret, Vt., where all his children were born. He afterwards moved to Barnard, Vt., where he d. Oct. 16, 1849. He m. in 1806 Lucy Payne, who was b. in 1773, and d. in 1850. Issue:

1. Almira,	b. Jul. 20, 1808.	d. Jul. 29, 1883.
2. Miranda.	b. Jul. 25, 1811.	
3. George C. 2d.	b. Mch. 16, 1816.	

Of these children, **Almira**[7] m. in 1856 William Sterling, and lived at Woodstock, Vt. No issue.

JUDGE JABEZ DELANO HAMMOND

2. **Miranda**[7] m. in 1833 A. Nelson Williamson, and lives at Hartland, Vt. Issue: Alonzo N., Myra, Burkley, Addie, Albert, and Clarence.

Alonzo N., a physician, lives at New London, Conn., and makes a speciality of epilepsy and allied diseases. He was formerly Assistant to the chair of Theory and Practice of Medicine in the Medical Dept. of the University of New York.

†–8–3. **George C. 2d**[7] bought and now lives on the farm formerly owned by Capt. Bicknell, his aunt Priscilla's husband. He was formerly a school-master and farmer, and more recently a newspaper correspondent at Barnard. He m. Sept. 15, 1851, Mary A. Swift, who was b. in 1820 and d. in 1883, and a granddaughter of Rose Hammond. Rose Hammond, who was probably a daughter of Nathan 3d, m. Peleg Briggs at Rochester, Mass., and had a daughter Florina. Peleg Briggs afterwards moved from Rochester to Woodstock, Vt., where Florina m. Dr. Thomas Swift, and had Mary A. Issue:

1. Lucy F.,   b. Oct. 29, 1852.
2. Carrie S.,   b. Sep. 16, 1854.   d. Oct. 17, 1870.
3. Emma A.,   b. Oct. 27, 1857.   d. Jun. 22, 1864.
4. George C. 3d, b. Mch. 18, 1860.
5. Bertha B.,   b. Oct. 25, 1863.

Of the above children, Carrie and Emma d. young; and Lucy, George C. 3d, and Bertha are all single, and all reside at Barnard, with their father. **George C. 3d**[3] manages the farm.

11.—CALVIN HAMMOND OF CHATHAM, MASS.

†. **Calvin Hammond**[5] of Dartmouth, fourth son of Jabez[4] [John,[3] Benjamin,[2] William[1]], settled in Chatham, Mass. He m. Dec. 15, 1765, Patience Young of Chatham, and had issue:

1. John,   b. Mch. 15, 1766.   d. Aug. 8, 1839.
2. Mary,   b.   d.
3. Stephen, b.   d.

†–2. **Mary**[6] m. Jun. 20, 1790, Samuel Young of Chatham, and had: Patience, Ebenezer, Samuel, and Molly. 3. **Stephen,**[6] who was a sailor, probably died at sea, unmarried.

13

†–1. **John,**[6] during the War of 1812–14, was taken from a fishing vessel off Chatham, and forced to act as pilot of a British privateer for several weeks, but was finally landed at Chatham, He m. May 15, 1788, Hannah Wing, lived in Chatham, and had issue :

1. Elizabeth,	b. Nov. 2. 1788.	d.
2 Calvin,	b. Aug. 18, 1790.	d. Jun. 7. 1854.
3. Luther.	b. Jan. 10, 1792.	d. Mch. 9, 1854.
4. John, Jr.,	b. Oct. 23, 1793.	d. Apr. 2. 1864.
5. Stephen,	b. Jul. 24, 1795.	d. Aug. 9, 1871.
6. William,	b. Jun. 19, 1799.	d. about 1829.
7. Elisha,	b. Aug. 2. 1801.	d. Sep. 13, 1888.
8. Zebedee,	b. Aug. 21, 1803.	
9. Hannah,	b. Sep. 6. 1805.	d. Mch. 7, 1886.

The sons in this family were mariners and masters of vessels, and resided at Chatham unless otherwise stated. Of the above children :

1. **Elizabeth**[7] m. William Davis, *alias* William Blount, of England, and had issue as follows : Sylvester, William F., Luther. Harriet, Otis W.. and Emily.

William Davis, *alias* Blount, when a young man, was on board the British ship " Guerrierre " when she was captured by the U. S. Frigate "Constitution," and called himself William Blount, probably to escape impressment in the English service.

9. **Hannah**[7] m. Aug. 11, 1834, Francis Patterson of Chatham, and had issue as follows : Arzelia A., Amelia F., Frederick A.

†–1–2. **Calvin,**[7] oldest son of John, m. Jan. 2, 1817, Deborah Eldridge of Chatham. Issue :

1. Amon,	b. Feb. 1, 1819.	d. Jan. 22, 1889.
2. Calvin,	b. Aug. 11. 1822.	d. Dec. 7. 1846.
3. Susanna,	b. Nov. 30, 1824.	d. Oct. 25, 1828.
4. Anthony,	b. Oct. 28, 1826.	d. May 29. 1831.
5. Susanna,	b. Dec. 22. 1828.	
6. Joshua G.,	b. Dec. 5. 1831.	
7. Anthony,	b. Nov. 15, 1833.	d. Jun. 10, 1836..
8. Darius E.,	b. Sep. 27, 1835.	

Of these children, 2. **Calvin**[8] never married and was lost overboard in Block Island Sound, Dec. 7, 1846, and **Joshua G.,**[8] also single, is an invalid residing at Chatham.

5. **Susanna**[8] m. 1st, in 1840, James M. Wixon of Dennis, Mass. Issue : James H. She m. 2d, Dec. 13, 1868, Jesse Gills of Chatham. No issue.

†-1-2-1. **Amon,**[3] a store-keeper in Chatham, and an active member of the Methodist Church. He m. 1st, Jul. 21, 1846, Rhoda Taylor, but by her had no issue.
He m. 2d, Oct. 11, 1847, Sarah Gould, and had issue:

    1. Amon F.,   b. Oct. 9, 1852.
    2. Myra,   b. Jul. 31, 1858.   d. Mch. 14, 1864.

Amon m. 3d, Jun. 6, 1868, Widow Charlotte Hodges.
He m. 4th, Sep. 3, 1877, Widow Adelaine Young. No issue by the third and fourth marriages.

†-1-2-1-1. **Amon F.,**[9] a grocer's clerk at Chatham, m. Nov. 2, 1874, Leonora F. Smith, and had issue:

    1. Florence G.,   b. Aug. 8, 1875.   d. Oct. 30, 1882.
    2. Edith R.,   b. Mch. 25, 1877.
    3. Walter S.,   b. Dec. 14, 1878.
    4. Laura G.,   b. Jun. 25, 1882.
    5. Russell C.,   b. Mch. 5, 1888.

†-1-2-8. **Darius E.,**[8] captain of a coasting schooner, m. Jul. 10, 1856, Helen M. Clark, and had issue:

    1. Darius C.,   b. Jan. 20, 1857.
    2. Stillman C.,   b. Jul. 27, 1862.
    3. Carrie B.,   b. Nov. 9, 1867.
    4. Sarah A.,   b. Feb. 11, 1870.
    5. Susie M.,   b. Jun. 1, 1876.
    6. Hannah G.,   b. Jan. 22, 1879.

Of these children, 1. **Darius C.**[9] m. Mch. 14, 1886, Hannah Bearse, and lives at Chatham. No issue: 3. **Carrie B.**[9] m. Jul. 18, 1889, Andrew H. Bearse, and has a son Harry.

†-1-3. **Luther,**[7] second son of John, m. Mch. 1817, Sally Gould of Chatham, and had issue:

    1. Stephen G.,   b. Feb. 28, 1818.
    2. Caroline,   b. Nov. 5, 1819.   d.
    3. Luther, Jr.,   b. Oct. 10, 1822.   d. Jul. 22, 1876.
    4. Azubah G.,   b. Nov. 22, 1825.   d. Nov. 4, 1860.
    5. Sarah M.,   b. Feb. 24, 1828.   d. Sep. 17, 1854.
    6. Franklin D.,   b. Feb. 24, 1830.   d. Jun. 23, 1864.
    7. Angenette W.,   b. Mch. 12, 1833.

Of these children, 2. **Caroline**[8] m. Feb. 5, 1843, Solomon Doane of Eastham, and had issue: Fuller G., Ella M., and Clara J.

    4. **Azubah G.**[8] m. Nov. 1846, Alonzo Nye, lived at Chatham, and had: Harriet E.

5. **Sarah M.**[6] m. Jul. 6, 1848, Winslow Loveland, a ship captain, and had : Cleora and Sarah W.

7. **Augenette W.**[8] m. Aug. 9, 1853, Benjamin H. Stinson, and lives at Jamaica Plain, Mass. Issue : Walter B., Wilbur H., Luther H., Sarah J., Benjamin F., Benjamin C., and Benjamin F.

†–1–3–1. **Stephen G.,**[8] captain in the merchant service, lives at Somerville, Mass. He m. Dec. 31, 1840, Susan E. Nickerson, and had issue as follows :

1. Emma C.,	b. Feb. 17, 1842.	d. Aug. 4, 1850.
2. Asenath E.,	b. Mch. 17, 1844.	d. Feb. 17, 1851.
3. Lauretta S.,	b. Mch. 15, 1846.	d. Dec. 15, 1848.
4. Stephen G., Jr..	b. Sep. —, 1851.	

†–1–3–3. **Luther Jr.,**[8] a captain in the merchant service, m. 1st, Aug. 1846, Emeline Young. Issue :

1. Edmund Y.,	b. Jul. —, 1852.
2. Luther E.,	b. Jan. 22, 1854.

Luther Jr. m. 2d, Jan. 5, 1865, Hannah G. Sparrow, but had no other issue.
Of these children, 1. **Edmund Y.**[9] a mariner, m. Dec. 25, 1872, Loella Maker of Brewster, Mass., and had issue :

1. Florence E.,	b. Apr. 10, 1877.
2. Elsie G.,	b. Aug. 12, 1881.

2. **Luther E.,**[9] dry goods dealer and hotel keeper, m. Aug. 30, 1877, Hannah J. L. J. Hammond, daughter of Isaac L. Hammond. Issue :

1. Mertis J.,	b. Jun. 18, 1878.
2. Harvey E.,	b. Aug. 13, 1879.

†–1–3–6. **Franklin D.**[8] a mason by trade, served as a nine months' man in Co. E, 43d Reg't. He afterwards re-enlisted and died Lieut. of Co. A., 58th Reg't M. V. M. He m. Oct. 1850, Bathsheba S. Nickerson, who d. Aug. 28, 1884. Issue :

1. Marianna A.,	b. Feb. 7, 1851.	
2. Emma C.,	b. Jan. 30, 1853.	
3. Mary E.,	b. Apr. 7, 1856.	d. Aug. 7, 1859.
4. Franklin D., Jr.,	b. Mch. —, 1858.	
5. Alanson,	b. Dec. 4, 1871.	d. May 13, 1875.

Of these children, **Franklin D. Jr.,**[9] who has never married, is a freight agent at Chicago.

1. **Marianna A.,**[9] m. Sep. 20, 1871, Frank C. Wood of Freedom, N. H., who is a dry goods merchant in East Boston. No issue.

2. **Emma C.**[9] m. Mch. 1874, George B. Bent, and resides at Detroit, Mich. Issue: Alanson M., Rena W., Lillian E., George B. Jr., C. Lester, and Lettie E.

†-1-4. **John Jr.,**[7] third son of John, m. Sep. 16, 1817, Mercy Hopkins of Chatham, and had besides David W., Rebecca W., and Abba M., who d. young, issue as follows:

1. David W.,	b. Nov. 13, 1820.	d. Aug. 17, 1884.
2. George T., }	b. Nov. 24, 1823.	d. Dec. 4, 1891.
3. John, }		d. Aug. 23, 1824.
4. John F.,	b. Nov. 3, 1825.	d. Jan. 11, 1892.
5. Isaac L.,	b. Jul. 15, 1827.	d. Oct. 5, 1859.
6. William,	b. Jul. 11, 1829.	
7. Dorcas D.,	b. May 30, 1831.	d. Aug. 23, 1888.
8. Abba M.,	b. Aug. 29, 1834.	
9. Mercy A.,	b. Sep. 27, 1838.	
10. Eleonora M.,	b. Jul. 4, 1842.	

Of these children, 7. **Dorcas D.**[9] m. Jan. 18, 1854, Clarington E. Robbins of Harwich, Mass, and had issue: Susan J. and Mercy C.

8. **Abba M.**[9] m. Aug. 5, 1885, David G. Patterson of East Boston, and lives at Roxbury, Mass. Issue not known.

9. **Mercy A.**[9] m. Nov. 24, 1861, Everett Patterson of Nantucket, and lives at East Boston. Issue:

1. Everett Hartwell,	b. Jun. 22, 1863.	d. Mch. 31, 1869.

10. **Eleonora M.**[8] m. Aug. 27, 1872, Fuller G. Doane, and lives at East Boston. Her children were: Fuller E. C., electrician, East Boston, and Carrie G. G.

†-1-4-1. **David W.,**[8] a captain in the coasting service, m. Dec. 3, 1844, Harriet Eldridge of Chatham. Issue:

1. Calvin,	b. Mch. 27, 1847.	
2. Harriet A.,	b. Jan. 26, 1848.	d. Oct. 8, 1880.
3. Minnie B.,	b. Nov. 11, 1854.	d. Feb. 11, 1857.

1. **Calvin,**[9] a house and sign painter at Chatham, m. Sep. 2, 1869, Susie Rogers of Chatham. Issue:

1. Hattie M.,	b. Apr. 23, 1870.
2. E. Hartwell,	b. Jan. 14, 1872.

2. **Harriet A.**[9] m. Jul. 14, 1868, David V. Terhune of Nova Scotia, but had no issue.

†–1–4–2. **George T.**[8] was captain of a fisherman, and was drowned off Chatham, Dec. 4, 1891. He m. 1st, Feb. 4, 1847, Marinda Bearse and had issue :

    1. Samuel A.,   b. Nov. 14, 1847.   d. Jun. 4, 1851.

George T. m. 2d, Feb. 26, 1856, Adelie A. Yale of Connecticut, who d. Feb. 13, 1892. No other issue.

†–1–4–4. **John F.**,[8] a fisherman and mariner, m. 1st, Dec. 6, 1849, Mehitable Gills. Issue :

    1. Julia A.,   b. Sep. 15, 1852.
    2. Adelia M.,   b. Jul. 14, 1856.   d. Apr. 25, 1876.
    3. Isaac L. 2d,   b. Feb. 23, 1861.
    4. Mattie,   b. Mch. —, 1868.   d. Dec. 14, 1870.

1. **Julia A.**[9] m. Jan. 1873, Elijah T. Harding, and had issue : Walter C. and Bertha F.

3. **Isaac L. 2d,**[9] a mariner, m. Nov. 19, 1885, Lizzie E. Ryder of Chatham, and had issue :

    1. Jessie L,   b. Jul. 23, 1889.   d. May 3, 1890.

John F. m. 2d, Apr. 22, 1868, Almeda Hamilton. No other issue.

†–1–4–5. **Isaac L.**[8] was a captain in the coasting service, and was lost at sea Oct. 5, 1859. He m. Feb. 6, 1851, Hannah Reynolds, and had issue as follows :

    1. Susan J.,   b. Jan. 2, 1852.   d. Sep. 12, 1852.
    2. Hannah J. L. J.,   b. Jan. 7, 1859.   d. Aug. 30, 1877.

2. **Hannah J. L. J.**[9] m. Aug. 30, 1877, Luther E. Hammond, son of Luther Jr. Her children were : Mertis J. and Harvey E.

†–1–4–6. **William,**[8] sixth son of John Jr., and captain of a fisherman, m. Aug. 22, 1858, Mercy Atkins of Chatham, and had ten children :

    1. Isaac W.,   b. Dec. 10, 1859.   d. Mch. 23, 1860.
    2. Rebecca A.,   b. Aug. 4, 1862.
    3. John W.,   b. Sep. 20, 1864.
    4. Twins,   b. Sep. 24, 1866.   d. Sep. 24, 1866.
    5. Cyrenah,   b. Aug. 27, 1868.   d. Dec. 12, 1870.
    6. Eleonora L.,   b. Mch. 16, 1871.
    7. Elmer F.,   b. Jan. 19, 1873.
    8. George T.,   b. Nov. 10, 1874.
    9. Ezra N. A.,   b. Aug. 17, 1876.

Of these children, 2. **Rebecca**[9] is a dressmaker at Chatham; 3. **John W.**[9] is a sea captain, and was recently in the employ of the Boston Tow Boat Co.; 7. **Elmer**[9] is a house and ship-carpenter at East Boston; 8. **George,**[9] in the employ of the Boston Tow Boat Co., is also engaged in studying marine engineering; 6. **Eleonora**[9] and 9. **Ezra**[9] reside at Chatham.

†–1–5. **Stephen,**[7] fourth son of John, m. Jan. 18, 1820, Betsey Ryder of Chatham, and had issue :

1. Alpheus A.,	b. Jul. 9, 1821.	
2. Rebecca R.,	b. Dec. 21, 1822.	d. Oct. 31, 1848.
3. Hannah W.,	b. Feb. 9, 1827.	d. in infancy.
4. Hannah W.,	b. Jan. 9, 1828.	
5. Stephen W., Jr.,	b. Feb. 20, 1829.	d. in infancy.
6. Stephen W., Jr.,	b. Oct. 24, 1830.	
7. Seth W.,	b. in 1835.	d. in infancy.
8. Seth W.,	b. May 14, 1837.	

Of these children, **Rebecca R.**[8] m. Feb. 2, 1844, Robert Eldridge of Chatham. Her children were : Robert A., Laura A., and Rebecca H.

4. **Hannah W.**[8] m. Jan. 7, 1851, Samuel Harding, and lives at Ansonia, Conn. Mr. Harding is a carpenter, and was drummer of the 58th Reg't M. V. M. Her children are : Corinna T., Mary W., George H., and Samuel E. T.

Hannah W. was formerly a school-teacher, and was leader of a church choir when 16 years of age.

†–1–5–1. **Alpheus A.,**[8] who is a mariner, m. Feb. 2, 1847, Rebecca Eldridge, and had issue :

1. Albert W.,	b. Jun. 19, 1849.

1. **Albert W.,**[9] a fisherman, m. 1st, Jan. 18, 1877, Clarinda H. Folger of Nantucket, and had :

1. Clarence A.,	b. May 18, 1878.

Albert W. m. 2d, Aug. 31, 1879, Sarah Folger, sister of Clarinda. Issue :

2. Florence M.,	b. Mch. —, 1880.
3. Willie,	b. Aug. —, 1882.

†–1–5–6. **Stephen W. Jr.,**[8] captain of a fisherman, m. Aug. 16, 1854, Eunice A. Rogers of Orleans, Mass., and had :

1. Adelbert S.,	b. Dec. —, 1862.

†-1-5-8. **Seth W.,**[8] school-committeeman, school-teacher, and justice of the peace, Chatham, m. Oct. 30, 1877, Addie L. Ellis. Issue:

1. Francis E.,   b. Jan. 10, 1879.
2. Arthur S.,   b. Aug. 11, 1880.
3. Edna M.,   b. Feb.   6, 1882.

†-1-6. **William,**[7] fifth son of John, m. May 5, 1820, Reliance Wing of Chatham, and had issue:

1. Rebecca,   b. Sep.   8, 1821.   d. Nov. 7, 1878.
2. William, Jr.,   b. Sep. 10, 1823.
3. Alexander,   b. Apr.   7, 1827.   d. Oct. 27, 1828.

1. **Rebecca**[8] m. Feb. 2, 1842, Albert Hardy of Chatham, and had issue:

1. Albertina,   b. Nov. 27, 1845.

1. **Albertina**[9] m. Jul. 7, 1881, William A. Prince of Southhold, N. Y. Issue not learned.

†-1-6-2. **William Jr.**[8] is a carpenter, and lives at Boston Highlands. He m. Apr. 14, 1846, Rhoda A. Harding, who was b. Nov. 23, 1823. Issue:

1. Everett B.,   b. Nov. 20, 1847.
2. William C.,   b. Feb. 13. 1849.   d. Mch. 24, 1850.
3. William C.,   b. Oct.   5, 1851.
4. Albinus A.,   b. Oct.   6, 1853.   d. Apr. 25, 1855.
5. Mary E.,   b. Nov. 11, 1856.   d. Apr. 28, 1859.
6. Addison R.,   b. Oct. 30, 1866.

Of these children, who were born at Chatham, Mass., **Everett**[9] is a carpenter, and **William C.**[9] a teamster. Both reside in Boston, and are single.

6. **Addison R.,**[9] who is a plumber in Boston, m. May 11, 1891, Elizabeth M. Carney of Boston. No issue.

†-1-7. **Elisha,**[7] sixth son of John, m. Jan. 29, 1824, Lydia Allen of Harwich, and had issue:

1. Eveline,   b. Jan.   6, 1828.
2. Lydia A.,   b. Sep. 17, 1829.
3. Almira,   b. Dec.   1, 1831.
4. Elisha. Jr.,   b. Nov. 23, 1833.
5. Albert S.,   b. Sep. 17, 1837.
6. Marcelia,   b. Feb.   7, 1844.

Of these children, 1. **Eveline**[8] m. 1st, Nov. 29, 1848, William F. Blount of Barnstable, Mass. Her children, by this marriage, were : William F., Emma C., Horace A., and Henry G.

Eveline m. 2d, Feb. 26, 1863, Josiah R. Dill, and had : Hattie F. b. Oct. 24, 1868.

2. **Lydia A.,**[8] who is a dealer in dry goods, m. Jun. 14, 1849, Mark C. Chase, and had issue : Mark, Annette, and Mary E.

3. **Almira**[8] m. Feb. 6, 1852, Roland R. Badger of Sharon, Vt. Her children were : Clara J., Emma, and Maria.

6. **Marcelia,**[8] formerly a teacher in Chatham, m. Feb. 25, 1868, Watson R. Baker of Harwich. She has a son Walter W., b. Jan. 21, 1875, who entered Dartmouth College in Sep. 1891.

†-1-7-4. **Elisha Jr.,**[8] captain of a fisherman, m. Apr. 25, 1859, Lydia E. Allen of Harwich, and had issue :

1. Mary T.,	b. Aug. —, 1861.	d. Oct. 24, 1864.
2. Mary C.,	b. Nov. 16, 1864.	
3. Cora E.,	b. Mch. 23, 1867.	

3. **Cora E.**[9] m. Apr. 6, 1888, Orrin H. Eldridge, and had two children.

†-1-7-5. **Albert S.,**[8] captain of a fisherman, m. Nov. 27, 1862, Sarah R. Snow, and had issue :

1. Marcus A.,	b. Aug. 22, 1863.
2. Walter J.,	b. May 29, 1874.
3. Angie M.,	b. May 30, 1878.
4. Herbert C.,	b Sep. 9, 1887.

Of these children of **Albert S., Marcus A.** and **Walter J.** are fishermen.

4. **Herbert C.,**[9] a tailor, m. Jul. 30, 1890, Susie M. Mayo. No issue.

†-1-8. **Zebedee,**[7] seventh son of John, m. Oct. 28, 1827, Betsey Fessenden of Brewster, Mass., and had issue :

1. Ann E.,	b. Feb. 22, 1828.	
2. Celistia F.,	b Aug. 18, 1830.	b. Apr. 13, 1870.
3. Cyrus A.,	b. May 13, 1833.	d. Jul. —, 1855.
4. Isabell B.,	b. Nov. 4, 1836.	
5. Lucy M.,	b Aug. 24, 1839.	d. Feb. 8, 1860.
6. Charles H.,	b. Nov. 5, 1841.	

Of the above children, **Cyrus A.**[6] was drowned on the Grand Banks; and **Lucy M.**[8] was a teacher at Chatham.

2. **Celistia**[8] m. Aug. 1851, Reuben Eldridge of Chatham, and had Cyrus, b. Dec. 31, 1858.

4. **Isabel B.**[8] m. Mch. 2, 1859, George T. Snow, carpenter at Chatham. Her children are: Rebecca T., Charles E., George E., Lucy I., and Susan B. Charles is a conductor, and George a brakeman, on the Chatham Branch R. R.

6. **Charles H.**[6] is a fisherman, and keeper of the Monomoy Light-house, Chatham. He m. Dec. 15, 1864, Dorinda Howes. Issue: 1. Celia F., b. Nov. 7, 1871.

13.—JOHN HAMMOND OF SOUTH WOODSTOCK, VT.

†. **John Hammond**[5] fifth son of Jabez' [John,[3] Benjamin,[2] William'], was born in what is now New Bedford, Jan. 20, 1749, and d. at South Woodstock, Vt., Aug. 1814. He moved from New Bedford to South Woodstock in Sep. 1782, where he was a farmer, his father going with him. He m. 1st, Lois Wood, by whom he had three sons who d. in infancy; and ten daughters as follows :

Mary,[6] who m. Spaulding Shepard; **Eunice,**[6] who m. Jesse Royce; **Hannah,**[6] who m. a Mr. Tyler; **Deborah,**[6] who m. E. Bigelow; **Dinah,**[6] single; **Laura,**[6] who m. Abner Abbot; **Drusilla,**[6] who m. William Sterling; **Lois,**[6] single; and two other daughters, who d. in infancy. Nothing further is known of these daughters.

John m. 2d, Lucy [Woods] Wing, by whom he had a son :

14. John Winslow,   b. May 17, 1807.   d. Nov. 5, 1888.

14. **John Winslow,**[6] who lived and died at Claremont, N. H., worked for a time in his younger days at West Wareham, Mass. He afterwards sailed from New Bedford in the whale fishery business, until he became and continued master of a vessel for several successive voyages, in which business he was always lucky. At the age of 80 he was hale and hearty, had most of his teeth, and could read without the aid of glasses.

Capt. John m. Sep. 14, 1846, Vienna Call, who was b. in 1813, and d. Oct. 13, 1885. Issue :

1. John Winslow 2d, b. Oct 31, 1847.
2 Gardner Merritt, b. Mch. 23, 1850.   d. Feb. 4, 1868.
3. Marcella E., b. Mch. 13, 1856.

†–14–1. **John Winslow 2d**[7] lives on his father's farm in Claremont, N. H., and has been twice married. He m. 1st, May 28, 1877, Mary McLaughlin, who d. Sep. 10, 1878. Issue :

    1. Catha,   b. May 29. 1878.

He m. 2d, Oct. 24, 1880, Gertrude J. Smith, and had further issue :

    2. Gardner Winslow,   b. Jun. 9 1881.

†–14–3. **Marcella E.**[7] m. Aug. 1879, Horatio N. Webster of Leeds, Eng., and lives at Newport, N. H. Issue :

    1. Horatio N , Jr.,   b. Feb. 11. 1881.
    2. Roger,   b. Jan. 16, 1886.

14.—ELIJAH HAMMOND OF RUTLAND AND OAK-HAM, MASS.

†. **Elijah**[5] **Hammond**, sixth son of Jabez[4] [John,[3] Benjamin,[2] William[1]], was born in the old town of Dartmouth, (now New Bedford), Mass., Mch. 4, 1751, and died at Oakham, Mass., Apr. 20, 1815. He served in the War of the Revolution, being a Sergeant in the 5th Mass. Reg't. He also acted a portion of the time as clerk, or private secretary, to General Washington. For one year he was confined on board a British prison-ship, where he underwent many hardships. He received an honorable discharge, and at the same time was honored with a badge of merit. His discharge — which was signed by General Washington himself — reads : " For faithful and honorable service, five years and upwards.
Given at Head-quarters the eleventh day of June, 1783."
He moved from New Bedford to Rutland, and afterwards to Oakham, Mass. He m. 1st, in 1777, Mrs. Sarah [Cutting] Harrington, who d. Mch. 4, 1794. Issue :

1. Elijah 2d,   b. Apr. 7, 1778.   d. Mch. 8, 1845.
2. Sarah,   b. Oct. 6, 1783.   d. in 1841.
3. Susannah,   b. Dec. 4, 1785.   d. May —, 1856.
4. Betsey,   b. Feb 8, 1787.   d. Jun. 23, 1840.
5. Abigail,   b. May 19. 1788.   d.
6. John,   b. Aug 19. 1790.   d. Apr. 1, 1871.
7. Aurelia,   b. Aug. 21. 1791.   d. Feb. 7, 1873.

The above children were born in Rutland, Mass. Elijah m. 2d, Eunice Davis, who was b. in 1754. Issue by the second marriage :

    8. Isabella,   b. in   1797.   d. Jan. 1. 1831.

Of these children, 2. **Sarah,**[6] who lived and d. in South Boston, m. Ira Draper of Spencer, and had issue : Fidelia, Octavia, Aurelia, Hammond, and James.

3. **Susannah**[6] m. James Glezen and lived many years in Beechwoods, Penn., where her children were born. They afterwards moved to Petersburg, Ind., where they both died. Mr. Glezen was b. in Holden, Mass., in 1777, and d. near Petersburg, Ind., Feb. 1840. Issue : Martha, Elijah Hammond, Susannah A., James, Caroline A., Joseph P., Edward A., Hamilton W., and Charles O.

4. **Betsey**[6] m. Joseph Phinney of Boston, and had issue : Ann Jane; and Laura, who m. Freeman Hunt, and had : Frederic, Laura, Helen, and Emma. Betsey lived in South Boston, but d. at Worcester at her brother John's.

5. **Abigail,**[6] called Nabbe, m. Ebenezer Cobb, and lived and d. in Philadelphia. Issue : Mary, Sarah, Ebenezer, and Joseph Phinney.

7. **Aurelia**[6] m. Ezra Maynard and lived and d. at Oakham, Mass. No issue.

8. **Isabella**[6] m. Nov. 20, 1816, Roswell Taylor of Oakham, where she lived and died. Issue : Caroline, Isabella L., Ann Jane, Elizabeth, and Mary.

Caroline, who m. Artemas Maynard now deceased, lives in Oakham.

†-1. **Elijah 2d,**[6] b. at Rutland, Mass., was in early life a merchant in Philadelphia, where he married, and where his children were born. In 1819 he moved to Petersburg, Pike Co., Ind., where he bought a farm, and where he d. Mch. 8, 1846. He was County Judge for a number of years, and a strong member of the Masonic Fraternity. He m. at Philadelphia, May 15, 1806, Mary Pollock, who d. in Petersburg, Feb. 25, 1842. Issue :

1	Albert,	b. Aug. 13, 1807.	d. Jun. 2. 1842.
2	Susanna,	b. May 14. 1809.	d. Oct. 3. 1819.
3	John,	b. Jun 24, 1811.	d.

4. Perry C.,	b. Sep. 26, 1813.	
5. Lester,	b. Jun. 14, 1816.	d. Dec. 27, 1851.
6. Jane,	b. Aug. 3, 1818.	d. Apr. 3. 1860.
7. Aurelia,	b. Feb. 8, 1827.	

Of these children, 6. **Jane,**[7] who lived and d. at Ireland, Dubois Co., Ind., m. Aug. 24, 1837, James Stewart, a farmer. Issue: Albert H., Elizabeth, Harry, Elijah, Aurelia, Amanda, Mary F., and Ethelbert.

7. **Aurelia,**[7] who resides in Helena, Ark., m. Nov. 22, 1848, George D. Jaquess, a physician and druggist. Issue: Mary, Luther, J. Wilkes, Ethelbert and Lorrentus, twins, and Aurelia G.

†-1-1. **Albert,**[7] oldest son of Elijah 2d, was a merchant at Petersburg, Ind. He m. Aug. 1, 1831, Elizabeth Case, and had issue:

1. Susan,	b. in 1832.	d. in 1834.
2. John M.,	b. Jan. 16, 1835.	
3. Elijah,	b. Aug. 1, 1836.	d. in 1859.
4. Reuben C.,	b. Jan. 6. 1839.	
5. Sarah Jane,	b. Oct. 19, 1840.	d. in infancy.
6. Amanda,	b. Oct. 18, 1841.	d. Aug. 24, 1855.

†-1-1-3. **Elijah,**[8] second son of Albert, received the Degree of M. D. at Louisville, Ky., in the Winter of 1857. He afterwards practised medicine at Edwardsport, Ind., where he died in the Spring of 1859. He m. ———— ———— , but left no issue.

†-1-1-4. **Reuben C.**[8] served one year as musician in the 27th Ind. Vols., during the late Civil War. He has never married, and is now engaged in the general insurance business in Petersburg.

†-1-1-2. **John M.,**[8] oldest son of Albert, enlisted as musician in the 27th Ind. Vols., and received his discharge after serving one year. He then raised a company of volunteers, which was afterwards a part of the 65th Reg't, and served as Captain until compelled on account of ill health to resign in Dec. 1863. Since the War he has lived at Evansville, Ind. He m. Apr. 23, 1853, Elizabeth Huffer, who d. Oct. 29, 1884. Issue:

1. Salem P.,	b. Apr. 22, 1854.	
2. Albert,	b. Mch. 24, 1856.	
3. Lida M.,	b. Nov. 17, 1858.	
4. Charles L.,	b. Mch. 23, 1861.	d. Mch. 31, 1891.

Of these children, 1. **Salem P.**[9] is a jeweler at Petersburg. He m. Sep. 19, 1881, Josie L. Chaffee, and had issue :

1. Lizzie,	b. Feb. 17, 1886.
2. Nnna,	b. Jul. 31, 1889.
3. Aura,	b. Feb. 13, 1892.

2. **Albert**[9] second son of John M., keeps a boarding-house in Chicago, Ill. He m. in Nov. 1887 Maggie Keernan of Chicago, but has no issue.

3. **Lida M.**[9] m. Feb. 28, 1883, Clarence Parker, and lives at Petersburg. Issue : Merle, Bessie, and Cade.

4. **Charles L.**[9] was a painter at Petersburg. He m. Jul. 16, 1890, Anna Pentecost, and d. without issue.

†–1–3. **John,**[7] second son of Elijah 2d, was a farmer at Petersburg. He m. Apr. 13, 1843, Jane Stewart, who d. Feb. 26, 1892. Issue :

| 1. William A., | b. Apr. 28, 1844. | d. Oct. 23, 1864. |
| 2. John, Jr., | b. Sep. 30, 1846. | |

1. **William A.**[8] was a Sergeant of Co. G., 65th Ind. Vols., from Jul. 15, 1862, to Jan. 21, 1864. He afterwards lived at Petersburg, and died on account of wounds and disabilities received in the service.

2. **John Jr.**[8] is a merchant in Petersburg. He m. Jun. 30, 1880, Lillie B. Tellie, and had issue :

1. Horace A.,	b. Jan. 6, 1882.	
2. Ida,	b. Aug. 28, 1884.	
3. Agnes,	b. Jun. 28, 1886.	
4. John,	b. Apr. 20, 1888.	d. in infancy.
5. Courtney E.,	b. Oct. 28, 1889.	
6. Omer Tellie,	b. May 8, 1891.	

†–1–4. **Perry C.,**[7] third son of Elijah 2d, is a merchant at Petersburg, firm of P. C. Hammond & Sons. He m. 1st, Sep. 20, 1837, Nancy Edmonson, and had issue :

1. Theodore E.,	b. Jul. 2, 1838.	d. Jul. —, 1878.
2. Oliver A.,	b. Dec. 14, 1840.	
3. Oscar,	b. Oct. 24, 1841.	d. in infancy.
4. Albert,	b. Aug. 8, 1843.	d. young.
5. Mary Florence,	b. Aug. 23, 1845.	
6. Almira,	b. May 23, 1847.	d. in infancy.
7. Perry C., Jr.,	b. Apr. 17, 1850.	
8. Reddick,	b. Aug. 13, 1852.	d. young.

Perry C. m. 2d, Feb. 19, 1857, Caroline Gilbreath, and had further issue:

9. Ida Belle,	b. Dec. 2, 1857.	
10. Lola,	b.	d. in infancy.

Of these children, 9. **Ida Belle**[8] resides with her parents in Petersburg.

1. **Theodore E.,**[9] oldest son of Perry C., enlisted in Co. H, 24th Ind. Vols., Jul. 6, 1861, and served in the Quartermaster's Dept. till Sep. 1863. He was then transferred to the 53d U. S. Colored Troops as Regimental Quartermaster, serving until Mch. 1866. He was afterwards an accountant at Petersburg. He m. in 1865 Sallie Hart of Milliken Bend, La., and had issue: Maggie and Flora.

Maggie[9] and **Flora**[9] are both married and live somewhere in Mississippi.

2. **Oliver A.,**[8] second son of Perry C., who served one year as musician in the 27th Ind. Vols., is now a merchant at Petersburg in company with his father and brother. He m. Nov. 7, 1877, Laura Watt, who d. Feb. 9, 1888. Besides Flora, Reddick and Willie O., who d. in infancy, he has issue:

1. Carrie,	b. Sep. 29, 1878.
2. Hugh W.,	b. Sep. 2, 1880.

3. **Mary F.**[8] m. Nov. 7, 1866, Alexander R. Byers, M. D., a physician at Petersburg. Dr. Byers, b. Jun. 15, 1829, received the degree of M. D. from the Medical College at Evansville, Ind., in Mch. 1854; served as Surgeon of the 65th Reg't Ind. Vols., from Aug. 1862 to Mch. 1865; member Pike Co. Ind. Med. Society; Ind. State Med. Society; and the American Med. Association. Issue:

1. Henry W.,	b. Sep. 21, 1867.	
2. Frank H.,	b. Mch. 20, 1869.	d. in infancy.
3. Anna M.,	b. Jul. 24, 1870.	d. Oct. 27, 1887.
4. Perry H.,	b. Apr. 28, 1872.	
5. John A.,	b. Dec. 24, 1873.	
6. Oliver A.,	b. Feb. 6, 1875.	
7. Ethel May,	b. Aug. 20, 1876.	

7. **Perry C. Jr.**[9] is a merchant at Petersburg, firm of P. C. Hammond & Sons. He m. Sep. 17, 1888, Sarah Bruner. No issue.

†-1-5. **Lester,**[7] fourth son of Elijah 2d, was a farmer at

Petersburg. He m. Aug. 23, 1838, Nancy Case, and had issue :

1. Mary J.,	b. about	1839.	d. about 1850.
2. Eliza A.,	b. Mch.	8, 1841.	
3. Theophilus,	b. Jul.	1, 1843.	d. Feb. 9. 1875.
4. Erastus,	b.		d. in infancy.
5. Oscar,	b. Jan.	29 1848.	
6. Elizabeth A.,	b. Mch.	27. 1850.	
7. Lester Helen,	b. Jun.	9, 1852.	d. Feb. 12, 1875.

2. **Eliza A.**[8] m. 1st, May 18, 1859, Posey Ashby, and had : Frances Evaline, and George B. McClellan, both of whom, with their father, died in Aug. 1864. Eliza m. 2d, Feb. 1865, William H. Dye. Issue : William, Ebenezer, and Mary Alice Belle. They reside in Caldwell Co., Tex.

6. **Elizabeth A.**[8] m. Sep. 19, 1865, William H. R. Snyder, and lives at Monroe City, Ind. Issue : Grace, Emma, Kate, Mary, Helen, and Oscar.

7. **Lester Helen**[8] m. Nov. 10, 1872, Elias Osborn Jr., and lived at Petersburg, Ind. Issue : A daughter that d. in infancy.

3. **Theophilus,**[8] oldest son of Lester, served from Aug. 1862 to Feb. 1863, in Co. K, 12th Ky. Cavalry, when he was discharged on account of ill health. After the War he carried on farming, and d. at Island 76, Mississippi River, Arkansas. He m. Aug. 13, 1862, Julia A. G. Dye, and had issue :

1. John L.,	b. May 18, 1863.	d. Jan. 3, 1885.
2. Nora,	b. Apr. 7, 1870.	

John L.[9] m. ——— ———, and d. at Monroe City, Knox Co., Ind., without issue ; and **Nora E**[9] resides, single, at Monroe City.

5. **Oscar**[8] served as bugler one year and nine months in Co. F, 10th Ind. Cavalry. He is now Superintendent and General Agent of the Prudential Life Insurance Co. of America, and resides at Terre Haute, Ind. He m. May 14, 1882, Jennie Tislow, née Davisson, and had issue :

1. Lester Davisson,	b. Jun. 23, 1883.
2. Harry Byars,	b. Dec. 31, 1884.
3. Barney Alexander,	b. May 8, 1890.

†-6. **John,**[6] second son of Elijah 1st, was b. in Rutland, Mass., Aug. 19, 1790. He afterwards moved to Oakham,

JOHN HAMMOND

Mass., and later to Worcester, where, after many years, he finally d. Apr. 1, 1871.

Although he kept much aloof from public life he was at one time one of the Overseers of the Poor of the City of Worcester, and was a member of the State Legislature in 1841.

He was noted for his sound common sense in business matters, his integrity of character, and his inflexibility of purpose in what he considered right or proper. But few men had more influence in shaping the development and prosperity of his adopted city than himself.

One of his peculiarities was a decided proneness to have all business matters take effect from April 1st. So noticeable was this that during his last illness, — which dated from Nov. 26th, — a friend remarked that "Mr. John Hammond would live until the first of April, and then he would die." And as a singular coincidence his death occurred on that date.

John m. 1st, Jun. 30, 1818, Adalina A. Stone, who was b. Oct. 29, 1798, and d. in Worcester, Jun. 3, 1846. Issue:

1. Elijah 3d,	b. Oct. 4, 1819.	
2. Otis S.,	b. Oct. 9, 1821.	d. Jun. 30, 1880.
3. Joseph P.,	b. Aug. 13, 1823.	
4. Adalina A.,	b. Aug. 29, 1825.	
5. Louise B.,	b. Mch. 10, 1828.	
6. Susan M.,	b. Sep. 17, 1833.	d. Aug. 2, 1854.
7. John R.,	b. Nov. 13, 1838.	d. Nov. 16, 1841.
8. Fred'c Hunt,	b. Jul. 1, 1843.	

John m. 2d, Dec. 1846, Mrs. Susan [Stone] Robinson, who was b. Apr. 28, 1804, and d. May 7, 1880. No other issue.

†-6-1. **Elijah 3d,**[7] oldest son of John, is a farmer, and lives at Worcester, Mass. He m. Dec. 19, 1843, Caroline N. Felton, who was b. in Barre, Mass., Dec. 9, 1821, and d. Jun. 6, 1882. Issue:

1. Adaline Sturgis,	b. Jan. 17, 1845.	
2. Alice Maria,	b. Dec. 19, 1849.	
3. Ellen Caroline.	b. Jan. 12, 1853.	
4. John,	b. Dec. 8, 1856.	d. Mch. 6, 1864.
5. Albert Elijah,	b. Dec. 16, 1859.	d. Mch. 6, 1864.

Of the children of Elijah 3d, **Alice**[8] and **Ellen**[8] live at home, both single; and **Adaline**[8] m. Sep. 10, 1867, Vernon Long, and lives in Buffalo, N. Y. Issue: Vernon H., Blanche S., Albert E., Frank E., and Alice.

14

†–6–2. **Otis S.,**[7] second son of John, was Head Clerk in the Freight Depot of the Boston & Albany R. R. at Worcester, Mass., and was much respected. He m. Oct. 12, 1847, Lydia Spooner, who d. at Graniteville, S. C., Mch. 10, 1892. Issue :

  1. Jennie Adaline,   b. Sep. 16, 1857.

Jennie Adaline[8] m. Aug. 22, 1883, Alvin Etheridge, and resides at Graniteville, S. C. Issue : Rodney Hammond and Ruth Elizabeth.

†–6–3. **Joseph P.,**[7] third son of John, is a farmer at Worcester, Mass. He m. 1st, Jun. 2, 1855, Ellen N. Robbins, who d. Apr. 22, 1874. Issue :

  1. John Frank,   single; Barre, Mass.

Joseph P. m. 2d, Jun. 14, 1876, Eliza A. Young. No other issue.

†–6–4. **Adaline Aurelia,**[7] oldest daughter of John, m. Oct. 8, 1846, Joseph Belyea, who d. Nov. 4, 1860, and lives in Clinton, Mass. Issue :

  1. Ida Louise.   b. Nov. 25. 1847.
  2. Albert John,   b. Dec. 8, 1852.   d. Aug. 12. 1854.

Ida Louise[8] m. Oct. 14, 1873, George H. Burtis, and lives in Worcester. Issue : Albert and Fred, twins, and Helen Louise.

†–6–5. **Louise B.,**[7] second daughter of John, m. Sep. 10, 1847, B. Frank Lee, who is a dealer in provisions in Worcester. Issue : Carrie and George P.

†–6–6. **Susan M.,**[7] third daughter of John, m. May 30, 1854, David White, and lived at her father's in Worcester. No issue.

†–6–8. **Fred'c Hunt,**[7] youngest son of John, was a farmer, and lives at Worcester. He m. May 8, 1866, Alice J. McFarland. Issue :

  1. Cora S.,   b. Jun. 18, 1868.
  2. Eliza A.,   b. Jan. 20, 1872.
  3. Myra L.,   b. Apr. 7, 1883.
  4. Fred'c Hunt, Jr.,   b. Oct. 16, 1886.

All of Fred's children are single, and all reside at Worcester.

II.—ELNATHAN HAMMOND OF NEWPORT, R. I.

†. **Elnathan⁴ Hammond**, second son of John,³ [Benjamin,² William¹], was born at Rochester, Mass., Mch. 7, 1703, and died at Newport, R. I., May 24, 1793, æ. 90. He was a sea captain in the merchant service, sailing from Newport, his place of residence. "His descendants cherish his memory with peculiar regard, retain his portrait, point to his former residence still standing in Thames Street, recall his character as a sea captain in the best commercial period of the town, and his active interests in the Congregational Church."

To the Memorandum Book kept by him, beginning Jan. 1, 1737, are the descendants of "William of London" indebted for the accurate information they possess of their early ancestors. Except for the Genealogical history contained in this book the line of William of London would have been inevitably swamped in the line of "William of Watertown," Mass. This valuable relic is a pocket memorandum book, long preserved in Vermont in the family of the grandson and namesake of the original owner, now in possession of Rev. John D. Hammond of San Francisco, Cal., a descendant of Capt. Elnathan Hammond.

The first inscription in respect to date in this reverend relic reads :

"Elnathan Hammond, his Memorandum Book, Feby 1755. Memorandum of some things I have observed, yᵗ I think remarkable and of some things I have thought so in the course of my reading."

On the fly-leaf is formally inscribed :

"This memorandum Book I have given to my grand-son, Elnathan Hammond, May yᵉ 15th, 1781, and I desire that he may have the possession of it after my Decease: Witness my Daughter Elizᵗʰ Sprague.   ELNATHAN HAMMOND."

"The portion of the book which with Genealogists has gained in vitality by time, is of course that in which the family history is disclosed, nor in this probably is the spirit misrepresented, which in a patriarchal way provided the mode of preserving it. The grave of Capt. Hammond, in the old Burying ground [Newport], is with those members of his family, finding their place in dust with his own, while traces of his filial spirit, in this record restore the place of his ancestral line in remembrance, and that of his venerated ancestress who brought it over."

The Genealogical history is prefaced with the following introduction :

"A short Record of our Family, by Elnathan Hammond, copied from a Family Record of my father's, Mr. John Hammond of Rochester, 1737, and continued, beginning the year at the 1st of January."

"William Hammond, born in the city of London, and there married Elizabeth Penn, sister of Sir William Penn, had children : Benjamin their son born 1621, Elizabeth, Martha and Rachel their daughters, all born in London. William Hammond died there and was buried. Elizabeth Hammond, widow of William Hammond, with her son Benjamin and three daughters, all young, left a good estate in London, and with several Godly people came over to New England in troublesome times in 1634, out of a conscious desire to have the liberty to serve God in the way of his appointment. They had with them the Rev. Mr. Lothrop, their minister, A. D. 1634. Settled in Boston, and there died 1640, had an honorable burial and the character of a very Godly woman.

Benjamin Hammond, their son, removed to Sandwich and there married Mary Vincent, daughter of John Vincent. She was born in England in 1633. Benjamin Hammond married to Mary Vincent 1650. Had born :

> Samuel, their son, 1655.
> John, their son, Nov. 30, 1663.
> Nathan, their son, 1670.
> Benjamin, their son, Nov. 1673.
> Had two daughters, died young.

Benjamin Hammond, with his wife and four sons, moved to Rochester and there died, aged 82 years, 1703. Mary his widow died 1705."*

Capt. Elnathan Hammond m. 1st, Dec. 27, 1728, Mary [Rogers] Wignall. She was a daughter of John Rogers of Newport, and was b. Aug. 24, 1700, and d. Oct. 20, 1749. Issue :

1. John Arnold,	b. Feb.	9, 1731.	d. Jun.	—, 1781.
2. Abigail,	b. Sep.	20, 1733.	d. Jan.	15, 1734.
3. Elnathan,	b. Jan.	17, 1736.	d. Dec.	4, 1737.
4. Abigail,	b. Feb.	15, 1737.	d.	
5. Elnathan, Jr.,	b. May	11, 1738.	d. Sep.	22, 1763.
6. Joseph,	b. Apr.	13, 1739.	d.	
7. Nathaniel,	b. Jun.	2, 1740.	d. Mch.	—, 1777.
8. Mary,	b. Sep.	22, 1741.	d. May	7, 1767.
9. Elizabeth,	b. May	25, 1743.	d.	
10. Susannah,	b. Jun.	18, 1744.	d. Aug.	24, 1780.

Capt. Elnathan m. 2d, Sep. 5, 1750, O. S., Elizabeth [Vernon] Cox, daughter of Samuel Vernon, Esq., and b. at Newport, Aug. 5, 1709. No living issue.

* Philip Battell, *Historical and Genealogical Register*, Jan. 1876.

CAPT. ELNATHAN HAMMOND.

Of the above children the first **Abigail**[5] and the first **Elnathan**[5] d. young; and **Elnathan Jr.,**[5] **Joseph,**[5] and **Mary**[5] d. single.

4. **Abigail**[5] m. Sep. 13, 1759, Jacob Richardson, and lived at Newport, R. I., where her husband was at one time postmaster. Issue: Mary Ann, Elizabeth Vernon, John Stevens, Nathaniel Hammond, Jacob Jr., Abby Hammond, Elnathan Hammond, Anstis Elizabeth, and George Washington. A descendant of Abigail in the fourth generation,—George H. Richardson,—is a resident of Newport, and Assistant Secretary of the Newport Historical Society.

9. **Elizabeth**[5] m. Jan. 20, 1773, Nathaniel Sprague, and lived at Rochester. Issue: Luce, Micah, and Nathaniel.

10. **Susannah**[5] m. Jan. 29, 1767, Caleb Lyndon, and d. at Rehoboth, Mass., Aug. 24, 1780. They had three sons and three daughters.

1.—JOHN ARNOLD OF NEWPORT, R. I.

†-1. **John Arnold**[5] m. Jun. 6, 1754, at Newport, R. I., Mary Scott, who is said to have been a niece of Benjamin Franklin. After his marriage he went with his family to Cornwallis, Nova Scotia, with the intention of founding a settlement there. He afterwards returned and engaged on the patriot side of the Revolution, was captured aboard a ship, taken to New York, and died a prisoner in the Hospital sometime in Jun. 1781. Issue:

1. Elnathan.	b. Dec. 16, 1760.	d.
2. Daughter,	b.	d. young.

†-1-1. **Elnathan,**[6] b. at Newport, R. I., m. Nov. 5, 1790, Deborah Carr, b. Jun. 10, 1760, and daughter of John Carr Jr. of North Kingston, R. I. Elnathan, moved to Lanesboro', Mass., and afterwards to Middlebury, Vt., where most of his children were born. Issue:

1. Lucinda,	b. May 8, 1792.	d. Jan. 19, 1853.
2. John Arnold,	b. Jul. 18, 1794.	d. Feb. 20, 1882.
3. Jane.	b. Oct. 27, 1795.	d. Mch. 19, 1850.
4. William,	b. Apr. 2, 1797.	d. May 27, 1858.
5. Emma,	b. May 4, 1799.	d. Apr. 1, 1886.
6. Edwin,	b. May 20, 1801.	d. Dec. 31, 1870.
7. Abigail,	b. Jan. 30, 1803.	

Of these children, **Abigail**[7] never married, and is living at Middlebury at the age of 90.

1. **Lucinda,**[7] b. at Lanesboro', Mass., m. Leonard Whedon of Bridport, Vt., where she lived a few years, but d. at Brattleboro'. No issue.

3. **Jane**[7] m. Levi Sperry of Cornwall, Vt., and d. Mch. 19, 1850, without issue.

5. **Emma**[7] m. Sep. 13, 1832, Elijah Birge of Middlebury. A few years before her death, she moved to Essex Junction, Vt., where she d. Apr. 1, 1886. Issue: Cyrus. Cyrus, who is a farmer at New Haven, Vt., m. Nov. 10, 1857, Marietta Elizabeth Gibbs. Issue: Walter Frederic, Frankie W., Freddie Wallace, Emma Clara, and Marietta E. Gibbs.

†-1-1-2. **John Arnold,**[7] oldest son of Elnathan, was a farmer at Middlebury, Vt. He m. Mch. 11, 1824, Fannie B. Keeler of Middlebury, who d. Apr. 2, 1870. Issue:

1. Martha H.,	b. Jun. 12, 1825.	
2. Helen,	b. Aug. 8, 1826.	d. Apr. 2, 1832.
3. Mariette.	b. Oct. 12, 1827.	
4. Helen Jane.	b. Apr. 29, 1836.	

Of these children, **Helen Jane**[8] resides, single, at Middlebury, Vt.

1. **Martha H.**[8] m. Dec. 12, 1851, Lucius Shaw, and resides at Middlebury. No issue.

3. **Mariette**[8] m. Feb. 17, 1848, Alonzo Raymond, and resides at Fond du Lac, Wis. Issue:

1. Fannie A.,	b. Jan. 4, 1849.	
2. Henry K.,	b. Apr. 17, 1851.	
3. Helen M ,	b. Jul. 24, 1853.	d. May 19, 1879.
4. Martha A.,	b. Feb. 22, 1857.	
5. Edwin A.,	b. Apr. 11, 1861.	

†-1-1-4. **William,**[7] second son of Elnathan, was a farmer at Middlebury, Vt. He m. Dec. 12, 1835, Sally Olmstead, who d. Dec. 13, 1873. Issue:

1. Elizabeth E.,	b. Apr. 3, 1836.
2. Henry W.,	b. May 3, 1837.

1. **Elizabeth E.**[9] m. Feb. 14, 1866, Josiah E. Dewey, and resides at Middlebury, Vt. No issue.

2. **Henry W.**,[2] who is a farmer at Middlebury, m. Sep. 16, 1862, Abbie Martin. Issue:

1. Martenia,	b. Jan. 16, 1864.
2. John W.,	b. Apr. 5, 1867.
3. William,	b. Dec. 1, 1870.
4. Dora E.,	b. Aug. 5, 1873.

Of these children, **Martenia**[3] m. Jun. 16, 1886, Willis Cady, and resides at Middlebury. Issue: Ralph Hammond, b. Aug. 29, 1891.

†–1–1–6. **Edwin**,[7] third son of Elnathan, was a farmer at Middlebury, and was noted for the high degree of perfection to which he bred the Atwood family of Spanish merino sheep in America. He m. Dec. 29, 1825, Alpa Olmstead, who d. May 1, 1871. Issue:

1. Edwin Seymour,	b. Nov. 7, 1827.
2. George,	b. May 31, 1836.

†–1–1–6–1. **Edwin Seymour**[8] is a farmer, and resides at Marinette, Wis. He m. 1st, Oct. 5, 1848, Julia A. Cady, who d. Aug. 5, 1850. Issue:

1. Julia E.,	b. May 13, 1849.	d. May 5, 1851.

Edwin S. m. 2d, Apr. 29, 1851, Rebecca Stewart, and had further issue:

2. Eva Julia,	b. May 11, 1852.	
3. Ed. Rice,	b. May 14, 1854.	d. Oct. 3, 1889.
4. Hattie Lou.,	b. May 5, 1858.	d. Jan. 17, 1886.
5. Dee Holeyoke,	b. Dec. 2, 1863.	

Of these children, **Eva Julia**[9] m. Nov. 3, 1874, Kelsey Theodore Waters, who was b. Jan. 11, 1846. Eva resides at Marinette, Wis., and has a son Theodore Hammond, b. Jun. 10, 1878.

4. **Hattie Louwella**[9] m. Oct. 24, 1885, Sandford J. Heafield, and lived at Marinette, Wis. No issue.

†–1–1–6–2. **George**,[8] second son of Edwin, is an extensive farmer and breeder of Spanish merino sheep at Middlebury, Vt. At the death of his father, the farm and flock came into his hands and has since been under his management and control. He has always been identified with the agricultural interests of his State, and at an early age became Secretary of Addison County Agricultural Society, which office he held for many years. He was also General Superintendent of the

Vermont State Agricultural Society, and one of its Directors for nearly 20 years. He served on the Board of Selectmen of his town over 12 years; was Postmaster under Garfield; and represented his town in the General Assembly of Vermont in the years 1878–79, during which he was Chairman of the Committee on Claims. He was nominated in County Convention in 1888 by acclamation for State Senator for two years, was elected by a full vote, and served as Chairman of the Committee on Rail Roads, and also served as Committee on Highways and Bridges, and Grand List. At the State Convention held at Burlington in 1888 to elect Delegates to the National Republican Convention at Chicago, he was elected alternate for ex-Secretary of War Proctor.

Mr. Hammond was one of the founders of the Vermont Atwood Merino Sheep Club, and has been its Secretary since its birth, and Treasurer all but the first two years. He spent most of the years 1888–90 in South America, and was in Buenos Ayres at the time of their revolution.

Mr. Hammond m. 1st, Sep. 16, 1858, Almeda L. Geer, who d. at San Francisco, Cal., Feb. 17, 1875. Issue:

    1. George E.,   b. Aug. 11, 1859.
    2. William Fred,   b. Mch. 27, 1861.
    3. H. S. Randall,   b. Feb. 12, 1864.

George Hammond m. 2d, Nov. 1, 1877, Jennie M. Morrison. No further issue.

1. **George E.**[9] is a book-keeper for the Thomson-Houston Electric Co., and resides at Chicago. He m. May 9, 1882, Addie Virginia Cowles, and has issue:

    1. Meeda Cowles.   b. May 12, 1883.
    2. Tom See,   b. Mch. 11, 1888.

2. **William Fred,**[9] who is a farmer at Middlebury, Vt., m. Nov. 1, 1880, Nellie Atwood. Issue:

    1. Bessie.   b. Feb. 1, 1882.   d. Feb. 4, 1882.
    2. Grace,   b. Dec. 15, 1883.

3. **Randall**[9] is General Agent for William Deering & Co., manufacturers of mowers and reapers. His place of business is Boston, Mass., and his residence, Leicester Junction, Vt. He m. Sep. 1, 1887, Florence Eliza Huntley, who was b. Feb. 10, 1865, at Whiting, Vt. No issue.

GEORGE HAMMOND.

7.—NATHANIEL OF NEWPORT, R. I.

†-7. **Nathaniel[5] Hammond,** fifth son of Capt. Elnathan, was b. at Rehoboth, Mass., and lived at Newport, R. I. He was a sea captain in the London trade, and d. in Jamaica, West Indies, Mch. 1777. He m. Nov. 27, 1769, Elizabeth Pabodie, who d. in Pharsalia, Chenango Co., N. Y., Mch. 1811. She was a daughter of Benjamin and Abigail [Lyon] Pabodie, and was directly descended from John Alden and Priscilla Mullins. Issue:

1. Benjamin,	b. Jan. 15, 1771.	b. Jan. —, 1858.
2. John,	b. Jun. —, 1773.	b. Oct. —, 1867.
3. Abigail,	b.	d. young.

†-7-1. **Dea. Benjamin[6]** was b. at Rehoboth, Mass., and d. at Norwich, Chenango Co., N. Y. He was a cabinet-maker and wheelwright at Newport, R. I., and Pharsalia, N. Y., where he moved about 1809, and made his home with his son John. He m. about 1790-91, Sarah Nichols, who was b. at Newport, R. I., Feb. 1771, and d. at Norwich, N. Y., Jan. 1858, æ. 84. Besides Polly, Joanna, Betsey, and Mary, who d. in infancy, they had issue:

1 Benjamin Pabodie,	b. Apr. 5, 1794.	d. Feb. 19, 1876.
2. Samuel Nichols.	b. about 1796.	d. about 1848.
3. John,	b Sep. 6, 1804.	
4. Abigail Southworth.	b. in 1806.	d. in 1869.
5. Sarah Nichols.	b. about 1808.	d. in 1865.

Of these children, who were all born at Newport, R. I., 5. **Sarah N.,[7]** who never married, lived at Norwich, N. Y., with her brother John, and d. at Middleton, Wis., with her sister Abigail in 1865.

†-7-1-1. **Benjamin Pabodie[7]** was a farmer at Onondaga, N. Y., where he lived and died. He m. Jul. 4, 1838, Lucinda Wilcox of Onondaga, who d. there Mch. 24, 1876, æ. 63. Issue:

1. Sarah E.,	b. Feb. 4, 1845.	
2. George W.,	b. Aug. 25, 1847.	d. Nov. 2, 1877-8.
3. Henry C.,	b. Feb. 25, 1850.	d. Feb. 24, 1876.

Of these children, **Sarah E.[8]** m. Jun. 10, 1876, Edward Tofield, who is a farmer and boatman at Oswego, N. Y. No issue.

2. **George W.,**[8] who was a farmer and lived and d. at
Utica, N. Y., m. May 14, 1876, Lucy Young, and had one
child :

> 1. Katie,   b. Oct. 22, 1878.

3. **Henry C.**[8] never married, was a farmer, and lived
and d. at Onondaga, N. Y.

†-7-1-2. **Samuel Nichols**[7] was a mechanic and farmer
at Claverack, Columbia Co., N. Y.. After some years he
sold his farm and opened a dry goods and grocery store. He
afterwards moved to Covington, Ky., where he died without
issue, though twice married. He m. 1st, about 1821, Allida
De La Matyr, who was born and married at Claverack, and died
there about 1833. He m. 2d, about 1835-6, Fanny [Ray]
McElleran, who was b. in Norwich, and d. in Brooklyn, N. Y.,
without issue by this marriage, though there were two children
by her former marriage with Mr. McElleran.

†-7-1-3. **John,**[7] who lived at Norwich, Chenango Co.,
N. Y., learned the trades of tanner and shoemaker, and later in
life was a dealer in hides, leather, boots, shoes, etc. He m.
Jul. 12, 1831, Elizabeth Owen, who was b. in Goshen, Orange
Co., N. Y., Dec. 10, 1810, and d. Aug. 6, 1887, at Norwich,
N. Y., without issue. John now resides at Greene, Chenango
Co., N. Y.

†-7-1-4. **Abigail Southworth**[7] m. 1st, at Pharsalia,
N. Y., in 1824, Rev. Augustine Anderson, a Methodist clergyman, who was b. in Penn Yan, Yates Co., N. Y., in 1802, and
d. Oct. 10, 1856, at Hartland, Niagara Co., N. Y. Mr. Anderson, who was a member of the Genesee Conference, and ordained
in 1825, preached all through western New York and northern
Pennsylvania, and afterwards in many places in Michigan.
Issue : Emory, Hester Ann, Sarah Maria, Charles H., Nettie A.

Of these children, **Emory,**[8] b. at Avoca, N. Y., in 1835,
m. in 1855, Melissa A. Smith, and had : Everett A., William
H., and Rose R. He d. at Granger, N. Y., in 1876, and his
widow, and his children, Everett and Rose, reside at Rochester,
N. Y. **Everett**[9] is a reporter for the press, and is said to be
an able young man.

Hester A.[8] d. at Jerusalem, N. Y., in 1851, when quite
young.

Sarah M.,[8] b. at New Hudson in 1841, m. in 1858, William W. Stone, and resides at Jamestown, N. Y. Her children are: Clarence A. and Nettie A.

Charles H.,[8] b. at New Hudson about 1843, m. in 1861–2, Sarah J. Heller, and lived at Little Valley, N. Y., where he d. in 1869. His children were: Elizabeth, and Florence who d. young.

Nettie A.,[8] b. at New Hudson in 1846, m. in 1871, Robert A. Prescott, and resides at Jamestown, N. Y. No issue.

Abigail [Hammond] Anderson m. 2d, in 1858, Rev. Henry De La Matyr, and d. without further issue, at Middleton, Wis., in 1869.

†–7–2. **John,**[6] second son of Capt. Nathaniel, was b. at Rehoboth, Mass., and died with his daughter Ruth at New Hudson, Alleghany Co., N. Y. He was a cabinet-maker and wheelwright at Newport, R. I., and Pharsalia, N. Y., where he moved about 1808. He m. Freelove Gardner Albro of Newport, who was b. in 1774 and d. Feb. 17, 1850. Issue:

1. Nathaniel,	b. in	1799.	d. Oct. 31, 1864.
2. Penelope Remington,	b. in	1801.	d. Jun. 5, 1855.
3. Abigail Lyon,	b. Nov. 28, 1803.		d. Feb. 15, 1858.
4. Stephen Yates,	b. Sep. 14, 1809.		
5. Ruth Waldron,	b. Oct. 31, 1811.		

Of these children, Nathaniel, Penelope, and Abigail were b. in Newport, R. I., and Stephen and Ruth in Pharsalia, N. Y. **Penelope R.,**[7] who was an invalid and an earnest Christian, lived with her brothers, Nathaniel and Stephen, and died with her brother Nathaniel at Scio, Alleghany Co., N. Y.

†–7–2–1. **Nathaniel,**[7] oldest son of John, who was a Congregational clergyman, preaching at Scio, Belmont, and Wellsville, N. Y., d. at Ossian, Livingston Co., N. Y. He was a man of decided views, strong convictions, and a good reasoner and sermonizer. He m. Mch. 24, 1850, Marilla Pearse, and had issue:

1. William C.,	b. Feb. 22, 1852.	d. Apr. 4, 1855.
2. Mary Julia,	b. Apr. 21, 1856.	

Mary Julia[8] resides at Akron, Erie Co., N. Y., never having married.

†-7-2-3. **Abigail Lyon,**[7] second daughter of John, known as Abba, was a superior woman, and a member of the Methodist Episcopal Church, and d. at Middleton, Wis., Feb. 15, 1858. She m. at Pharsalia, N. Y., Aug. 9, 1821, Rev. Henry De La Matyr, a Methodist clergyman, who d. at Bishop, Inyo Co., Cal., Sep. 20, 1889. Her children were : John Henry, b. Aug. 1822 ; David, b. Dec. 1823 ; Gilbert, b. Jul. 1825 ; Jane, b. 1827 ; George, b. 1829 ; Rebecca, b. 1832 ; Walter, b. 1835 ; Elias, b. 1837.

Of these children, **John,**[8] **David,**[8] **Gilbert,**[8] and **George**[8] were clergymen in the Methodist Episcopal Church; **Jane**[8] m. Rev. George Chester, a Methodist clergyman, deceased, and now resides, with her son George, at City Point, Fla. ; **Rebecca**[8] m. Rev. James Thomas, and resides with her daughter at Washington, D. C. ; **Walter,**[8] for many years Principal of Public Schools in Wisconsin, is now engaged in mining in western Colorado : **Elias**[8] is a physician, practising in Oakland and San Francisco, Cal.

Of these four sons, David d. in 1848, at New Hudson, N. Y. ; George and John, having retired from the ministry, reside at Bishop, Inyo Co., Cal.

Gilbert,[8] who has been a member of the Genesee, East New York, Nebraska, St. Louis, and South-East Indiana Conferences, while in Indianapolis was elected to the 46th Congress of the United States. In 1883 he entered the Colorado Conference, was stationed in Denver for six years, was then transferred to the East Ohio Conference, and stationed at Akron, O., in 1889, where he now resides.

†-7-2-4. **Stephen Yates,**[7] second son of John, a Methodist clergyman, was licensed to preach in 1850, joined the Geneva Conference in 1857, and was a faithful preacher of the Gospel to many Churches in western New York. On account of ill health, he was obliged to give up the ministry, and removed to Binghamton, N. Y., in 1891, where he now resides. He m. 1st, Feb. 21, 1833, Martha Adams, daughter of Darius Adams, who was b. May 14, 1809, and d. Apr. 16, 1863. Issue :

1. John Dempster,   b. May 9, 1841.
2. Charles Darius,   b. Mch. 1, 1844.

Stephen Y. m. 2d, Oct. 8, 1866, Mary [Chamberlayne] Parsons, who was b. Dec. 20, 1833, and had further issue :

3. Mary Stephenia,   b. Jul. 7, 1868.

Of these children, John was b. at Norwich, Chenango Co.; Charles Darius at Rushford, Alleghany Co.; and Mary at Lyndonville, Orleans Co., N. Y.

1. **John Dempster,**[5] oldest son of Stephen Yates, graduated from Alleghany College, Meadville, Penn., with the degree of A. B. in '65; later received the degree of A. M. from the same College; and the degree of D. D. from Union College in '83; afterwards moved to Carson City, Nev., where he was a clergyman in the Methodist Episcopal Church; and was also Grand Secretary of the Grand Lodge and Grand Chapter of Masons; and about 1888 removed to San Francisco, Cal., where he now resides. Dr. Hammond is a member of the California Annual Conference of the Methodist Episcopal Church, and has for a number of years had charge of the San Francisco Depository of the Methodist Publishing House. He m. at Springville, N. Y., Nov. 29, 1866, Sarah E. Powers, daughter of Rev. Philander Powers, who was b. in Bath, N. Y., Feb. 26, 1843. Issue:

    1. Henry Powers,   b. Jun. 4, 1871
    2. Anne Ruth,   b. Jan. 10, 1878.

Of these children, born at Carson, Nev., **Henry Powers**[9] is a member of the University of California, class of '93.

2. **Charles Darius,**[5] second son of Stephen Yates, served in the War of the Rebellion in a New York regiment, being employed as a telegraph operator. He was afterwards a telegraph operator at Susquehanna, N. Y., later train-despatcher at Albany, and finally was elected Superintendent of the Delaware & Hudson Canal Co. R. R., which position he now holds, residing at Albany, N. Y. He m. Jan. 29, 1866, Elnora Babcock, daughter of Brayton Babcock, M. D., of Friendship, N. Y., who was b. Nov. 24, 1844. No issue.

3. **Mary Stephenia,**[5] only daughter of Stephen Yates, resides at Schenectady, N. Y. She m. May 15, 1889, William L. Hall, who is Foreman of the Freight Dept. of the Delaware & Hudson Canal Co. R. R. Issue: 1. Ruth, b. Jun. 11, 1890.

†-7-2-5. **Ruth Waldron,**[7] youngest daughter of John, resides with her daughter Olivia at Akron, Erie Co., N. Y. She m. Feb. 17, 1831, Walter Adams, a farmer, who d. at

Akron, Sep. 27, 1877, æ. 75. Issue: Olivia E. A., Byron, Emily, Harriet, Mary, and Frank.

Of these children, **Olivia**[8] m. H. H. Newton, and resides at Akron, N. Y.; **Byron**,[8] single, lives at Belpre, O.; **Emily**,[8] or Emila, m. L. A. Stevens, Methodist minister, and resides at Perry, N. Y.; **Harriet**[8] m. C. G. Stevens, Methodist minister, and resides at Akron, N. Y.; **Mary**[8] m. Robert Crawford, a physician, and resides at Lu Verne, Minn.; and **Frank**[8] m. Clara Kelsey, and resides at Unadilla, N. Y.

III.—BENJAMIN HAMMOND 3d, OF ROCHESTER, MASS.

†. **Benjamin**[4] **Hammond 3d**,* third son of John,[3] [Benjamin,[2] William[1]], was born at Rochester, Mass., Dec. 1, 1704, and died there Jul. 19, 1758. He built a house near that of his father, afterwards known as the Seth Mendell Place, and taken down in 1856 by John Mendell, son of Seth. He was a man of irreproachable character, and was much respected in his native town, where he held many responsible offices, being also a captain of militia. He was an active member of the Congregational Church, in whose prosperity he took a deep interest. He did not forget that his ancestors left home and friends, crossed the Atlantic, and settled in the wilds of New England, for the freedom of worshiping according to the dictates of their own consciences. He m. about 1730 Priscilla, daughter of the late Samuel Sprague of Rochester, who d. Oct. 23, 1778, æ. 83. She was a superior woman, endowed with great benevolence, and with a mind ever alive to the benefits of the poor and helpless, who found in her a friend ever ready to aid them. Issue:

1. Ruth,	b. Mch. 7, 1732.	d. Aug. 12, 1758.
2. Nathaniel,	b. Jul. 27, 1734.	d. Feb. 1, 1827.

* [Extract from the Will of Benjamin Hammond 3d of Rochester, Mass.]

In the Name of God, Amen: I, Benj. Hammond of Rochester, in the county of Plymouth, in New England, Yeoman, under bodily infirmity, but in the exercise of my reason, through God's Goodness, Do make this my last Will and Testament.

And 1st., I desire to give my whole self, soul and body, to God in Jesus Christ, humbly begging his merciful acceptance, and pardon of my many sins and Reconciliation with God through the great sacrifice that was given for the remission of sins.

As touching my outward estate my will is that my true and loving wife, Priscilla, be honorably supported at equal cost between my two sons, Nathaniel and Enoch, and to live with that child she likes best.

Benjamin Hammond House.

3. Enoch,	b. Mch. 13, 1735.	d. Mch. 12, 1800.
4. Priscilla,	b. Oct. 31, 1740.	d. Jun. 19, 1758.
5. Hannah,	b. Dec. 25, 1743.	d. Aug. 28, 1758.

Priscilla, widow of Benjamin Hammond, m. 2d, in 1763, Rev. Thomas West, first pastor at North Rochester.

Of the above children, Ruth, Priscilla, and Hannah all d. single at Rochester.

2.—NATHANIEL OF ROCHESTER, MASS.

†-2. **Nathaniel,**[5] oldest son of Benjamin 3d, was endowed with great strength of body and mind. He engaged in a variety of occupations, such as teaching school winters, and freighting to the neighboring seaports of Nantucket, Newport, etc. He was Selectman and Assessor of Rochester for 19 years; delegate of the Constitutional Convention in 1780; member of the Legislature three years; and Moderator of the annual town meetings of Rochester many years. During the War of the Revolution, he united heart and hand in the cause, and raised a company of militia, of which he was appointed captain. He married young, and settled on a farm inherited from his wife's father, situated in the northerly part of Hammondtown. He m. 1st, in 1756, Phebe, daughter of Nathan Hammond, who d. May 10, 1801, æ. 63. He m. 2d, in 1803, Elizabeth, daughter of Jacob Hathaway, who d. Jan. 13, 1854, æ. 92. Capt. Nathaniel Hammond d. Feb. 1, 1827, æ. 93, without issue.

3.—ENOCH OF ROCHESTER, MASS.

†-3. **Enoch,**[5] second son of Benjamin 3d, was a man of large benevolence, which was extended to all around him, as he studied the good of friends and neighbors. He was Selectman and Assessor of Rochester for over 20 years; Moderator of the annual town meeting for many years; held many other important town offices; and was also a noted land surveyor. In the time of the Revolutionary War, the care of the soldiers' wives was consigned to him, his deep interest in them giving him the name of the "Father of the Town." His memory was cherished with much respect by those of the community who knew him personally.

He m. Jan. 7, 1762, Drusilla, daughter of Rev. Thomas West of North Rochester. She was b. Sep. 2, 1742, and d. Nov. 28, 1814, æ. 72.   Issue:

1. Benjamin,	b. Aug 26, 1763.	d. Jul. 7, 1836.
2. Ruth,	b. Feb. 12, 1765.	d. Nov. 8, 1765.
3. Thomas,	b. Aug. 17, 1766.	d. May 1, 1804.
4. Nathaniel,	b. Jun. 26, 1768.	d. Jul. 8, 1838.

†-3-1. **Benjamin,**[6] oldest son of Enoch, was for many years engaged in the merchant service between Boston and Liverpool. He was a man of much mechanical ingenuity, and built the house in which he afterwards lived, which contained many fine pieces of furniture, and other specimens of his handicraft in wood-work. He m. Jan. 24, 1793, Elizabeth Pope, daughter of Samuel and Elizabeth Pope of Fairhaven. She was b. in Fairhaven, Jun. 1767, and d. in Mattapoisett, Nov. 16, 1856, æ. 89.   Issue:

1. Drusilla,	b. Apr. 11, 1794.	d. Jun. 5, 1801.
2. Sylvia,	b. Mch. 30, 1796.	d. Apr. 5, 1857.
3. Elizabeth,	b. Jun. 4. 1799.	d. Oct 2. 1876.
4. Drusilla,	b. Sep. 23, 1801.	d. Feb. 13, 1871.
5. Thomas,	b. Apr. 11, 1804.	d. Jun. 8, 1809.
6. Thomas Penn,	b. Jun. 8, 1807.	d. Dec. 6, 1879.

Of these children, the first Drusilla and the first Thomas died young; and **Sylvia,**[7] **Elizabeth,**[7] and the second **Drusilla,**[7] who were women of more than ordinary ability, died single at Mattapoisett. Elizabeth was a tailoress, and Drusilla was a woman of some literary talent.

†-3-1-6. **Thomas Penn,**[7] son of Benjamin, was a man of good judgment, untiring energy, and great perseverance, and was much respected for his integrity of character. He was a farmer and stone-worker, living on the old homestead. In his younger days he was an ensign in the State Militia, his sword and plume being still preserved in his old home. His judgment as an appraiser of land was frequently sought; and later in life he served as Selectman of the town of Mattapoisett. He m. Jan. 10, 1839, Jane [Bullen] Mendell, daughter of Samuel and Jane [Smith] Bullen of Farmington, Me. She was b. in Farmington, Jan. 23, 1804, and d. at Mattapoisett, Apr. 4, 1881, æ. 77.   Issue:

Dec 24 1907

1. Charles Benj ,	b. Nov. 25, 1839.	
2. Roland,	b. Feb. 14, 1842.	
3. Edward Leslie,	b. Nov. 11, 1844.	
4. Wm. Garrison,	b. Mch. 13, 1848.	d. Dec. 13, 1890.
5. Twin daus.,	b. Jun. 13, 1850.	d. in infancy.

The Author's Old Home.

†-3-1-6-1. **Charles Benjamin,**[3] oldest son of Thomas Penn, was for many years engaged in the whale fishery, sailing from Marion, Mattapoisett, and New Bedford. He has been in nearly all parts of the maritime world, and good luck always attended him. In the Fall of 1862, while in the bark Ocean Rover of Mattapoisett, the vessel with 850 bbls. of sperm oil was captured and burned off the Western Islands by Capt. Semmes of the Privateer Alabama, and all hands put into the ship's boats to shift for themselves. They landed on one of the Western Islands, afterwards reached Fayal, and were sent to Boston by the American Consul. The owners and crew were afterwards remunerated for their loss out of the $15,000,000 awarded the United States under the Treaty of Washington for damages caused to American shipping by privateers sent out by the Confederacy.

During his last voyage he was first officer of the bark Hunter of New Bedford, sailing in the Arctic and Pacific Oceans, and making a complete voyage around the world.

Charles B. is a farmer, and resides in Hammondtown, Mattapoisett. He m. Aug. 15, 1871, Euphemia F. Dexter of Mattapoisett, who was b. Mch. 6, 1845. Issue:

1. Phemie Dexter,	b. Jan. 27, 1873.		
2. Sadie Alton,	b. May 9. 1875.		
3. Maria Mendell,	b. Dec. 31, 1877.		
4. Carrie Eunice,	b. Aug. 1, 1880.	d. Feb. 17, 1881.	
5. Chas. Stillman,	b. Jun. 29, 1883.		

Of these children, **Phemie Dexter**[2] m. in 1890 Byron P. Dunn of Mattapoisett, where they now reside. Issue: Carrie Hammond, b. Jun. 8, 1891.

†-3-1-6-2. **Roland,**[3] second son of Thomas Penn, in early life was a teacher in the public schools of Mattapoisett. In Sep. 1862 he enlisted as a private in Co. I, 3d Reg't M.V. M., going into camp "Joe Hooker" at Lakeville, Mass. The Reg't in Oct. took steamers for the Dept. of North Carolina, where it remained during its term of service, nine months, taking part in the battles of Whitehall, Kingston, and Goldsboro', which are inscribed on its flag. The Reg't left New Berne for Boston, in Jun. 1863, and was mustered out at camp Joe Hooker on the 26th of the same month. Roland entered Tufts College in the Fall of '64, from which he graduated with honor in Jul. '68. After serving a year as Principal of Guilford Academy, Laconia, N. H., he commenced the study of medicine in the

15

Fall of '69 with Dr. William E. Sparrow of Mattapoisett, and entered the Medical Dept. of Harvard University in Nov. '70. He received the degree of M. D. in Jun. '72, and commenced the practice of medicine in Bellingham, Mass., in Aug. '71. While in Bellingham, Dr. Hammond was Chairman of the School Committee, and Superintendent of Schools for ten successive years, and was Town Clerk and Auditor of Accounts three years. In Apr. 1882 he removed to the city of Brockton, Mass., where he now resides, a practitioner of medicine. He was Justice of the Peace from Jul. 1880 to Jul. 1887; and a member of the School Committee of Brockton during the years 1886-7-8. He is a Fellow of the Mass. Med. Society; member of the Grand Army of the Republic; and of the various Masonic Orders in Brockton, being a Past Master of St. George Lodge, A. F. & A. M. He is also the author of this Genealogy.

Dr. Hammond m. Sep. 25, 1873, Mary Lucinda, oldest daughter of Martin and Lydia [Coburn] Rockwood of Bellingham, who was b. Feb. 3, 1847. Issue:

    1. Roland, Jr.,   b. Jul. 29, 1875.

Roland Jr.[9] is a member of the Brockton High School, and was recently employed in the dry-goods store of Asa Whitman, Campello.

    †-3-1-6-3.   **Edward Leslie,**[8] third son of Thomas Penn, is a farmer and a dealer in milk and meats, and resides at Mattapoisett. On his farm is a knoll which was once an Indian burying-ground. He is a man of untiring energy and great endurance. He m. in 1873, Abbie [Bolles] Mendell, widow of the late John Mendell, who was b. Dec. 5, 1841, and d. Apr. 8, 1892. Issue:

    1. Arthur Thomas,   b. Dec. 6, 1873.
    2. Henry Leslie,   b. Mch. 23, 1876.   d. Jun. 19, 1876.

Arthur[9] resides at home, and works with his father, being also a member of the Fire Department.

    †-3-1-6-4.   **William Garrison,**[8] fourth son of Thomas Penn, commenced active life with a short whaling cruise in the Atlantic Ocean. After some years of ill health he entered the employ of Snell & Atherton, manufacturers of shoe tools in Brockton, Mass. In the Spring of 1879 he returned to the old homestead in Mattapoisett, and assumed charge of the farm,

and the care of his parents during the remainder of their lives. He m. Oct. 3, 1883, Emily [Snow] McDougal, who was b. Feb. 11, 1837. He d. Dec. 13, 1890, without issue.

†-3-3. **Thomas,**[6] second son of Enoch, graduated from Harvard College and settled in New Bedford, where he was an attorney-at-law, and where he d. May 1, 1804. He m. Sep. 24, 1792, Sarah, daughter of John and Martha [Tillinghast] Slocum of New Bedford. She was b. Nov. 11, 1772, and d. Oct. 15, 1859, after a 2d marriage to Capt. Roland R. Crocker of New Bedford. Issue:

1. Henry George,	b. Feb. 14, 1794.	d. Sep. 7, 1869.
2. Martha Slocum,	b. Aug. 2, 1798.	d. Apr. 26, 1830.
3. William Penn,	b. Dec. 23, 1801.	d. Jun. 10, 1802.

2. **Martha Slocum**[7] m. Oct. 26, 1818, Asa N. Burnham, who d. Jun. 5, 1830, and lived in Union Springs, New York. Issue:

1. Thomas Hammond,	b. Nov. 14, 1819.	d. in 1853.
2. Norman Huntington,	b. Jun. 12, 1821.	d. Oct. 1, 1842.
3. Sarah Crocker,	b. Apr. 14, 1830.	d. Nov. 30, 1834.

1. **Thomas Hammond**[7] Burnham left a son, Norman Hammond Burnham, b. Apr. 17, 1848.

†-3-3-1. **Henry George,**[7] oldest son of Thomas, was a sailor in the merchant service in his younger days. Later in life he went to Cayuga Co., N. Y., and lived at Union Springs until the time of his death. He m. Ellen Lowry of this place, who was b. Jan. 10, 1807, and d. May 29, 1874. Issue:

1. Rowland Crocker,	b. Mch. 3, 1829.	
2. Martha Slocum,	b. Dec. 22, 1830.	d. Jan. 3, 1872.
3. James Lowry,	b. Oct. 13, 1833.	
4. Thomas Slocum,	b. May 1, 1839.	d. Jun. 30, 1866.
5. Sarah Joanna,	b. Jan. 15, 1841.	d. Apr. 13, 1883.
6. Elizabeth Earl,	b. Nov. 9, 1842.	d. May 2, 1860.

Of these children, **Thomas,**[8] a promising young man, d. at the age of 27, and **Elizabeth**[8] at the age of 18, both single.

1. **Rowland Crocker,**[8] oldest son of Henry G., is a farmer at Union Springs on the homestead of his father. He m. Jan. 4, 1865, Cynthia E. Coe, who was b. Dec. 25, 1834. Issue:

1. Lillian E.,	b. Oct. 10, 1865.
2. Fred U.,	b. Mch. 31, 1867.

3. Charles H.,	b. Jul. 15, 1868.	d. Nov. 28, 1868.
4. Flora E.,	b. Jul. 3, 1869.	
5. Harriet C.,	b. Dec. 22, 1870.	
6. Sarah E.,	b. Dec. 2. 1873.	
7. Louis J.,	b. Jun. 10, 1875.	d. Apr. 3, 1876.

Of these children, **Lillian**[9] and **Hattie**[9] are teachers in the public schools of the State, and all are single.

2. Martha Slocum,[8] oldest daughter of Henry G., m. Apr. 22, 1857, Curtis N. Coe, who was b. at Grange, Alleghany Co., N. Y., Jun. 20, 1829.   Issue:

1. Ellen H.,	b. Aug. 3, 1861.
2. Elizabeth H.,	b. Jul. 7, 1864.
3. Curtis Henry,	b. Sep. 23. 1869.

Besides the above, there were Hannah and Thomas, who d. in infancy.

3. James Lowry,[8] second son of Henry G., is a carpenter, and lives at Union Springs. He m. Dec. 22, 1858, Hannah Shank, who was b. Dec. 16, 1836.   Issue:

| 1. Thomas Slocum, | b. May 23, 1862. |
| 2. James Eugene, | b. Jul. 10, 1864. |

James Eugene,[9] second son of James L., m. Feb. 16, 1888, Mary E. Frawley, and lives at Pueblo, Col.   Issue:

| 1. Henry G., | b. Dec. 23, 1888. | d. Jun. 12, 1892. |
| 2. Naomi, | b. Jul. 13, 1891. | d. Jan. 13, 1892. |

5. Sarah Joanna,[8] second daughter of Henry G., m. Nov. 30, 1860, William H. Van Sickle, an extensive farmer of Union Springs, who was b. May 12, 1836.   Issue:

| 1. Henry Hammond, | b. Sep. 10, 1863. |
| 2. Rowland, | b. Jul. 31, 1874. |

Mr. Van Sickle m. 2d, Feb. 12, 1885, Nellie H. Burlew. **Henry H.,**[9] son of William Van Sickle, m. Mch. 22, 1885, his cousin, Elizabeth H. Coe, daughter of Curtis N. Coe, and resides in Wellington, Kan. Issue: Curtis William.

†–3.–4.   **Nathaniel Esq.,**[6] third son of Enoch, lived on the old homestead, where his father and grandfather had lived before him, and was a farmer and Justice of the Peace.   He m. 1st, Oct. 23, 1791, Lucy Barstow, daughter of Gideon and Jane Barstow.   She was b. Mch. 25, 1772, and d. Oct. 20, 1802.   Issue:

| 1. Enoch, | b. Feb. 25, 1793. | d. Mch. 9, 1793. |

2. Priscilla Sprague, b. Jan. 13, 1795.　d. Mch. —, 1844.
3. Enoch,　b. Jul. 21, 1798.　d. in　1816.
4. Rufus,　b. Sep. 26, 1800.　d. Jul. 25, 1801.

Nathaniel m. 2d, Oct. 30, 1803, Priscilla, daughter of Noah and Eunice Hammond, who was b. Jul. 21, 1783, and d. Dec. 12, 1820. Issue:

5. Rufus,　b. Aug. 7, 1805.　d. Aug. 10, 1854.
6. William Penn,　b. Sep. 23, 1807.　d. Oct. 14, 1807.
7. John Wilkes,　b. Oct. 22, 1808.　d. Sep. 23, 1843.
8. Lucy Barstow,　b. Mch. 16, 1810.　d. Apr. 20, 1810.
9. Nathaniel,　b. Feb. 24, 1813.　d. Jun. 28, 1870.
10. Elizabeth Pope,　b. Nov. 9, 1815.　d. Jan. 8, 1870.
11. Benjamin,　b. May 11, 1818.

Of these children, **Priscilla Sprague**[7] m. Jul. 3, 1816, Lazerus LeBaron, son of Rev. Lemuel LeBaron, minister in Mattapoisett. Lazerus was a farmer, and lived on the Lot Jones place in Mattapoisett. Issue:

1. Enoch Hammond.　b. Apr. 5, 1817.　d. Mar. 9, 1892.
2. Jane Loring.　b. Jul. —, 1818.
3. Lucy Barstow.　b. Dec. —, 1826.
4. Elizabeth Allen,　b. Jun. —, 1831.

Of Priscilla's children, **Enoch Hammond**[8] m. Florilla, daughter of Capt. Joseph Taber of Mattapoisett. Issue: Sarah, Enoch, Alonzo, Charles, Joseph, and Jennie.

†–3–4–5. **Rufus**,[7] fourth son of Nathaniel, was a ship-carpenter at Mattapoisett, and was drowned in the harbor by the capsizing of a boat. He m. Lucy, daughter of James Purrington, but had no issue.

†–3–4–10. **Elizabeth Pope**,[7] youngest daughter of Nathaniel, m. Jul. 1844, Lazerus LeBaron, who afterwards moved to Turner, Me., where he d. Jul. 29, 1864. Issue:

1. Francis,　b. Oct. 22, 1850.
2. Alton S.,　b. Jan. 10, 1854.

Of these children, **Francis**[8] is a contractor; and **Alton S.**[8] is a commission merchant, residing at Newton Centre, Mass.

†–3–4–7. **John Wilkes**,[7] sixth son of Nathaniel, was a ship-carpenter, and lived at Mattapoisett. He m. Feb. 8, 1835, Maria Louisa, daughter of Dr. Wilbur Southworth, who d. Apr. 10, 1886. Issue:

1. John Wilkes, Jr.,　b. Dec. 16, 1837.
2. Eudora Frances,　b. Dec. 5, 1839.

Of these children, **Eudora Frances**[8] m. Dec. 26, 1869, Hiram R. Johnson, who was b. Oct. 19, 1839, and is a machinist at Somerset, Mass. No issue.

†-3-4-7-1. **John Wilkes Jr.**[8] entered Tufts College in '57, and graduated at the head of his class in '61. After that he taught school until Sep. '62, in which month, being then the Principal of the High School in Tisbury, he one morning resigned, bidding farewell to the school, and enlisted as a private in Co. I, 3d Reg't M. V. M. He served with his company in North Carolina, returning with the regiment to Boston, Mass., in Jun. '63, at the expiration of his term of service, nine months. He then taught school, and in the Fall of '64 began the study of law in the Law School at Harvard University, and in the office of Sweetser & Gardner in Boston. He was admitted to the Bar at Cambridge in Feb. '66, and practised law in Cambridge and Boston, being City Solicitor of Cambridge from 1873 to 1886. In Mch. 1886 he was appointed to a seat upon the Bench of the Superior Court of Massachusetts, where he now is. He has resided in Cambridge since Mch. 1866.

Judge Hammond m. Aug. 15, 1866, Clara Ellen, daughter of Prof. Benjamin F. Tweed of Cambridge, Mass., who was b. Apr. 2, 1842. Issue:

1. Frank Tweed, b. Mch. 1, 1870.
2. Clara Maria, b. Jul. 21, 1881.
3. John Wilkes, Jr , b. Aug. 7, 1884.

Of these children, **Frank Tweed,**[9] a graduate of the Academical Dept. of Harvard University, is at present a student of law.

Judge Hammond received the honorary degree of LL.D. from Tufts College in Jun. 1891.

†-3-4-9. **Nathaniel,**[7] seventh son of Nathaniel, was a ship-carpenter, and lived at Mattapoisett. He m. Feb. 13, 1839, Mary, daughter of Larnet and Polly [Dexter] Hall. Issue:

1. Martha Burnham, b. Jan. 1, 1840. d. Sep. 23, 1840.
2. Nathaniel Herbert, b. Aug. 3, 1841. d. Jul. 7, 1862.
3. Larnet Hall, b. Mch. 20, 1844. d. Feb. 19, 1876.
4. Thomas West, b. Jun. 26, 1850.
5. Mary Eliza, b. Nov. 13, 1858. d. Feb. 27, 1862.

Of these children, **Nathaniel Herbert**[8] d. at the age of 21, and **Larnet Hall**[8] at the age of 32, both single.

JUDGE JOHN W. HAMMOND.

†–3–4–9–4. **Thomas West,**[8] in early life a physician, afterwards studied and practised law at Minneapolis, Minn., from 1885 to 1889, when he moved to Tacoma, Wash., where he now resides. He m. Dec. 23, 1876, Desire, daughter of Edwin and Mary [Hiller] Purrington of Mattapoisett, who was b. Mch. 3, 1858. Issue:

1. Nathaniel Herbert,   b. Oct. 16, 1878.
2. Edith May,   b. May 19. 1881.
3. Thomas West, Jr.,   b. Jul. 28, 1887.
4. Carrie Murphy,   b. Jun. 3, 1890.

†–3–4–11. **Benjamin,**[7] eighth son of Nathaniel, was a blockmaker, and formerly lived in Fairhaven, Mass. He m. 1st, Oct. 1839, Elizabeth, daughter of Job Randall of Mattapoisett, who d. Oct. 1856. Issue:

1. Sophia Adelaide,   b. May 6, 1841.
2. Joshua Bowles,   b. Feb. 22, 1847.

Benjamin m. 2d, Jul. 12, 1858, Mary Ann Briggs, who d. Nov. 4, 1892. Benjamin moved to Turner, Me., in 1859, where now he resides. Issue:

3. Hart Briggs,   b. May 31, 1860.

1. **Sophia Adelaide**[8] m. Nov. 6, 1859, Wilson B. Hudson, a sailmaker at Mattapoisett, who was b. Jul. 27, 1838, and d. Oct. 6, 1886. Issue: Elizabeth Peakes and Helen Bourne, both of whom d. young.

†–3–4–11–2. **Joshua Bowles,**[8] oldest son of Benjamin, is a farmer and carpenter, and lives at South Hanson, Mass. He m. Jan. 31, 1864, Tamar Bourne, who was b. Apr. 17, 1846. Issue:

1. Joshua Wilson,   b. Dec. 12, 1864.
2. Nellie Elizabeth,   b. Aug. 31, 1866.
3. Francis Alton,   b. Sep. 2, 1868.
4. George Albert,   b. May 17, 1872.
5. Hattie Leslie,   b. Jul. 22, 1876.

Of the above children, 1. **Joshua Wilson**[9] is a freight clerk for the Old Colony R. R., and resides at South Hanson. He m. Jul. 30, 1890, Eliza Miriam Dearborn, who was b. at Chelsea, Mass., Jun. 19, 1873. Issue:

1. Lillie Frances,   b. Apr. 29, 1892.
2. Gilbert Wilson,   b. Aug. 20, 1893.

2. **Nellie Elizabeth**[9] m. 1st, Mch. 1, 1882, John W. Lane, who d. Jul. 14, 1884, without issue She m. 2d,

Dec. 30, 1888, George W. Tarr, a shoemaker, b. at Gloucester, Mass., Oct. 28, 1856. Issue: Hattie Leslie, b. Jul. 5,
1889; and Lottie Mildred, b. Oct. 24, 1892.

3.　**Francis Alton**[9] resides at South Hanson, and is fitting
for college; and **George Albert**[9] is a farmer at South Hanson.

†–3–4–11–3.　**Hart Briggs**,[9] youngest son of Benjamin,
is a farmer, and resides at Turner, Me. He m. Sep. 26, 1885,
Minerva Stella Davis, who was b. in Naples, Me., Feb. 25,
1865. No issue.

IV—ROWLAND[4] HAMMOND OF PLYMPTON, MASS.

†.　**Rowland**[4] **Hammond,** fourth son of John,[3] [Benja-
min,[2] William[1]], was b. at Rochester, Oct. 30, 1706, and d.
at Plympton (now Carver), Mass., Jun. 16, 1788. He
moved to what is now North Carver in 1739, and was a farmer
and sheep-raiser. He m. 1st, in 1731, Ann Winslow, daughter
of Dea. Samuel Winslow of Rochester, who was b. in 1709
and d. in 1734. Issue:

1. Rowland 2d,	b. in 1731.	d. Sep. 7, 1810.
2. George.	b. Jun. —, 1734.	d. Jan. 14, 1782.

Rowland m. 2d, Sep. 4, 1737, Lydia Bonum, who was b.
in 1698, and d. Jan. 23, 1756.

He m. 3d, May 5, 1757, Mary Southworth, who d. Mch. 3,
1788. No issue by the second and third marriages.

†–1.　**Dea. Rowland 2d**,[5] who never married, outlived
his brother, Capt. George, and after the latter's death brought
up his children. When Rowland became old his brother's
children cared for him.

†–2.　**George**,[5] second son of Rowland, who was a captain
of militia, was a farmer on the homestead of his father at
Carver, Mass. He m. 1st, Nov. 1759, Lucy Sturtevant, who
was b. in 1737, and d. Aug. 25, 1772. Issue:

1. Lydia,	b. Nov. 15, 1760.	d.
2. Anna,	b. Apr. 18, 1762.	d.
3. Molly,	b. Mch. 17, 1764.	d. Jul. 20, 1785.
4. Lucy,	b. May 20, 1766.	d. May 9, 1842.
5. George 2d,	b. May 4, 1768.	d. about 1795.
6. Hannah,	b. Aug. 1, 1770.	d. Sep. 1, 1810.

Capt. George m. 2d, Nov. 1773, Betsey Thomas, who d. Mch. 20, 1787. Issue :

7. Betsey,	b. Mch. 28, 1774.	d. Sep. 20. 1851.
8. Thomas,	b. Jun. 6. 1776.	d. Dec. 9. 1825.
9. Benjamin,	b. Dec. 10, 1778.	d. Dec. 2. 1825.
10. Priscilla.	b. Jan. 8, 1781.	d. Nov. 13. 1826.

Of Capt. George's children, **Molly**[6] never married, and died at Carver, Mass.

1. **Lydia,**[6] oldest daughter of Capt. George, lived and d. in Minot, or West Minot, Me. She m. Nov. 9, 1780, James Murdoch, who was b. in 1754, and d. at Springfield, Me., in 1850. Issue : James, George, Lucy, Mary, Hannah, Lydia, and Clarissa.

2. **Anna,**[6] second daughter of Capt. George, who was quite a poetess, lived, and died in middle life, at New Gloucester, Me. She m. Nov. 18, 1779, Dr. William Bridgham, who was b. in 1756, and, after marrying a second time, d. Aug. 4, 1837, æ. 81. Issue : Dr. William Jr., Joanna, Dr. Thomas, Lucy, George, Caroline, and Nancy. This was quite a noted family.

4. **Lucy,**[6] fourth daughter of Capt. George, lived and d. at Hebron, Me. She m. Aug. 2, 1787, Samuel Roland Bridgham, brother of Dr. William, who was b. in 1763, and d. Jul. 4, 1837, æ. 74. Issue : Mercy, Samuel Roland, Alexander, Sophia, Derrick, Thomas, Stafford, and Dr. Roland Hammond.

5.—GEORGE HAMMOND 2d, OF WORCESTER CO., MASS.

†. **George**[6] **Hammond 2d,** oldest son of Capt. George,[5] [Rowland,[4] John,[3] Benjamin,[2] William[1]], was b. at Plympton, Mass., now Carver, May 4, 1768, and moved after his marriage, probably to some part of Worcester Co., perhaps Worcester, where he died of an acute illness about 1795. He had the reputation of being an intelligent and thrifty man, and is said to have acquired money rapidly after going to Worcester Co. He m. Oct. 2, 1788, Lucy Southworth of Plymouth, Mass.,

who a few years after his death m. Capt. Nathaniel Luther.* The family afterwards moved to Windsor, Berkshire Co., Mass., where Lucy, widow of George Hammond, died about 1830. Issue :

1. George, Sr.,	b. May 20, 1790.	d. Dec. 30, 1869.
2. Rowland,	b. in 1792.	d.

†-2. **Rowland,**[7] second son of George, who was a carpenter, lived first for some years in Canada. About 1818–19 he moved to Gorham, Ontario Co., N. Y., where he afterwards lived, and where he probably died. He m. about 1816 Lydia Crane, and had issue :

1. Samuel,	b. in 1818.	d.
2. Henrietta,	b. in 1820.	d.
3. Nath'l Walter,	b. about 1822.	d.

But little is known in regard to these children, the following scanty information being all that it has been possible to obtain.

1. **Samuel**[8] is said to have learned the trade of shoemaker while living in Canada. He afterwards, in company with his father-in-law, is said to have carried on the manufacture of shoes at Hartford, or New Haven, Conn., and later to have had an extensive shoe establishment, perhaps a shoe store, in Boston, Mass. Sometime after 1840, he went to St. Louis and married, and returned to Connecticut. His wife afterwards died in Boston, and a few years later he went to California, and may be living there now.

2. **Henrietta**[8] married, and perhaps lived in Canada, nothing further being known of her.

3. **Nathaniel Walter,**[8] after residing some years with his mother, went to Canada, it is said, to live with his mother's brother, and afterwards attended school there. In the time of the California gold fever he started for that State. The vessel, after leaving some South American port, was never heard from, and is supposed to have been lost in doubling Cape Horn. Still it is possible that he escaped and may be now living.

---

* Lucy [Southworth] Hammond's children by Capt Luther were: Calvin Hammond, Harvey, Louisa, and Lydia. Of these children, Calvin m. Fanny Younglove, daughter of Judge Younglove, and lived at or near Naples, Ontario Co., N. Y. Harvey m. 1st, Anise Blodgett, and 2d, a daughter of Judge Younglove. Louisa m. Henry Porter; and Lydia m. 1st, a Mr. Ferris, and 2d, a Mr. Gritman.

(1.)—GEORGE SR. OF CRAWFORD CO., OHIO.

†-1. **George Sr.,**[7] oldest son of George 2d, learned the trade of carpenter and cabinet-maker with David Carlisle, with whom he afterwards moved to Geneva, N. Y. Here he worked at his trade some years with Resolved White, and accumulated enough property to buy a farm in Gorham, Ontario Co., N. Y. In 1822 he moved to what is now Auburn township, Crawford Co., Ohio, where he pre-empted 160 acres of land, which is now owned and occupied by his son George Jr. He was a member of the Baptist Church, and was a man much esteemed and respected by his neighbors. He m. 1st, in the Winter of 1812, Sarah P., daughter of Daniel White, one of the descendants of Resolved White, who came over in the Mayflower in 1620. Sarah P. White, b. in Pomfret, Conn., moved to Windsor, Berkshire Co., Mass., and later to Gorham, N. Y., where she was afterwards married to George Hammond. She d. at Auburn, O., Apr. 4, 1840. Issue :

1. Albert,	b. Feb. 25, 1813.	d. Mch. 23, 1886.
2. Alfred,	b. Jul. 6, 1815.	d. Aug. 28, 1840.
3. Harvey,	b. Mch. 12, 1818.	d. Sep. 6, 1846.
4. Anna,	b. Sep. 12, 1820.	
5. George, Jr.,	b. Jun. 26, 1824.	
6. Rowland W.,	b. Oct. 24, 1829.	d. Feb. —, 1866.
7. Sarah.	b. Sep. 28, 1833.	d. Mch. 9, 1854.

George Hammond Sr. m. 2d, in 1841, Mrs. Abigail [Gambell] Grnesbeck, but had no further issue.

Of the children of George Sr., Albert, Alfred, Harvey, and Anna were born at Gorham, N. Y., and George, Rowland, and Sarah at Auburn, O.

†-1-1. **Albert,**[8] oldest son of George Sr., a farmer and a man of fine reputation, lived at Likens, Crawford Co., O. He m. Aug. 1834 Catherine Gruesbeck, who d. at Likens, Feb. 26, 1864, æ. 47. Issue :

1. Almira,	b. Mch. 12, 1835.	
2. Alvira,	b. Feb. 24, 1839.	
3. Philora,	b. Nov. 18, 1842.	
4. Orlando,	b. Sep. 5, 1847.	d. Oct. —, 1848.
5. Ellen D.,	b. Sep. 3, 1848.	
6. Lucy,	b. Aug. 22, 1851.	

Of these children, 1. **Almira**[9] m. 1st, Oct. 19, 1854, James Miller, who d. May 5, 1864. Issue : Albert H., Izora, Alvira, Elbert Philip, and Frances Marion.

Almira m. 2d, Dec. 13, 1872, Jacob Johnson, and lives at Plankton, Crawford Co., O. Issue : Corma Ellis.

2. **Alvira**[9] m. Feb. 24, 1859, Jacob Rhodes, and lives at Bloomville, Seneca Co., O. Issue: Eva A., Elmer E., Charles, Nellie, Odessie, Nettie G., and Ira D.

3. **Phidora**[9] m. Apr. 6, 1862, J. Wesley Parks, and lives at Balsam Lake, Polk Co., Wis. Issue: Alva D., Ira H., Olive, and Ella.

5. **Ellen Delora**[9] m. Mch. 12, 1868, Sidney Brown, and lives at St. Croix, Polk Co., Wis. Issue: Bertha, Inez M., Olive, Frank H., Mary M., and Ada O.

6. **Lucy**[9] m. Dec. 13, 1878, James Ely, and resides at Balsam Lake, Polk Co., Wis. Issue: James Alton and Nellie Floy.

†–1–2. **Alfred,**[8] second son of George Sr., a substantial farmer and respected citizen, lived formerly at Tiro, Crawford Co., but moved to Likens in 1844. He m. Nov. 9, 1837, Julia A. Hulse, and had issue:

    1. Calvin,   b. Sep. 25, 1838.

†–1–2–1. **Calvin,**[9] a machinist, m. at Tiffin, Ohio, Sep. 14, 1856, Eva Stroup, and resided at Likens and Bloom, Ohio, and Paris, Mich. Issue:

    1. Rowland W.,   b. Oct. 30, 1857, at Likens, Ohio.
    2. Eloda Ann,   b. Dec. 1, 1860, at Bloom. Ohio.
    3. Mary Jane,   b. Dec. 13, 1868, at Paris, Mich.

Of these children, **Rowland W.,**[10] a farmer at Likens, m. Aug. 22, 1880, Sarah E. Miller. Issue:

    1. Albert,   b. May 22, 1881.   d. Apr. 25, 1886.
    2. Lydia May,   b. Oct. 19, 1882.
    3. Ralfela M.,   b. Mch. 25, 1884.   d. Apr. 19, 1886.
    4. Hattie Bell,   b. Feb. 5, 1886.
    5. Altie Pearl,   b. Aug. 8, 1888.

2. **Eloda A.**[10] m. in 1881 Daniel Livensparger, and lives at Bloomville, Seneca Co., Ohio. Issue: Daisy May, Lewis Earl, Ethel, Roy, Mary, Jacob, and Harvey; all dead, except Ethel and Roy.

3. **Mary J.**[10] m. Nov. 6, 1887, George W. Fortny, and resides at Carothers, Seneca Co., Ohio. Issue:

    1. Adelbert,   b. Oct. 2, 1888.

ANNA HAMMOND NEWKIRK

†–1–3. **Harvey⁶ Hammond,** who remained single, resided the most of his life with his father, whom he assisted in his farm-work, which he was obliged to relinquish on account of failing health. He was a great reader and a kind and obedient son.

†–1–4. **Anna,**⁵ oldest daughter of George Sr., moved to Ohio in Feb. 1822. At the age of 17, her mother's failing health caused the care of her father's family to devolve principally upon her. After her father's second marriage in 1841, she taught school a few terms. She m. Jul. 2, 1846, Cornelius L. Newkirk, and went to Leroy, Calhoun Co., Mich., where she resided eight years, and where her three oldest children were born. In 1854 the family moved to Occola township, Stark Co., Ill., where the next two children were born. In 1869 the family removed to Macon Co., Mo. Mr. C. L. Newkirk, who was in early life a teacher, d. May 11, 1886. Issue:

1. Garrett,   b. May   3, 1847.
2. Sarah Amelia,   b. May   1, 1851.
3. Mary Ella,   b. Mch. 25, 1854.
4. John Alfred,   b. Oct. 18, 1856.
5. George H'd,   b. Oct. 3, 1859.

Of these children, 2. **Sarah,**⁹ who is single, resides at Goldsberry, Mo.

1. **Garrett,**⁹ b. in Leroy, Mich., graduated in 1868, from the Rush Medical College, Chicago; practised medicine eight years in Macon Co., Mo., and Woodford Co., Ill.; medicine and dentistry two years. Since then dentistry exclusively, taking a course in the Chicago College of Dental Surgery, in which institution he was afterwards Professor of Hygiene and Dental Irregularities. He m. Dec. 1872, Martha E. Martin, and is a dentist at Chicago, Ill. Issue:

1. John M.,   b. Oct. 30, 1879.

3. **Mary Ella**⁹ m. in 1883, Dr. Charles Van Wye, and lives at Browning, Mo. Her children are: Mattie and Alfred.

4. **John Alfred**⁹ m. in 1890 Jennie Russell and resides at Ethel, Mo. No issue.

5. **George Hammond Newkirk**⁹ m. in 1888, Florence Wright, resides at Goldsberry, Mo., and has a son, Earle.

†–1–5. **George⁵ Hammond Jr.,** a successful farmer

and genial man, lives at Tiro, Crawford Co., Ohio. He m. 1st, in 1846, Amelia Gruesbeck, who d. Feb. 1851. Issue:

1. Emma,   b. Apr. 27, 1847.
2. Fillmore,   b. Jun. 9, 1849.

George Jr. m. 2d, in the Spring of 1855, Mary Lewis, who d. Apr. 1882, and by whom he had two daughters:

3. Irene,   b Sep. 27, 1856.
4. Sarah,   b. Nov. 17, 1863.

George Jr. m. 3d, in 1883, Alice Victoria Melaron, by whom there is no issue.

Of these children, **Emma**[9] m. Nov. 25, 1866, Rev. B. Frank Crouse, a Lutheran clergyman, b. Mch. 16, 1840. Their present residence is Muncie, Delaware Co., Ind. Issue: Corbie C., Justus H., Lulu A., Thirzie F., and Emma May. Corbie m. Mch. 16, 1891, Frank W. Jordan, and lives in Nebraska.

2. **Fillmore,**[9] an industrious farmer, resides at Ida Grove, Ida Co., Iowa. He m. 1st, Feb. 25, 1872, Josephine Crouse, who was b. in Auburn, Ohio, Oct. 24, 1871, and d. Sep. 27, 1880. Issue:

1. Charles Ellsworth,   b. Apr. 19, 1873, in Auburn, Ohio.
2. Geston Lyle,   b. Sep. 9, 1874, in Auburn, Ohio.
3. Norah Amelia,   b. Mch. 14, 1876, in Auburn, Ohio.

Fillmore m. 2d, Dec. 9, 1882, Ellan Boney, who was b. Jun. 13, 1852, at Beaver, Pa. Issue:

4. Maude May,   b. Feb. 12, 1884, in Ripley, Huron Co., Ohio.

Charles Ellsworth[10] is now attending a commercial college in Omaha, Neb.

3. **Irene,**[9] second daughter of George Jr., m. Nov. 29, 1877, Theo. C. Gruesbeck, and lives in Lorane, Whitley Co., Ind. No issue.

4. **Sarah,**[9] who is single, lives with her sister, Irene, in Lorane, Ind.

†–1–6. **Rowland W.**[9] **Hammond,** a teacher and later in life a merchant, was a scholarly and well-read man. He was also quite a politician, and during the ten or eleven years that he resided in Wyandotte Co., Ohio, held town or county office nearly all the time. He afterwards removed to Galion, Ohio, where he engaged in mercantile pursuits. He m. in

1851, Martha J. Miller, and both d. in Kirby, Wyandotte Co., Ohio. She, in Oct. 1865, and he in Feb. 1866, leaving their four girls orphans. Rowland Hammond and wife are buried at Galion, Ohio. Issue:

1. Emeline,	b. May 9, 1852.
2. Sarah Matilda,	b. Feb. 12, 1854.
3. Amelia,	b. May 30, 1857.
4. Ida J.,	b. Aug. 31, 1862.

Of these children, 1. **Emeline**[9] m. Oct. 31, 1857, Ross Cuykendoll, and resides at Plymouth, Richmond Co., Ohio. Her children are: Fred, Frank, and May.

2. **Sarah Matilda**,[9] or Tillie as she is called, m. Sep. 27, 1873, John Brokaw, and resides at Plymouth, Ohio. Her children are: Guy L., Gertie, and Ida.

3. **Amelia**[9] m. Oct. 1874, m. George Rittenowe, resides at Missoula, Montana, and has a son:

1. Clifford Hammond,	b. Oct. 17, 1878.

4. **Ida J.**[9] m. Oct. 21, 1880, Mahlon A. Thomas, and resides at Fostoria, Ohio. No issue.

†–1–7. **Sarah Hammond**,[5] the pet of the family, resided with her father until her marriage to Henry Van Orsdoll, Aug. 7, 1851. They resided at Columbia City, Ind. Issue:

1. Anna Amelia,	b. Feb. 3, 1853.	d. Apr. 14, 1856.
2. George Hammond,	b. Feb. 27, 1854.	

George Hammond Van Orsdoll,[9] b. in Whitley Co., Ind., near Columbia City, m. in that city, Jul. 19, 1881, Sarah E. Thatcher, and now lives in Marion, Grant Co., Ind. His children are: Walter Hammond, Lorena Evaline and Vivian Zoe.

[MENDELL NOTE.]

6.—HANNAH OF ACUSHNET, MASS.

†–2–6. **Hannah**,[6] fifth daughter of Capt. George, after her marriage, lived near the "Half Way Ponds" in Plymouth, Mass. After the birth of her third child Seth, the family removed to what is now Acushnet, Mass., where she afterwards

lived, and where she d. Sep. 1, 1810. She m. Oct. 2, 1791, Ellis Mendell, who was b. Mch. 20, 1763, and d. Jun. 12, 1849, and was a son of Seth and Mary Mendell. Issue :

1. Mary,	b. Jan. 28, 1793.	d. Jun. 9, 1878.
2. Lucy,	b. Oct 30, 1794.	d. Oct. 12, 1821.
3. Seth,	b. Nov. 29, 1796.	d. Feb. 9, 1836.
4. George.	b. Sep. 4, 1798.	d.
5. John,	b. Sep. 15, 1800.	d. Apr. 7, 1811.
6. Hannah,	b Aug. 18, 1802.	d. Jun. 1, 1834.
7. Anna,	b. May 15, 1804.	d. May 15, 1808.
8. Ellis,	b. Jun. 27, 1806.	d.
9. Lydia,	b. Jan. 11, 1809.	d. May —, 1810.

Of Hannah's children, **Mary**[7] m. Capt. Silas Stetson, and lived at North New Bedford. Issue : George M., Lucy, Henry, Mary M., Lucy M., Thomas S., Betsey S., and Hannah.

2. **Lucy**[7] m. Saulisbury Blackmer, and lived at New Bedford. Issue : Hannah, Seth, and Charles.

4. **George**[7] m. Jane Allen, and lived at Acushnet. Issue : Albert A., George H., Katie, Lucy, Hannah, Augustus H., and Henry Russell.

6. **Hannah**[7] m. Peleg H. Stetson, and lived at New Bedford. Issue : Capt. Charles, Nancy Bourne, and Jane S.

8. **Ellis**[7] m. Catherine Allen, and lived at Acushnet. Issue : Mary, Jennie, Seth, and Ellis.

3. **Seth,**[7] oldest son of Hannah, was a captain of militia, and lived in Mattapoisett on the Enoch Hammond place, afterwards the residence of his son, Nathaniel Hammond, Esq. He m. Dec. 3, 1822, Jane Bullen, daughter of Samuel and Jane [Smith] Bullen of Farmington, Me. Issue :

1. John,	b. May 20, 1824.	d. Jan. 24, 1865.
2. Henry,	b. Aug. 20, 1826.	d. Oct. 16, 1828.
3. Henry 2d,	b. Jul. 8, 1829.	d. Mch. 19, 1885.
4. Maria,	b. Dec. 4, 1831.	d. Jun. 2, 1841.
5. Ellis,	b. Jun 11, 1834.	
6. Jane,	b. Aug. 1, 1836.	d. Jul. 15, 1838.

Of these children, Henry, Maria, and Jane d. young.

1. **John**[8] was a farmer and store-keeper, and inherited his father's homestead. He m. 1st, about 1849, Sarah L. Barstow, who was b. Apr. 27, 1826, and d. Apr. 27, 1857. Issue :

1. Lucy Ann,	b. Jan. 5, 1851.

John m. 2d, Jun. 20, 1858, Abbie Bolles, who was b. Dec. 5, 1841, and d. Apr. 8, 1892. Issue:

2. Clara,	b. Jul. 15, 1859.	d. Oct. 24, 1885.
3. Charles S.,	b. Nov. 29, 1861.	
4. John Clifford,	b. Feb. 5, 1863.	d. Oct. 24, 1865.
5. Ellis L.,	b. Apr. 9. 1865.	

Of John's children, 1. **Lucy Ann**[9] m. Jun. 19, 1870, Robert B. Stratton, and lives at Santa Barbara, Cal. No issue.

3. **Charles Stetson**[9] formerly Supt. of the Economic Electric Manufacturing Co., Brockton, Mass., is now Electrician for the New Bedford Electric Railway. He m. Dec. 6, 1888, Carrol B. Dennis of Mattapoisett, Mass., and had issue:

1. Annie Dennis,	b. Dec. 4, 1891.
2 John Dennis,	b. Sep 12, 1893.

4. **Ellis Lincoln**[9] is an expressman and lives at Mattapoisett. He m. Jan. 1, 1890, Madie A. Clark. No issue.

3. **Henry 2d,**[8] third son of Seth, was in early life a whaler, sailing from New Bedford. He was afterwards a farmer at Amboy, Oswego Co., N. Y., where he d. Mch. 19, 1885. He m. Jan. 3, 1857, Martha J. Stewart, who was b. Jul. 30, 1833. Issue:

1. Charles,	b. Jun. 30. 1859.	d. Feb. 8, 1861.
2. George,	b. Nov. 4. 1861.	
3. Henry H'd,	b. Aug. 22. 1864.	
4. Mary,	b. Aug. 6, 1867.	
5. Ellis,	b. Oct. 6. 1871.	

Of the above children, 3. **Henry**[9] is a locomotive engineer on the Rome & Watertown R. R., New York.

2. **George,**[9] who is a farmer at Amboy, m. Feb. 3, 1887, Helen Stacy. Issue:

1. Henry Babcock.	b. Nov. 1, 1891.

5. **Ellis,**[8] fourth son of Seth, is assistant postmaster at Mattapoisett. He m. May 6, 1858, Mary A. Slocum, who was b. at New Bedford, Aug. 22, 1837. Issue:

1. Jane Crapo,	b. Jul. 9, 1859.	
2. Henry,	b. Sep. —, 1862.	d. Sep. —. 1862.
3. Kate Clifford,	b. Mch. 4, 1863.	
4. Harriet Maria,	b. Mch. 7, 1868.	

Jennie is a telegraph operator at Mattapoisett; **Kate,** a dressmaker; and **Harriet** a typewriter at New Bedford.

16

†-2-7. **Betsey,**[6] sixth daughter of Capt. George, lived and died at Barnard, Vt. She m. Mch. 30, 1791, Capt. Ebenezer Atwood, who was b. in 1773, and d. Apr. 24, 1841. Issue:

1. Betsey H'd,	b. Jan. 21, 1800.	d. Nov. 22, 1863.
2. Ebenezer,	b. Mch. 29, 1802.	d. Jan. —, 1869.
3. Priscilla,	b. Jun. 10, 1804.	d. Mch. 12, 1812.
4. George H'd,	b. May 24, 1810.	
5. Joseph,	b. Sep. 19, 1813.	d. Jan. 21, 1814.

1. **Betsey Hammond,**[7] who lived at Barnard, m. May 20, 1823, John Tucker, who was b. Sep. 3, 1798, and d. May 7, 1874. Issue: Lucian A., Priscilla W., Lucian C., Caroline M., Betsey A., Abbie, and Ebenezer A.

Of these children, **Eben A.,**[8] who is a farmer at Barnard, m. Oct. 24, 1865, Mary E. Richmond, and has a daughter Carrie M.

2. **Ebenezer,**[7] oldest son of Betsey, who was a farmer at Barnard, m. Apr. 1, 1824, Elvira Tucker, who was b. at Barnard, Jun. 12, 1805, and d. at Malone, N. Y., Apr. 17, 1871. Ebenezer was in the Legislature many years, and held other public offices. Issue: Joseph Foster, Seth, Thomas Hammond, George Alexander, Elizabeth Penn, Charles, John Tucker, Nancy Ann, Oliver Augustus, Ebenezer, Irving Herbert, Myron Winslow, and Lucia Elvira.

Of these children, **J. Foster**[8] is a thriving and successful farmer at Malone, N. Y. He m. Dec. 20, 1849, Sarah A. Parker, and has a daughter Lizzie, b. Mch. 1865.

4. **George Hammond,**[7] second son of Betsey, is a farmer at Malone, N. Y. He m. 1st, Mch. 20, 1834, Mary N. Culver, who was a descendant on her father's side from Henry Adams who settled at Braintree, Mass., about 1640. Issue: Emma, Elizabeth, William Penn, George A., Samuel, Benjamin Hammond, Parker, Mary J., Caroline Ward, and Addie G. George Hammond m. 2d, Jan. 1, 1876, Josepha F. [Thompson] Tucker. No further issue.

Of these children, the five sons all served in the late Civil War.

Samuel,[8] the third son, graduated at the Albany Law School in 1867; practised law at Adell, Iowa, '68 to '71; moved to Ellsworth, Kan., and practised law from '71 to '83; prosecuting attorney for two years, and Mayor of Ellsworth for several

successive terms ; in '83 retired from practice of law, and settled
in North Easton, Mass. Samuel m. 1st, Dec. 23, 1871, Mrs.
Minnie Brown, and had Samuel, and two daughters, who d. in
infancy. He m. 2d, Jul. 31, 1879, Mrs. Mattie A. Levering,
and had a daughter Carrie.

8.—THOMAS HAMMOND OF CARVER, MASS.

†. **Thomas,**[6] second son of Capt. George[5] [Rowland,[4]
John,[3] Benjamin,[2] William[1]], was a farmer, inheriting his
father's homestead. He m. Dec. 25, 1800, Persis Cobb, who
was b. Aug. 21, 1780, and d. Apr. 9, 1851. Issue :

1. Anna Winslow,	b. Jan. 25, 1802.	d. Mch. 11, 1830.
2. Betsey Thomas,	b. Dec. 1, 1803.	d. Oct. 11, 1843.
3. Thomas, Jr.,	b. Jan. 10, 1806.	d. Sep. 2, 1864.
4. Persis Cobb,	b. Nov. 13, 1807.	d. Mch. 31, 1851.
5. Mary,	b. Jan. 20, 1810.	d. Nov. 30, 1882.
6. Almira,	b. Mch. 2, 1812.	d. Jul. 22, 1833.
7. Melissa Cobb,	b. Mch. 16, 1814.	d. Jan. 16, 1894.
8. William,	b. Mch. 20, 1816.	d Nov. 15, 1837.
9. George Winslow,	b. Apr. 26, 1818,	d. Nov. 2, 1881.
10. Nehemiah Cobb,	b. Jul. 23, 1820.	d. Mch. 30, 1845.
11. Roland,	b. Jun. 29, 1822.	d. Jul. 29, 1824.

Of Thomas's children, Rowland d. young ; and **Amira,**[7]
William,[7] and **Nehemiah**[7] d. single. **William**[7] was a
shoemaker, and **Nehemiah**[7] a physician.

1. **Anna Winslow,**[7] oldest daughter of Thomas, who
lived at Carver, m. Sep. 29, 1825, Earl Shaw, who was b.
May 31, 1799, and d. Mch. 11, 1830. Issue : **Anna,**[8] who
m. 1st, Dr. Charles A. King of Carver, and had : Sarah
Austin. She m. 2d, Joshua L. Nash of Abington, Mass., and
had : Emma Hammond and Alice Louise.

2. **Betsey Thomas,**[7] second daughter of Thomas, lived
at Boston and at Easton, Mass. She m. May 13, 1832,
Daniel Reed, who was b. Mch. 22, 1797, and d. Oct. 2, 1879.
Issue : Charlotte Augusta (?), Almira Hammond, Melissa
Cobb, Olive Janette, and Thomas.

4. **Persis Cobb,**[7] third daughter of Thomas, who lived at
Easton, Mass., m. Feb. 10, 1828, Daniel Reed, who, after her
death, married her sister Betsey Thomas. Issue : Persis Hammond, who resides, single, at Easton Centre, Mass.

5. **Mary,**[7] fourth daughter of Thomas, lived at North
Carver, Mass. She m. Apr. 19, 1832, Thomas Cobb, who
was b. Aug. 17, 1808, and d. Aug. 25, 1886. Issue: Mary
Thomas, Almira Hammond, and Rev. Solon.

Of Mary's children, **Mary**[8] m. Rodolphus Crocker, and
had a daughter Juliette; **Almira**[8] m. William H. Barrows,
and has a grandson Dudley Hammond Barrows, living in New
York City; **Rev. Solon,**[8] who is a clergyman at Erie, Penn.,
m. Hannah D. Anthony, and has a son: Willie Anthony.

7. **Melissa Cobb,**[7] sixth daughter of Thomas, lived many
years in Boston, but afterwards moved to Cottage City, Mass.,
where she d. Jan. 16, 1891. She m. Dec. 31, 1837, Samuel
Virgin, who was b. Jul. 4, 1808. Issue: Charlotte Augusta
and Rev. Samuel Henderson.

Of Melissa's children, **Charlotte Augusta**[8] m. Dec. 6,
1887, Sylvester J. Lee, and lives at Cottage City; **Rev.
Samuel Henderson**[8] m. Dec. 24, 1868, Isadore F. Blodgett
of Boston, and is a clergyman in New York City. Issue:
Mabelle Hammond, Frederic Oakham, and Edith Meriam.

9. **George Winslow,**[7] second son of Thomas, was a
farmer, and lived for a time at Hardwick, Mass. He afterwards
moved to and died at Winchester, N. H. He m. Nov. 29,
1865, Lucia Bert, who was b. Dec. 27, 1831. No issue.

†–3. **Thomas Jr.,**[7] oldest son of Thomas, was a farmer
on the old homestead at Carver, Mass. He m. Jun. 16, 1833,
Lydia Shaw, who was b. Mch. 1, 1811. Issue:

1. Lucian Thomas,	}	b. Sep. 10, 1834.	d. Jul. 30, 1862.
2. Lydia Maria,			
3. William,		b. Jun. 30, 1842.	d. Sep. 6, 1893.
4. Charlotte Eliz.,		b. Jun. 20, 1849.	

Of these children, **Lucian Thomas**[8] was a Sergeant in
the 2d Inf. M. V. M., and d. at Harrison's Landing, Va.

2. **Lydia Maria**[8] m. Apr. 9, 1862, Benjamin W. Rob-
bins, and lives at North Carver. Issue: Annie Hammond,
John Sprague, Lucian Thomas, Evelyn Florence, and Maurice
Fletcher.

4. **Charlotte Elizabeth,**[8] who resides at North Carver,
m. Nov. 24, 1874, Andrew R. Eames, a farmer, who was b.
Aug. 21, 1845, and d. Apr. 21, 1882. Issue: Embert Hathaway, Mabelle Hortense, and Flora Isabel.

†-3-3. **William**[9] was a boot and shoe dealer at Sedalia, Mo. He m. Oct. 6, 1869, Harriet V. Richardson, who was b. Aug. 12, 1846. Issue:

1. William Lee,	b. Aug. 15, 1871.	d. Jun. 4, 1881.
2. Lucian T.,	b. Jun. 16, 1873.	d. Jun. 1, 1881.
3. Grace,	b. Jul. 11, 1877.	d. Jun. 15, 1881.
4. Mary Richardson,	b. Feb. 22, 1879.	d. Jun. 14, 1881.
5. Alice Maud,	b. Nov. 30, 1880.	
6. Ralph Dana,	b. Jan. 30, 1883.	
7. Irving Richardson,	b. Jul. 9, 1885.	
8. Harriet Lydia,	b. Jul. 29, 1887.	

Of these children, William Lee was born at East Bridgewater, Mass., and the others, except the youngest, at Nebraska City, Neb.

9.—BENJAMIN HAMMOND OF EAST CARVER, MASS.

†. **Benjamin**[6] **Hammond**, third son of Capt. George,[5] [Rowland,[4] John,[3] Benjamin,[2] William[1]], was a farmer, and lived at East Carver, Mass. He m. in the Fall of 1803, Hannah Sturtevant, who was b. in Nov. 1779, and d. Mch. 11, 1870. Issue:

1. Priscilla P.,	b. Aug. 28, 1804.	d. Feb. 23, 1887.
2. Lucy,	b. May 18, 1806.	d. Aug. 29, 1892.
3. Benjamin, Jr.,	b. Apr. 8, 1808.	d. Jan. 31, 1891.
4. Josiah S.,	b. May 10, 1810.	d. Nov. 28, 1886.
5. Hannah,	b. Jun. 16, 1813.	d. Jun. —, 1857.
6. George,	b. Jun. 21, 1815.	
7. Roland,	b. Sep. 15, 1818.	d. May 19, 1819.

1. **Priscilla P.,**[7] oldest daughter of Benjamin, who lived in Plymouth, Mass., m. Apr. 1821, Reuben Sherman, who was b. Mch. 28, 1797, and d. Apr. 25, 1879. Issue: Elizabeth D., Priscilla, and Reuben.

2. **Lucy,**[7] second daughter of Benjamin, who lived in Carver, m. Oct. 1824, Benjamin Ransom, who was b. Aug. 23, 1806, and d. Apr. 27, 1864. Issue: Benjamin, and Dr. Nathaniel Morton of Taunton.

5. **Hannah,**[7] third daughter of Benjamin, who lived in Plymouth, Mass., m. in 1841 Roland E. Cotton of Plymouth, who was b. Jan. 4, 1802, and d. Feb. 27, 1856. Roland Cotton was one of the famous line of Cottons, who filled the

position of Register of Deeds at Plymouth for 133 years in succession. Issue: Hannah Sophia, Sarah Louisa, and Augusta Delfthaven.

†–3. **Benjamin Jr.,**[7] oldest son of Benjamin, was a farmer, and lived on his father's place in East Carver. He m. Jul. 31, 1831, Mary Sherman, who was b. Mch. 10, 1809. Issue:

1. Mary Ann,	b. Aug. —, 1832.
2. Henry Taber,	b. Jan. 25, 1834.
3 Susan Augusta,	b. Dec. 2, 1835.
4. Maria Thompson,	b. Nov. 23. 1837.
5. Lucy,	b. Aug. 15, 1839.
6. Sarah A.,	b Jan. 17, 1842.
7. Julia Francis,	b. Apr. 20. 1853.

Of these children, **Sarah**[9] and **Julia**[8] have never married, and reside with their mother at East Carver. There was also a daughter **Cordelia,**[8] who d. young, Aug. 8, 1852.

1. **Mary Ann,**[8] who resides at East Carver, m. Apr. 1866, Lorenzo Shaw, who was b. Jul. 1823. No issue.

2. **Henry Taber,**[8] only son of Benjamin Jr., was formerly a sailor, but is now a lumberman, residing at East Carver. He m. Mch. 31, 1858, Betsey Shaw, who was b. Jul. 19, 1835. Issue:

1. Walter Franklin,	b. Oct. 2, 1858.
2. Arnold Lester,	b. Jun. 30, 1873.

3. **Susan Augusta,**[8] second daughter of Benjamin Jr., m. Jan. 11, 1879, Thomas Hathaway, and resides at Middleboro', Mass. No issue.

4. **Maria Thompson,**[8] third daughter of Benjamin Jr., who resides at Brockton, Mass., m. Aug. 28, 1860, Junius Blanchard, a book-keeper, who was b. Aug. 28, 1836. Issue: Eunice Capen, b. Jul. 27, 1862. **Eunice Capen**[9] m. Dec. 12, 1888, Horace M. Locke, a physician, and lives in Brockton. Issue: 1, Dean Jewett, b. Feb. 14, 1890; 2. Louise, b. Jun. 12, 1892.

5. **Lucy,**[8] fourth daughter of Benjamin Jr., who resides at Plymouth, Mass., m. Apr. 9, 1862, Benjamin Whiting, who was b. Aug. 13, 1839. Issue: Herbert Franklin, b. Aug. 13, 1871.

JOSIAH S. HAMMOND, M.D.

†–4. **Josiah S.,**[7] second son of Benjamin, graduated in medicine at Dartmouth College, N. H., in 1834. He settled in Plympton, Mass., where he practised his profession nearly half a century, and d. at the ripe age 76, much respected. Dr. Hammond m. 1st, at New Bedford, Mch. 5, 1835, Mary A. Taber, who d. soon after, without issue. He m. 2d, Nov. 25, 1838, Betsey Parker, who was b. May 9, 1818. Issue:

1. Josiah P.,	b. Nov. 24, 1839.
2. William Penn,	b. Sep. 25, 1841.

†–4–1. **Josiah P.,**[9] oldest son of Dr. Josiah, is a farmer, and lives at Plympton, Mass. He has been Town Clerk of Plympton for a number of years, and has held many other important town offices. He m. 1st, Jul. 3, 1864, Celia Myrtis Bisbee, who d. Mch. 3, 1884. Issue:

1. Myrtis Bisbee,	b. Apr. 11, 1865.	
2. Rachel M.,	b. Jul. 4, 1867.	d. Mch. 7, 1891.
3. William Penn,	b. Jun. 16, 1869.	
4. Arthur B.,	b. Jul. 20, 1878.	

Besides the above children, Amy F., Fred W., and Grace E. d. young.

Josiah P. m. 2d, Oct. 21, 1885, Martha Young, and had further issue:

5. Roland Orr,	b Mch. 24, 1889.

Of Josiah Parker's children, **Myrtis Bisbee**[9] m. Dec. 23, 1888, Josiah A. Holmes, and lives at Brockton. No issue.

2. **Rachel M.**[9] m. Feb. 5, 1883, Elmer Bradford, and lived at Plympton. Issue: Blanche Myrtis, b. Oct. 30, 1885.

3. **William P.**[9] is a machinist, and lives at West Lynn, Mass. He m. Nov. 22, 1891, Lucia J. Snow.

†–4–2. **William Penn,**[ ] second son of Dr. Josiah S., is a successful physician, residing at Charlestown, Mass. He graduated from Amherst College, class of '69, and took his M. D. at Harvard in '73, ranking well in his class. He m. Sep. 17, 1873, Sarah Abbie [Harrub] Cole, who was b. Jun. 24, 1846. Issue:

1. Bessie Parker,	b. Jul. 9, 1874.

†–6. **George,**[7] third son of Benjamin, was a farmer, and for many years resided at North Abington, Mass. In 1864 he moved to Lockeford, Cal., where he now resides at the ripe age

of 77. He m. 1st, Nov. 6, 1834, Susanna Shaw, who was b.
Apr. 21, 1816, and d. Nov. 29, 1874. Issue:

1. Delia Marcella,   b. May 30, 1836.
2. Susan Lucretia,   b. Jan. 13, 1839.
3. Roland George,   b. May 16, 1842.
4. Josiah Shaw,   b. Sep. 10, 1844.
5. Horace Alfred,   b. Aug.   7, 1847.
6. Hannah Sturtevant,   b. Dec. 12, 1849.
7. Clara Cobb,   b. Nov.   8, 1853.   d. Nov. 12, 1889.
8. John Culver,   b. Oct. 19, 1856.

The above children were born at North Abington, Mass.
George Hammond m. 2d, Mch. 19, 1866, Mrs. Mary J.
[Bartlett] Smith. No other issue.

1. Delia Marcella,[8] oldest daughter of George, m.
Apr. 30, 1885, Dr. Dean J. Locke, who was b. Apr. 16, 1823,
and d. May 4, 1887. They reside at Lockeford, San Joaquin
Co., Cal. Issue: Luther Jewett, Ada, Horace Mann, M. D.,
Harvard '86, Nathaniel Howard, Ida, Mary, William Williard,
Hannah, John Calvin, Edward Moor, Eunice, George Ham-
mond, and Theresa.

2. Susan Lucretia,[8] second daughter of George, who
also lives at Lockeford, m. May 15, 1859, George Shepley
Locke, a farmer, who was b. Oct. 30, 1830. Issue: Sarah
A. J., Elmer Hammond, George Franklin, Wallace H., Almy,
Lilla, John G., Mertice, Franklin Hammond, and Almy G.

†–6–3. **Roland George,**[8] oldest son of George, is a
farmer, residing at Lockeford, Cal. He m. Nov. 12, 1876,
Rebecca Taylor, who was b. Nov. 15, 1856. Issue:

1. Alice Edna,   b. Oct.   8, 1877.   d. Jun. 15, 1884.
2. Alberta Josephine,   b. Aug. 24, 1879.
3. George,   b. Feb.   6, 1881.
4. Estella May,   b. May   21, 1883.
5. Ina Pearl,   b. Aug. 18, 1885.
6. Nellie,   b. Dec. 10, 1890.

†–6–4. **Josiah Shaw,**[8] second son of George, graduated
from the State Normal School, California, in '68, and from the
Cooper Medical College, San Francisco, in '73, and is now a
physician residing at Butte City, Montana. He m. Dec. 25,
1867, Ann Eliza Simpson, who was born at St. Louis, Mo.,
Sep. 23, 1851. Issue:

1. Emma Louise,   b. Jul.   4, 1869.
2. Kate T.,   b. Apr.   3, 1871.

3. Hattie,	b. Jan. 13, 1873.	
4. Delia,	b. Oct. 6, 1881.	d. Sep. 1, 1891.
5. Nelson,	b. Sep. 22, 1883.	
6. Benjamin,	b. Jun. 5, 1885.	

†–6–5. **Horace Alfred,**[5] third son of George, is an engineer, and lives at Oakland, Cal. He m. 1st, Apr. 7, 1880, Dolly McGregor, who was b. in San Francisco in 1857, and d. in Oakland, Cal., Nov. 25, 1884. Issue:

1. Amy Evelyn, b. Oct. 9, 1881.

Horace Alfred m. 2d, Nov. 20, 1886, Anna Elizabeth Hayes. No issue by the second marriage.

6. **Hannah Sturtevant,**[5] third daughter of George, who lives at Lodi, Cal., m. Mch. 17, 1867, Thomas Bush Geffroy, a farmer, who was b. in Newport, R. I., Apr. 4, 1834. Issue: Mabel, Carrie, Bertha, Arthur, Richard, Susie, and Amy.

7. **Clara Cobb,**[5] who lived at Cahto, Cal., m. Jun. 24, 1872, Rev. Orville Allen Ross, who was b. at Uxbridge. Mass., Oct. 8, 1852. Issue: Nettie Taylor, Eva, Orville Clarence, Edith, Talford Allen, and Arthur Hastings.

Orville A. Ross, his wife Clara, and his son Arthur, were all killed, Nov. 12, 1889, near Lockeford, Cal.

†–6–8. **John Culver,**[5] fourth son of George, is a farmer at Lockeford, Cal. He m. Sep. 21, 1872, Lucie Jane Coil, who was b. in Lincoln, Ill., Dec. 25, 1864. Issue:

1. Horace Coil. b. May 2, 1883.
2. Alice Ethel, b. Oct. 2, 1884.

†–2–10. **Priscilla,**[6] youngest daughter of Capt. George, was b. at Carver, Mass., Jan. 8, 1781, and d. there Nov. 13, 1826. She m. Mch. 22, 1804, Gen. Ephraim Ward, who was b. in 1778, and d. at Carver, Apr. 10, 1856, and was a Brigadier in the Mass. Vol. Militia. Issue:

1. Eliab,	b. Jul. 1, 1805.	d. May 12, 1892.
2. Priscilla,	b. Apr. 19, 1808.	d. Oct. 17, 1871.
3. Ephraim,	b. Oct. 15, 1810.	d. Dec. 25, 1873.
4. Betsey.	b. Jan. 16, 1813.	d. Sep. 4, 1811.
5. George,	b. Sep. —, 1815.	d. Aug. 29, 1856.
6. Mary,	b. Mch. 9, 1818.	d. Sep. 18, 1841.

Of these children, **Mary**[7] d. single at the age of 23 at Carver.

1. **Eliab**[7] graduated from Dartmouth College, class of '31,

and later was a Brigadier in the State Militia. He afterwards became a successful lawyer and Justice of the Peace, residing at Middleboro', Mass. He represented the town in the Legislature during several sessions, and was elected to the Senate in 1843. He retired from active life some years before his death. He was a remarkably well-preserved man for one of his years, his mind being as bright and active as that of a much younger man.

His advanced age and retentive memory enabled him to render very material assistance in the preparation of this Genealogy, and the writer recalls many pleasant interviews with him on the subject. He m. Oct. 17, 1862, Prudence Holmes, who was b. Feb. 17, 1806, and d. Sep. 17, 1875. No issue.

2. **Priscilla**[7] m. Mch. 21, 1835, Peleg H. Stetson of New Bedford, who was b. Jan. 1800, and d. Jan. 26, 1867. Issue:

 1. Mary,   b. Sep. —, 1838.   d. Jul. —, 1861.
 2. Sprague,   b. Feb. 12, 1841.

Sprague,[8] who is a farmer at Lakeville, Mass., m. Dec. 13, 1864, Thalia Weston, who was b. May 2, 1841. Issue: George Ward and Jane. **George Ward**[9] is a graduate of Dartmouth College, and an attorney at Middleboro' and Boston.

3. **Ephraim**[7] was also a graduate of Dartmouth College, and a lawyer of some note at Middleboro'. He m. 1st, Nov. 1850, Margaret Washburne of Frankfort, Me., who was b. in 1821, and d. in 1884. Issue: Mary Helen, b. in 1855, and d. in 1885.
Ephraim m. 2d, a Mrs. Van Arne, but had no other issue.

4. **Betsey**[7] m. May 27, 1841, Horace Holmes, who was b. in 1809, and d. in 1855, and lived at Kingston, Mass. Issue: Mary Ward, b. Jul. 1842.

5. **George**[7] m. Oct. 1, 1840, Caroline L. Leonard, b. May 28, 1817, and lived at Lakeville, Mass. No issue.

V.—JOHN HAMMOND JR. OF ROCHESTER, MASS.

†. **John**[4] **Hammond Jr.,** fifth son of John,[3] [Benjamin,[2] William[1]], born at Rochester, Mass., Sep. 4, 1716, and died there Dec. 20, 1785, succeeded to and carried on his

father's farm. He married about 1740, Mary Ruggles, daughter of Timothy Ruggles, second minister in Rochester, and had issue :

1. Elizabeth,	b. Jan. 9, 1742.	d.
2. Timothy,	b. Feb. 25, 1744.	d. Dec. 4. 1783.
3. Elnathan,	b. Jul. 20, 1746.	d. Jan. 16. 1750.
4. Molly,	b. Feb. 10. 1750.	d.
5. John 3d,	b. Jul. 16. 1753.	d. Dec. —, 1753.
6. John,	b. Nov. 2. 1756.	d.
7. Benjamin,	b. Mch. 30, 1759.	d.
8. Hannah,	b. Jan. 19, 1763.	d. Jan. 2. 1793.

Of these children, **Elnathan**[5] and the first **John**[5] d. young ; **Hannah**[5] died single, at the age of thirty ; and **Molly,**[5] **John,**[5] and **Benjamin,**[5] all single, lived on the "Old Homestead." They adopted two young people, **Abel Howes** and **Deborah Ruggles,** who afterwards married and assumed the care of these old people, and received the farm as a compensation. Hence the "Old Homestead" is now known as the "Howes Place."

†–1. **Elizabeth**[5] m. Sep. 17. 1769, Rev. Bezaliel Shaw, who was b. in 1738, graduated from Harvard College in 1763, and preached at Nantucket, Mass. They had one daughter, **Elizabeth,**[6] who was b. in 1772, m. Dr. Andrew Craigie of Cambridge, and d. there May 7, 1841.

2.—TIMOTHY OF ROCHESTER, MASS.

†–2. **Timothy,**[5] who inherited the northern part of his father's farm, m. Sep. 25, 1767, Deborah, daughter of Roger Hammond, who was b. Oct. 15, 1746. Issue :

1. Timothy 2d,	b. Aug. 10, 1768.	d. Oct. 20, 1851.
2. Betsey,	b. Feb. 12, 1770.	d.
3. Deborah,	b. Jun. 1, 1773.	d.
4. Susannah R.,	b. Nov. 3, 1776.	d.

Of these children, 2. **Betsey**[6] m. Feb. 12, 1795, Ebenezer Rogers, and lived on the "Caswell place" in "Hammondtown," in what is now Mattapoisett. No issue.

3. **Deborah**[6] m. in 1799, Asa Swift of Wareham, and lived in Fairhaven, Mass. Issue :   John and Asa or Aseph.

4. **Susannah Ruggles**[6] m. Aseph Price, who was a sailor, and son of Thankful Hammond (daughter of Nathan Hammond), and Asa Price. They lived in Mattapoisett, but had no issue.

†-2-1. **Timothy 2d,**[6] who resided on his father's place, m. Jun. 1791, Betsey LeBaron of Plymouth, Mass., who d. Jan. 18, 1854, æ. 90, and had twelve children:

1. Deborah,	b. Jan. 9, 1793.	d. in	1886.
2. Mary,	b. Dec. 1, 1795.	d. Jul. 23, 1861.	
3. Bezaliel Shaw,	b. Dec. 12, 1797.	d.	
4. LeBaron,	b. Feb. 14, 1799.	d. Dec. 4, 1879.	
5. Ebenezer Rogers,	b. Mch. 6, 1801.	d.	
6. Timothy,	b. Dec. 19, 1803.	d. in	1838.
7. Elizabeth Rogers,	b. Apr. 2, 1805.	d.	
8. Andrew Craigie,	b. Apr. 5, 1808.	d. Mch. 3, 1889.	
9. Samuel W.,	b. Apr. 23, 1810.	d.	
10. Frederick H.,	b. Jun. 15, 1812.	d. Jul. 7, 1859.	
11. Emily,	b. Sep. 4, 1814.		
12. Harriet W.,	b. Sep. 2, 1816.		

1. **Deborah,**[7] when a girl went to live with Dr. Andrew Craigie in Cambridge. She afterwards m. Daniel Hastings and lived in Boston, and d. in Brattleboro', Vt., in 1886. Issue: Francis E., Daniel, Louis W., Horace, Emily, and Isabella.

2. **Mary**[7] m. 1st, Jul. 19, 1832, Moses Davis, a mariner, and son of Mercy Hammond (daughter of Moses Hammond), and Joseph Davis, and lived in "Hammondtown," Mattapoisett. Issue: Lemuel and Thomas, twins, and Mary Elizabeth.

Mary m. 2d, James Hammond, son of Capt. Gideon Hammond. No issue.

3. **Bezaliel Shaw,**[7] a bachelor, known as "Shaw," in early life was in the merchant service. Later he was a dealer in crockery and glassware in Boston. Afterwards he went to New Orleans and engaged in trading, and died there more than thirty years ago.

†-2-1-4. **LeBaron,**[7] second son of Timothy 2d, also in the merchant service, sailing from New York City, afterwards kept a market in Brooklyn, N. Y., where he d. Dec. 4, 1879. He m. Maria Weed of New York City, who was b. Apr. 13, 1811, and d. Oct. 19, 1888, and had issue:

1. Emily Attaline,	b. Apr. 27, 1833.	
2. Maria Louisa, ⎰	b. Feb. 8, 1835.	d. Jul. 13, 1880.
3. Mary Eliza, ⎱		

4. Ann Augusta,	b. Feb. 7, 1838.	
5. Josephine,	b. May 7, 1840.	d. Jan. 25, 1842.
6. Rachel Frances,	b. Oct. 25, 1841.	
7. George LeBaron,	b. Jan. 24, 1843.	
8. William Henry,	b. Dec. 12, 1845.	d. Aug. 8, 1847.
9. Harriet Almira,	b. Nov. 12, 1847.	d. Sep. 22, 1855.
10. Georgianna Weed.	b. Mch. 15, 1850.	d. Jan. 22, 1880.
11. Ella Elizabeth,	b. May 12, 1852.	
12. Caroline Adelaide,	b. Jul. 1, 1854.	

Of these children, Josephine, William H., and Harriet A. d. in childhood; and Mary Eliza, Rachel Frances, and Ella Elizabeth are all single.

1. **Emily A.**[8] m. May 2, 1855, John W. Haskins, and had issue: John Wesley, Minnie Louise, Josephine Weed, and Florence LeBaron.

2. **Maria L.**[8] m. Jun. 1, 1858, Jeremiah V. Spader, and had issue: Annie Vanderbilt, Louise Hammond, Nellie Vanderbilt, Charles Furman, and Willard Burtis. Louise H. m. Nov. 29, 1884, George D. Selden, and has Maria Louise and George D.

4. **Ann A.**[8] m. Aug. 7, 1866, Stephen M. Ostrander, but has no issue.

7. **George L.**[8] m. Oct. 22, 1867, Jennie Eisenhart, is a ship-chandler in New York City, and resides in Brooklyn. Issue:

1. George LeRoy,	b. Sep. 26, 1878.	d. Jun. 29, 1882.
2. Edna Virginia.	b. Nov. 30, 1882.	d. Nov. 29, 1890.
3. Jessie LeBaron,	b. Mch. 19, 1885.	

10. **Georgianna W.**[8] m. Apr. 20, 1871, Tennis D. Huntling, and had issue: Grace Madison, Ethel LeBaron, and George Hammond.

12. **Caroline A.**[8] m. Oct. 10, 1877, Frank W. Chadsey. No issue.

†-2-1-5. **Ebenezer Rogers,**[7] third son of Timothy 2d, in early life was a cooper in the whaling service, and lived at Fairhaven, Mass. He m. about 1827, Lovica Jenney, who was b. in 1814, and d. May 31, 1862, and had one child:

1. George Frank, b. Dec. 11, 1831.

Eben R. afterwards went South, became a trader on the Mississippi River, and probably d. at New Orleans. He is said to have married a second time, and probably had further issue.

1. **George Franklin**[8] was a mate in the whaling service, and lived at Fairhaven. He m. Jun. 26, 1856, Abbie E. Wing of Acushnet, Mass., who was b. Aug. 12, 1834, and had issue as follows:

1. John Jenney,	b. May 4, 1861.
2. James Wing,	b. Sep. 29, 1867.

6. **Timothy,**[7] fourth son of Timothy 2d, a bachelor, engaged in the merchant service from New York City, and residing there died in the Hospital on Staten Island about 1838.

7. **Elizabeth R.**[7] m. John West, lived in New Bedford until her husband's death, after which she lived with her brother LeBaron in Brooklyn, N. Y., and worked at cap-making. She d. without issue, probably at Newark, N. J.

8. **Andrew C.,**[7] in early life was in the coasting service, sailing from New Bedford and New London. He afterwards went to Cincinnati, Ohio, and learned the carpenter's trade. He m. Aug. 13, 1837, Eliza J. Henderson, who d. in 1868. Issue:

1. Elizabeth,	b. Sep. 14, 1838.	d. Sep. 17, 1839.
2. Horace H.,	b. Mch. 23, 1841.	d. Feb. 22, 1849.
3. Charles F.,		
4. Albert F.,	b. Dec. 2, 1842.	d. Feb. 2, 1849.
5. Frederick,	b. Jun. 26, 1844.	d. Jul. 10, 1845.
6. Cornelia E.,	b. Dec. 14, 1847.	d. Jul. 11, 1848.
7. Horace A.,	b. Jul. 2, 1852.	d. Mch. 1, 1885.

9. **Samuel W.,**[7] a bachelor, was a cabinet-maker at New Bedford. He afterwards went South, and probably died at Macon, Ga.

10. **Frederick H.**[7] in early life was engaged in the whaling service, and afterwards for eleven years was a spar-maker at East Boston. He moved to Malden, Mass., about 1855, and d. there Jul. 7, 1859. He m. 1st, Mary Ann Pierce of Lynn, Mass. No issue.

He m. 2d, Sarah Redman [Pratt] of Malden, and had issue:

1. Franklin Henry,	b. May 28, 1854.	
2. Frederick,	b. Jun. 10, 1856.	d. Jun. 10, 1856.
3. Samuel Wing,	b. Oct. 18, 1857.	

Frank H.[8] and **Samuel W.**[8] reside at Malden.

11. **Emily**[7] never married, and lives with her sister Harriet at Hammondtown.

12. **Harriet W.**[7] m. Apr. 21, 1855, Marshall Howes, and lives on her father's place in Hammondtown. Issue: Frank LeBaron and Harriet Emma.

Frank[8] m. Sally Crapo, lives at New Bedford, and has: Edwin, Harry, Annie Ruggles, Hattie, and Charles Crapo.

Emma[8] m. James Jay of New Bedford, and has no issue.

JABEZ HAMMOND'S FAMILY RECORD.

"a. tru copy taken of from my old Count may – 17 – 1765.
February–12–1727 a record of nams and Berths of my father
and mother and my self and my wives and all their children.

my Honered father John Hammond was Born in ye – –	1663
my Honered mother mary Hammond was Born – – –	1674
I Jabez Hammond was Born febury – ye – 27 –	1699
and was mared to Sary Lathrop Aprell – – 14 – –	1725
my wife Sary Hammond was Born december – 31 –	1703
and ouer first Child Joshua was Born Aprel – 1	1726
and died ienuery – 2 the same year – 1726	
ouer Second Child Hanah July the – 20 – – – – –	– 1727
and died the – 9 – day of June – 1730	
our third child Zilpha was Born Agust – 10 –	1729
and died iune – 18 – 1730	
ouer forth Child rebeka was Born febury – 14 –	1730
ouer fifth Child Lothrop was Born Aprel – 24 –	1732
and died in Jaimacer novmber – 26 – 1756	
my sixth Child Sary was Born october – 15 –	1734
and died in noumber – 19 – 1734	
my wife Sary died in noumber – 9 – 1734	
i mared my Second wif Abegal fane may – 12 –	1736
my second wife Abegal was Born – 22 – may – –	1714
our first Child fane was Born may the 20 – –	1737
our second Child Sary was Born march – 24 – –	1739
our third Child Jabez was Born June – 9 –	1741
our forth Child Luther was Born Aprell – 8 –	1744
our fifth Child Calvin was Born december 29 –	1745
our Sixth Child Roda was Born noumber: 16 –	1747
our Seventh Child John was Born ienuery – 20 –	1749
our eight child Eligah march – 4	1751
our ninth Child gorg was Born Agust – 19	
our tenth Child Caleb was Born decen	
our eleventh Child Ruth was born	
and died in the – 11 of december – 1	
ouer twelfth Child Abegal was	

Monday ye 23d day of Sept 178
and wife re moved to wood sto
and His wife Abigil aged 68
A Record of Berths and deaths of my famely.

JABEZ HAMMOND."

As showing something of how the early settlers lived, and
what they lived on, we give below the obligation of Thomas F.
Hammond to his parents:

Know all men by these Presents that I Thomas Faunce Hammond of Reading in Windsor County and State of Vermont, for
and in consideration of five hundred and forty eight Dollars to me
in hand paid by Faunce and Mary Hammond of Reading in
Windsor County and State of Vermont, the receipt whereof I do
acknowledge, do covenant and agree with them the said Faunce
and Mary Hammond, that from this time forth I will yearly keep
one Cow for them on suitable grass and hay; that the House in
which they live shall be constantly at their service; That I will
find them in suitable fire-wood for one fire in said house; That I
will pay them yearly twenty pounds of Flax; That I will pay
them yearly ten pounds of wool; That I will pay them yearly
thirty pounds of sugar; That I will pay them yearly four Bushels
of Wheat; That I will pay them yearly four bushels of Rye;
That I will pay them yearly two Barrels of Cider; That I will
pay them yearly six bushels of Apples; and that I will also pay
them ten Dollars in Cash yearly; and likewise, that I will yearly
prepair one acre of tillage Land suitable for a crop which shall
be constantly for their benefit.

Provided also, that the above privileges shall not extend to the
benefit of their heirs or assigns after their Decease.

In testimony of the fulfilment of the above obligation I have
hereunto set my hand and seal, this twentieth day of March in the
year of our Lord, one thousand eight hundred and seven.

THOMAS F. HAMMOND [Seal.]

In presents of
Simeon Currier

Filed on the back: "Thomas F. Hammond's Obligation to
Faunce and Mary Hammond."

PART IV.

NATHAN HAMMOND, THIRD SON OF BENJAMIN.

†. **Nathan³ Hammond,** third son of Benjamin² of Sandwich, [William¹ of London], born at Sandwich, in 1670, was a farmer, and lived in the northern part of Hammondtown, in the old town of Rochester. The house which he built was on the east side of the road opposite the residence of Nathaniel Dunham. He married 1st, the widow Alice Dexter, daughter of Capt. Seth Pope of Fairhaven, Mass. Issue :

1. Nathan 2d,	b. Apr. 5, 1699.	d.
2. Susanna,	b. Mch. 24, 1701.	d.
3. James,	b. Jul. 31, 1702.	d.
4. Sarah,	b. Mch. 15, 1704.	d.

Nathan m. 2d, Feb. 5, 1720, Elizabeth Bourne of Swansea. He m. 3d, Feb. 1825, Meribah Delano. No issue by the second and third marriages.

Of Nathan's children, nothing further is known of **James⁴** and **Sarah⁴**; **Susannah⁴*** m. Mch. 14, 1722, her cousin Barnabas Hammond, son of Samuel. Issue : Elizabeth, James, Mary, and Ellis.

I.—NATHAN 2D, OF ROCHESTER, MASS.

†–1. **Nathan 2d,⁴** lived on his father's farm, and was a farmer. He m. Nov. 16, 1727, Sarah Snow, who was b.

* For further record see Genealogy of Barnabas Hammond, page 111.

17

Mch. 20, 1703, and a daughter of Nicholas and Lydia [Shaw] Snow of Rochester. Issue:

1. Alice,	b. Sep. 3, 1728.	d.
2. Joshua,	b. Mch. 29, 1730.	d.
3. Lydia [Lois?],	b. Feb. 7, 1732.	d.
4. Phebe,	b. Apr. 5, 1734.	d. May —, 1801.
5. Sarah,	b. Apr. 24, 1736.	d.
6. Susannah,	b. Jun. 28, 1738.	d.
7. Mary,	b. Jul. 12, 1742.	d.
8. Thankful,	b.	d.

Of these children, **Alice, Joshua,** and **Sarah** probably d. young; and Lois or Louisa, Phebe, Susannah, and Thankful received the old homestead by inheritance, Mary having probably received her part previously.

3. **Lois,** or **Louisa,** m. May 29, 1764, Nathaniel Merrick (or Myrrick) of Hardwick, Mass. She had a daughter Phebe, who probably m. Paul Russell, as her heirs were Russells.

4. **Phebe** m. Jun. 17, 1758, Capt. Nathaniel Hammond, who was b. Jul. 27, 1734, and a son of Benjamin and Priscilla [Sprague] Hammond. Phebe lived on the Nathaniel Dunham place in Hammondtown, and d. without issue.

6. **Susannah** m. Mch. 16, 1764, Nathaniel Besse, and lived on the Andrew Dunham place in Hammondtown. Issue: Lavinia, Martha, Lois, Joshua, Nathan, Nathaniel, and James. Joshua Besse m. Betsey Roper, and had a daughter Artemisia who m. Andrew Dunham, father of Nathaniel and Andrew Dunham of Mattapoisett. Lavinia lived, single, and d. in Hammondtown at a ripe old age.

7. **Mary** m. Aug. 29, 1767, Seth Barlow. Mary lived to the north of her father's place, and had a son Seth Jr.

Seth Jr. m. Mary Tinkham, and had a daughter Ruth, who m. Capt. Russell Snow, and had: Elliot and Mary.

8. **Thankful** m. Asa (or Aseph) Price, and lived in Fairhaven, Mass. Issue: Asa Jr. and Thankful. Asa Price Jr. m. Susannah Hammond, daughter of Timothy Hammond 1st, but had no issue.

PART V.

BENJAMIN 2D, YOUNGEST SON OF BENJAMIN.

†. **Benjamin³ Hammond,** fourth son of Benjamin,²
[William¹], was born in Sandwich, Mass., Nov. 1673, came
to Rochester, Mass., with his brothers about 1680–84, and
settled on the west bank of the Mattapoisett River, in what
was afterwards known as "Hammondtown," and died at Rochester, Mch. 29, 1747. He was a man of superior abilities and
acquirements for that time, and filled with honor many public
stations; was Selectman and Assessor 14 years, Representative
in the Legislature two years, and is said to have held commission as Justice of the Peace under Queen Anne. He was
also a noted land surveyor, and in company with Benjamin
Crane of Taunton, is said to have surveyed and laid out many
of the towns in Plymouth and Bristol Counties. He m. Elizabeth Hunnewell, daughter of Capt. Hunnewell of New Hamp-
shire, and had seven sons and one daughter that grew to
maturity and married. Of the sons, six settled in Rochester,
and one, Polypus, in Newport, R. I.   Issue:

1. Polypus,	b. Nov. 29, 1702.	d. Feb. 5, 1773.
2. Josephus,	b. May 6, 1703.	d. in 1779.
3. Antipas,	b. Jul. 16, 1704.	d. Mch. 29, 1773.
4. Barzillai,	b. Mch. 9, 1706.	d.
5. Israel,	b. Oct. 15, 1707.	d. in 1800.
6. Mary,	b. Sep. 25, 1709.	d.
7. Elisha,	b. about 1712-15.	d.
8. Roger,	b. in 1722.	d. Sep. 29, 1758.

Of these children, 6. **Mary⁴** m. Apr. 10, 1740, Rev. Elisha
Tupper, and had issue: Jean, Mehitabel, Thankful, and Abigail.

I.—POLYPUS HAMMOND OF NEWPORT, R. I.

†-1. **Polypus,**[4] who was a captain, had land on Matta-poisett Neck given him by his father, but afterwards moved to Newport, R. I. He m. 1st, Oct. 13, 1734, Sarah Mumford, who was b. in 1708, and d. Feb. 21, 1771. Both died and were buried in Newport. Issue :

1. Mumford,	b. in	1735.	d.
2. Elizabeth,	b. in	1736.	d. May 19, 1751.
3. Abigail,	b. in	1737.	d. Aug. 1, 1802.
4. Mary,	b. about	1739.	d.
—5. Stephen,	b. Jun. 8, 1740.		d.
6. Anna, ⎱	b. Jul. 18, 1742.		d.
7. Sarah, ⎰			d. Feb. 26, 1762.
8. Anstris,	b. Dec. —, 1744.		d. Sep. 21, 1745.
9. Anstris,	b. Nov. —, 1746.		d.

Capt. Polypus m. 2d, Mch. 29, 1751, Bathsheba Randall, and had further issue :

10. Consider,	b. in	1755.	d.
11. Mary,	b. Aug. 11, 1756.		d.
12. Polypus, Jr.,	b. about	1758.	d.

Of the above children, the two sons **Mumford**[5] and **Stephen,**[5] and some of the daughters, d. single ; **Abigail**[5] d. single at New Bedford ; **Anna**[5] m. Apr. 3, 1777, Rev. Jonathan Moore ; another daughter m. a Mumford, and a third m. a Peck ; of **Consider**[5] and **Mary**[5] nothing further is known.

12.—POLYPUS JR. OF ROCHESTER, MASS.

12. **Polypus Jr.**[5] m. Nov. 7, 1784, Maria Benson at Middleboro', lived at Rochester, and had issue :

1. Hannah,	b. Jul. 13, 1785.	d.
2. Sarah,	b. Jan. 26, 1788.	d.
3. Polypus,	b. Sep. 25, 1791.	d.
4. Samuel,	b. May 11, 1798.	d.

Nothing further is known of the children of Polypus Jr.

II.—JOSEPHUS HAMMOND OF ROCHESTER, MASS.

†. **Josephus**[4] **Hammond,** second son of Benjamin 2d,[3] [Benjamin,[2] William[1]], was a farmer, and lived in the " Church

Neighborhood" in Rochester, Mass. He m. 1st, Thankful
Winslow of Rochester, and had issue as follows :

1. Pernall,	b. Mch. 24, 1735.	d.
2. Edward,	b. May 8, 1738.	d. May 11, 1802.
3. Thankful,	b. Jan. 2. 1740.	d.
4. Zuriah,	b. Apr. 22, 1742.	d.
5. Josephus, Jr.,	b. Jun. 14, 1744.	d. Jan. 12, 1745.

Josephus m. 2d, Jan. 18, 1753, Mary Bourne, and had
further issue :

6. Josephus 2d,	b. Dec. 31, 1758.	d.

Of Josephus's children, **Pernall,** or **Parnell,**[5] m. in 1755
Paul Sears Jr. Issue not known.

3. **Thankful**[5] m. Jan. 13, 1760, John Stevens, and lived
in Rochester. Issue : Josephus, John, Micah, and William ;
Mehitable, Mary, Sarah, and Phebe.

4. **Zuriah**[5] m. Jan. 15, 1761, Stephen Bennett, and probably lived in Rochester. Issue not known.

6. **Josephus 2d**[5] lived in Wareham, but nothing further
is known of him.

2.—EDWARD OF MARION, MASS.

†-2. **Edward,**[5] who was a Captain in Col. Cotton's Reg't
in 1775, lived in Sippican, or what is now the town of Marion.
He m. Jun. 17, 1762, Mary Lombard (sometimes called
Lambert), daughter of Caleb Lombard, who d. Oct. 3, 1833,
æ. 88. Issue :

1. Thankful,	b. Mch. 22, 1763.	d.
2. Caleb,	b. Nov. 17, 1765.	d.
3. Nathaniel 3d,	b. May 7, 1768.	d. Feb. 15, 1830.
4. Stephen,	b. Oct. 8, 1770.	d.
5. Betsey,	b. Apr. 23, 1773.	d.
6. Thomas Nathan,	b. Nov. 23, 1775.	d.
7. William,	b. Jun. 21, 1778.	d.
8. Ethan Allen,	b. Dec. 24, 1780.	d.
9. Edward,	b. Mch. 2, 1784.	d.
10. Polly,	b. Jul. 28, 1787.	d.

Of these children, **Thankful**[6] m. Feb. 27, 1780, Elnathan
Foster of Rochester, but lived at New Bedford ; of **Caleb**[6]
nothing further is known ; and **Edward**[6] probably d. single.

5. **Betsey**⁶ m. 1st, Sep. 21, 1794, Job Blankenship of Marion, and had a son Job, who was a sea captain, and known as Capt. Job. She m. 2d, Seth Hammond 3d, who was probably a son of Barnabas and Mary [Clark] Hammond, but had no further issue.

10. **Polly**⁶ m. Jan. 12, 1814, Josiah Baker of Cape Cod, town of Dennis.

†–2–6. **Thomas Nathan,**⁶ fourth son of Edward, m. Aug. 11, 1799, Louise Delano of Marion, and is said to have gone "Out West," nothing further being known of him.

†–2–8. **Ethan Allen,**⁶ sixth son of Edward, who was a sailor living on "Great Neck," Marion, m. in 1802, Deborah Delano of Marion, and had issue:

1. Ethan Allen,   b. Sep. 27, 1806.   d. Jun. 3, 1823.
2. Harper Delano,   b. May 13, 1809.   d. Feb. 10, 1824.

Of these sons, **Ethan Allen**⁷ died at the "Sailor's Snug Harbor," N. Y., and **Harper Delano**⁷ was lost at sea.

†–2–3. **Nathaniel 3d,**⁶ second son of Capt. Edward, who was a sailor in the merchant service, lived in Marion, and was drowned in the Harbor there Feb. 15, 1830. He m. Feb. 2, 1794, Sylvia Blankenship, and had issue:

1. Betsey,   b. Sep. 7, 1794.   d. May 16, 1795.
2. Caleb,   b. Apr. 20, 1796.   d. Sep. 1, 1819.
3. Reuben B.,   b. Apr. 17, 1799.   d. Aug. 12, 1829.
4. Philip F.,   b. Jul. 18, 1801.   d. Oct. 1, 1833.
5. George B.,   b. Oct 28, 1803.   d. May 9. 1869.
6. Nathaniel,   b. Nov. 2, 1807.   d. Jun. 13, 1839.

Of these children, **Betsey**⁷ d. in infancy; **Caleb**⁷ probably d. single; and **Nathaniel,**⁷ who never married, was a sailor in the coasting service.

3. **Reuben Blankenship,**⁷ who lived in Marion, m. Eliza Hadley, but left no issue.

4. **Philip Farmer,**⁷ who also lived in Marion, m. Eliza P. Blankenship, and d. without issue.

†–2–3–5. **George Blankenship,**⁷ who was a shoemaker at Marion, m. in 1826, Mary C. Ellis of Fairhaven, who was b. Jul. 7, 1807, and d. Nov. 16, 1853. Issue:

1. Mary L.,   b. Jan. 16, 1827.   d. Apr. 16, 1878.
2. Reuben B.,   b. Mch. 12, 1830.   d. Nov. 20, 1855.

3. John,   b. Feb. 16, 1833.   d. Apr. 30, 1892.
4. George E.,   b. Apr. 12, 1836.   d. Apr. 12, 1837.
5. Lydia E.,   b. Dec. 3, 1838.   d. Nov. 27, 1858.
6. Martin Van B., b. Sep. 26, 1842.
7. Sylvia,   b. Aug. 18, 1845.
8. Ellen F.,   b. Aug. 2, 1852.   d. Feb. 26, 1853.

Of these children, **1. Mary Lombard,**[8] who lived in New Bedford, m. Jun. 26, 1855, John R. Lewis of New Bedford, who was b. May 3, 1827, and d. Jun. 26, 1862. Issue: Charles W., Ellis M., and John R. Jr. **Ellis**[9] m. Jan. 30, 1890, Lillian T. Baker, and lives at Woods Holl.

2. Reuben Blankenship[8] m. Aug. 27, 1854, Sylvia A. Maxim, and lived at Fairhaven. No issue.

6. Martin Van Buren,[8] who is a carpenter at Fairhaven, m. Feb. 5, 1872, Rhoda E. Rounseville, who was b. Sep. 1, 1848. Issue:

1. Martin Van B., Jr., b. Jul. 6, 1876.   d. Jul. 6, 1876.
2. Edna C.,   b Sep. 2, 1879.

7. Sylvia[8] m. Dec. 8, 1865, Savery C. Braley of Fairhaven, who was b. Feb. 23, 1844. Issue: Susan, Frank, Mattie A., John K., Charles R. and Willie A. twins. **Mattie A.**[9] m. Lawrence P. Tiernan, lives in Boston, and has a son Charles S. b. Jun. 21, 1891.

†–2–3–5–3. **John,**[8] who was a harness maker at Acushnet, m. Oct. 25, 1858, Mary A. Braley of Fairhaven, who was b. Apr. 22, 1833. Issue:

1. Sarah J.,   b. Jul. 16, 1859.   d. Jan. 9, 1879.
2. Mary C.,   b. Nov. 5, 1860.   d. Mch. 22, 1862.
3. John E.,   b. Jan. 24, 1863.
4. Frank S.,   b. Nov. 12, 1864.   d. Oct. 15, 1865.
5. George A.,   b. Jan. 21, 1867.
6. Alonzo H.,   b. Dec. 6, 1868.
7. Josephine C., b. Jan. 22, 1871.
8. James A.,   b. Jul. 11, 1873.   d. Jun. 18, 1882.
9. Mercy E.,   b. Sep. 13, 1875.

Of John's children. **5. George A.**[9] lives at Acushnet, and m. Apr. 17, 1890, Hattie A. Hart. Issue:

1. Chester A.,   b. Aug. 21, 1891.

6. Alonzo H.[9] lives in Acushnet, and m. Nov. 1, 1891, Isabel Braley. No issue.

7. Josephine[9] lives at Acushnet, and m. Dec. 9, 1886, Frank R. Ward, who was b. Jul. 22, 1860. Issue:

1. Willard D ,   b. Jan. 1, 1890.
2. Samuel C.,   b. Oct. 7, 1891.

†-2-4. **Stephen,**[6] third son of Capt. Edward, was a sea captain in the merchant service, and lived at Rochester. He m. Jul. 30, 1798, Betsey Blankenship, daughter of Charles Blankenship, who d. Aug. 3, 1830. Issue :

1. Henry,	b. May 6, 1799.	d. Dec. 24. 1808.
2. Charles B.,	b. Jul. 11, 1801.	d. Jun. 8, 1839.
3. Polly,	b. Sep. 11, 1803.	d. Nov. 18, 1812.
4. Stephen, Jr.,	b. Sep. 29, 1805.	
5. Betsey B.,	b. Aug. 26. 1807.	d. in 1880.
6. Henry,	b. Aug. 3, 1809.	d. Jun. 3, 1850.
7. William,	b. Oct. 28, 1813.	d. Feb. 7, 1892.
8. Joseph,	b. Nov. 3, 1816.	d.
9. Caleb,	b. Jan. 4, 1820.	d. in 1885.
10. James F.,	b. Apr. 24, 1822.	

Of these children, **Henry**[7] and **Polly**[7] d. young : **Betsey**[7] lived single at Marion ; **Joseph**[7] left home at the age of 17, and perhaps went West, nothing further being known of him.

†-2-4-2. **Charles Blankenship**[7] was a sea captain and lived at Marion, but d. at New Orleans. He m. Jun. 26, 1836, Eliza P. [Blankenship] Hammond, widow of Philip Farmer Hammond, and had issue :

1. Lizzie,   b. in 1838.   d. in 1856, single.

†-2-4-4. **Stephen Jr.**[7] was a carpenter and lives in Marion. He m. Oct. 16, 1829, Lydia B. Richmond of Marion, who was b. May 16, 1807. Issue :

1. Stephen E.,	b. Jun. 9, 1831.	d. about 1858.
2. Beuretta.	b. Apr. 21, 1834.	d. in 1880.
3. Charles E.,	b. Feb. 5, 1836.	d. in 1857.

Of these children, **Stephen E.,**[8] who was a physician, d. in Mexico, single. **Charles E.**[8] also never married ; and **Beuretta**[8] m. Matthew Hiller of Mattapoisett, and had issue : Lydia R., Willie H., Emerson B., Charles E., and Ira R.

†-2-4-6. **Henry**[7] was a sea captain living at Marion, and d. of sunstroke at Appalachicola, Fla. He m. Aug. 14, 1838, Lydia Butler Clifton of Marion, and had issue :

1. Jennison,   b. Mch. 12, 1843.

1. **Jennison**[8] entered the U. S. Navy, Sep. 18, 1861, at New Bedford, Mass., and continued in the service until the ship, the U. S. S. Brandywine, was burned at the Navy Yard,

Norfolk, Va., Sep. 3, 1864. Since that time he has been employed in the Navy Yard, at Norfolk, as clerk, except from Jun. 11, 1885 to Apr. 22, 1889. He m. Mch. 7, 1865, Rebecca J. Langley, who was b. Apr. 23, 1836. Issue:

1. Mary Clifton,   b. Dec. 31, 1865.
2. Lydia Frances,   b. Jan. 14, 1868.   d. Aug. 11, 1874.
3. Jennie Eldredge, b. Jun. 22, 1875.

Of these children, **Mary Clifton**[9] m. Jun. 8, 1887, Walter L. Massenburg.

†-2-4-7. **William,**[7] who in early life was a sea captain, and later a farmer and carpenter, lived at Mattapoisett, where he died. He m. in 1832, Jane, daughter of Prince and Martha Snow, and had issue:

1. William Henry,   b. Aug. 4, 1842.   d. Jun. 4, 1847.
2. Dulcina,   b. May   4, 1844.   d. Jul. 6, 1847.
3. James F.,   b. Feb. 17, 1852.

3. **James F.,**[8] who is a machinist at Mattapoisett, m. Apr. 29, 1871, Rebecca, daughter of Abner P. and Lydia [Conkeal] Cowen. Issue:

1. William Henry,   b. Jul. 26, 1872.

†-2-4-9. **Caleb**[7] was formerly a dentist in New Bedford, which occupation he was obliged to relinquish on account of ill health, and he afterwards became a sailor. He m. Jan. 1, 1846, Mary Knights of New Bedford, and had a daughter, **Elizabeth,**[8] who, the last known of her, lived in Boston.

†-2-4-10. **James F.**[7] was a carpenter, and a captain of a coasting vessel, and lived at Newport, R. I. He m. Catherine Spooner, and had issue:

1. Emma,   b. about 1866.
2. Charles, b. about 1870.

Nothing further is known of these children.

†-2-7. **William,**[6] fifth son of Capt. Edward, was a sailor and lived in Rochester, near the Marion line, and was drowned in Marion Harbor, Aug. 10, 1813. He m. Oct. 21, 1802, Nancy Clifton of Marion, and had issue:

1. Edward,   b. Aug. 1, 1805.   d. Aug. 2, 1870.
2. Louisa,   b. in   1809.   d. Jun. 29, 1874.
3. Nancy,   b. about   1812.   d. Aug. 22, 1831.

Of these children, **Nancy**[7] d. single; and **Louisa**[7] m. Gideon Barlow of Mattapoisett. Issue: Charlotte, Edward Newton, and Gideon Barstow.

†-2-7-1. **Edward,**[7] only son of William, was a ship-builder at Nantucket. He m. Nov. 14, 1830, Susan Cobb of Nantucket, who was b. Nov. 30, 1811, and still living. Issue:

1. George F.,	b. Sep. 1, 1831.	d. Apr. 16, 1863.
2. Edward C.,	b. Aug. 6, 1833.	
3. James Nye,	b. Dec. 27, 1836.	
4. Susan Cobb,	b. Nov. 10, 1839.	d. Dec. 17, 1873.

Of these children, 4. **Susan Cobb**[8] m. May 12, 1869, Thomas Bates of Nantucket. No issue.

†-2-7-1-1. **George F.,**[8] oldest son of Edward, was also a ship-builder at Nantucket. He m. Oct. 20, 1853, Mary A. Coffin, who was b. Jan. 31, 1833. Issue:

1. George Edward,	b. Jan. 2. 1856.	d. Apr. 28, 1856.
2. Charles F.,	b. Aug. 28, 1860.	

2. **Charles F.**[9] is a dealer in dry goods at Nantucket. He m. May 21, 1885, Mary F. Coffin, who was b. May 7, 1864. Issue:

1. Charles C.,	b. May 8, 1886.

†-2-7-1-2. **Edward C.,**[8] second son of Edward, is a jeweler in Boston, and lives at 22 Chester Square. He m. May 29, 1859, Sarah Hallett, who was b. Sep. 1837. No issue.

†-2-7-1-3. **James Nye,**[8] third son of Edward, is foreman of the jobbing and repairing departments of the American Watch Co., Waltham, Mass. He m. Dec. 25, 1865, Delia Newton Sherman, who was b. Oct. 27, 1841. Issue:

1. Grace,	b. Mch. 8, 1868.
2. Florence,	b. Jun. 16, 1870.
3. James C.,	b. Apr. 13, 1875.

III.—ANTIPAS HAMMOND OF ROCHESTER, MASS.

†. **Antipas**[4] **Hammond,** third son of Benjamin 2d,[3] [Benjamin,[2] William[1]], was a farmer and settled on Mattapoisett Neck, northeast of the residence of the late Hiram Hammond. He was a lieutenant of militia, and for seven years one of Selectmen and Assessors of Rochester. He m. Dec. 21, 1736, Abigail Swift, and had issue as follows:

1. Jireh,	b. Dec. 5, 1737.	d. Apr. 29, 1773.
2. Hunnewell,	b. Aug. 9, 1740.	d. Nov. 2, 1807.
3. Abigail,	b. Mch. 24, 1742.	d.
4. Joseph,	b. Sep. 5, 1747.	d.
5. Elizabeth,	b. Jan. 18, 1752.	d.
6. Benjamin,	b. Apr. 5, 1756.	d. Jun. 16, 1843.

The will, proved Jun. 7, 1773, mentions the four sons.
Jireh[5] and **Hunnewell**[5] are given the homestead.

Of the above children, **Jireh** and **Abigail** probably lived
and d. single, in Rochester.

2. **Hunnewell**[5] was a farmer and lived near the Hiram
Hammond place. He m. Nov. 26, 1778, Mary Andrews, who
d. Apr. 1829, between 80 and 90 years of age. No issue.

4. **Joseph**[5] m. Feb. 23, 1769, Rachel Winslow, and is
said to have moved to the State of New York, all trace of him
afterwards being lost. Issue: Abigail, Matilda, Nancy, Antipas, and Stephen.

5. **Elizabeth**[5] m. Dec. 8, 1773, Job Haskell, farmer,
and lived on Mattapoisett Neck. Issue: Job Jr., Abigail,
Hunnewell, and Roxellana.

Of these children, **Hunnewell**[6] m. in 1802 Lucy Ellis.
Abigail,[6] commonly called Nabby, who was quite a literary
woman, m. Charles Bruce Freeman of Mattapoisett, and had:
Job, Mary, Eveline, Lucy, Sally, and Abigail Jr. Of Abigail's
children, **Abigail Jr.**[7] m. a Lamson, and lived at Madison,
Ind.; and **Sally**[7] m. James Shaw, lived on Mattapoisett Neck,
and had: William, Bruce Freeman, John, Richard, Elizabeth,
and Nathaniel.

6.—BENJAMIN OF ROCHESTER, MASS.

†-6. **Benjamin**[5] was a farmer and lived on Mattapoisett
Neck, his farm adjoining that of his brother-in-law, Job Haskell.
He m. Oct. 22, 1780, Lydia Haskell, who d. Aug. 1841, æ. 81.
Issue: 1. Elihu; 2. Abiah; 3. Leonard, b. Jun. 13, 1789,
d. Apr. 2, 1864; 4. Aseneth; 5. Joanna; 6. Joseph.

There was also an adopted daughter, Mary Ann, b. May 13,
1803, and d. Oct. 8, 1884. Of the above children of Benjamin
Hammond, **Elihu**[6] d. at 19, **Aseneth**[6] at 22, and **Joanna**[6]
at 20, all single.

252 HAMMOND GENEALOGY.

2. **Abiah[6]** m. William Moore, son of Rev. Jonathan Moore, and lived and d. at New Orleans. Issue: Jonathan, Benjamin, Sarah, Lucy, and others that d. in infancy.

6. **Joseph,[6]** who was a farmer, m. 1st, Hannah Dean, daughter of Abiel Dean, and had issue: Hunnewell, Lydia, and others. Joseph afterwards moved to Ohio (perhaps Cincinnati), where his wife, Hannah, died. He afterwards married three times, and had many children.

Of Joseph's children, **Hunnewell[7]** d. a few years since in Ohio; and **Lydia[7]** m. a Hervey, or Harvey, and lived at Steubenville, Ohio. Nothing further is known of Joseph.

Mary Ann,[7] said to have been adopted by Aseneth, lived at Mattapoisett. She m. Jan. 8, 1823, Josiah Robinson, fisherman and miller, who was b. Dec. 5, 1799, at Harwich, Mass., and d. Jun. 11, 1883, at Mattapoisett. Issue:

1. William,	b. Oct. 18, 1823.	d. Aug. 25, 1825.
2. Joseph H.,	b. May 10, 1825.	
3. Abbie P.,	b. May 1, 1828.	d. Mch. 6. 1893.
4. Martha,	b. May 11, 1830.	d. Jun. 10, 1885.
5. Mary E.,	b. Sep. 5, 1833.	
6. Josiah,	b. Sep. 13, 1837.	d. Jan. 17, 1890.
7. William,	b. Jul. 3, 1839.	d. Dec. 26. 1858.
8. Benjamin F.,	b. Jan. 18, 1842.	
9. Sarah M.,	b. Apr. 18, 1844.	d. Sep. 19, 1845.

Of these children, **William[8]** died in Cuba, single, and **Abbie,[8]** also single, resided up to the time of her death at Mattapoisett.

2. **Joseph[8]** m. Hannah Harlow of Plymouth, lives at Mattapoisett, and has: Charles and Florence.

4. **Martha[8]** m. Marcus Bartlett LeBaron, lived at Mattapoisett, and d. without issue.

5. **Mary[8]** m. John Jenney of Fairhaven, lives at Hammondtown, and has one daughter: Olivia, or Livie.

6. **Josiah[8]** m. Lucy Caswell, who was a granddaughter of Mary Hammond and Elisha Caswell, and d. without issue.

8. **Benjamin F.[8]** is one of the Overseers at State Farm at Bridgewater. He m. 1st, Nov. 13, 1866, Amelia L., daughter of Joseph J. Hammond, who d. May 9, 1883. Issue:

1. Harry L., b. Oct. 6, 1867. d. Mch. 8, 1886.

Benjamin m. 2d, Sep. 16, 1891, Isabel Estella Roberts of Belfast, Me., formerly a teacher.

†–6–3. **Leonard,**[6] commonly called "Uncle Leonard," and second son of Benjamin, in youth a carpenter, later engaged in mercantile pursuits at Mattapoisett. He afterwards became a Government contractor, and built several light-houses, viz. : Ned's Point Light, Mattapoisett; Gay Head Light, Martha's Vineyard; besides several at the mouth of the Mississippi River. For many years he conducted the hotel in Mattapoisett known as the "County House." He m. Jan. 6, 1813, Asenath Cushman, who was b. Jan. 7, 1793, and d. Oct. 18, 1854. Issue :

1. Joseph F.,	b. May 8, 1814.	d. Feb. 28, 1817.
2. Jos. Frank,	b. Mch. 16, 1818.	d. Nov. 18, 1856.
3. Abiah M.,	b. Oct. 19, 1819.	d. Nov. 23, 1874.
4. Thomas C ,	b. Dec. 20, 1823.	d. May 23, 1851.
5. George Fred,	b. Oct. 5, 1824.	
6. Ann E.,	b. Nov. 24, 1827.	
7. Jane L.,	b. Oct. 14, 1832.	
8. Leonard,	b. Oct. 14, 1833.	d. in infancy.

Of Leonard's children, **Abiah M.**[7] m. 1st, May 10, 1845, Simeon Fish, a cabinet-maker at Mattapoisett. Issue : Edward. Abiah m. 2d, William H. Babcock, and moved to Walla Walla, Wash., where she afterwards died. Issue : A daughter, name not learned.

6. **Ann E.**[7] resides in Malden, Mass. She m. Dec. 19, 1844, Caleb King of Rochester, dry-goods merchant, who was b. Dec. 6, 1820, and d. Jan. 3, 1893. Issue : Caleb L., Robert, and George.

7. **Jane L.,**[7] who resides in Malden, m. Sep. 2, 1851, William Taylor of Mattapoisett, a furniture dealer. Issue : William L., b. Sep. 16, 1852.

†–6–3–2. **Joseph Frank**[7] was a ship-rigger, and resided at Mattapoisett. He m. May 1842, Lurana K. Harlow of Middleboro', who was b. Jun. 28, 1822. Issue :

1. Benj. Frank,	b. Oct. 15, 1846.	
2. George K.,	b. Sep. 28, 1848.	d. Sep. 28, 1851.
3. Georgia,	b. Oct. 11, 1853.	
4. Thomas,	b. Apr. 7, 1856.	

Of these children, **Georgia**[8] m. Nov. 24, 1876, Charles H. Hiller of Mattapoisett, who was b. Aug. 25, 1852. Issue : Hope Barstow.

4. **Thomas,**[8] son of Joseph Frank, lives in Buffalo, N. Y., and is in the employ of his brother, Benjamin Frank.

†-6-3-2-1. **Benjamin Frank**[6] has been in the diamond, watch and jewelry business at Buffalo, N. Y., 23 years, and has a second store at Tonawanda, N. Y. He is also special partner in the firm of Whittet, Barrett & Co., engineer's supplies, Buffalo, N.Y., and is interested in several smaller ventures. He m. Oct. 26, 1870, Ella M. Gould of Buffalo, and had issue:

1. Lawrence Tillson,   b. Jul. 29, 1871.
2. Bessie Livingston,   b. Jan. 28, 1873.
3. Harlow,   b. Jun. 2, 1876.
4. Clifford Robson,   b. Jun. 22, 1878.

†-6-3-4. **Thomas C.**[7] third son of Leonard, was a storekeeper at Mattapoisett. He m. Nov. 19, 1845, Susanna A. Delano of Marion, who was b. Apr. 26, 1825, and d. May 10, 1891. Issue:

1. Helen T.,   b. Dec. 12, 1846.

1. **Helen T.**[8] m. May 11, 1871, Charles T. Leonard of Rochester, and lives at Minneapolis, Minn.

Susanna [Delano] Hammond m. 2d, Dr. Seth Haskell of Rochester, and had a daughter, Lucy Fessenden, who d. at the age of 10.

†-6-3-5. **George Fred**[7] is a retired seafaring man, and resides at Mattapoisett. He m. 1st, Jan. 29, 1847, Abbie M. Sears, daughter of Joseph and Susan Sears, who was b. Mch. 21, 1828, and d. May 16, 1864. Issue:

1. Georgianna L.,   b. May 5, 1848.   d. Aug. 20, 1848.

George F. m. 2d, Sep. 30, 1866, Abbie H., daughter of Stephen and Eunice [Cannon] Snow, who was b. Jan. 3, 1834. Issue:

2. Frederic L.,   b. Nov. 23, 1869.

2. **Fred L.**[8] is a clerk in the employ of Denison Tag M'f'g Co., Boston, and was recently one of the Registrars of Voters of that city.

IV.—BARZILLAI HAMMOND OF ROCHESTER, MASS.

†. **Barzillai**[4] **Hammond,** fourth son of Benjamin 2d,[3] [Benjamin,[2] William[1]], sometimes referred to as the "Wizard," was a farmer, and lived near the southwesterly part of the late

Hiram Hammond farm, Mattapoisett Neck. He was a Selectman and Assessor of Rochester for several years. He m. 1st, Jun. 18, 1725, Mary Barlow, and had a large family as follows :

1. Nathaniel,	b. Jun.	5, 1726.	d.
2. Elizabeth,	b. Oct.	19, 1728.	d.
3. Benjamin,	b. May	5, 1730.	d.
4. Moses,	b. Nov.	15, 1731.	d in 1800.
5. Stafford,	b. Sep.	9, 1733.	d. Jul. 15, 1809.
6. Hannah,	b. Apr.	26, 1735.	d.
7. Micah,	b. Mch.	1, 1738.	d.
8. Lucie,	b. Jul.	26, 1741.	d.
9. Sarah,	b. May	1, 1743.	d.
10. Elisha,	b. Feb.	4, 1750.	d.

Barzillai m. 2d, Aug. 16, 1750, Anna Tobey, and had further issue :

11. Mary.	b. in 1755.	d. Oct. —, 1832.	

Barzillai m. 3d, Mch. 25, 1759, Sarah Doty, but had no other issue.

The will mentions Moses, Stafford, Lucy, Sarah, Elisha, and Mary.

Of Barzillai's children, nothing further is known of Nathaniel, Elizabeth, Benjamin, Hannah, Micah, and Lucie, and they probably d. young.

9. **Sarah**[6] m. a Jenne; and **Elisha**[5] is said to have moved to the State of New York, but nothing further is known of him.

11. **Mary**[5] m. Dec. 2, 1773, Nathan Briggs of Wareham, who d. May 25, 1817, æ. 69. Mary resided at Wareham, and had issue : Anna, Sally, Mary, Nathan and Hannah, twins, Elizabeth, Lydia, Sylvanus and Abigail, twins, and Elisha. Of these children, **Nathan**[6] m. Mary Davis, daughter of Joseph and Mercy [Hammond] Davis, and had a son, Nathan, who m. Almira, daughter of Nathaniel Dunham of Hammondtown. They reside on the old homestead of Nathan Hammond, grandson of William Hammond of London.

4.—MOSES OF ROCHESTER, MASS.

†-4. **Moses**,[5] third son of Barzillai, who was a farmer and lived in Hammondtown, m. Apr. 1, 1756, Mercy Howes, or House, and had issue :

1. Alice,	b. Sep. 17, 1757.	d.
2. Joshua.	b. Jun. 14, 1758.	d.
3. Moses, Jr.,	b. Apr. 3, 1761.	d.
4. Stephen,	b. Mch. 25, 1763.	d.
5. Abel,	b. May 3, 1765.	d.
6. Mercy M.,	b. Jun. 7, 1767.	d. Mch. 4, 1829.
7. Mehitable,	b.	d.

Moses m. 2d, Jun. 26, 1772, Mehitable Barlow. No other issue.

The will, proved Jun. 18, 1800, mentions Alice, Joshua, Moses, Mehitable, and Mercy.

Of the above children, nothing further is known of Joshua, Moses Jr., Stephen, Abel, or Mehitable, and they probably d. young; and **Alice**[6] m. Feb. 6, 1777, James Blankenship Jr.

6. Mercy M.[6] m. Mch. 15, 1787, Joseph Davis of Rochester, who was b. in 1756, and d. Feb. 20, 1821. Issue: William, Elizabeth, Joseph, Mercy, Rebecca, Moses, Mary, Sylvia, Eliza, Alice, Alden, and William. Of Mercy's children, **Moses**[7] m. Mary, daughter of Timothy Hammond; **Mary**[7] m. Nathan Briggs, as stated above; and **Alice**[7] m. a Tucker, and was the mother of Dr. H. A. Tucker, whose summer residence is at Cottage City, Mass.

5.—STAFFORD OF ROCHESTER, MASS.

†-5. **Stafford,**[5] fourth son of Barzillai, was a farmer, and built and occupied the house now owned by William Tripp on Mattapoisett Neck. He m. 1st, Aug. 2, 1761, Hannah Doty, who was b. in 1735, and d. Apr. 30, 1793. Issue:

1. Prince,	b.	d.
2. Asa,	b.	d.
3. Christopher,	b. Jun. 15, 1770.	d. Apr. 10, 1842.
4. Alden,	b. about 1773.	d.
5. Betsey,	b. Sep. 17, 1775.	d. Mch. 4, 1869.

Stafford m. 2d, Rachel Hathaway, but had no other issue.

†-5-1. **Prince,**[6] oldest son of Stafford, who lived at Fairhaven, m. Nov. 22, 1795, Elizabeth Jenney of that town, and had issue:

1. Lucy,	b. in 1796.	d. Sep. —, 1886.
2. Betsey J.,	b. Feb. 12, 1798.	d. Jan. 1, 1871.
3. Sophia,	b. in 1800.	d. in 1870.

Of these children, **Lucy**[7] m. in 1823 John Aiken, and had Joseph and John Francis; **Betsey**[7] m. Oct. 12, 1819, Abram Barker, and had six sons and five daughters; **Sophia**[7] m. Feb. 22, 1826, Alanson Goodwin, but had no issue.

†–5–4. **Alden**,[6] fourth son of Stafford, was in early life a sea captain in the coasting trade; and afterwards lived and d. in Acushnet, Mass. He m. Sarah Rounseville, and had issue:

1. Lucy,   b. in 1805.   d. Oct. 27, 1880; single.

†–5–5. **Betsey**, or **Elizabeth**,[6] only daughter of Stafford, who lived at Mattapoisett, m. May 27, 1798, Cook Brownell, a farmer, who was b. Sep. 17, 1775, and d. Aug. 31, 1859. Issue:

1. Stafford.   b. in   1799.   d. Mch. 16, 1848.
2. Hannah.   b. Jun. 4. 1803.   d. Aug. 22, 1893.

1. **Stafford**[7] was a prominent sea captain in the Liverpool and South American trade, sailing from Mattapoisett and New York, and at one time commanded the brig Massachusetts.

2. **Hannah**,[7] who lived at Mattapoisett, m. 1st, in 1826 Benjamin Dexter, but had no issue.
She m. 2d, in 1833, Barker K. Sheffield, and had a son, Elliott, whose name was afterwards changed to Stafford Brownell, and who d. Jul. 4, 1858. She m. 3d, in 1849, Joseph W. Snow, but had no further issue.

†–5–3. **Christopher**,[6] third son of Stafford, inherited his father's place on Mattapoisett Neck, and was a farmer. He m. Nov. 18, 1802, Abigail Pierce, who was b. May 3, 1778, and d. Jan. 18, 1847, and had issue:

1. Edmond Doty,   b. Jan. 28, 1804.   d. Aug. 25, 1827.
2. Hiram.   b. Jul. 3, 1806.   d. Jul. 23, 1811.
3. Eliza W.,   b. May 2, 1808.   d. Mch. 18, 1888.
4. Anna Briggs.   b. Oct. 13, 1809.   d. Jul. 17, 1877.
5. Abigail P.,   b. Apr. 20, 1811.   d. Apr. 21, 1858.
6. Hiram M.,   b. Mch. 25, 1813.   d. May 24, 1885.
7. Roxellana H., b. Mch. 1, 1815.   d. Mch. 17, 1888.
8. Loring P.,   b. Nov. 19. 1819.   d. Dec. 17, 1877.

Of these children, Edmond Doty, a sailor, was drowned at sea, and the first Hiram d. young.

†–5–3–3. **Eliza W.**[7] lived in Mattapoisett, and m. Sep. 23, 1834, William L. Bourne, a carpenter, who was b. Feb.

18

22, 1808, and d. Mch. 25, 1867, and was a son of John and
Mary [Savery] Bourne.   Issue:

1. George W.,	b. Jun. 3, 1835.	
2. Edmond L.,	b May 9, 1837.	
3. Abbie E.,	b. Jan. 21, 1840.	d. Feb. 25, 1891.
4. Mary L.,	b. Mch. 14, 1842.	
5. Ann Eliza,	b. Dec. 9, 1844.	

Of Eliza's children, **George W.**[8] m. Sep. 6, 1856, Helen
A. Ellis, but has no issue.

2. **Edmond L.**[8] m. 1st, Lucy Purrington, and 2d, Eliza
[Hall] Briggs, but has no issue.

3. **Abbie**[8] m. Sep. 6, 1860, Capt. Charles F. Keith of
Mattapoisett, and had :   Willlie and Charlie.

4. **Mary L.**[8] m. Jan. 2, 1866, Heman G. Holmes, and
has no issue.

5. **Annie E.**[8] m. Sep. 26, 1871, Joseph T. Sampson,
who d. Jul. 25, 1891, and has a son :   Andrew.

†–5–3–4. **Anna Briggs,**[7] second daughter of Christopher, lived at Fairhaven, Mass., and m. Nov. 15, 1835, Alborn
Allen of that town, and had one child that died young.

†–5–3–5. **Abigail P.,**[7] who resided at Arkwright, N. Y.,
m. Apr. 21, 1835, Washington Sheopard of that town, who
was b. Nov. 29, 1806. Issue: Rollin L., Allen M., Setina
L., Galusha H., and Adeline and Adelaide, twins.

†–5–3–7. **Roxie Haskell**[7] m. Jan. 1, 1843, Amos T.
Pierce of Fairhaven, where they resided.   No issue.

†–5–3–6. **Hiram M.,**[7] fourth son of Christopher, was a
farmer, and lived on Mattapoisett Neck on the Antipas Hammond farm. He m. Sep. 23, 1847, Mary, daughter of Abraham
and Hannah [Stevens] Shaw, who was b. Jun. 28, 1823.
Issue :

1. Hannah S.,	b. Mch. 15, 1852.	
2. Abram S.,	b. Sep. 10, 1853.	
3. Hiram C..	b. Feb. 20, 1858.	
4. Stafford B ,	b. Sep. 14, 1861.	d. Jan. 17, 1864.

Of these children, **Hannah**[8] lives with her mother on the
old homestead.

2. **Abram S.,**[8] who is a farmer and lives on Mattapoisett Neck, m. May 1887, Mrs. Alice W. Ashley of New Bedford. No issue.

3. **Hiram C.,**[8] who is a laborer and lives in Mattapoisett Village, m. Jan. 17, 1883, Alecia L., daughter of James and Mary [King] Small, who was b. Nov. 21, 1862. Issue:

   1. Lillian M.,   b. Jun. 19, 1884.   d. Nov. 19, 1887.

†–5–3–8. **Loring P.,**[7] son of Christopher, m. Permelia S. Snow of Swanzey, N. H., daughter of Ivory and Vilura [Slate] Snow, who was b. Mch. 31, 1827. Issue:

   1. Emma L.,   b. Mch. 8, 1856.

1. **Emma**[8] is a seamstress, and lives in Springfield, Mass.

†–5–2. **Asa,**[6] second son of Stafford, who lived in Fairhaven, m. Oct. 14, 1787, Sarah Jenney of that town, and had issue:

1. Michael,	b.	d.
2. Hannah,	b.	d.
3. Sally,	b. Jul. 10, 1795.	d. Feb. 16, 1876.
4. William,	b. in 1800.	d. in 1883.
5. Almira,	b.	d.

Of these children, 2. **Hannah,**[7] who lived and d. in New Bedford, m. 1st, Oct. 22, 1812, William Lane of New Bedford. She m. 2d, John Chase of New Bedford. No issue by either marriage.

3. **Sally,**[7] who lived in Fairhaven, m. about 1815, Salathiel Eldridge of that town. Issue:

1. Sarah Ann,	b. Aug. 21, 1816.	d. May 12, 1878.
2. Betsey,	b. Feb. 8, 1818.	d. Jun. 18, 1840.
3. Maria,	b. May 10, 1822.	d. Jul. 10, 1842.

Of Sally's children, **Sarah Ann**[8] m. John Terry of New Bedford, and had Lydia and Clarence; **Betsey**[8] m. Barnabas Ewer Jr. of Fairhaven, and had Frederic; and **Maria**[8] m. Franklin Hatch of New Bedford, but left no issue.

5. **Almira,**[7] m. about 1815 Thomas Kelley of New Bedford, where they resided. Issue: Asa Hammond, William, Jane, Amanda, Nancy, and Hannah. Asa Hammond Kelley is a cooper at New Bedford.

†–5–2–1. **Michael,**[7] or **Mitchell,**[7] oldest son of Asa, lived and d. at Fairhaven, Mass. He m. about 1807 Melintha

Wood of Fairhaven, who d. at Randolph, Mass., Sep. 29, 1860. Issue:

1. Samantha,	b. in	1818.	d. May 15, 1835.
2. Lydia H.,	b Jul. 14, 1819.		d. Mch. 16, 1860.
3. Asa Russell,	b. in	1825.	d. Jan. 28, 1868.

After the death of Michael, Melintha, with her children, moved from Fairhaven to Randolph, where she became a milliner, and where she afterwards died, and was buried in the Central Cemetery.

Of Michael's children, **Samantha**[8] never married, and d. and was buried at Randolph.

2. **Lydia H.**[8] m. Mch. 28, 1838, Archibald Woodman of Poultney, Vt., who d. at Melrose, Mass., Feb. 17, 1872, æ. 56. Lydia, who lived and d. at Randolph, had issue: John, Abbie S., Eliza R., George, Annie, Annie 2d, and Irvin.

Of Lydia's children, **Abbie S.** m. Dec. 14, 1859, Ira W. Porter, and lives at Mobile, Ala. **Eliza R.** m. Nov. 25, 1862, Frank Porter, who is a druggist at Randolph, Mass.

3. **Asa Russell,**[8] youngest son of Michael, was a pattern-maker, and lived the latter part of his life at Reading, Mass., where he died and was buried. He m. 1st, Jan. 1, 1851, Lucy T. Leonard, and had issue:

1. Irving.	b. Aug. 27, 1852.	d. May 8, 1853.

Asa m. 2d, at Providence, R. I., Patience M. Stark of Concord, N. H., who died a few months later without issue.

He m. 3d, Oct. 13, 1866, Caroline [Stowell] Bartlett of Reading, Mass. No issue.

(1.)—WILLIAM HAMMOND OF WAUCONDA, ILL.

†. **William**[7] **Hammond,** second son of Asa[6] [Stafford,[5] Barzillai,[4] Benjamin 2d,[3] Benjamin,[2] William[1]] was born at Fairhaven in 1800, and died at Wauconda, Ill., in 1883. He became a seaman at a very early age, and later a master in the merchant service. His first voyage, when he was only 15, was with Capt. Washington Decost, in the ship Euphrates, between New York and Liverpool. The ship was wrecked and came to New Bedford for repairs, and lay in port at the time of the September gale of 1815. His last voyage was in the ship Minerva of Bedford. After that he moved to the State of New

York, and from there to Wayne, and afterwards to Wauconda, Ill., where he purchased a farm. He m. 1st, Sep. 29, 1822, Lucy H. Tallman of New Bedford, who d. Apr. 14, 1839. Issue :

1. Lucy,	b.	d.	young.
2. Roland R. C.,	b. Jul. 15, 1823.	d. about 1843.	
3. Rhoda.	b	d.	young.
4. Betsey T.,	b. Aug. 5, 1830.		
5. William T.,	b. Feb. 10, 1832.		
6. James H.,	b. Jun. 1. 1833.		
7. Joseph T.,	b. Nov. 5, 1835.		
8. Virginia,	b. about 1837.	d.	young.

Capt. William Hammond m. 2d, Dec. 6, 1838, Lucinda Boutwell, who was b. at Zoar, Cattaraugus Co., N. Y., Aug. 12, 1821. Issue :

9. Edwin,	b. Sep. 7, 1839.	d. Jun. 9, 1863.	
10. Kate,	b. Nov. 25, 1841.		
11. Jackson,	b. Apr. 11, 1844.	d. Mch. 27, 1861.	
12. Frank,	b. Aug. 16, 1847.		
13. Charles B.,	b. Mch. 6, 1849.	d. Nov. 30, 1866.	
14. Nellie,	b. Dec. 22, 1851.		
15. Rollin,	b. Jun. 15, 1855.		
16. Carrie D.,	b. Jan. 7, 1862.		

The first set of children, except the last two, were b. at New Bedford, Mass. The second set were all b. at Wayne, Du Page Co., Ill.

†-2. **Roland Robinson Crocker,**[3] was lost from a whale-ship, in the river De La Plata, when about 20 years of age. He was single, and was named after Capt. Roland Robinson Crocker of New Bedford.

†-4. **Betsey T.,**[3] who resides at Elgin, Ill., m. Oct. 16, 1847, John Wait, who was b. in Oxford, Mass., Dec. 10, 1811, and is a blacksmith. Issue : William Tyler, Lucy E., Clara B., and Cora May.

†-5. **William Tallman**[3] went to live with his maternal grandparents when two years of age ; and was away from his parents until 22 years old : at 16 went to sea for ten years ; in 1852 went to his parents' house in Illinois for the first time ; and in April 1859 left there for the coast of California ; in 1860 went to Oregon, remaining there ten years, and then to Washington Territory.

He now resides at Lewisville, Clark Co., Wash., and is a farmer and stock-raiser. He m. Dec. 1862, Sarah Ann Wallis, née Lotspeich, of Oregon, who was b. Dec. 27, 1835. Issue :

1. Samuel Tallman,	b. Oct. 28, 1865.	
2. Clarence Howland.	b. Mch. 10, 1867.	d. Jun. 4, 1890.
3. Joseph Osmin,	b. Feb. 21, 1869.	
4. Felix Neal,	b. Oct. 9, 1870.	
5. Henry Oliver.	b. Nov. 27, 1872	
6. Chancy Lotspeich,	b. Sep. 17, 1874.	
7. Bird,	b. May 8, 1876.	
8. Herman,	b. Sep. 12, 1879.	d. Jun. 22, 1888.

Of the above children, the first four were b. in Oregon, and the others in Washington, and all are single. **Samuel**[9] and **Joseph**[9] are farmers; **Felix**[9] a blacksmith; and **Clarence**[9] was engaged in steamboating.

†–6. **James Howland,**[9] resides at Amador City, Amador Co., Cal., and is a miner. He m. 1st, Jul. 15, 1856, Nancy McGurk, who was b. Jun. 1832, and d. Jul. 1866. Issue:

1. William T.,	b. Apr. 19, 1858.	
2. James H.,	b. Jan. 19, 1860.	
3. Francis Joseph,	b. Feb. 6, 1862.	
4. Sarah Elizabeth,		d. Nov. 4, 1885.

James Howland m. 2d, Oct. 12, 1871, Eliza M. Joy of Nantucket, who was b. Oct. 28, 1848, and had further issue:

5. Florence J.,   b. Oct. 30, 1873.

Of James's children, **Sarah E.**[9] d. single, at the age of 23.

1. **William T.,**[9] who resides at San Francisco, m. Nov. 1876–7, Maggie Marden, and had issue:

1. Elsie V.,	b. Sep. 25, 1879.
2. Edna B.,	b. Aug. 10, 1883.
3. Will. T.,	b. Aug. —, 1890.
4. Alpha,	

2. **James H.,**[9] who resides at Gutter Creek, Amador Co., Cal., m. Jun. 17, 1882, Katie Fitzgerald. Issue:

1. Willie,	b. Mch. 19, 1883.
2. Frank,	b. Sep. 21, 1888.
3. Ethel,	b. Jun. 27, 1890.

3. **Francis,** or **Frank,**[9] third son of James Howland, resides at Barberton, South Africa, where he is electrician in a quartz mill. He m. Apr. 1889 Margaret M. Steele of Dundee, Scotland. No issue.

†–7. **Joseph Tallman**[9] resides at Dennison, Grayson Co., Tex., and is a farmer. He was a private in Co. E, 9th Minn. Vols., and was a prisoner of war eleven months. He

m. Dec. 14, 1862, Frances Marion Hathaway, who was b.
Oct. 1842, and had issue :

    1. Edwin A.,   b. Nov. 22, 1863.
    2. Esther Louisa,   b. Aug. —, 1870.   d. Feb. —, 1871.
    3. Helen May,   b. May 18, 1872.

  1. **Edwin A.,**[9] who resides at Dennison, m. May 22,
1886, Edith Belle Kinnie. Issue :

    1. Joseph Tallman,   b. Apr. 16, 1887.

  Of Capt. William's children by the second marriage, **Jackson**[9] d. at Wayne, Ill., single ; **Edwin**[9] was a member of
Co. C, 127th Reg't Ill. Vols., and d. at Milliken's Bend, single,
Jun. 9, 1863, and is buried there ; and **Carrie,**[9] single, lives
with her mother at Wauconda, Lake Co., Ill.

  †–10. **Kate,**[9] who resides at Wellington Avenue, Lake
View, Ill., m. Nov. 29, 1865, Edward M. Barnard, who was
b. Oct. 27, 1828. Issue :

    1. Edward M., Jr.,   b. Dec. 11, 1866.
    2. Louie,   b. Oct. 27, 1868.

  †–12. **Frank,**[9] who is a farmer at Warrenville, Ill., m.
Aug. 26, 1868, Carrie Mulnix, who was b. Apr. 23, 1839.
Issue :

    1. Carrie Dell,   b. Mch. 12, 1877.

  †–13. **Charles B.**[9] resided at Clyde, Cook Co., Ill., but
is buried at Wayne, Ill. He m. Jan. 3, 1872, Lizzie Holmes,
who was b. Aug. 18, 1846. No issue.

  †–14. **Nellie,**[9] who resides at Clyde, Ill., m. Oct. 15,
1873, Peter McDonald, builder and contractor, who was b.
Jul. 14, 1842. Issue :

    1. Lulu Irene,   b. Dec. 26, 1874.
    2. Grace Edna,   b. Apr. 9, 1877.
    3. George Allan,   b. Nov. 24, 1879.

  †–15. **Rollin**[9] lives at Wakefield, Neb., and is a cabinet-
maker. He m. Sep. 15, 1880, Nellie Clawson, who was b.
Jan. 19, 1861. Issue :

    1. Genevieve,   b. Jun. 24, 1886.

V.—ISRAEL HAMMOND OF ROCHESTER, MASS.

†. **Israel[4] Hammond,** fifth son of Benjamin 2d,[3] [Benjamin,[2] William[1]], was a farmer and lived in Hammondtown, Mattapoisett. He m. in 1736, Elizabeth Wilbur, who was b. in 1712, and d. in 1802. Issue:

1. David,	b. Sep. 27, 1738.	d. Apr. 20, 1821.
2. Ruth,	b. May 31, 1740.	d.
3. Sarah,	b. Oct. 6, 1741.	d. Nov. 17, 1741.
4. Gideon,	b. Mch. 30, 1743.	d.
5. Israel,	b. Jun. 3, 1745.	d. Sep. 14, 1745.
6. Alice,	b. Nov. 11, 1846.	d. Oct. 16, 1755.
7. John,	b. Sep. 23, 1748.	d. Sep. 24, 1828.
8. Noah,	b. Jun. 8, 1750.	d. Aug. 27, 1834.
9. Elizabeth,	b. Dec. 9, 1752.	d.
10. Mary,	b. Sep. 15, 1754.	d. Feb. 21, 1834.

Of these children, Sarah, Israel, and Alice died young; **John[5]** and **Mary[5]** d. single; **Elizabeth[5]** probably married, but nothing further is known of her, nor of **Ruth[5]**; and **Gideon[5]** m. Apr. 15, 1768, Abigail Barlow, but there is no further record of him.

†-1. **David,[5]** oldest son of Israel, who was a farmer at Hammondtown, m. Dec. 5, 1764, Elizabeth Annable. Issue:

1. Israel,	b. Sep. 23, 1765.	d. young.
2. Ephraim,	b. Dec. 23, 1771.	d. young.
3. David,	b. Jul. 12, 1776.	d. young.

8.—NOAH OF ROCHESTER, MASS.

†-8. **Noah,[5]** fifth son of Israel, was a noted blacksmith and lived at Hammondtown, and was thrice married. He m. 1st, May 31, 1777, Eunice Hammond, daughter of Josiah Hammond 2d, who d. Feb. 15, 1785, æ. 27. Issue:

1. Rebecca,	b. Feb. 14, 1779.	d. in 1868.
2. Elizabeth,	b. Feb. 12, 1781.	d. in 1870.
3. Priscilla,	b. Jul. 21, 1783.	d. Dec. 12, 1820.

He m. 2d, Nov. 9, 1786, Lydia [Churchill] Barlow, who d. May 15, 1804, and had further issue:

4. Noah,	b. Jul. 24, 1787.	d. in 1803.
5. Amittai B.,	b. Aug 30, 1789.	d. Oct. 17, 1874.
6. Israel,	b. Feb. 13, 1792.	d. May 22, 1839.

Noah m. 3d, Sep. 1804, Abigail Palmer, widow, who d. in 1816. No other issue.

†-8-1. **Rebecca,**[6] oldest daughter of Noah, m. Apr. 25, 1800, Benjamin Barstow, a ship-carpenter at Mattapoisett. Issue:

1. Benjamin Frank,   b. Mch. 23, 1801.   d. Sep. 17. 1866.
2. Nathan H.,   b. Oct. 5, 1807.   d. Jan. 13, 1892.
3. Henry,   b. Dec. 3, 1817.
4. Susan C. B.,   b. May 29, 1820.

Of these children, **Benjamin Franklin,**[7] who was postmaster many years at Mattapoisett, m. about 1835, Sarah S. Drew of Fairhaven, and had: Benjamin, Lizzie, Sophia, and Edwin.

2. **Nathan H.,**[7] who was a ship-carpenter at Mattapoisett, m. Dec. 26, 1829, Mary, daughter of Reuben and Mary [Toby] Dexter, and had: Helen, Carrie, Lizzie, Mary, Nathan, and Mary Y.

3. **Henry,**[7] who was formerly a ship-carpenter at Mattapoisett, m. Jan. 2, 1842, Mary, daughter of Andrew and Sarah [Clark] Southworth, and had: Sarah and Henry.

4. **Susan C. B.**[7] m. May 18, 1850, David H., a shipcarpenter, and son of Eliakim and Mary Cannon, and had: Mary, Dana, Nathan, and Lawrence.

†-8-2. **Elizabeth**[6] m. in 1799 Richard Whittemore, and had seven daughters: Eunice Hammond, Harriet, Mary Hammond, Rebecca, Priscilla, Caroline, and Elizabeth Hammond. Of these daughters: Eunice Hammond m. David Wilbur of Plympton; Mary Hammond m. Seth Wilbur of Brockton; and Elizabeth Hammond m. Lothrop Shurtleff of Middleboro'. All three left families.

†-8-3. **Priscilla**[6]* m. Oct. 20, 1803, Nathaniel Hammond, Esq., son of Enoch, and had issue:

1. Rufus,   b. Aug. 7, 1805.   d. Oct. 10, 1854.
2. John Wilkes,   b. Oct. 22, 1808.   d. Sep. 23, 1843.
3. Nathaniel,   b. Feb. 24, 1813.   d. Jun. 28, 1870.
4. Eliz. Pope,   b. Nov. 9, 1815.   d. Jan. 8, 1870.
5. Benjamin,   b. May 11, 1818.

There were also William Penn and Lucy Barstow who d. in infancy.

* See Family of Nathaniel Hammond, Esq., p. 212.

†–8–6. **Israel,**[6] who was a farmer in Hammondtown, m. Jul. 1830, Joanna, daughter of Seth Burgess, who d. Nov. 1881. Issue :

    1. Georgianna,   b. Nov. —, 1837.   d. Apr. 11, 1893, single.

†–8–5. **Amittai B.**[6] Selectman, Assessor, and Overseer of Poor of Rochester 29 years, and of Mattapoisett 6 years ; declined further office in both towns ; member of Legislature in 1833 and 1856 ; member of Constitutional Convention 1853 ; Justice of the Peace 42 years ; and Deacon and member of the Congregational Church many years. He m. Jul. 15, 1823, Lucinda White, who d. Oct. 13, 1869. Issue :

    1. Noah,   b. Jul. 27, 1824.   d. Sep. 11, 1825.
    2. Lydia Churchill, b. Feb. 12, 1827.   d. Feb. 13, 1857.
    3. John C.,   b. Jan. 27, 1829.   d. Aug. —, 1847.
    4. Noah,   b. Feb. 8, 1833.   *d. Mar. 1, 1894.*

Of these children, Noah and John C. died young, and **Lydia Churchill**[7] d. at the age of 30, single.

†–8–5–4. **Noah,**[7] of Mattapoisett, Selectman, Assessor, and Overseer of the Poor 18 years ; chairman of the three boards many years ; Justice of the Peace 28 years ; Justice to issue Warrants and take Bail in Criminal cases 10 years ; Notary Public since 1888 ; school teacher from 1857 to 1866 ; surveyor of land and conveyancer many years ; has large practice in Probate Courts as executor and administrator ; and member of the Legislature of 1894. He m. Jun. 2, 1861, Martha Mayhew Dexter, who was b. Jul. 12, 1837. Issue :

    1. Allen Dexter,   b. Jun. 4, 1871.
    2. Clara Lucinda,   b. Dec. 23, 1872.

1. **Allen Dexter**[8] is a graduate of the Medical Department of Boston University, class of '93, and is one of the out-door physicians of the Homœopathic Medical Dispensary, Boston.

VI. – ROGER HAMMOND OF ROCHESTER, MASS.

†. **Roger**[4] **Hammond,** seventh son of Benjamin 2d,[3] [Benjamin,[2] William[1]], was a farmer in Hammondtown, and lived on the west bank of Mattapoisett River, a little north of

NOAH HAMMOND.

the late Alvah Shurtleff house, on the homestead of his father.
He m. Apr. 15, 1744, Charity, daughter of Josiah and Mary
[Barlow] Hammond, who d. Jul. 27, 1803, æ. 87. Issue:

1. Olive.	b. Apr. 13, 1745.	d.
2 Deborah,	b. Oct. 15, 1746.	d.
3. Anna,	b. in 1748.	d.
4. Benjamin,	b. Jul. 7, 1752.	d Oct. 17, 1754.
5. Thankful,	b. Sep. 7, 1754.	d.
6. Roger, Jr.,	b. in 1756.	d. Mch. 28, 1760.

†-1. **Olive**[5] m. Jan. 5, 1764, Stephen Wing, and lived
on the late Alvah Shurtleff farm in Hammondtown. Issue:
seven sons, and three daughters, Anna, Harriet, and Sophia.

Of Olive's daughters: **Anna**[6] m. Royal Hathaway, and
lived at the Head-of-the-River, Acushnet, Mass., but had no
issue; **Harriet**[6] m. Capt. John LeBaron, Mattapoisett, no
issue; and **Sophia**[5] m. Capt. Seth Freeman, Mattapoisett,
and left no issue.

†-5. **Thankful**[5] m. Jul. 12, 1781, Dr. Samuel Cheever
of Eastham, Mass., and probably had issue.

2.—DEBORAH OF ROCHESTER, MASS.

†-2. **Deborah,**[5]* second daughter of Roger, lived in Hammondtown, and m. Sep. 25, 1767, Timothy Hammond, son of
John Hammond Jr. Issue:

1. Timothy 2d,	b. Aug. 10, 1768.	d. Oct. 20, 1851.
2. Betsey,	b. Feb. 12, 1770.	d.
3. Deborah,	b. Jun. 1, 1773.	d.
4. Susannah,	b. Nov. 3, 1776.	d.

VII.—ELISHA HAMMOND OF ROCHESTER, MASS.

†. **Elisha**[4] **Hammond,** sixth son of Benjamin 2d,[3] [Ben-
jamin,[2] William[1]], was a farmer, and lived on the Stephen
Bowles place in Hammondtown, his farm adjoining that of his
father. He was for several years one of the Selectmen and

* For further record of Deborah's children, see Genealogy of John Jr., p. 234.

Assessors of the town of Rochester. He m. Jan. 24, 1741,
Elizabeth Haskell, and had issue :

1. Ebenezer,	b. May 9. 1743.	d. in 1815.
2. Joanna,	b. May 18, 1745.	d.
3. Susanna,	b. Oct. 7, 1747.	d.
4. Anstris,	b. Feb. 27, 1750.	d.
5. Hannah,	b. Jun. 18, 1755.	d. in 1831.
6. Abigail,	b. in 1760.	d.
7. Elisha,	b. in 1763.	d.
8. Elizabeth,	b.	d.

Of these children, **Joanna**[5] m. 1st, Capt. Allen, and 2d,
Peras Clark; and **Susanna**[5] m. Apr. 6, 1772, Wyatt Barlow
of Hardwick, Mass.

4.   **Anstris,** or **Anstrus,**[5*] m. 1st, Apr. 1778, Silas Jenney of Fairhaven, but had no issue : Anstris m. 2d, Jun. 6,
1787, Seth Hammond Jr. of East Fairhaven, and had :   Elisha,
Elihu, and Betsey.

5.   **Hannah**[5] m. Daniel Pratt, and d. in 1831 ; of **Abigail**[5]
and **Elisha**[5] nothing further is known ; and **Elizabeth**[5] m.
Benjamin Wilkes of Rochester.

†–1.   **Ebenezer,**[5] oldest son of Elisha, b. at Rochester,
Mass., lived in New Bedford in 1774, and in Petersham, Mass.,
in 1786, where he probably died. He m. Nov. 23, 1766,
Deborah Terry of New Bedford, and had issue : 1. Sarah ;
2. Joanna ; 3. Elizabeth : 4. Elisha ; 5. Deborah : 6. Patience ; 7. Abigail ; and 8. Ebenezer, b. Apr. 20, 1786, and
d. May 1847.

Of these children, 1. **Sarah**[6] m. Stephen Leach of Hornby,
(or Hunby), Steuben Co., N. Y.; 2. **Joanna**[6] m. Smith
Turner of Narraganset and Royal Grant, N. Y.; 3. **Elizabeth**[6] m. Dea. Brigham of Hornby, N. Y.; 5. **Deborah**[6]
m. Oliver Woodward of W. Bridgewater, Mass.; 6. **Patience**[6]
m. Azariah Poley of Hornby, N. Y.; and 7. **Abigail**[6] m.
Jabez Whipple of New Salem.

4.—ELISHA HAMMOND OF COLUMBIA, S. C.

†.   **Elisha**[6] **Hammond,** oldest son of Ebenezer,[5] Elisha,[4]
[Benjamin 2d,[3] Benjamin,[2] William[1]], was born at New Bed-

* For further record of Anstris's children, see Genealogy of Seth Hammond Jr.,
page 21.

ford, Oct. 10, 1774, and died at Macon, Ga., Jul. 9, 1829.
He graduated at Dartmouth College in 1802; moved to South
Carolina in 1803; was elected Professor of Languages in the
University of South Carolina, at Columbia, in 1805; and was
chosen President of the same in 1816. He was also Principal
of Bethel Academy at Macon, Ga. He m. in 1806 Catherine
Fox Spann of Edgefield, S. C., and had issue:

1. James Henry,	b. Nov. 15, 1807.	d Nov. 13, 1864.
2. Caroline Augusta,	b. Nov. 11, 1809.	d. May —. 1847.
3. M. C. Marcellus,	b. Dec. 12, 1814.	d. Jan. 23, 1876.
4. John Fox,	b. Dec. 7, 1821.	d. Sep. 29, 1886.

†–2. **Caroline Augusta,**[7] only daughter of Elisha, m.
at Silverton, S. C., Feb. 1845, Rev. Ezekiel Foster Hyde,
who was b. in Colburn, Canada West, May 1, 1814, and d.
at Anderson, S. C., Oct. 22, 1884. Of their issue, Catherine Spann, b. Jan. 19, 1846, is living at Beech Island, S. C.,
single.

†–1. **James Henry,**[7] oldest son of Elisha, was b. in
the District of Newberry, S. C., Nov. 15, 1807, and d. at
Redcliff, Beech Island, S. C., Nov. 13, 1864. He was fitted
for college by his father, who was a fine scholar with unusual
gifts as a teacher, and in 1823 entered the junior class of the
University of South Carolina, and graduated fourth in a class
of distinguished merit in 1825. Mr. Hammond adopted the
profession of law, and was admitted to the Bar in 1828. He
was elected to Congress in 1834, where he made a vigorous
speech against the Abolition movement. Failing health obliged
him to leave Congress, after which he traveled in Europe two
years for his health. In 1842 he was elected Governor of
South Carolina, and, under his administration, the arsenals at
Charleston were converted into military academies on the plan
at West Point. In 1855 Gov. Hammond removed a few miles
from his plantation to Beech Island, in the Edgefield District,
to a place which he named Redcliff. In 1857, without his
knowledge, he was elected to the U. S. Senate to fill the
vacancy occasioned by the death of Judge Andrew Pickens
Butler. At this time he had been out of political life for nearly
fifteen years. Gov. Hammond was a very strong supporter of
the doctrine of States Rights; but failing health did not permit
him to take any active share in our great struggle. "In private
life Senator Hammond was affable and genial, warm in his
friendships and devoted in his affections. Famous writer, able

governor, and great senator,—at home he was the plain and unpretending country gentleman and planter, easy of access to all. Very fond of the company of friends and neighbors, his conversational powers were something more than excellent —they were brilliant. His hospitality was princely, and there were few admitted to his intimacy who did not feel the spell of his musical voice as he held them in the thrall of his glittering eye." He m. Jun. 23, 1831, Catherine E. Fitzsimons, and had issue :

1. Harry.	b. Mch 30, 1832.	
2. Edward Spann,	b. Jun. 26, 1834.	
3. Paul Fitzsimons,	b. Mch. 27, 1838.	d. Dec. 17, 1887.
4. Katherine,	b. Sep. 26, 1840.	d. Nov. 20, 1882.
5. Elizabeth.	b. Oct. 4, 1849.	

†-1-1. **Major Harry,**[8] oldest son of James Henry, b. at Columbia, graduated at the University of South Carolina, 1851 ; graduated Medical Dep't, University of Pennsylvania, Philadelphia, 1855 ; traveled in Europe 1856–7 ; Professor of Natural Sciences, University of Georgia, 1859–60 ; entered 14th Reg't S. C. Vols., Oct. 1861, as Assistant Commissary ; appointed Major and Brigade Quartermaster in Gen. Maxey Gregg's (afterwards McGowan's) Brigade 1862 ; served in the field with the Army of North Virginia from that date until paroled at Appomatox Court House 1865 ; since that date planter at Beech Island ; author of several essays and speeches, and the Hand-Book of South Carolina. Major Hammond m. Nov. 22, 1859, Emily Cumming, and had issue :

1. Julia Bryan,	b. Aug. 24, 1860.
2. Catherine Fitzsimons,	b. Feb. 17, 1867.
3. Henry Cumming,	b. Dec 10, 1868.
4. Christopher Cashel Fitzs,	b. May 24, 1870.
5. Alfred Cumming,	b. Jan. 11, 1873.

These children are all living and are all single. **Henry Cumming**[9] is an attorney at Augusta, Ga.

†-1-2. **Edward Spann,**[8] second son of James Henry, graduated University of Georgia, 1852 ; graduated Medical Dep't, University of Pennsylvania, 1855 ; member of Legislature, South Carolina, 1858–9 ; served on General Bonham's Staff with the rank of Major, 1861 ; planter in Mississippi and Virginia ; editor *Richmond Whig*, 1863–4 ; since then planter in Aiken, and attorney at Aiken Court House, S. C. He m. 1st, Jun. 20, 1861, Marcella Christiana Morris of Lynchburg, Va., who d. Jun. 12, 1878. Issue :

1. Elizabeth Delaware,   b. Aug. 9, 1866.

He m. 2d, Oct. 12, 1882, Laura Hanson Brown, *née* Dunbar, and had issue :

2. William Dunbar,   b. Sep. 1, 1883.
3. James Henry,   b. Feb. 4, 1885.

Of these children. **Elizabeth Delaware**[9] m. Sep. 29, 1885, Albert Evarts Willis of Williston, S. C., and had issue :

1. Marcella Celeste Willis,   b. Jul. —, 1886.
2. Albert Edwin,   b. May —, 1888.

†-1-3. **Paul Fitzsimons**,[8] third son of James Henry, cotton planter, Aiken Co., S. C. ; served on Gen. Kirby Smith's and Gen. Breckenridge's Staffs 1862-3 ; member of the first re-construction Convention of South Carolina 1865 ; author of several speeches and pamphlets, and of a biography of his father ; for many years noted as a most successful cotton and rice planter in Aiken Co., S. C. ; and, while he lived, a power in his community on account of his mental abilities and moral qualities. He m. Nov. 9, 1858, Loula M. Comer, and had issue :

1. Marcus Claude,   b. Aug. 5, 1859.
2. Maria,   b. Mch. 2, 1861.   d. Jun. 16, 1882.
3. Celeste,   b. Nov. 25, 1862.
4. Catherine Fitzsimons,   b. Jun. 29, 1864.   d. Dec. 12, 1864.
5. James Henry,   b. Oct. 23, 1865.
6. Caroline Victoria,   b. Dec. 9, 1867.
7. Frank Lyttleton,   b. May 18, 1869.   d. Oct 6, 1869.
8. Kate Gregg,   b. Aug. 16, 1870.

Of these children, 1. **Marcus Claude**,[9] who is a clerk at Savannah, Ga., was b. at Macon, Ga., and the others at Beech Island, S. C.

2. **Maria**[9] m. Dec. 3, 1878, Alphius Philip Cassin, and had issue :

1. Maria Celeste,   b in 1880.
2. Cornelius Philip,   b. Apr. —, 1882.

3. **Celeste**[9] m. Feb. 16, 1880, Calbraith Butler Lamar, and had issue :

1. Sarah Adams,   b. Mch. 12, 1881.

†-1-4. **Katherine**,[8] oldest daughter of James Henry, m. 1st, Oct. 10, 1861, James Gregg of Graniteville, S. C., who d. Apr. 19, 1876. She m. 2d, Apr. 13, 1878, William E. McCoy of Augusta, Ga. No issue by either marriage.

†-1-5. Elizabeth, [5] youngest daughter of James Henry, m. Dec. 7, 1871, William Raiford Eve, cotton planter at Beech Island, S. C. Issue:

1. Catherine Fitzsimons,   b. Sep. 15, 1872.
2. Edward Armstrong,   b. Oct. 27, 1873.
3. Sarah Jane,   b. Aug. 17, 1875.
4. Annie Hampton,   b. Oct. 20, 1876.
5. William Raiford, Jr.,   b. Jul. 4, 1878.
6. James Hammond,   b. Jan. 16, 1880.
7. Elizabeth Hammond,   b. Oct. 5, 1882.
8. Henrietta,   b. Nov 22, 1884.
9. Christopher Cashel,   b. Sep 20, 1886.   d. Sep. 21, 1886.
10. Aphra,   b. Sep. 19, 1887.   d Sep. 20, 1887.
11. Henry Harford,   b. Oct. 23, 1888.

†-3. Marcus Claudius Marcellus, [7] second son of Elisha, was b. at Newberry, S. C., Dec. 12, 1814, and d. at Beech Island, Jan. 23, 1876. He graduated at the U. S. Military Academy in 1836, and was assigned to the 4th Inf., as 1st Lieutenant, Nov. 7, 1839; resigned, Dec. 31, 1842, on account of illness; 1842–46, cotton planter in Georgia; Paymaster in the Mexican War until Apr. 15, 1847, when he resigned again on account of ill health; returned to a plantation at Hamburg, S. C.; thence to Athens, Ga., in 1860, and to Beech Island in 1863; member of State House of Representatives 1856–7; author of various essays on agriculture, etc., and of "A Critical History of the Mexican War," 1843–49.[*] Maj. M. C. M. Hammond m. Jul. 12, 1842, Harriet Pamelia Davies of Augusta, Ga., who was b. Jul. 11, 1821, and d. Oct. 31, 1880. Issue:

1. Katherine Spann,   b. Jun. 25, 1843.
2. Charles Davies,   b. Mch. 11, 1845.
3. Anne Sarah,   b. Oct. 1, 1846.
4. M. Claudius M.,   b. Apr. 1, 1849.   d. Sep. 1, 1852.
5. Thomas Taylor,   b. Oct. 28, 1850.
6. James Henry,   b. Jul. 30, 1855.
7. William Gilmore S.,   b. Dec. 11, 1858.   d. Feb. 28, 1892.

†-3-1. Katherine S., [8] who resides at Beech Island, m. Dec. 15, 1864, James R. Randall of Baltimore, a poet and writer for the press. Issue: Harriet Davies, Aubrey DeVere, Marcus Hammond, Ruth Marie, Caroline Louise, Maryland Henry Campbell, and Elizabeth Yeatman.

†-3-2. Charles Davies [8] was a soldier, teacher and planter, and lived for some years with his father. He is now a

[*] From Appleton's Cyclopedia of American Biography, by permission.

merchant and planter at Allen's Station, on the Savannah & Augusta R. R., Ga. He m. Sep. 20, 1888, Lizzie Chance, but has no issue.

†-3-3. **Ann Sarah**[9] m. Apr. 4, 1882, George O. Walker of Beech Island, who is a miner. Issue :

    1. Harry Hammond,   b. Sep. 24, 1883.
    2. Stella,   b. Mch. 5, 1886.

†-3-5. **Thomas Taylor**,[9] a clerk in the National Bank at Augusta, Ga., m. Jun. 17, 1884, Bessie Day of Augusta. Issue :

    1. Claude Randall,   b. Mch. —, 1885.

†-3-6. **James Henry**,[8] railway employe at Atlanta, Ga., m. Aug. 1882, Lizette Gosti of Genoa, Italy. Issue :

    1. Ruby Elvira,   b. Aug. 10, 1883.
    2. Guido,   b. Jul. 2, 1886.
    3. Rene,   b. Aug. —, 1888.

†-3-7. **William Gilmore Sims**,[9] railway employe at Hamburg, S. C., m. Feb. 1882 Sarah Rountree of Beech Island. Issue :

    1. Helen May,   b. Jul. 26, 1882.
    2. Reuben Chas. Marc,   b. Oct. 26, 1883.   d. Aug. 9, 1884.
    3. Willie Gilmore. Jr.,   b. Feb. 14, 1885.
    4. Hal Rayford,   b. Nov. 23, 1886.   d. Nov. 30, 1886.

†-4. **John Fox**,[7] M. D., third son of Elisha, was b. in Columbia, S. C., Dec. 7, 1821, and d. at Poughkeepsie, N. Y., Sep. 29, 1886; graduated, University of Virginia; Medical College, Augusta, Ga.; and in 1841 at the Medical Dep't, University of Pennsylvania; Assistant Surgeon, U. S. Army, Feb. 16, 1847; Major and Surgeon, Feb. 26, 1861; Brevet Lieutenant Colonel Mch. 13, 1865, for "faithful and meritorious service during the War"; Lieutenant Colonel, Jun. 26, 1876; in 1849 had medical charge of troops infected with cholera on Western frontier; served in Florida, from Nov. 1852 till Oct. 1853, during an epidemic of yellow fever; in 1862 was Medical Director of the 2d Army Corps, Potomac, and was present at the siege of Yorktown and the principal battles of the Peninsula.[*]

Dr. Hammond m. Apr. 15, 1863, Caroline E. Lawrence, who was b. in New York City, Jun. 1, 1842. Issue :

[*] From Appleton's Cyclopedia of American Biography, by permission.

| 1. Katharine Betts, | b. Mch. 24, 1864. |
| 2. Elizabeth Percy, | b. Mch. 17, 1865. |

Of these daughters, **Elizabeth Percy,**[x] the younger, m. Aug. 11, 1886, George Loomis Taylor, who was b. at Bangor, Me. Mrs. Taylor and family reside at Munich and Tegernsee, Bavaria, Germany. Issue: Loomis Hammond, Lucy Curtis, and Romaine Goddard.

Mrs. Caroline E. Hammond, widow of John Fox, and her daughter **Katharine,**[5] also reside at Munich.

8.—EBENEZER HAMMOND OF EDGEFIELD, S. C.

†. **Ebenezer**[6] **Hammond,** second son of Ebenezer,[5] [Elisha,[4] Benjamin 2d,[3] Benjamin,[2] William[1]], was born in Petersham, Mass., Apr. 20, 1786, and died in Jackson Co., Ark., May 1847. He joined his brother Elisha in South Carolina in 1812, where he finished his education, and afterwards studied medicine with Dr. Meredith William Moon of Newberry, S. C. He m. in 1814 Maria, daughter of Dr. Moon, who died in Jackson Co., Ark., Apr. 1847. Issue:

1. William Meredith,	b. Nov. 4, 1817.	d. Feb. —, 1844.
2. Dennis Fletcher,	b. Dec. 15, 1819.	d. Oct. 31, 1891.
3. Charlotte Eliza,	b. Sep 19, 1821.	
4. Elisha Quincy,	b Mch. 25, 1824.	d. Mch. 17, 1887.
5. Lydia Antoinette,	b. Jan. 7, 1826.	d. Feb. —, 1849.
6. Harriette Maria,	b. Jan. 20, 1828.	
7. Eben Francisco,	b. Dec. —. 1829.	d. Jun. —, 1885.
8. Sommerfield George,	b. Jan. 14, 1831.	d. Feb. —, 1848.
9. James Henry,	b. Dec. 6, 1832.	d. about 1863.
10. Catherine M.,	b. Oct. 13, 1834.	d. Jun. —, 1848.
11. M. C. Marcellus,	b. Apr. —, 1836.	

Of these children, all but three of whom were b. at Edgefield, **William M.**[7] was a merchant, and d. single at Memphis, Tenn.; and **Sommerfield G.**[7] and **Catherine Melissa**[7] both d. single in Jackson Co., Ark.

†-3. **Charlotte Eliza,**[7] oldest daughter of Ebenezer, resides at Gainesville, Ga. She m. 1st, May 7, 1840, David B. Douglas, who d. in Jackson Co., Ark., Nov. 1848. Issue: Benjamin Ebenezer, William A., Carolina, and Cathleen. Eliza, with her children, returned to Georgia in Nov. 1849. She m. 2d, Jul. 4, 1853, George N. Johnson, who was wounded in the battle of Missionary Ridge, and d. at Rock Island.

Issue: George and Fletcher. Eliza m. 3d, in 1873, Burpe Camp, who d. in 1877. No other issue.

†-4. **Elisha Quincy,**[7] third son of Ebenezer, served with distinction in the late Civil War, and was afterwards a farmer in Coweta Co., Ga. He m. Jan. 19, 1869, a widow, whose maiden name was Jane Robinson. Issue:

    1. Helen May,   b. Dec. 10, 1871.

†-5. **Lydia Antoinette**[7] was b. in Lincoln, Ga., and d. in Jackson Co., Ark., Feb. 1849. She m. in 1846, Patrick Henry Dandridge, who d. Jan. 1849 without issue.

†-6. **Harriette Maria,**[7] third daughter of Ebenezer, lives at Gainesville, Ga. She m. Nov. 16, 1858, Elijah Elmore, a Lutheran clergyman, who d. May 1877. No issue.

†-7. **Ebenezer Francisco,**[7] commonly called Frank, served with bravery and distinction in the late Civil War; was on Gartrell's staff; was shot five times; and once had a silk handkerchief drawn through his body. He was afterwards a farmer, and d. in De Kalb Co., Ala., Jun. 1885. He m. Dec. 21, 1859, in Spalding Co., Ga., Mary A. Barfield, who now lives at Gainesville, Ga. Issue:

    1. Harriet M.,   b. Oct. 7, 1860.   d. Oct. 21, 1865.
    2. Mary E.,   b. Dec. 29, 1861.   d. Mch. 5, 1862.
    3. William E.,   b. May 5, 1863.
    4. James H. M.,   b. Sep. 9, 1865.
    5. Eliza Amanda,   b. Jul. 16, 1867.
    6. Pickens Taylor,   b. Dec. 9, 1871.
    7. John Sommerfield,   b. Sep. 13, 1873.
    8. Walter Francisco,   b. Aug. 31, 1877.

Of these children, **William**[8] and **Walter**[8] are farmers; **James**[8] is a clerk, and lives near his mother; **Pickens**[8] and **Sommerfield**[8] are carrying the mail from Atlanta to Guntersville, Ga.; and **Eliza**[8] lives with her mother in Gainesville.

†-9. **James Henry,**[7] sixth son of Ebenezer, was a lawyer the latter part of his life, and was a grand man. He was a Civil Engineer and Acting Captain in the late Civil War, and was wounded in the battle of Chickamauga in Sep. 1863, and died soon after at his home in Newnan, Coweta Co., Ga. He m. in 1860 Mary E. Robinson, and d. without issue.

†-11. **Marcus Claudius Marcellus,**[7] youngest son of Ebenezer, is a store-keeper and postmaster at Tyre, Douglas

Co., Ga. He was distinguished for his bravery in the late
Civil War. He m. 1st, Sep. 23, 1863, Sallie Roberts of
Fayette Co., Ga., who d. Feb. 22, 1877. Issue:

   1. Claudice Maria,   b. Jul. 6, 1864.
   2. Henry Sommerfield,   b. Dec. 25, 1867.

Marcellus m. 2d, Oct. 15, 1882, Maggie Kinney of Carrol
Co., Ga. Issue:

   3. Hugh Lavender,   b. Jun. 20, 1885.
   4. Eliza Ruby May,   b. Sep. 19, 1891.

Of these children, **Claudice**[5] m. Dr. Gustavus A. Mitchell,
and lives at Flowery Branch, Hall Co., Ga.; and **Sommerfield**,[5] who has never married, is a druggist in Covington, Ga.

†-2. **Dennis Fletcher,**[7] second son of Ebenezer, was
b. in Edgefield District, S. C., Dec. 15, 1819, and d. at
Orlando, Fla., Oct. 31, 1891. In early life he moved to Newnan, Ga., where his marked ability soon placed him in the
front rank of the lawyers of that section. Soon afterwards he
was made Judge of the Superior Court of the Coweta Circuit,
which position he held from 1855 to 1862, when he resigned
and moved to Atlanta, and resumed the practice of his profession. After the War, when the disorganized elements of
Atlanta society came together and attempted to restore the
reign of law and order, Judge Hammond was one of the
strongest factors in the work of reform. He was elected
Mayor of Atlanta in 1871, and his administration has been
frequently referred to as a model. He never sought political
preferment, and promptly declined a unanimous nomination to
Congress.

Judge Hammond was a man of indomitable will and great
energy, and had a fund of general information and mother wit
rarely found. It was no uncommon occurrence for him to keep
Court, Jury and lawyers convulsed with laughter for hours,
without seeming to try to do so.

Judge Hammond was a representative of the old school of
Southern gentlemen. With all the advantages of birth and
education, he remained all his life a man of the people and the
masses loved and honored him. He make a spotless record in
three states,—in South Carolina, Florida, and Georgia,—and his
death is sincerely regretted by all who ever knew him. His
memory will long be cherished, and the younger members of
the Bar will always have him pointed out to them as a model

JUDGE D. FLETCHER HAMMOND.

lawyer and Judge. He has stamped the impress of his courage and devotion to duty upon the public mind and conscience, and many of our later reforms had their starting point with him. Singularly modest and unassuming, with a child-like simplicity, and plainness of manners and speech, he was a refreshing character in this world of art. A clear and discriminating mind, a sound and well-balanced judgment, trained and matured by discipline, honesty, uprightness and integrity of character, a confiding faith and trust in God,—these were the weapons with which he fought the battles of life. Combined with his keen wit, there was a devout and serious sentiment, and he was ever fond of reading and expounding the Scriptures.

In later years Judge Hammond moved to Orlando, Fla., where he practised his profession in company with his son Edward M., and where he was residing at the time of his death.

Judge Hammond m. Sep. 1844, Adelene Robinson, who survives him. Issue :

1. Octavia,	b. Dec. 18, 1845.
2. William Robinson,	b. Oct. 25, 1848.
3. John Dennis,	b. May 12, 1850.
4. Edward Marcellus,	b. Oct. 29, 1853.

Of these children, **Octavia**[3] m. Jan. 14, 1868, Augustus D. Adair. Mr. Adair is senior member of the firm of A. D. Adair & McCarty Bros., dealers in cotton and fertilizers at Atlanta, Ga. Issue : Adelene, Laura and Augusta, twins, and Alfred.

†–2–2. **William Robinson,**[7] oldest son of Judge Hammond, is an attorney-at-law, and resides at Atlanta. He was elected Judge of the Superior Court of the Atlanta Circuit, in Nov. 1882, to fill an unexpired term, and was re-elected for a full term of four years in Nov. 1884. In Nov. 1885 he resigned, and resumed the practice of law in Atlanta. He m. Oct. 1870 Laura Rawson, but has no issue.

†–2–3. **John Dennis,**[8] second son of Judge Hammond, entered the University of Georgia in '67 ; from which he graduated with the degree of A. B. in '70 ; received a license as a Methodist local preacher in Atlanta in '71 ; joined the North Georgia Annual Conference in '72 ; afterwards entered Drew Theological Seminary, Madison, N. J., from which he graduated with the degree of B. D. in '75 ; again entered the North

Georgia Conference, and preached at various places in the State until '86: was then transferred to the Methodist Episcopal Church, St. Louis, Mo., and in Jun. '88 received the degree of D. D. from Central College, Fayette, Mo.; and in the same year was elected and confirmed President of Central College, which position he now fills.

He m. Sep. 10, 1879, Lydia Hardy of Elizabeth, N. J. Issue :

1. Frances,   b. Jul. 14, 1883.
2. Henry Dennis,   b. Oct. 4, 1887.
3. Katherine,   b. Sep. 1, 1889.

†-2-4. **Edward Marcellus,**[8] youngest son of Judge Hammond, is an attorney-at-law, and resides at Orlando, Fla. He was elected a member of the Florida Senate in Nov. 1888, which position he still fills. He m. 1st, Dec. 10, 1879, Henrietta Hardy, who was b. Aug. 13, 1854, and d. Nov. 23, 1883 without issue. Hon. Edward M. m. 2d, Dec. 22, 1890, Jennie Sweetapple of Orlando, formerly of Montreal, Canada. Issue :

1. Henry Sweetapple,   b. Dec. —, 1891.

JOHN COTTON'S DEED TO JOHN HAMMOND—1693.

To All People unto whom this present Deed of sale shall come, John Cotton of Plymouth in the Province of Massachusetts Bay in New England, minister of the Gospel, sendeth greeting, Know ye that the said John Cotton with the full & free consent of Joanna his wife, for & in Consideration of the summe of twenty foure pounds lawful money of New England to them secured in law at the time of the ensealing of these presents, to be paid by John Hammond of Rochester in the County of Barnstable in the Province aforesaid, the security for which twenty foure pounds they doe hereby acknowledge, & with which valuable consideration, they are fully satisfied & contented, Have granted, bargained, sold, aliened, enfeoffed, conveyed & confirmed by these presents, doe fully, freely & absolutely grant, bargain, sell, aliene, enfeoffe, convey & confirm unto the said John Hammond, his Heirs & Assigns forever, All that their whole right, title, interest, estate, proportion, Dividend, claim & demand whatsoever which they or either of them now have, may, might, should or ought at any time here-

after to have had of, in or unto, A certaine tract of land lying &
being at Rochester in the County and Province aforesaid, which
said land is a Halfe share, that is to say, the one halfe of a three
& thirtieth part of the whole township of said Rochester, whether
divided or undivided, all arable pasture & wood land, marish,
meadows, trees, woods, under woods, waters, feedings, com-
monages, rights, liberties, priveledges, commodityes & appurtenances whatsoever of in & unto the said halfe share belonging
or upon the same & every part thereoff standing, lying or growing
howsoever butted or bounded, To Have & to hold the above
granted premises & every of the same to him the said John Hammond, his Heires & Assignes, to his & their only proper use,
benefit & behoofe forever: And the said John Cotton & Joanna
his wife for themselves, their Heires, Executors, Administrators,
& every of them doe hereby covenant & promise to & with the
said John Hammond, his Heires, Executors, Administrators, &
Assignes in manner following, namely, That at the time of the
Ensealing & Delivery of these Presents, they the said John Cotton
and Joanna his wife were the true, proper & lawful owners of this
Halfe share of land & of all the appurtenances, rights, liberties &
priveledges & commodyties thereunto belonging & had in themselves good right, full power & lawful Authority to alienate, sell,
dispose, convey & assure their Estate, right, title & interest of, in
& unto the said halfe share of land & unto every part & parcell
thereof as is above expressed: And that the said bargained
premises are free & cleare & clearly acquitted & discharged of &
from all former & other gifts & grants, bargaines, sales, mort-
gages, entailes, joyntures, powers of thirds, titles, troubles, charges
& encumbrances whatsover: And that the said John Hammond,
his Heires & Assignes shall & may from henceforth forever lawfully, peacefully & quietly have, hold, use, occupy, possesse &
enjoy the above bargained premises & every part & parcell thereoff
without the least lett, hinderance, deniall, suibe , trouble,
eviction or expulsion of them the said John & Joanna Cotton or
either of them, their or either of their Heires, Executors, Administrators or any other person or persons from by or unto them or
by either of their meanes, consent, title or procurement: And
lastly, that the said John Cotton & Joanna his wife or either of
them shall at any time hereafter upon the request or demand of
the said John Hammond, his Heires, Executors or Assignes doe
any such further Act or Acts, thing or things, device or devices in
the law whatsoever as may be lawfully or reasonably advised or
required for the more full & cleare confirming & sure making of
the above bargained premises unto the said John Hammond, his
Heires or Assignes according to the true intent & meaning hereoff:
In Witnesse whereoff the said John Cotton & Joanna his wife
have hereunto set their hands & seales this tenth day of June, one
thousand six hundred ninety & three, And in the fifth yeare of the

Reigne of our Soveraigne Lord & Lady, King William & Queen Mary.

Signed sealed & delivered   JOHN COTTON [Seal.]
    in the presence of us
      Samuel Jougam.

The   marke of   JOANNA COTTON [Seal.]
    Joanna King.

      Province of the Massachusetts Bay, Plymouth ss.

At His Majesty's Superior Court of Judicature held at Plymouth for the County of Plymouth on the last Tuesday of April Anno Domini 1732 – – –

Josiah Cotton Esq' son of the within named John Cotton late of Plymouth, Clerc, and Joanna his wife both deceased, made Oath That he well knew his parents' handwriting, and that he verily believes his Father John Cotton wrote the within Deed himself, and that he and his wife signed and executed the same.

              Att. Samuel Tyler, Clerc.

    Plymouth ss: March 2, 1757. Received & Recorded with the Record of Deeds for the County of Plymouth. Book 44. Folio 61 – – –

                    ℣ Jno. Cotton, Reg'.

                                2/10.

ADDENDA.

Joseph J. Hammond, page 118. line 36, d. Dec. 16, 1893.
Charles S. Mendell, page 225, line 9, is now Supt. of the New Bedford Electric Railway.
Lydia Butler Clifton, page 248, line 37, d. Dec. 31, 1893.

ERRATA.

Page 1, lines 3 and 6, *for* Abby *read* Abbey.
Page 41, line 4, *for* Frank^2 *read* Frank^3.
Page 76, line 8, *for* Snockley *read* Shockley.
Page 97, line 16, *for* Francis *read* Frances.
Page 103, line 30, *for* Francis *read* Frances.
Page 177, lines 14 and 15, *for* Peleg *read* Joseph.
Page 220, line 4, *for* Phidora *read* Philora.
Page 232, line 15, *for* 1885 *read* 1855.

INDEX OF HAMMONDS.

Females are indexed under their maiden names.

Deborah, 235
Deborah, 235
Deborah, 236
Deborah, 267
Deborah, 268
Deborah P., 98
D. Fletcher, 276
Delia, 55
Delia, 101
Delia M., 48
Delia M., 232
Dewitt C., 48
Dinah, 186
Dora Inez, 150
Dorcas D., 181
Dor E., 52
Dorus, 71
Drusilla, 186
Drusilla, 208
Drusilla M., 24
Dwight, 161
Dwight S., 142

E

Ebenezer, 13
Ebenezer, 268
Ebenezer, 274
Ebenezer F., 275
Ebenezer R., 237
Eben. Paul, 53
Edith Bird, 144
Edgar B., 26
Edmister, 28
Edmund, Baron, 2
Edmund S., 142
Edmund Y., 180
Edson Dana, 16
Edward, 245
Edward, 250
Edward C., 250
Edward E., 162
Edward L., 210
Edward M., 19
Edward M., 278
Edward S., 270
Edward W., 118
Edward W., 162
Edwin, 53
Edwin, 112
Edwin, 199
Edwin, 263
Edwin A., 262
Edwin F., 112
Edwin Fitch, 43
Edwin G., 45

Edwin Jr., 113
Edwin P., 139
Edwin P. Jr., 140
Edwin S., 199
Edwy E., 36
Effie, 107
Eleonora, 181
Eleonora, 183
Eliakim, 56
Elias, 118
Elihu, 22
Elihu, 251
Elijah, 100
Elijah, 187
Elijah, 189
Elijah G., 26
Elijah G., 103
Elijah, 2d, 108
Elijah, 3d, 193
Eliphel, 14
Elisha, 22
Elisha, 30
Elisha, 184
Elisha, 255
Elisha, 267
Elisha, 268
Elisha, 268
Elisha C., 103
Elisha, Jr., 185
Elisha Q., 275
Eliza, 22
Eliza, 34
Eliza, 106
Eliza, 147
Eliza, 164
Eliza, 273
Eliza A., 118
Eliza A., 192
Eliza Ann, 67
Eliza B., 114
Eliza D., 24
Eliza L., 107
Eliza W., 257
Elizabeth, 3
Elizabeth, 14
Elizabeth, 14
Elizabeth, 17
Elizabeth, 22
Elizabeth, 22
Elizabeth, 40
Elizabeth, 63
Elizabeth, 64
Elizabeth, 81
Elizabeth, 84
Elizabeth, 87

Elizabeth, 111
Elizabeth, 111
Elizabeth, 124
Elizabeth, 130
Elizabeth, 134
Elizabeth, 169
Elizabeth, 178
Elizabeth, 197
Elizabeth, 208
Elizabeth, 211
Elizabeth, 235
Elizabeth, 249
Elizabeth, 251
Elizabeth, 257
Elizabeth, 264
Elizabeth, 265
Elizabeth, 268
Elizabeth, 268
Elizabeth, 272
Elizabeth A., 43
Elizabeth A., 89
Elizabeth A., 192
Elizabeth A., 97
Elizabeth D., 271
Elizabeth E., 198
Elizabeth F., 171
Elizabeth H., 19
Elizabeth H, 116
Elizabeth J., 42
Elizabeth J., 58
Elizabeth L, 79
Elizabeth M., 166
Elizabeth P., 3
Elizabeth P., 213
Elizabeth P., 274
Eliz. Rogers, 238
Ella Aug., 144
Ella Eliz., 237
Ella H., 159
Ellen, 164
Ellen, 193
Ellen A., 18
Ellen Delora, 220
Ellis, 111
Elmer, 183
Elmer E., 56
Elmer E, 138
Elmina A., 69
Elmina E., 164
Elnathan, 108
Elnathan, 197
Elnathan, 197
Elnathan, 235
Elnathan, Capt. 4
Elnathan, Sr., 195

Elnathan, Jr., 197
Eloda A., 220
Elon A., 151
Elon Oscar, 159
Elon O. E., 150
Elsie, 108
Elsina, 55
Elvira Thos., 143
Elwyn E., 161
Emeline, 223
Emery, 33
Emily, 68
Emily, 238
Emily A., 25
Emily A., 237
Emma, 62
Emma, 69
Emma, 154
Emma, 164
Emma, 198
Emma, 222
Emma, 259
Emma A., 145
Emma C., 181
Emma F., 65
Emma I, 20
Emma King, 121
Emma Lu., 156
Emma Maria, 43
Emma S., 37
Emma Sarah, 157
Enoch, 207
Ephraim, 67
Ephraim, 68
Erasmus W., 156
Ernest, 36
Ernest, 53
Ernest Mark, 161
Esther, 42
Ethan Allen, 216
Ethan A , Jr., 246
Etta, 107
Etta Susie, 151
Eudora F., 214
Eugene, 55
Eugene H., 82
Eugene Lynn, 65
Eunice, 57
Eunice, 108
Eunice, 109
Eunice, 123
Eunice, 186
Eunice, 264
Eva, 165
Eva Julia, 199

Philip, 170
Philip Delano, 172
Philip Faunce, 246
Philora, 220
Phineas, 14
Pickens, 275
Polly, 29
Polly, 31
Polly, 85
Polly, 113
Polly, 246
Polly, 248
Polypus, 244
Polypus, Jr., 244
Prince, 37
Prince, 256
Priscilla, 87
Priscilla, 108
Priscilla, 112
Priscilla, 176
Priscilla, 213
Priscilla, 233
Priscilla, 265
Priscilla P., 229
Priscilla S., 213

R

Rachel, 3
Rachel F., 237
Rachel M., 231
Ralph, 67
Ralph Perry, 155
Randall, 200
Rasselas A., 169
Rasselas W., 156
Ray Benson, 154
Rebecca, 29
Rebecca, 33
Rebecca, 107
Rebecca, 108
Rebecca, 131
Rebecca, 174
Rebecca, 183
Rebecca, 184
Rebecca, 265
Rebecca H., 119
Rebecca R., 183
Reuben B., 246
Reuben B., 247
Reuben C., 189
Reuben W., 58
Rezin, 3
Rhoda, 131
Rhoda, 173
Richard, 108

Richard G., 138
Robert, 124
Robert, 146
Robert C., 106
Robert C., 2d, 107
Roger, 99
Roger, 111
Roger, 266
Roger, Jr., 99
Roger Wing, 120
Roland, 209
Roland G., 232
Roland, Jr., 210
Roland Orr, 231
Roland R. C., 261
Rollin, 263
Rosabell A. A., 45
Rosa Belle, 60
Rosamond, 11
Rosanna, 104
Rose, 99
Rose, 177
Rowland, 216
Rowland, 218
Rowland, 227
Rowland C., 211
Rowland, 2d, 216
Rowland W., 222
Rowland W., 2d, 220
Roxie Haskell, 258
Ruby, 171
Rufus, 213
Ruth, 14
Ruth, 33
Ruth, 40
Ruth, 57
Ruth, 57
Ruth, 64
Ruth, 111
Ruth, 131
Ruth, 132
Ruth, 264
Ruth A., 32
Ruth Alice, 66
Ruth Ann, 68
Ruth Waldron, 205

S

Salathiel, 38
Salem P., 190
Sally, 30
Sally, 32
Sally, 51
Sally, 132

Sally, 259
Samantha, 260
Samuel, 11
Samuel, 20
Samuel, 29
Samuel, 40
Samuel, 52
Samuel, 56
Samuel, 58
Samuel, 61
Samuel, 123
Samuel, 125
Samuel, 218
Samuel, 262
Samuel Albro, 141
Samuel D., 46
Samuel, Jr., 61
Samuel, Jr., 71
Samuel N., 202
Samuel W., 238
Samuel W., 2d, 238
Samuel, 2d, 28
Samuel, 3d, 28
Sarah, 35
Sarah, 41
Sarah, 62
Sarah, 84
Sarah, 86
Sarah, 92
Sarah, 101
Sarah, 130
Sarah, 131
Sarah, 188
Sarah, 222
Sarah, 223
Sarah, 230
Sarah, 241
Sarah, 242
Sarah, 255
Sarah, 268
Sarah A., 146
Sarah Ann, 44
Sarah Ann, 80
Sarah Agnes, 97
Sarah B., 117
Sarah E., 30
Sarah E., 114
Sarah E., 201
Sarah E., 262
Sarah Eliz., 80
Sarah Eliz., 118
Sarah J., 59
Sarah Joanna, 212
Sarah L., 134
Sarah Lovina, 152

Sarah Lovina, 160
Sarah M., 180
Sarah M., 223
Sarah N., 201
Sarah S., 147
Sarah Shaw, 120
Sarah T., 115
Sarah W., 120
Sarah W., 122
Seneca, 54
Seneca, 56
Seth, 12
Seth, 31
Seth, 36
Seth, 78
Seth, Jr., 21
Seth, Jr., 31
Seth, Jr., 268
Seth Oscar, 84
Seth W., 184
Seth, 2d, 21
Seth, 3d, 32
Seth, 3d, 34
Seth, 3d, 246
Shubael, 103
Shubael, Jr., 104
Silas, 17
Silvanus, 123
Sommerfield, 275
Sommerfield, 276
Sommerfield G., 274
Sophia, 101
Sophia, 120
Sophia, 257
Sophia A., 215
Stafford, 256
Stanley, 49
Stella, 173
Stephen, 62
Stephen, 104
Stephen, 146
Stephen, 153
Stephen, 177
Stephen, 244
Stephen, 248
Stephen E., 248
Stephen F., 155
Stephen F., 160
Stephen G., 180
Stephen H., 149
Stephen, Jr., 147
Stephen, Jr., 248
Stephen W., 183
Stephen W., Jr., 183

INDEX OF OTHER NAMES.

Females are indexed under their maiden names.

BAILEY.

———, 77

BAKER.

J. F., Mrs., 149
Josiah, 246
Lillian T., 247
Watson R., 185

BALDWIN.

A. Webster, 157
Carrie M., 157
Emma E., 157
Henry, 149

BALL.

Patty, 133

BARBOUR.

William P., 71

BARDEN.

Anna, 103

BARFIELD.

Mary A., 275

BARKER.

Abram, 257

BARLOW.

Abigail, 264
Clarissa, 109
Gideon, 249
Hannah, 23
Hannah, 111
Lydia, 264
Mary, 98
Mary, 99
Mary, 108
Mary, 255
Mehitable, 109
Seth, 242
Seth, Jr., 242
Wyatt, 268

BARNARD.

Edward M., 263

BARNES.

Anna, 78
Ida J., 142

BARNUM.

George W., 68

BARRELL,

Ellen C., 84

BARROWS.

Dudley H., 228
William H., 228

BARRY.

Ellen, 96

BARSTOW.

Benjamin, 265
Benjamin F., 265
Henry, 265
Lucy, 212
Nathan H., 265
Sarah L., 224
Susan C. B., 265

BARTLETT.

Caroline, 260
Elias H., 18
Mary J., 232

BASSET.

Nellie, 53

BATES.

Edgar B., 106
Mary, 89
Mary, 97
Thomas, 250

BATTEY.

Clarissa A., 103

BAXTER.

Emaline, 51
Julia E., 52

BAYLEY.

Royal L., 169

BEARSE.

Andrew H., 179
Clarence, 25
Hannah, 179
Marinda, 182

BELDING.

Sophie, 122
Willard J., 122

BELLOWS.

Caroline F., 152

BELYEA.

Ida Louise, 194
Joseph, 194

BENNETT.

Charles O., 122
Cordelia, 106
Robert, 118
Sophia L., 64
Stephen, 245

BENSON.

Hannah, 100
Jabez, 100
Maria, 244

BENT.

George B., 181

BENTON.

Lizzie M., 141
S. J., 141

BERT.

Lucia, 228

BERTINE.

Josephine M., 73

BESSE.

Nathaniel, 242

BICKNELL.

Abigail, 176
Fannie, 176
Jabez H., 176
John S., 176
John S., Jr., 176
Sophia, 18

BIRD.

John H., 172

———, 17

BIRGE.

Cyrus, 198
Elijah, 198

BISBY.

Celia M., 231

BISHOP.

Betsey, 167
D. B., 164
Helen, 46
Samuel, 71

BLACKMER.

Saulisbury, 224

BLAKE.

Laltmer S., 25

BLANCHARD.

Eunice C., 230
Julia A., 161
Junius, 230

BLANKENSHIP.

Betsey, 248
Catherine, 114
Eliza P., 246, 248
Elizabeth, 34
Harriet, 116
James, Jr., 256
Job, 246
Ruby, 113
Sylvia, 246

BURTON.
Harriet A., 110
Rachel, 110

BUTTERFIELD.
Eliza, 64

BYERS.
Alexander R., 191

C

CADY.
C. Elbert, 65
Julia A , 199
Willis, 199

CALL.
Vienna, 186

CAMP.
Burpe, 275

CAMERON.
Fred. M., 174

CAMPBELL.
John A., 150
Maria S., 40

CANNON.
David H., 265
Hallet M., 109
Henry, 120

CAREY.
Ebenezer, 71
George L., 51

CARLETON.
Henry, 132

CARNEY.
Elizabeth M., 184

CARR,
Deborah, 197
Lydia P., 90

CARROLL.
Abigail, 86

CARVER.
Chandler, 30

CASE.
Elizabeth, 189
Nancy, 182

CASGRAIN.
Charles W., 97

CASON.
Elizabeth, 3

CASSIN.
Alphius P., 271

CASWELL.
Elisha, 14
Lucy, 252

CHADSEY.
Frank W., 237

CHADWICK.
Barnabas, Jr., 123
Ellen A., 35

CHAFFEE.
Joel W., 151
Josie L., 190
Namena S., 151
Onia F. W., 151

CHAMBERLAIN.
Lucinda, 148

CHAMBERLAYNE.
Mary, 204

CHANCE.
Lizzie, 273

CHANDLER.
Eliza H., 83
Eunice, 25
Frances A., 150

CHAPMAN.
John, 145

CHASE.
Elizabeth A., 35
John, 37
John, 259
Mark C., 185

CHEEVER.
Samuel, 267

CHENEY.
Parmelia, 48

CHESTER.
George, 204

CHILCOTE.
Mordecai F., 134

CHILDS.
Hattie, 76

CHIPMAN.
Abigail, 15

CHRISTIAN.
Stephen, 86

CHURCH.
Hearty, 76

CHURCHILL.
Lydia, 264

CLAPP.
Abigail, 79

CLARK.
Amanda, 82
Ann E., 142
Clarissa, 44
David, 12
Edwin W., 80
Emaline S., 53
Frank E., 157
Harry A., 121
Helen M., 179
Madie A., 225
Mary, 34
Peras, 268
Temperance. 108
William T., 173

CLAWSON.
Nellie, 263

CLEMENT.
Robert, 169

CLEVELAND.
Ida. 169

CLIFF.
Carrie C., 52

CLIFTON.
Jirch, 34
Lydia B., 248
Nancy, 101
Nancy, 249

CLOBB.
F. M., 164

CLOSE.
Clarissa, 40
James, 41
Nathaniel, 63

COBB.
Almira, 228
Ebenezer, 188
James N., 33
Mary, 228
Persis, 227
Solon, 228
Susan, 250
Thomas, 228

DAVIS (cont'd).
Minerva S., 216
Moses, 236
Moses, 256
William. 178
William II., 164

DAVISSON.
Jennie, 192

DAY.
Bessie, 273

DEAN.
Amos, 174
Amos II'd, 174
Frederic A., 174
Hannah, 252
Henry N., 74
Joanna, 174
Josephine, 174
Mary B., 174
Nathaniel, 174
Nathaniel W., 174

DEARBORN.
Eliza M., 215

DEARDON.
William II. II., 105

DEISS.
George T., 80

DeLAMATYR.
Allida, 202
David, 204
Elias. 204
George, 204
Gilbert, 204
Henry, 203-4
Jane, 204
John, 204
Rebecca. 204
Walter, 204

DELANO.
Beulah, 101
Deborah, 246
Harper, 111
Louise. 246
Meribah, 241
Priscilla, 170
Sally P., 115
Susanna A., 254

DELOUNAY.
Margaret. 78

DeMORANVILLE.
Edson. 34

DENNIS.
Carrol B., 225

DEWEY.
Josiah E., 198

DEXTER.
Alice, 241
Benjamin, 257
Daniel, 24
Euphemia F., 209
Martha M., 266
Mary, 265
Mary A., 23
Susan, 25

DICKINSON.
Mary J., 159

DILL.
Josiah R., 185

DILLINGHAM.
Edward II., 22

DINWIDDIE.
Jane, 175

DIVOLL.
Julia, 83

DOANE.
Fuller G., 181
Laura, 26
Solomon, 179

DODGE.
Nancy P., 89

DOE.
Nellie M., 143

DOHERTY.
Nellie E., 85

DOTEN.
Edward, 20

DOTY.
Richard, 104
Sarah, 255

DOUGLASS.
David B., 274

DOW.
Emily F., 88

DOWNER.
Susan, 141

DRAPER.
Arvilla. 169
Ira. 188

DREW.
Sarah S., 265

D'ROSIA.
Laura M., 151

DUDLEY.
D. Willard, 159

DUGAW.
Andrew, 45

DUNBAR.
Elisha, 77
Laura II., 271

DUNHAM.
Almira, 255
Nathaniel, 255
Sidney A., 53

DUNKIN.
Esek, 71

DUNN.
Byron P., 209
Joseph, 82

DUNNING.
Amanda, 69

DWINELL.
Albert, 160
Clarence R., 159

DYE.
Julia A. G., 192
William II., 192

DYER.
Helen L., 176

E

EAMES.
Andrew R., 228

EDMISTER.
Elizabeth, 28

EDMONDS.
Thomas, 143

EDMONSON.
Nancy, 190

EDSON.
Sarah, 15

EILER.
Annie K., 17

EISENHART.
Jennie. 237

GARDNER.
Allen, 153
David G., 152
Lois, 57
Lydia, 12
Moses, 78

GARHING.
Carrie, 55

GASTON.
Athelston, 64
Eben, 63

GEER.
Almeda L., 200

GEFFROY.
Thomas P., 233

GELETT.
John, 25
Rebecca, 119

GERMAINE.
Libbie, 157

GESSLER.
Frances L., 137

GETCHEL.
Ada M., 36

GIBBS.
Marietta E., 198

GIBSON.
Johnson, 107
Robert W., 72

GIFFORD.
Alden, 87
Fear, 122
George P., 87
Hannah, 37
Nancy R., 26
Peleg W., 118
Reuben, 122

GILBREATH.
Caroline, 191

GILLS.
Jesse, 178
Mehitable, 182

GLASGOW.
Joseph, 59

GLEZEN.
James, 188

GLOVER.
William P., 40

GODDARD.
George H., 94
Eliza, 168
Nancy M., 168

GOLDSMITH.
John, 87

GOODRICH.
Ruth, 67

GOODWIN.
Alanson, 257

GORHAM.
Jabez, 31
Jane, 33

GORTON.
John, 55

GOSLING.
Martha, 143

GOSTI.
Lizette, 273

GOULD.
Daniel, 67
Ella M., 254
George W., 88
Sally, 179
Samuel N., 22
Sarah, 179

GRAHAM.
Lizzie, 154

GRANNIS.
Almira, 45
Levi, 44

GRAVES.
Simeon, 107

GREEN.
Amy, 70
Leo, 41
Louisa, 171
Lydia, 170
Maria, 122
Polly, 71
Stephen, 75
Susan, 103

GREENE.
William A., 35

GREENFIELD.
Thomas, 17

GREGG.
James, 271

GREGORY.
Susan, 164
Theodorus, 109

GREY.
Richard, 57
Sarah, 60

GRIFFITH.
Obed, 14

GRINNELL.
Cornelius, 118

GROSS.
Phœbe E., 41

GRUESBECK.
Abigail, 219
Amelia, 222
Catherine, 219

GUNTHER.
Laura, 102

GURNEY.
William A., 35

H

HACKET.
Asa, 14

HADLEY.
Eliza, 246
Stephen, 15

HADSELL.
Georgia, 68

HAIGHT.
Joseph, 57

HALE.
Mary E., 161
William D., 65

HALL.
Abigail, 166
David, 120
Eliphalet, 104
Eliza, 258
James M., Jr., 114
Mary, 214
Minnie, 102
William L., 205

HALLETT.
Sarah, 250

HAMILTON.
Almeda, 182
Edwin L., 68
Helen H., 43
Warren G., 81

HANCOCK.
Mariette, 171

HANDY.
Gamaliel, 22
George, 21

HANEY.
William, 34

HANNAFORD,
Jennie E , 124

HAPGOOD,
Mary L., 141
Salome F., 141

HARD.
Charles F. N., 83

HARDING.
Elijah T., 182
Rhoda A., 184
Samuel, 183

HARDY.
Albert, 184
Albertina, 184
Edmund, 92
Henrietta, 278
Lydia, 278

HARKINS.
Harry, 88

HARLOW.
Hannah, 252
Lurana K., 253

HARRINGTON.
Parmelia, 160
Sarah, 187

HARRUB.
Sarah A., 231

HART.
George A., 37
Hattie A., 247
Sallie, 191

HARTER.
Frank H., 172

HARTSHORN.
J. Willard, 157

HARTWELL.
James L., 141
Mary E., 141

HARVEY.
Frank, 30
———, 252

HASKELL.
Abigail, 251
Elizabeth, 268
Hunnewell, 251
Job, 251
Joseph, 130
Lydia, 251
Palmer, 31
Seth, 109
Seth, 254

HASKINS.
Isaac, 30
John W., 237
Orpha B., 32
Ruby A., 33

HASTINGS.
Daniel, 236
Jennie, 161

HATCH.
Celia, 82
Franklin, 259
Joanna, 123
Rebecca, 124
Ruth, 123

HATHAWAY.
Abigail, 74
Bennajah, 31
Elizabeth, 207
Emma, 66
Frances M., 263
Gardner, 105
Mary, 11
Noah, 31
Royal, 267
Sally, 100
Samuel W., 75
Thomas, 230

HATTLESTONE,
Betsey P., 115

HAWLEY.
George B., 90
Sally, 133

HAYDEN.
Joseph, Jr., 77

HAYES.
Anna E., 233

HAYWARD.
Martin, 80

HAZARD.
Annie T., 26

HEADLE.
Lucy M., 165

HEAFIELD.
Sanford J., 199

HELLER.
Sarah J., 203

HENDERSON.
Eliza J., 238

HENDRICK.
Asa, 19

HENDY.
Susie E., 66

HENRY.
Almeda, 47
Anna, 167

HERVEY.
———, 252

HICKEY.
John, 44

HICKS.
Caroline, 73

HIGGINS.
Ann, 19
Maggie L., 173
Mary, 47

HILL.
Frank, 51
Sadie, 80

HILLER,
Charles H., 253
Matthew, 248

HILLMAN.
Hulda, 113

HINCKLEY.
William, 88

HINDS.
Mary F. W., 151

HITCH.
Emma, 71
Nelson A., 71

HOAG.
Ruby A., 76
Stephen C., 73

HODGE.
Isannah, 82

HODGES.
Charlotte, 179
Sarah, 115

HODSKINS.
Damon H., 62

HOFFMAN.
Lavina, 45
Minnie, 56

HOLBROOK.
Charles E., 148

HOLLIS.
John F., 84

HOLMES.
Annie P., 53
David E., 61
Heman G., 258
Horace, 234
Ida C., 60
Josiah A., 231
Lizzie, 263
Mary, 132
Prudence, 234
Thomas, 29

HOOPER.
Sarah E., 79

HOPKINS.
Mercy, 181

HORN.
Jane, 165
Jemima, 164

HOSMER.
Granville, 93

HOUSE,
Mercy, 255

HOVEY.
Ivory, 6
Olive, 111

HOWARD.
Lydia, 114
Parmelia, 115

HOWE.
Jane L., 92
Malana, 50

HOWELL.
Henry D., 143

HOWES.
Abel, 235
Dorinda, 186
Emma, 239
Frank LeB., 239
Idella C., 24
Marshall, 239
Mercy, 255

HUBBARD.
William H., 32

HUBBELL.
Myron, 62

HUDSON.
Wilson B., 215

HUFFER.
Elizabeth, 189

HULSE.
Julia A., 220

HUMPHREYS.
Frank, 137

HUNNEWELL.
Elizabeth, 243

HUNT.
Ada, 36
Oliver, 35

HUNTER.
Catherine A., 164

HUNTLEY.
Florence E., 200

HUNTLING.
Tennis D., 237

HURD.
Amy A., 44
Louisa A., 45

HUSTON.
Sarah, 92

HYDE.
Annie E., 85
Catherine S., 269
Ezekiel F., 269
George E., 85
James, 85
Lydia, 61

HYLAND.
Henry, 85

I

INGERSOLL.
John N., 68

INSCO.
James H. C., 59

IRISH.
Sarah P., 27

J

JACKSON.
Nancy, 104

JACOBS.
Thomas, 48

JACQUES.
William M., 143

JAMES.
Caroline, 149

JAQUESS.
George D., 189

JAY.
James, 239

JENKINS.
John, 23

JENNE.
Jehaziel, 74
———, 255

JENNEY.
Anstris H'd, 21
Elizabeth, 13
John, 252
Jonathan, 14
Lovica, 237
Lydia, 111
Mary, 14
Prince, 77
Sarah, 259
Silas, 268

JENNISON.
Sumner H., 46

JIPSON.
Norton W., 160

JOHNSON.
George N., 274
Henry E., 85
Hiram R., 214
Jacob, 219
Rebecca, 84
Samuel, 107
William W., 59

JONES.
Samuel, 77
Sarah, 12
Sylvester, 41
Walter, 144

JORDAN.
Frank W., 222

JOY.
Eliza M., 262

JUDSON.
Clark, 45
Edward G., 144

K

KEELER.
Fannie B., 198

KEERNAN.
Maggie, 190

KEITH.
Charles F., 258

KELLEY.
Asa H'd, 259
Mary, 33
Thomas. 259
———, 46

KELSEY.
Clara, 206

KEMPTON.
Elijah, 77

KENDALL.
David. 133
Ellen F., 160

KENDRICK.
Alfred, 109

KENNEDY.
Andrew, 144
Joseph, 144

KENNEY.
Jacob, 14

KERR.
Alexander, 67

KEYES.
———, 117

KING.
Caleb, 253
Charles A., 227
Harriet S., 121
Susan B., 88

KINNEY.
Maggie, 276

KINNIE.
Edith B., 263

KIRBY.
Cynthia, 76

KNAPP.
Jared, 147
Mary, 171
Susan A., 46

KNIGHTS.
Mary, 249

KNOX.
Henry C., 60

KOEPKA.
Charles, 45

L

LACY.
Elizabeth. 115
Henry, 146

LAIRD.
Charles K., 175
Horatio N., 175
Julia, 174
Samuel. 174
Samuel, Jr., 174

LAMAR.
Calbraith B., 271

LAMBERT.
Mary, 245

LAMSON.
———, 251

LANDERS.
Ephraim, 14

LANE.
John W., 215
William, 259

LANGLEY.
Rebecca J., 249

LANPHIER.
Susan M., 169

LARABLE.
Martin, 60

LARUE.
Eliza J., 138

LASHER.
John, 58

LAVARE.
Lavina A. T., 86

LAWRENCE.
Caroline E., 273
Martha L., 97

LAWTON.
Russell T., 103

LEACH.
Eliza Ann, 19
Jane, 120
Stephen, 268

LeBARON.
Alton, 213
Betsey, 236
Enoch H'd. 213
Francis, 213
John, 267
Lazerus, 213
Lemuel, 6
Mary, 109
M. Bartlett, 252

LEE.
B. Frank. 191
Gilbert W., 97
Sylvester J., 228

LEONARD.
Caroline L., 234
Charles T., 251
Enoch. 132
George E., 121
Jane, 121
Lucy T., 260
Mary, 26

LEROY.
Mary S., 152

LEVERING.
Mattie A., 227

LEWIS.
Ellis, 247
James. 114
John R., 247
Mariette, 46
Mary, 222

LIBBY.
Myra Belle, 92

LIFFLER.
William P., 159

LINCOLN.
Elizabeth, 79
Frank, 37

LITTLE.
Anna M., 106
Elsie N., 107
Renie W., 107

LIVENSPARGER.
Daniel, 220

LLOYD.
Almyra, 137

LOBB.
Laura, 98

LOBDELL.
Caleb, 40
Ruth, 42

LOCKE.
Dean J., 232
George S., 232
Horace M., 230

LOCKWOOD.
Joseph W., 70
Lydia, 72
Nathaniel, 72

LOMBARD.
Elizabeth, 21
Mary, 245

LONG.
Martha, 158
Vernon, 193

LONGLEY.
Edmond, 17

LORING.
Susanna, 78

LOTHROP.
Ebenezer, 130
Hope, 130
John, 9
Sarah, 131

LOUCKS.
Minnie, 63

LOVELAND.
Winslow, 180

LOVELL.
Betsey, 89
Eldredge, 104
Horace, 101

LOWRY.
Ellen, 211

LUCE.
John G., 101
Thomas S., 156

LUTHER.
Nathaniel, 218

LYNDON.
Caleb, 197

LYON.
Edgar M., 24
Frank M., 24
Gilbert, 24

LYONS.
Amanda, 53

M

MACK.
John, 77

MACOMBER.
Abbie A., 26
Harriet, 27
Louise, 114
Margaret, 56
Sally, 30
———, 57

MACY.
Sarah, 58

MAKER.
Loella, 180

MANCHESTER.
Lucy, 29

MANERING.
James H., 139
Rebecca A., 137

MANEY.
Kate, 110

MANN.
Gordon, 82
Josiah, 82
Loretta, 47

MARBLE.
Edwin, 18
Francis, 103

MARCY.
Sarah, 157

MARDEN.
Maggie, 262

MARK.
Ann, 43

MARRETT.
Ella, 151

MARTIN.
Abbie, 199
Martha E., 221

MASSENBURG.
Walter L., 249

MATHEWS.
Charlotte, 145
Maria, 146

MAXIM.
Henry T., 31
Sylvia A., 247
Zilpha, 105

MAYNARD.
Ezra, 188

MAYO.
Susie M., 185

McCOY.
William E, 271

McCRAY.
Josiah, 51
Samuel, 51

McDONALD.
Peter, 263

McDOUGAL.
Emily, 211

McELLERAN.
Fanny, 202

McFARLAND.
Alice J., 194

McGEORGE.
Eliza, 156

McGRATH.
Lewis, 153
Lovina, 153
Lucy, 152

McGREGOR.
Dolly, 233

McGURK.
Nancy, 262

McINTYRE.
Elizabeth, 148

McKEE.
Hattie A., 50

McKOY.
Hannah, 110

McLARON.
Alice V., 222

McLAUGHLIN.
Mary, 187

O

ODNEAL.
S. Ellen, 164
Walter H., 164

OLMSTEAD.
Alpha, 199
Sally, 198

ORCUTT.
Jane M., 32

OSBORN.
Demaris, 47
Elias, Jr., 192
Selick, 113

OSBORNE.
Lizzie, 85

OSTRANDER.
Stephen M., 237

OSWALD.
Charles B., 53

OTIS.
~ Charles, 81

OWEN.
Elizabeth, 202

P

PABODIE.
Elizabeth, 201

PAINE.
Sarah, 115

PALMER.
Abigail, 265
Ann, 59
Theodore D., 174
Titus, 57

PARKER.
Amos L., 151
Bessie, 231
Betsey, 231
Clarence, 190
Elizabeth, 77
Francis A., 20
Sarah A., 226

PARKS.
J. Wesley, 220
Loretta, 58

PARLOW.
Lucinda, 13

PARMENTER.
Helen, 20

PARSONS.
Lizzie D., 51
Mary, 204

PARTRIDGE.
Newton, 144

PATTENGALL.
Eliza W., 24

PATTERSON.
David G., 181
Everett, 181
Francis, 178

PAYNE.
Elizabeth, 3
Lucy, 176

PEAKS.
Martin T., 85

PEARSE.
Marilla, 203

PECK.
———, 244

PECKHAM.
Ira, 58
Sapphira, 117

PENBERTHY.
Jane M., 75

PENN.
Elizabeth, 1, 9
William, 1
William, Sir, 1

PENTECOST.
Anna, 190

PERKINS.
Frances Belle, 97
Fred H., 148
Helen, 160
Ignatius, 147
Linda H., 148

PERRY.
Ebenezer, 130
Ella M., 102
Walter, 103

PETER.
Hannah M., 50

PHILIP.
King, 124

PHILLIPS.
Cloe, 116
Emma, 62

PHINNEY.
Joseph, 188

PHIPPS.
William S., 91

PIERCE.
Abigail, 257
Amos T., 258
Betsey, 46
Janette, 27
Mary, 35
Mary A., 238
Minnie A., 105
Orrin, 42

PINCIN.
Thomas, 77

PIPINGER.
Nathaniel, 54

PITTS.
Lemuel, 113

PLATT.
Albertus H., 43

POLEY.
Azariah, 268

POLLOCK.
Mary, 188

POMEROY.
Mary E., 167

POND.
Louise, 117
Mary, 52

POOLE.
Albert, 82

POPE.
Elizabeth, 208
James, 51
Mitchell, 132

PORTER.
Frank, 260
Ira W., 260

POST.
Adeline S., 36

POTTER.
Fanny, 55
Helen E., 93
Mary, 171

ROLFE.
Philip, 170

ROOD.
Mary, 63

ROSS.
Orville A., 233

ROUNSEVILLE.
Rhoda E., 247

ROUNTREE.
Sarah, 273
Sarah, 257

ROUSE.
James, 41

ROWE.
Mary, 149

ROWELL.
Charles W., 84

ROY.
Anne, 49

RUDE.
Mary, 63

RUGGLES.
Deborah, 235
Mary, 235
Timothy, 5

RUSSELL.
Daniel, 54
Jennie, 221
Laura, 165

RYDER.
Betsey, 183
Eben, 87
Lizzie E., 182

S

SAFFORD.
Emma, 142

SALABAR.
Y. C, 107

SALE.
James G., 134

SALSBURY.
Annie V. B., 26

SAMPSON.
Joseph T., 258

SANFORD.
John, 38

SARGEANT.
Albert, 162
Betsey, 167

SAULWATER.
Rachel, 56

SAUNDERS.
Edward, 25
John W., 66

SAVAGE.
George M., 165

SAVANAC.
Ada, 93

SAVERY.
Jacob B., 37
Sophia M., 101

SAWIN.
Mary, 160

SAYLER.
Lucy J., 140

SAYRE.
Theodore H., 141

SCARF.
Sarah E, 20

SCHARVES.
Sarah A., 35

SCHIMMERHORN.
George C., 50

SCHNELL.
Anna, 49

SCOTT.
Emma L., 65
Libby J., 159
Mary, 197

SEARS.
Abbie M., 254
Abby, 51
Paul, Jr., 245

SELDEN.
George D., 237

SERGEANT.
Aaron C., 115

SERRING.
Hannah H., 134

SHANK.
Hannah, 212

SHARPE.
Johnivry M., 17

SHAW.
Anna, 227
Betsey, 230
Bezaliel, 235
Earl, 227
Elizabeth, 235
Jacob, 67
James, 251
Lorenzo, 230
Lucius, 198
Lydia, 228
Mary, 258
Mary A., 112
Susanna, 232
Susannah, 119
William, 24

SHEDD.
Jane M., 142

SHEFFIELD.
Barker K, 257
Elliot, 257

SHELL.
William H., 81

SHEOPARD.
Washington, 258

SHEPARD.
Harriet E., 162

SHEPERD.
Elizabeth, 38
Hannah, 56

SHEPWARD.
Annie, 19

SHERMAN.
Asa, 77
Delia N., 250
Dorothy, 38
Louisa, 103
Mary, 230
Prudence, 13
Reuben, 229
Ruth, 114

SHERWIN.
Darius, 147

SHERWOOD.
Nancy J., 138

SHIMMEL.
Cecelia, 48

SHOCKLEY.
Joseph, 29

STEVENS (cont'd).
L. A., 206
Malana E., 156
Polly, 22
Sarah, 21

STEWART.
Charles, 144
Clinton, 144
Ella E., 144
Gussie A., 144
Harry, 144
Hettie, 144
James, 189
Jane, 190
Lizzie, 144
Lucy A., 144
Martha J., 225
Rebecca, 199
Samuel, 144
William W., 44

STILLSON.
Frank L., 172
Jane Ann, 171

STINSON.
Benjamin II., 180

STODDARD.
Miranda, 185

STONE.
Adalina A., 193
Alice, 141
Hannah, 146
Susan, 193
William W., 203

STONEMETZ.
Hannah, 175

STORING.
Nicholas II., 67

STORY.
John O., 20

STOWE.
Alice, 49

STOWELL.
Caroline, 260
Edvina A., 115
Mary A., 35

STRATTON.
Robert B., 225

STROUP.
Eva, 220

STUBBS.
James, 23

STUDLEY.
John, Jr., 84
R. Whitney, 104

STURTEVANT.
Hannah, 229
Lucy, 216
Martin L., 121

SUMNER.
Anna M., 68

SUNDERLAND.
Caroline, 72

SWEENEY.
Anthony, 136

SWEETAPPLE.
Jennie, 278

SWIFT.
Abigail, 250
Asa, 235
Charles J,. 67
John P., 124
Louis C., 124
Mary A., 177
Mary E., 102
Prince D., 124
Thomas, 99
Thomas, 177

SYLVESTER.
Lettie, 84

T

TABER.
Abigail, 13
Abigail, 21
A. French, 108
Charles A., 159
George R., 32
John M., 76
Mary, 38
Mary, 231
Tripp, 113

TALLMAN.
Hannah, 39
Lucy H., 261

TANNER.
Catherine A., 63

TARR.
George W., 216

TAYLOR.
Ellie S., 151
George L., 274
Rebecca, 232
Rhoda, 179
Rosetta, 106
Roswell, 188
William, 34
William, 253

TAZER.
Mary, 147

TELLIE.
Lillie B., 190

TERHUNE.
David V., 182

TERRY.
Deborah, 268
John, 259

THATCHER.
Sarah E., 223
William, 31

THAYER.
Laura, 62

THOMAS.
Betsey, 217
Charles, 114
James, 204
Mahlon A., 223
Margaret, 56
Mehitable B., 142

THOMPSON.
Clarinda, 73
Clarissa, 149
Gideon D., 156
Josepha F., 226

THORNE.
Jacob, 57
Phebe, 62

THURSTON.
Louise M., 16

TIBBALS.
Hulda, 64

TIERNAN.
Lawrence P., 217

TINKHAM.
Emeline, 26
Harry N., 28
Nelson, 25

TISLOW.
Jennie, 192

TOBEY.
Anna, 255
Desire, 29
Ella M., 102
Sylvanus, 14

TOFIELD.
Edward, 201

TORREY.
John D., 85

TOWER.
Clarence C., 150
Horace S., 87

TOWNSEND.
Francis, 144

TRAVERS.
Mary, 52

TREADWELL.
Sarah J., 174

TRIPP.
Abiel, 171
Annie M., 34
Rose, 1

TROW.
Harriet W., 90

TUCKER.
Eben A., 226
Elvira, 226
H. A., 256
Joel, 171
John, 226
Josepha F., 226
———, 256

TUPPER.
Elisha, 243
Samuel, 14

TURNER.
Jane, 49
Joseph, 12
Mary, 28
Ruth, 32
Smith, 268

TUTHILL.
Adelbert, 144

TWEED.
Clara E., 214

U

UNTERSEE.
Franz, 173

UPHAM.
Warren R., 18

V

VALLER.
Lois, 38

VAN ANTWERP.
Fela, 40

VAN ARNE.
Mrs., 234

VAN FROCKEN.
James S., 80

VAN HOVENBURGH.
Charles B., 61

VAN MARTER.
Sophie, 110

VAN METER.
Hannah, 134

VAN NESS.
Henry, 54
Wilampey, 54

VAN ORSDOLL.
George H'd, 223
Henry, 223

VAN PELT.
Alexander, 69

VAN SICKLE.
Henry H'd, 212
Rowland, 212
William H., 212

VAN WICKELL.
Addie D., 80

VAN WYE.
Charles, 221

VERNON.
Elizabeth, 196

VIAL.
Edwin, 121

VILES.
John R., 151
Nira M., 152

VINAL.
Abigail C., 85
Adeline, 85

VINAL (cont'd).
Carolina A., 86
Ezra, 85
Gideon, 86
Gideon, 86
John Fred, 86
John S., 85
Mary Ann, 85
Olive H., 85
Sarah, 86
William, 86

VINCENT.
Mary, 10

VIRGIN.
Charlotte A., 228
Samuel, 228
Samuel H., 228

W

WADDAMS.
Caleb, 63

WADSWORTH.
Norman, 40

WAGER.
Sylvanus, 41

WAIT.
Eliza, 60
Emily A., 58
John, 261

WAITE.
Sarah D., 169
Walter A., 162

WALDSMITH.
Eliza A., 175

WALKER.
George O., 273
Jarvis, 166

WALL.
Thomas H., 33
Walter, 85

WALLIS.
Sarah A., 261

WALTERS.
Margaret, 45

WAME.
Kate, 119

WARD.
Arabelle E., 46
Betsey, 234